Next page: Carel Willink,
*Landscape under a Rainy
Sky* (detail). 1943. Canvas,
90 x 120 cm. Collection
Stichting Van Baaren,
Utrecht (© Sylvia Willink).

THE

COUN

OW
TRIES

Arts and Society in Flanders

and the Netherlands

A Yearbook

1997-98

Published by the

Flemish-Netherlands Foundation 'Stichting Ons Erfdeel'

ontents

Chronicle

Visual Arts

ntwerp,

World Port and Provincial City

The name 'Antwerp' – or 'Antwerpen' as it is in Dutch – is related to the Middle Dutch '*aenwerp*', meaning alluvial land, but no true citizen of Antwerp will accept this modest explanation. In the local dialect the 'h' of, for example, 'hand' is not sounded, and so *clearly* 'Antwerpen' derives from '*Hand-werpen*', meaning 'Hand throwing'. This explanation of the name has its origin in the well-loved legend of the young hero Brabo, who freed the poor fishermen from the tyranny of the giant Antigoon. The giant would chop off and throw away the hand of any fisherman sailing down the River Scheldt who refused to pay a toll. After Brabo had defeated Antigoon, the Emperor allowed him to throw the giant's chopped-off hand from the tower of his stronghold, thereby demarcating the area of the new city. This legend comfortably links the origin of the city with the right to free navigation and liberation from tyranny.

However, alongside the Antigoon legend, which the romantic nineteenth century consecrated with the impressive statue of the hand-throwing Brabo on the main square, there also persists another die-hard Antwerp self-image, and this one does have a historical basis. During the sixteenth century Antwerp became a world capital and the memory of that golden age, when every burgher was a '*Sinjoor*' ('*seigneur*' in French, '*señor*' in Spanish), lives on to this day in the minds of the people. In 1993, when Antwerp was (again) the 'cultural capital of Europe' (see *The Low Countries* 1993-94: 272), a study of the city's image was carried out among the people of Antwerp and among 'non-*Antwerpenaren*'. It appeared that the inhabitants see themselves without hesitation as tolerant, humorous, intelligent and international, while the outside world was particularly aware of the provincial arrogance and narrow-mindedness of the people of Antwerp who, in their view, mistakenly believed that they lived in 'the capital of Flanders'.

A chequered history

According to the generally-accepted view of history, in the sixteenth century Antwerp became the successor to Bruges, which had been the

The Brabo fountain on the main square, by Jef Lambeaux (1887).

A View of Antwerp, plate from *Description de la Baronnie, chasteau, drefves, villages, Hame(...) & Bois et aultres appendances, terre et s(eigneu)rie de Beveren en flandres*, 1602. Antwerp, Arenbergarchief, LA 4413.

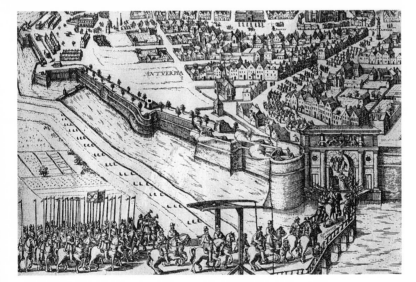

Entry of Alexander Farnese, Duke of Parma, at the head of his troops in Antwerp on 27 August 1585 (Koninklijke Bibliotheek, Brussels).

economic and cultural centre of the Low Countries under the dukes of Burgundy. After the conquest of Antwerp in 1585 by the troops of Alexander Farnese, the Italian governor of the Spanish Netherlands, the role of Antwerp was taken over by Amsterdam. But according to Fernand Braudel (*Civilisation and Capitalism*, 1979), that story is over-simplistic. He argues that Antwerp became the successor to both Bruges and Venice, and that during its brief golden age the city was the centre of the whole international economy. Antwerp was linked by busy trade routes to London, Lisbon, Cadiz, Genoa, Brazil, the Atlantic islands and to the coasts of Africa and Northern Europe.

Unknown Master, *Market
Day on Meir and Meir
Bridge in Antwerp*.
Late 16th century.
Panel, 90 x 140 cm.
Koninklijke Musea voor
Schone Kunsten, Brussels.

However, the prime movers in this spectacular upturn were not the
indigenous people but merchants from the Northern European Hanse cities:
the English, French and, above all, the Spanish, Italians and Portuguese. As
befitted an international seaport in times of growing religious tension, the
city of Antwerp was an example of religious tolerance. Braudel distinguishes
three periods: that of the Portuguese, dominated by the trade in pepper
(1501-1521), the Spanish period when the main commodity was silver from
the New World (1535-1557) and finally the years of rapid industrial growth
in Antwerp and the Netherlands (1559-1585). Between 1500 and 1568 the
city's population shot up from 44,000 to over 100,000 and the whole infrastructure was thoroughly modernised. This growing prosperity went hand in
hand with the disintegration of the traditional medieval social fabric,
creating a widening gap between rich and poor and, as a result of that, social
unrest and religious conflict. The estrangement between this modern, tolerant, early-capitalistic and increasingly Calvinistic metropolis and the
Catholic Spanish hierarchy eventually led to Antwerp's participation in the
uprising against the Habsburgs and the definitive end of its golden age.

The economic and intellectual elite fled to the free, up-and-coming North,
where they made a great contribution to the development of the Dutch
Republic, while the closing of the River Scheldt in 1609 sealed the material
fate of this port city. Curiously enough, Antwerp remained an important
centre of culture even in the seventeenth century: the Jesuits saw to the
modernisation of education, where great emphasis was placed on (Jesuit)
drama and mathematics as well as on the Greek and Latin classical writers.
This distinctly intellectual order also stimulated the blossoming of the
baroque in what was now the Antwerp of the Counter-Reformation. For

example, both the interior and the exterior of the Carolus Borromeus Church are among the finest examples of the so-called 'Jesuit style'. Indeed, Pieter Paul Rubens had a hand in the plans for the church's interior and made a series of remarkable paintings for it. This world-famous painter was also involved in the building of the Porta Regia on Vlasmarkt and, of course, in his own 'Rubens' House' (see *The Low Countries* 1996-97: 302).

But Rubens and his school (which included Otto van Veen) were not alone. There was Jacob Jordaens (who, among other things, drew up the plans for the St Anna Chapel and 'Jordaens' House'); there were also Antoon (later Sir Anthony) van Dyck, Ambrosius Francken, Maarten de Vos, Abraham Janssens and Jan Bruegel. True, the printing trade was by now almost entirely in Roman Catholic hands, but it produced a wealth of theological, Christian humanist, liturgical and devotional works. And religious sculpture reacted to the ravages of the Calvinist iconoclasm of 1566 by creating altars, pulpits, confessionals, communion rails and organ and rood screens of great artistic quality, as well as images of saints and representations of the Madonna (St Paul's Church, St James' Church and Carolus Borromeus). Even after the partition of the Low Countries in 1648, Antwerp remained an internationally-renowned centre of silver making (Abraham Lissau, Willem van der Mont, Johannes Moermans, Wierik Somers III and Han Herck) and of violin and harpsichord building (Hans Ruckers, Johan Daniel Dulcken and Pieter Borlon Jr.).

But the real revival came in the nineteenth century with Napoleon, who

The facade of the Carolus Borromeus Church.

began modernising and expanding the port. The River Scheldt was reopened in 1839 when the Netherlands and the new Belgian state signed the London peace treaty, and Antwerp gradually became one of the largest seaports in Europe. In the twentieth century, Antwerp, along with the rest of the country, was twice occupied by the Germans, but when liberated in 1944 it lost no time in resuming its role as a large naval and, later, trading port.

Containers, pipelines and diamonds

As an Allied supply port, the city suffered severe damage from flying bombs (the German V1 and especially V2 rockets) towards the end of the Second World War. However, it was possible to rebuild or restore the oldest buildings and streets so that today's visitors can easily form a picture of the city's rich history: from the medieval castle known as the 'Steen' and the high Gothic tower of the Cathedral of Our Lady (see *The Low Countries* 1993-94: 266), via the Town Hall and the guildhalls in Flemish Renaissance style, the baroque churches of St Paul and St Carolus Borromeus to the Art Nouveau houses that line Cogels-Osylei and even the single house designed

The Cathedral of Our Lady, seen from the south-east (Photo Provincial Government of Antwerp).

by Le Corbusier located near the first Canadian tank, now preserved as a monument, which signalled the liberation of Antwerp in September 1944. What visitors do not immediately see are the Plantin and Moretus printing works (see *The Low Countries* 1994-95: 236-243), the birthplace of the independent-minded sixteenth-century polemicist, poet and teacher Anna Bijns and the Ruusbroec Society's collection of mystical manuscripts, to mention just a few of the hidden treasures.

The visitor who wonders what the people of Antwerp do for a living need only pay a visit to the docks and the diamond district. It soon becomes clear that Antwerp is now first and foremost a container port, its quays stretching right up to the Dutch border. The port area is also home to a whole string of oil refineries, hence all the tankers travelling to and fro. So Antwerp lives on an increasing volume of world-wide container traffic and on the refining of crude oil. The port, which handled a hundred million tons of cargo in 1995, provides jobs directly or indirectly for some 106,000 people. Despite its distance from the North Sea – compared to Rotterdam or Zeebrugge, for example – Antwerp is still the second biggest port in Europe, a fact that is largely explained by its central location and its exceptionally high productivity (33 containers per hour). Antwerp is directly linked to Germany, Switzerland and France by motorways, the Scheldt-Rhine Canal and an extensive railway network. Thus in 1992 the port realised added value of 10 billion US dollars.

In contrast to these two recent forms of economic activity, the diamond trade is one of the oldest examples of a truly Antwerp industry. Today diamond processing and the diamond trade are the domain of Jewish and non-Jewish '*Antwerpenaren*', and of Indians and Africans. However, documents dating from 1465 prove that, as far as the Low Countries are con-

Art Nouveau in Antwerp:
Jacques de Weerdt's Hôtel
de Maître 'Quinten Metsys'
on Cogels-Osylei, Berchem,
1904.

The Antwerp docklands
(Photo by Guido Coolens).

cerned, this industry began in Bruges, though there were Flemish diamond cutters working in Paris as early as 1407. In 1483 we find the first mention of an Antwerp diamond cutter, Wouter Pauwels. In the sixteenth century merchants from Genoa, Venice and Portugal were largely responsible for the prosperity of Antwerp's diamond trade. After their expulsion from Spain (1492) and Portugal (1497), there were large numbers of Portuguese Jews working as diamond merchants in Antwerp. The tolerant religious climate that prevailed at the time partly accounts for this. However, the real heyday of the 'Antwerp diamond' began in 1871 with imports of rough diamonds from South Africa and the simultaneous mass immigration of Jews from Eastern Europe. Ever since, the traditionally immigrant district around Central Station has been known as the 'Jewish quarter' and the 'diamond district', for it is here that both the traditional religious life and the main economic activity of the Jewish immigrants is located (see *The Low Countries* 1995-96: 21-26). In these few streets with their hundreds of jeweller's shops, it is indeed (apart from diamonds and pearls) a question of 'all that glitters really is gold', even though the really important deals are done behind the closed doors of the Diamond Exchange and the Diamond Circle (which accounted for between 7 and 8% of Belgium's total exports in 1995). This area, which bears a remarkable resemblance to the orthodox Jewish streets of New York and Tel Aviv, is nevertheless typically 'Antwerp' for several reasons: in addition to Yiddish – which is in fact also spoken here by many non-Jews – one can also hear 'pure' Antwerp dialect, and it is a well-known fact that in the Kempen around Antwerp thousands of people make a living from industrial diamond processing. And one should not be deceived by appearances: though 80-85% of the Jews still work in the diamond industry, these days more than half of the diamond workers and traders are non-Jewish.

The diamond trade is one of the oldest examples of a truly Antwerp industry.

Antwerp multiracial or multicultural?

Today some 300,000 people live in the city and more than 600,000 in the Antwerp agglomeration. In addition to Jews, Indians and Africans, Antwerp is home to tens of thousands of Turkish and Moroccan immigrants. The majority of them have lived and worked in Antwerp for two generations or more, so that it is no exaggeration to speak of a 'multiracial' metropolis. Multiracial (or 'multiethnic'?) is however not the same as 'multicultural'; which is to say that these different ethnic communities live alongside each other rather than with each other. That is apparent, among other things, from their geographical distribution in the city and its suburbs and from the obviously different religious and cultural worlds in which these communities seek to preserve their own identity. Though the members of these ethnic groups come into contact on a daily basis at work and in public life (schools, public services, medical services), and though there is little or no sign of inter-ethnic violence, at present one cannot really speak of successful integration, let alone of a true 'multicultural' experience. Since the occasional friction that does arise usually concerns real or alleged social differences, it is understandable that political programmes that champion 'ethnic purity' meet with most success in those areas where the underprivileged, indige-

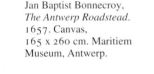

nous Antwerp citizens feel threatened by the visible presence of 'the others'.

Yet this does not explain everything: even in relatively homogeneous 'white' areas, sympathy for these programmes seems to be growing; with the result that during the last elections in 1994 almost 28% of the Antwerp electorate voted for a party, namely the Vlaams Blok, which advocates the 'organised repatriation' of these 'foreigners'. This electoral behaviour can be compared to reactions in other large European cities, but it may also have to do with the idiosyncratic political profile of the Antwerp electorate. Though the city has been ruled for more than seventy years by a coalition of Christian Democrats and Socialists (joined after the recent elections by Liberals, Greens and Flemish Nationalists), the people have often made a point of voting perversely: for example, in 1928 the Flemish activist August Borms was elected to Parliament while in prison serving a life sentence, and the extreme left-wing anarchist Leo Frenssen won a seat in Parliament and six seats in the city council.

I think that the success of the Vlaams Blok is partly explained by this tradition of political idiosyncrasy. After almost a century of centre-left government, people want to express their dissatisfaction with social degeneration and bureaucracy in the only way they believe really hits the political establishment. Unfortunately, in doing so they also give a licence to people who have elevated intolerance to a (political) programme and who take advantage of every mistake and every scandal within the majority party, without ever having to prove anything. It is impossible to predict whether this trend will continue – for the moment the Vlaams Blok has been pushed into opposition by a 'mammoth alliance' of all the other parties – but it is certainly a crucial challenge for all the democratic forces in the city.

Jan Baptist Bonnecroy,
The Antwerp Roadstead.
1657. Canvas,
165 x 260 cm. Maritiem
Museum, Antwerp.

Antwerp 1997: a postmodernist metropolis?

Meanwhile, Antwerp is still a European metropolis with much to offer in terms of national and international culture. The principal museums, churches and historic buildings are all within walking distance of each other, with the exception of Middelheim Park, the open-air modern sculpture museum that accommodates some three hundred works by modern artists from Rodin on (see *The Low Countries* 1994-95: 119-124). In the last twenty years more and more art galleries and workshops have been set up around these museums, including that of Panamarenko (see *The Low Countries* 1994-95: 181-185) and Bernd Lohaus. But Antwerp is also a theatre city offering a wide choice of traditional and experimental theatre and a Flemish Opera which the German quality weekly *Die Zeit* recently declared 'one of the best in Europe'. A Summer Arts Festival is organised every summer, with the Canadian Cirque du Soleil and the French Zingaro among the 1996 highlights. Autumn brings the Festival of Flanders which focused special attention on the Dutch and Flemish Polyphonists (see *The Low Countries* 1993-94: 39-50; composers such as Ockeghem lived and worked here) and attracted guest conductors like Anthony Rooley, Paul van Nevel and Giogi Savalas. In 1998 Middelheim will be mounting a major retrospective of the sculptor Henry Moore and in 1999 Antwerp, in association with London's National Gallery, will round off the twentieth century with a historic Anthony van Dyck exhibition featuring some eighty of his most famous works.

However, the culture of everyday life looks rather different: now that the traditional ideological denominationalism is steadily crumbling and the great historical distinction between 'Catholics', 'Socialists' and 'Liberals' has long been blurred, new forms of fragmentation are emerging in Antwerp. Without much effort one can grow up, go out, marry and have friends in a Turkish, Moroccan, Jewish or Flemish environment without ever once really talking to someone from another milieu. In the long term, spontaneous 'ghettoising' such as this can be of little good to a city which in its best periods was characterised by openness and hospitality. If this situation does not change, Antwerp will become a postmodern agglomeration of a convivial but narrow-minded provincial city surrounded by all kinds of exotic villages. Luckily there are a number of groups, both in the city council and in the districts, who dream of turning this world port back into a real world city, where the presence of so many different cultures is regarded as enriching and where an effort is made to stimulate the necessary interaction. This can be achieved through education; people must again be made aware of the city's rich international and interactive past and, without in any way seeking to decry the positive achievements of each community, people must learn to experience that internationalism in their own district without complexes. After all, this city became great through the 'alluvium' (the '*aenwerp*') of centuries of immigration, and not by tyrannising passing fishermen or restricting free development.

LUDO ABICHT
Translated by Alison Mouthaan-Gwillim.

FURTHER READING

ADRIAENSSENS, IVO (ed.), *Antwerp: Cultural Capital of Europe. Official Guide.* Mechelen, 1993.

ASAERT, GUSTAAF, F. SUYKENS *et al.*, *Antwerp, a Port for All Seasons.* Antwerp, 1986.

BLYTH, DEREK, *Flemish Cities Explored: Bruges, Ghent, Antwerp, Mechelen, Brussels and Leuven.* London, 1996.

BURKE, PETER, *Antwerp: A Metropolis in Comparative Perspective.* Ghent, 1993.

FARMILOE, KEN and PATRICK RYAN (comp.), *Antwerp.* Antwerp, 1993.

ISACKER, KAREL VAN and RAYMOND VAN UYTVEN (ed.), *Antwerp: Twelve Centuries of History and Culture.* Antwerp, 1986.

STOCK, JAN VAN DER (gen. ed.), *Antwerp: Story of a Metropolis, 16th-17th century.* Antwerp, 1993.

oney

and Excrement

The Psychology of Capital and the Marketplace

in Pieter Bruegel the Elder's 'Dulle Griet'

Pieter Bruegel the Elder (c.1525-1569) is beyond doubt the best-known Flemish painter of the sixteenth century. Little is known about his life, but from signatures and dates it is to some extent possible to survey his extensive oeuvre of paintings, drawings and engravings. Bruegel received his training in Antwerp in the husband-and-wife workshop of Pieter Coecke van Aelst and Mayeken Verhulst Bessemers. In 1551 he was accepted into the Guild of St Luke as a master. After this he travelled via France to Italy, returning to Antwerp about 1556.

Bruegel's paintings included religious subjects (e.g. *The Slaughter of the Innocents*) as well as genre scenes and landscapes. In this last category especially he proved himself an outstanding artist, for instance in his famous *The Fall of Icarus,* which centuries later provided W.H. Auden with the subject for his poem 'Musée des Beaux-Arts'. Bruegel's landscape drawings would be regarded as models of their kind long after the sixteenth century. His genre pieces, which earned him the name 'Peasant-Bruegel', often depict peasants dancing or brawling at fairs, wedding-feasts and other exuberant celebrations. With these works, of which his *Peasant Wedding* is probably the best known, he laid the foundations of a tradition which was to be continued in the first half of the seventeenth century by such Flemish painters as David Teniers the Younger and Adriaen Brouwer.

Bruegel achieved a fusion in his art of the new Italian models and the older traditions of Low Countries painting. He was particularly fascinated by the strange imagery of Hieronymus Bosch, which he extended and updated. Bruegel's themes, drawn to a great extent from literature, the theatre and from proverbs, always have an allegorical significance. Like Bosch, he cast light on the dark and hidden aspects of the human mind. The finest examples of this are his series of engravings, such as the *Seven Deadly Sins.* The painting *The Triumph of Death,* too, with all its horrors, displays close links with Bosch's iconography.

(Tr. Tanis Guest)

Pieter Bruegel the Elder started his career in Antwerp in 1551 as a master in the Guild of St Luke, where he quickly made a name for himself as a 'Second Bosch.'[1] Sometime in the early 1560s, he designed his most Bosch-like painting, the *Dulle Griet*. This surreal masterpiece transforms images from city life and folklore to represent a contemporary psychological hell. To understand it we must start with Antwerp, for the city at this time was *'a trading centre such as the world had never seen before or since, for never since has there been a market concentrating the trade of all commercial*

Pieter Bruegel the Elder,
Dulle Griet. c.1562.
Museum Mayer van den
Bergh, Antwerp.

nations.'² The Antwerp stock exchange, the Bourse, controlled the wealth of Europe, and in mid-century it was at the height of a boom. This boom was founded on new forms of credit, necessary to finance the high risks of sea-trading. The shift to credit allowed merchants to defer and interweave the consequences of their ventures, and citizens became used to the psychology of gambling on future profits. Like modern trading-floors, the Bourse was no sober club. Incidents of violence were not unknown and the building itself (new in 1531) was plagued by vandalism and graffiti. It was a centre for gossip and scandal of all kinds. '*He that will believe every nue that is blasted in Flanders among merchants shall have a mad head*,' commented the English spy Stephen Vaughan to Thomas Cromwell in a dispatch of 1535.

The boom produced an extraordinary atmosphere at the Bourse, where exchange activities were dominated by betting and chance. The validity of a contract from 1534 depended on the buyer marrying a nun or the daughter of a nun. Life-insurance fraud was common. A particularly macabre case in 1566 involved a bet on the specific cause of a death (poison). Against this background, the notorious bond in Shakespeare's *Merchant of Venice*, where Antonio stakes a pound of his own flesh against the success of a shipping venture, no longer appears so bizarre.³

Bruegel's working life was naturally affected by these developments. Private individuals, as well as guilds and corporations, now bought almost everything on credit, and the fortune of Bruegel's Guild rode on that of the

Bourse. In 1540, St Luke's moved their headquarters to the new building; by 1560, they had incorporated many luxury crafts supplying the market-place: mirror-makers, goldbeaters, embroiderers, organ builders.

What sorts of images were available to the artist to depict these changes in society and the status of money? For Bruegel, as for Rabelais and Shakespeare, firsthand acquaintance with the old folk world of ghosts, transformations and witchcraft went hand in hand with the new urban experience. At this cross-roads also sits the *Dulle Griet*, wherein a hell-mouth, two giants and a ship are set in a sinister mixture of town and landscape. Let us single out one of the strangest motifs: the giant scooping coins out of his eggshell rear. How is this image linked to the novel economic culture of sixteenth-century Antwerp?

Bizarre imagery was not itself unusual in Bruegel's *milieu*, where print-makers, painters and playwrights found a sophisticated city-wide audience for complex visual fantasies. Thus a Reformation broadsheet invents a surreal supernatural kitchen, while, at the other end of the market, an artist such as Joris Hoefnagel creates a sheet of visual puns about Bruegel's friend the geographer Ortelius. The '*rederijkers*', the theatre groups of the guilds, drew huge audiences for their displays of riddling flamboyance leavened with farce.[4]

As in the broadsheets and farces, the *Griet*'s dominant images come from the fracturing world of folk culture. Echoes of sinister tales can be heard in the earliest description (1600) of the painting: '*A Dulle Griet, who robs in front of hell, wears a vacant stare and is (cruel, or) strangely and weirdly dressed.*' The proverb, '*to rob in front of hell*', referred to women who feared neither death nor the devil, and 'Dulle Griet' was by extension a folk synonym for 'virago' or 'bitch.' The fluid image of Griet could be woven

Joris Hoefnagel, *Emblematic Composition in honour of Abraham Ortelius*. 1593. © Historische Musea / Stedelijk Prentenkabinet, Antwerp

Anonymous, *The Battle of the Breeches*. c.1550. (from M. de Meyer, *De Volks- en Kinderprent...* , 1942).

into a joke about the wife wearing the breeches, but in other, darker stories, she became a witch.[5]

The *Dulle Griet* also resembles the ornate dramas of Bruegel's '*rederijker*' colleagues, in that it invents allegorical characters to dramatise the big issues of the day. The painting could be both a rhetorical elaboration of the Griet folk-figure, and a sort of caricature on the state of Antwerp, to be captioned perhaps with a version of the proverb: '*Lady Antwerp Loots before Hell.*' The protagonists have been identified as figures from Antwerp's civic pageantry: the Maid of Antwerp, who wore red sleeves; and the Antwerp Giant, in helmet and breastplate (designed in 1534 by Bruegel's master Pieter Coecke).[6] These two appeared together in a festival tableau in 1561. Renaissance city governments often used giant figures, drawn from legends, in civic processions, to cow and impress the citizens. The Elizabethan George Puttenham described '*these midsommer pageants in London, where to make the people wonder, are set forth great and vglie Gyants, marching as if they were alive, and armed at all points.*'[7]

In Bruegel's painting, then, the Maid is satirised as a Dulle Griet, clutching her frying pan and treasure. The city's Giant is a monstrous '*Dukatenscheisser*', an excretor of ducats, dressed as a witch and burdened with signs representing money-madness. The hell-mouth and cauldron flanking them recall the punishment for avarice in Antwerp Hell-paintings; also that, according to Antwerp law, coiners of false money were boiled in oil or water. This parodic money-giant appears to function as a kind of town sign embodying a deformation in the life of the town.

These strange images broadly evoke Avarice; more precisely, they create visual poetry out of a complex of ideas and experiences to do with money, excrement, fraud and the bizarreries of consumption. In treating these themes, the *Dulle Griet* goes beyond satire. The play between real and unreal in the picture raises issues hotly contested at this time, in a lull between bitter religious wars and the witch-hunts which followed. Is a hell-mouth real? Is a *Dukatenscheisser*? Is a witch?

So what does Bruegel's *Dukatenscheisser* mean? Why represent it in this way? It seems that the key way in which Bruegel made the image contem-

The 'Dulle Griet' (detail from Dulle Griet)

porary was by unfolding and enhancing a surrealism already inherent in his folk material. Thus, Griet and the Giant are cross-dressers. In rural magic, this signifies that they are uncanny. In city-caricature, it is a shorthand for 'the-world-turned-upside-down'. It is also a mark of carnival-time. The giant's cross-dressing further identifies him as a kind of 'hagazussa' (witch), a boundary-figure who 'sits on the fence' between village and wilderness.[8] On the burning roof, by the giant's foot, a small man scrapes a kettle with a knife; he exemplifies a Flemish expression for 'scraping the bottom of the barrel' ('hij wil altijd het onderste uit de kan halen'). The proverb-illustration locks into a more complicated circle of dripping and dousing actions around the Giant. A woman steals from the huge purse; a hand douses her from a jug. The Giant spoons coins onto a woman who catches them in a bowl, the silver coins of Flanders (now tarnished black). As in Hoefnagel's rebus, these cameos help us understand the contexts of

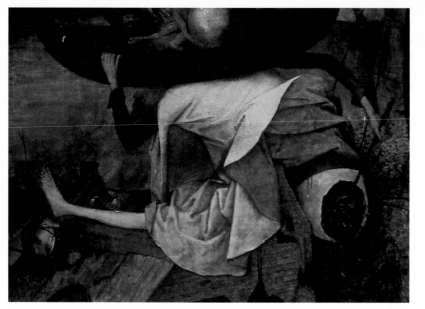

The *Dukatenscheisser* (detail from *Dulle Griet*).

Pieter Bruegel the Elder (workshop), *The Man with the Sack of Gold and his Flatterers*. 1568. engraving. From R. van Bastelaer, *Les Estampes de Bruegel l'Ancien* (1904).

theft and weird displacement of bodily functions that Bruegel intends for his Giant.

The idea of a *Dukatenscheisser* was probably not new; it is known in seventeenth-century folklore, and chocolate ones are still made in Germany. Tracts and allegories on the evils of money were also common in the 1550s. But when Bruegel animated these abstractions, he made the surrealism part of the meaning. Followers of Bosch had made similar images at Antwerp a few decades before, wherein huge hellish noses dribble money onto a cauldron of the damned. A print from Bruegel's atelier attacks those obsessed with money in the most directly scatological way. *The Man with the Sack of Gold and his Flatterers* (c.1568) is captioned: '*Why crawl up his hole when he opens his purse?*'. Much more subtly, in Bruegel's own *Battle between the Money-Banks and the Strong-Boxes*, coins are the body contents of the soldiers. His Money-Bank-men and Strong-Box-men may be interpreted as dehumanised men whose bodies have become constipated carapaces of wealth.

The forms of these fantasies are rooted in early modern psychology. Country people had customarily combined supernatural causes with everyday images to describe their unconscious lives, although they did not, naturally, think of it in these terms. They regarded dreams as a gate to the spirit world, the territory of ghosts, sleepers and the devil. The *Dukatenscheisser*'s coins – and Griet's treasure – appear also in this world. Freud commented that, '*in dreams in folklore, gold is seen in the most unambiguous way to be a symbol of faeces. If the sleeper feels the need to defecate, he dreams of gold, of treasure.*'[9] In dream-tales from many different regions, the connection between treasure and excrement is recognised in a comic punchline, when the dreamer wakes up. A fifteenth-century story is typical: '*My neighbour once dreamt that the devil had led him to a field to dig for gold, but he found none. The devil said, "It is there for sure, only you*

Pieter van der Heyden (after Pieter Bruegel the Elder), *The Battle Between the Money-Banks and Strong-Boxes*. c.1558. Koninklijke Bibliotheek Albert I, Prentenkabinet, Brussels.

cannot dig it up now..." The man asked that the place should be marked. The devil suggested, "*Just shit on it ... it will not occur to anyone that gold lies hidden here, and you will recognise the exact place.*" The man did so, then immediately awoke and felt that he had done a great heap in his bed ... Thus his dream-gold was turned to filth.' (Poggio, *Facetiae*)

The folk-treasure-dream formula is recognisably the seed of Bruegel's *Dukatenscheisser*, but such tales are relatively free of anxiety, whereas in the *Griet* anxiety is king. The simple coarse humour of the original idea has altered considerably. To understand why this should be so, we need the help of both the psychoanalysts and the historians of money.

Freud found that, for the very young infant, faecal matter is a prized substance. As the child is socialised, this valuation is suppressed and '*the child's interest in faeces is transferred in the adult onto another material which he learns to set above almost everything else – gold or precious metals.*'[10] When he is an adult, he will learn to value money as others do, and act accordingly. However, as the economy changes, similar expenditure may appear profligate in one generation and generous in the next. Georg Simmel explained how historical circumstance affects an individual's relationship to money: '*If the character of money as an ultimate purpose oversteps that intensity for an individual in which it is the appropriate expression of the economic culture of his circle, then greed and avarice emerge. I emphasise the dependence of these concepts on the current specific economic conditions, because the same degree of passion in acquiring and holding onto money may be quite normal in one context but may belong to the hypertrophied categories in another...*'[11]

Greed, avarice and other kinds of money-passions change in character and virulence, because changes in the economy alter the commonsense view of what is inappropriate and abnormal. The changing relationship between money inside and outside of the mind may turn on the ways in which money ceases to supply the same satisfactions as its infantile equivalent. Kovel argues that people compensate for the increasing abstractness of their money systems by making their unconscious configurations of money more sensuously real. 'Money diseases' evolve as money ceases to be material and becomes instead an invisible medium of credit, present in the world less as sensual heavy treasure than as a series of digits.

The position of money in the unconscious mind has indeed changed over the course of our economic history. The hermit Peter Damian (c.1007-1072) suffered a nightmare which reveals the clash between an older gift economy and a new commercial perception of precious metals as money. Peter received a gift of silver and found that his inner self regarded it as money: '*At night, when he was trying to recite psalms, his head felt dizzy and his intestines seemed to undulate with a swarm of vermin*'.[12] By the thirteenth century, the identification of body-contents with money was commonplace. Pope Innocent III compared the avaricious man to Hell, '*because both eat but do not digest, both receive but do not give back.*' Dante described Master Adam, a notorious false-coiner burned in 1281, as '*shaped like a lute, if only he had been cut short at the groin, from the part where a man is forked. The heavy dropsy which dispairs the members by ill disposal of the humors, so that the face does not answer to the belly, made him hold his lips apart*'. (*Inferno*, xxx, 49-56)

The skinny limbs and inflated belly are caused by a disease of the digestion, dropsy. Dropsy was a good metaphor for Master Adam's particular fraud: since (according to Aristotle) the body's digestion 'cooks' food, false coining was like bad digestion. So Dante makes counterfeiting a disease of the body politic's digestive system.[13]

The notions of digestion gone wrong, of evil cooking, and of fraud as demonic disorder were thus readily to hand in Bruegel's culture. To these, as an Antwerp man, he may have added a novel appreciation of money's endlessly deferred satisfactions. Money splits the original exchange of goods into two 'mutually indifferent acts,' so the conclusion (or consummation) of the transaction can be deferred almost indefinitely. The historian Agnew argues that this resulted in the wide-scale adoption, in the sixteenth century, of a modern speculative mercantile attitude towards the world: '(in) the expanded commerce of the sixteenth and seventeenth centuries ... the desire for liquidity ... suggested a simultaneous readiness and reluctance to transact – a threshold moment of indecision in the cycle of exchange, a moment frozen in the money form itself.'[14]

This attitude appeared in its most extreme form in the culture of the Antwerp Bourse. In this frame of mind, inherited associations of money-as-body-contents could be developed into convoluted and perverse images. For the first time then, Bruegel's *Griet* shows money, excrement, body-deformation and demons as connected in our dreams. That this configuration is still present in our culture is clear from Kovel's description of the neurosis of a late twentieth-century New York banker: '*Though he was unable to enjoy commodities.. he was fiendishly interested in money for its own sake, i.e. as part of himself... In sessions when Curtis talked of money.. sensations in his groin or neck or rectum – stabbing pains or moments of flushing – would occur. Sometimes he felt as if a warm fluid were incontinently running down his legs, (or) as though his insides would rise through his gorge and choke him. To say that Curtis was fiendishly interested in money is not an idle comment. (In) analysis.. we learned that for him, to be declining in wealth was to open the portals of his body, especially his anus, to demons. These were variously described, usually as powerful men who resembled people in real life; at times they had a purely fantastic aspect. They would come for him, nail him to a rack, pull his insides out to extract the precious stuff.*'[15]

Evidently, any system of money is an abstraction invented by human minds. Such a system itself operates upon the minds of people living in it and with it. As a money system grows in complexity and reaches higher levels of abstraction, so too the position of money in men's minds and in their dreams becomes increasingly complicated. The bizarre phenomenon of the Antwerp credit boom can be seen as a staging post in the long transformation of money into abstraction. So too, the money-excrement relations in Bruegel's image mark a sea-change in the way we dream about money. From the unproblematic peasant dreams of treasure to the nightmares of the twentieth century. The gigantic *Dukatenscheisser* – both comic and uncanny – makes visible a watershed in the history of dreams.

LOUISE S. MILNE

1. On Bruegel's career and works, see MARIJNISSEN, R. H. and M. SEIDEL, *Bruegel*. New York, 1984; on his relationship with Boschian themes, see MILNE, L. S., *Dreams and Popular Beliefs in the Imagery of Pieter Bruegel the Elder*. PhD diss., Boston University (1990).

2. The quotation is from EHRENBERG, R., *Capital and Finance in the Age of the Renaissance*. London, 1928, p. 234. On the merchants and their economy, see VAN DER WEE, H., *The Growth of the Antwerp Market and the European Economy (fourteenth-sixteenth centuries)*, 3v. The Hague, 1963; 'Anvers et les innovations de la technique financière aux XVIe et XVIIe siècles', *Annales: Economies, Sociétés, Civilisations* XXII (1967), pp. 1067-1089. Two colourful accounts of Antwerp at this period are J. Wegg's *Antwerp, 1477-1559* (London, 1916), and *The Decline of Antwerp Under Phillip of Spain* (London, 1924).

3. Prior to the mid-century boom, the financial structure of Antwerp was relatively primitive. In 1543, Charles V approved the practice of lending at interest – the main activity of the Bourse by the 1560s. On bizarre clauses in contracts see JEANNIN, PIERRE (a.k.a. Jean-Paul Clébert), *Les Marchands au XVIe siècle*. Paris, 1957.

4. See GIBSON, W., 'Artists and *Rederijkers* in the Age of Bruegel', *Art Bulletin* LXIII / 3 (September, 1981), pp. 426-446.

5. MILNE, L. S., 'Dreams and Pieter Bruegel the Elder's *Dulle Griet*'. In: SHETTER, W.Z. and I. VAN DER CRUYSSE (ed.), *Contemporary Explorations in the Culture of the Low Countries*. Lanham (MD), 1996, pp. 207-230.

6. SULLIVAN, M., 'Madness and Folly: Pieter Bruegel the Elder's *Dulle Griet*', *Art Bulletin* LIX (1) (1977), pp. 55-66.

7. Writing in his *Art of English Poesie*: '...but within they are stuffed full of brown paper and tow, which the shrewd boys underpeering do guilefully discover and turne to a great derision.'

8. DUERR, H.P., *Dreamtime: Concerning the Boundary Between Wilderness and Civilisation* (Tr. F. Goodman). Oxford, 1985, p. 46.

9. FREUD, S. and D.E. OPPENHEIM, *Dreams in Folklore* (Tr. from the M.S. of 1911 by B.L. Pacella). New York, 1958.

10. FREUD and OPPENHEIM, p. 37. The classic statement of this transference and its effects is Freud's 1908 essay 'Character and Anal Eroticism', in his *Collected Papers*, v.2. New York, 1959, pp. 45-50. Cf. also JONES, E., 'Anal-Erotic Character Traits'. In: *Papers on Psychosanalysis*. Boston, 1961, pp. 413-437; and the remarks in FREUD, S., *The Interpretation of Dreams* (The Standard Edition, ed. J. Strachey *et al.*, IV). London, 1953, p. 200; for bibliography up to 1977, see LITTLE, L. K., *Religious Poverty and the Profit Economy in Medieval Europe*. Ithaca, 1978, pp. 227-228, n. 86.

11. SIMMEL, G., *The Philosophy of Money* (Tr. T. Bottomore and D. Frisby). London / Boston, 1978, p. 238.

12. LITTLE, p. 73, 235-6, n. 11. For full references see MILNE (1990), pp. 158-184.

13. For this argument see DURLING, R., 'Deceit and Digestion in the Belly of Hell'. In: GREENBLATT, S. (ed.), *Allegory and Representation*. Baltimore / London, 1981, pp. 61-93.

14. AGNEW, J-C., *Worlds Apart. The Market and the Theatre 1550-1750*. Cambridge, 1986, p. 43-44. The original insight is in MARX, K., *Grundrisse* (Tr. M. Nicolaus). New York, 1973, pp. 148-49. For a non-Marxist critique coming to very nearly the same analysis of the displacement function in money, see SHACKLE, G.L.S., *Epistemics and Economics: A Critique of Economic Doctrines*. Cambridge, 1972, pp. 359-61.

15. KOVEL, J., *The Age of Desire*. New York, 1981, pp. 43-44.

Toleration

and Tolerance in the Netherlands

Maarten de Vos, *Bona Causa*. 16th century. Ink, 33 x 19.9 cm. Stedelijk Prentenkabinet, Antwerp.

The Dutch have long been convinced that their society displays the virtue of tolerance. For centuries they have cherished tolerance as a priceless heritage. Even today, when tolerance has come to be regarded as the hallmark of a decent society, they consider it their duty, on the grounds of tradition, to guard it with even greater care than, as they suspect, is customary in other states. In sixteenth- and seventeenth-century Europe, where tolerance was the exception rather than the rule, it was more securely anchored in the Netherlands than anywhere else. Today, of course, the Netherlands no longer occupies such a position. Tolerance is now the rule in many more states, and yet the idea persists in the Netherlands that the country still remains to a certain degree exceptional. It is more willing than others to deal with new problems – drugs, abortion, euthanasia, homosexuality, crime – in a spirit of comprehensive tolerance, convinced that the consequences of the principle must also be realised in these as yet not fully charted areas and that vacillating foreigners will, after a while, appreciate this. In other words, faithfulness to the Dutch heritage forces the present generation to take upon itself the risky role of pioneer.

Such ideas – and every nation cherishes a few – are of course to some degree mythical. It is by no means difficult to undermine generalisations about Dutch tolerance by pointing to examples of crass intolerance to be found in both past and present Dutch society. To take one such example, there seems no reason to regard the Dutch attitude toward the immigration of people from non-European cultures as in any way either particularly generous or particularly restrictive. There is simply nothing special about it, and that is not surprising: no country can allow an exceptional degree of hospitality and thus attract large numbers of immigrants who have been turned away elsewhere. Indeed, even in its drugs policy it is extremely difficult for the Netherlands to differ too radically from its European partners. Moreover, the loud opposition to the policy of tolerance which is growing in those urban areas where dealers and addicts are causing problems is leading to a more repressive approach. In the past few years there has been a growing degree of scepticism concerning the results of the libertarian tolerance of the sixties and seventies, and this is by no means confined to the far right, a grouping that in the Netherlands is in any case extremely small and totally unrepresentative. A wide spectrum of opinion is questioning whether this tolerance has not caused an unacceptable abandonment of norms: not freedom, but moral and social anarchy. Even the current left-wing-liberal coalition has felt it necessary to increase its prison capacity substantially and to maintain public order more forcefully than seemed required just a short time ago. The government continues to praise the value of tolerance with conviction; but, confronted with the eternal dilemmas which this brings with it, it is cautiously exploring its limits.

Eternal dilemmas indeed. We can clearly analyse the problematic character of toleration in Dutch history. The concept acquired pressing significance in the sixteenth century, the age of Erasmus. Then, it was completely clear: the increasingly numerous groups of Protestant subjects appealed to the Catholic government to tolerate, i.e. not to persecute them. That is the starting point: a minority, regarded as heretical by the government, requests the right to hold a divergent view in matters of religion and to preach this within its own circle. They do not ask that the government accord Protestant views equal status with those of Catholics, let alone that it embrace them. It must not, however, try to force those with different beliefs to abandon them. In essence, it is proposed that the government should tolerate the dissemination of religious beliefs that it regards as wrong and sinful within the state it governs. This is the principle of toleration in the strict sense of the word: by virtue of its supreme authority and despite its conviction that it possesses a monopoly on religious truth, the government is to permit some of its subjects to deny the truth of established religion. On the other hand, the subjects acknowledge the authority of the government – anyone who requests toleration is, after all, submitting himself to the authority of those who must grant it.

Bronze statue of Erasmus (1622) in Rotterdam.

The principle of toleration in this original meaning was never realised in the Netherlands. The absolute refusal of the government in the Low Countries to allow any latitude to Protestantism ultimately led to widespread unrest in the 1560s, and in the 1570s to a bitter and lengthy revolt. In 1581, the Northern provinces of the Low Countries abjured their allegiance to their prince, Philip II, who was also King of Spain, and in so doing they split away from the Southern provinces (later to become Belgium), which did not do so. In the late 1580s and 1590s the Northern provinces formed themselves into an independent state – the Dutch Republic – whose independence was finally formally conceded by Spain at the Treaty of Münster in 1648. This state was clearly Protestant, but, although the highest authorities in the country were members of the Protestant reformed church, this church was not established, and the Republic was famed for its toleration. What should we understand by this?

In the 1570s, the Protestant rebels conquered several important regions, in the first place Holland, which was already a highly urbanised area. In the towns and in the rural areas, Catholic administrators were, as far as possible, replaced by Protestants. Catholic churches were taken over by Protestants; the monasteries were dissolved; church property was nationalised: many priests, monks and nuns who remained faithful to the old religion left the country, sometimes under compulsion. There were several violent incidents, in which Catholics were the victims. Public Catholic worship was forbidden. Thus, the Protestant authorities no more applied the principle of toleration in the strict sense than their Catholic predecessors. That is to say, they recognised the freedom every human being possesses in his own conscience; neither pressure to conform nor persecution of dissenters formed part of the administrative apparatus of the Protestant authorities. In 1579 this was expressly stated in a short sentence in the Union of Utrecht, a treaty of union signed in Utrecht by those provinces, mainly from the North, which desired to pursue with vigour the war against the representatives of the prince, Philip II, despite their hopelessly confused situation. In the seventeenth and eighteenth centuries the text of this Union was regarded in the Republic as a kind of constitution and thus the passage concerning religion acquired the status of a principle. The relevant passage is Article 13, in which it is stated that each province has the right to choose the religious regime that seems best to it, on condition that *'each individual enjoys freedom of religion and no one is persecuted or questioned about his religion'*. There was to be no inquisition, either Catholic or Protestant, but, given the right of the provincial governments to determine the religion which was to prevail in each region, there was to be freedom of conscience only, not freedom of (public) worship.

The course of events in the Republic meant that in all seven of her constituent provinces Protestantism was recognised as the prevailing religion. However, it was a long time before Calvinist Protestantism, organised in the Reformed Church, could count on the support of a (small) majority of the population in a majority of the provinces. The Republic remained a country widely divided in matters of religion, in which there was a certain degree of

Emmanuel de Witte,
Interior of the Portuguese
Synagogue in Amsterdam.
1680. Canvas, 110 x 99 cm.
Rijksmuseum, Amsterdam.

latitude for Catholics, Jews, Baptists, Lutherans, all kinds of idiosyncratic sects and, in all probability, fairly large groups of people who took no active part in religious life at all. In evaluating this situation, contemporaries and historians alike have sought the answer to the central question of how this latitude came about. Why were those people in the Republic who did not wish to conform to the rules of the prevailing religion given more freedom to organise in their own church fellowships than was the norm in Europe in the seventeenth and first part of the eighteenth century?

There was no question of toleration in the sense of the word defined above. No government in the Republic ever promulgated an ordinance of principle in which it declared on the basis of its supreme authority that its subjects were free to profess a religion in public which it, the reformed government itself, regarded as false and sinful. If the government generally responded with extreme caution when confronted with flagrant evidence of unorthodoxy and urged by the Reformed Church to take measures against it, this was usually for reasons of practicality rather than principle. In the final analysis the government had to ensure peace and good order, and it realised that in a community as immensely heterogeneous as that of the Netherlands – and particularly, of course, in the great international commercial centre of the world that Holland was for a time – it was completely impossible to impose uniformity. There was the additional consideration that in the remarkably decentralised administrative system of the Republic, things which were forbidden in one province or town were permitted in another. A pastor who preached unorthodox sermons, an author who wrote unorthodox books and a printer who published them could, if exiled from one town, sometimes set up in another just a few miles away and carry on their business there untroubled.

One should not imagine, however, that relations were relaxed and peaceable. The seventeenth century was one which abounded in clamorous, bitter and often, to modern taste, crude polemic. Rigid dogmatism and unbending principle stood in the way of reconciliation. Those who involved themselves in the discussion on toleration were not concerned with the issue which preoccupied the much more sentimental eighteenth century – earthly happiness – but with the salvation of the soul, the horrors of eternal damnation, the complete insignificance of human beings in the face of God's omnipotence. And discussion there was in plenty. Jonathan Israel gives a lively summary of this fierce debate in his book *The Dutch Republic. Its Rise, Greatness and Fall* (1995). The origin of such discussions always lay in concrete doctrinal disputes, either within the Reformed Church itself, or between the Reformed Church and the government. Frequently the question of principle, whether public dissemination of views branded as sinful untruth by the Reformed Church was to be permitted, was narrowed down to the question of whether religious diversity would undermine political stability. Arguments of conscience and practice, of philosophy and politics, were constantly intertwined. The outcome was for a long time uncertain. Although from as early as the second half of the seventeenth century the Republic was both praised and blamed by foreign visitors as an island of religious toleration, actual practice in fact lacked any intellectual or juridical basis. No government had decreed that a coherent system of toleration should exist in the Republic. And no Dutch author would have been able to provide the necessary theoretical arguments for such legislation, arguments capable of convincing the Reformed Church.

Only in the eighteenth century was toleration truly raised to the level of a principle and valued in wider circles for its own inherent worth. There were two reasons for this. The first was the fact, which can be noted throughout Europe, that religious orthodoxy in general, whether Catholic or Calvinist, was being undermined and attacked in a variety of ways. The new natural sciences and new critical methods applied to ancient texts gave rise to serious doubts as to the truth of the Bible, with its strange tales of miracles and inexplicable contradictions. An intellectual climate thus developed in which the preacher who wished to ban all other beliefs on the basis of his own truth became less common and attracted less of a following. It became easier to assume that it is not wrong for Christians to interpret the Bible in different ways, and that Judaism and Islam may be respected even in a Christian community. Doubt, scepticism, a cautious relativism made Western societies, including the Netherlands, more tolerant than hitherto. But something else was also afoot. In the course of the eighteenth century there developed from a whole constellation of older notions a concept which would gain enormous significance: the concept of the Rights of Man, inherent and inalienable, which included the right to freedom of expression and

N. Bauer, *The National Assembly in The Hague on 13 August 1796*. This Assembly was in fact the first representative body of the people in the Low Countries.

religious worship. Has toleration ever received a more solid foundation than in the late eighteenth-century theories of the Rights of Man and the Citizen, which received their classic formulations in the American Declaration of Independence in 1776 and in the French Declaration of the Rights of Man and the Citizen in 1789? The Constitution of the Batavian Republic of 1798 was the Dutch expression of these ideas.

And yet penetrating critics saw even at the time that it was not so. It was very far from the case, they said, that the doctrine of the rights of man affirmed toleration. One concept in fact excluded the other. The brilliant revolutionary, Mirabeau, spoke these remarkable words during the debate on the 1791 constitution: *'I am not going to preach toleration. The most unlimited freedom of religion is in my eyes a right so sacred that the word toleration intended to express it, seems to me to convey a suggestion of tyranny. In fact, the existence of any authority which has the power to tolerate is an encroachment upon the liberty of thought, precisely because it tolerates and therefore has the power not to tolerate.'* And, in the same year, Tom Paine wrote in his *Rights of Man* (1791-1792): *'Toleration is not the opposite of intolerance but is the counterfeit of it. Both are despotisms. The one assumes to itself the right of withholding Liberty of conscience, and the other of granting it.'*

In principle, these thinkers are undoubtedly right; a state which recognises and respects human rights has no need of the concept of toleration. And yet that concept has, precisely in our own time, undergone an enormous expansion. In common usage it is applied to much more than religious freedom. The concept of toleration has become the concept of tolerance. The 'permissive society' of the sixties and seventies was also called a 'tolerant

A peace demonstration in Amsterdam on 21 November 1981: soldiers (mark the haircuts!) v. nuclear arms (Photo by José Melo).

society'. In education, in social and sexual relations, tolerance was regarded as the value which provided the grounds for this whole cheerful discarding of discipline. Now that certain negative effects of this are being widely lamented, it is being said that tolerance went too far in the preceding period and must be checked – and that, as Mirabeau and Paine showed, is precisely the possibility that the principle of toleration leaves open.

The use of the term is even more interesting when it is applied in situations where one would have expected an appeal to human or constitutional rights. In 1984 a fifteen-year-old black youth from the Antilles was murdered by a sixteen-year-old white youth. A small monument was erected in his memory and to serve as a warning: *'May Amsterdam, once the bulwark of toleration, continue to bear the torch of tolerance. Because his skin colour could not be tolerated, a child fell victim here to intolerance.'* The writer of this epitaph clearly did not regard the criminal law, which forbids murder, nor Article 1 of the Dutch Constitution of 1983, which forbids racial discrimination, as sufficient. Not juridical, but traditional ethical arguments must spur the people of Amsterdam to better behaviour. He did not realise that the tolerance that he praised – in his case the tolerance of a minority by a majority – is antithetical to the universal principles relating to human equality and rights, which he doubtless also espouses. But, in the final analysis, he was not wholly mistaken. In daily life, the practice of tolerance – by the majority in respect of the minority, the native population in respect of ethnic minorities, the solid citizen in respect of the vagrant, the addict, the underclass – is probably more meaningful than the concepts to be found in legal texts.

Any consideration of the history of toleration and tolerance in the Netherlands reveals a far from simple picture. Obviously: for both theory and practice are complex and unstable. Can this essay, therefore, have no conclusion? No, not really, but we shall nevertheless propose one. What links the Netherlands of the seventeenth century with the Netherlands of the twentieth is perhaps that people then as now attempt to keep their highly complex society afloat and stable, not by demanding as great a degree of uniformity as possible but, if we may so express it, by exploring the limits within which maximum freedom and tolerance must be contained in order to avoid the risk of disintegration and anarchy. And that was, then as much as now, perhaps more a practical question than one of speculation, theory and principle. Objections from abroad or from religious orthodoxy to the fairly liberal policy, in comparison with elsewhere, on the fundamental issues of abortion, euthanasia and drug addiction, are nowadays consistently parried by a resort to statistics: Dutch reluctance to enforce absolute prohibitions leads to fewer abortions, fewer addicts, a lower incidence of secret acts of euthanasia and pitiful suicides. This was the response which the Dutch in the seventeenth century sometimes gave to fierce criticism from abroad of the relative freedom granted to churches, sects, movements of all kinds, to the universities, the press, the stage: *'but look, the order in our towns is rather greater than less than in your country, and our trade is flourishing abundantly.'*

E.H. KOSSMANN
Translated by Lesley Gilbert.

andora's

Box

Political Culture in Belgium

The Kingdom of Belgium will never be the same again after that extraordinary summer and autumn of 1996. The arrest of Marc Dutroux and the subsequent shocking discovery of the bodies of children who had been abducted, sexually assaulted and murdered, so devastated Belgian society that a panic-stricken government felt duty-bound to promise radical reform. Faced with the mass outrage of the people of Belgium, the only remedy was to put an end to governmental inefficiency, over-politicised judicial authorities and the widespread culture of nepotism and (minor) corruption. The politicians' only alternative was an Italian-style debacle.

On 20 October 1996, 300,000 people took to the streets of Brussels. It was not the sort of demonstration where slogans were chanted; there were very few banners; no firecrackers exploded; no fists were waved threateningly in the air. It was a march by very ordinary people; most of them had never taken part in a demonstration before. Mothers, fathers, grandparents and children had reacted *en masse* to the appeal of the parents of the murdered and missing girls and were looking to express, calmly and with dignity, their abhorrence of the violence to which children in our society are subjected. The White March demonstrators – 'white' as the colour of innocence and hope – were also looking to impress upon the policy-makers that the judicial authorities are supposed to serve the people, and not vice versa. The White March of 20 October will go down in history as a silent cry of indignation at the distortions in society and the failure of government. But it was also a vociferous plea for greater justice, for child-friendliness, for humaneness.

The White March was a watershed in Belgian society, for on this occasion the demonstration was not headed by leaders of interest groups or political parties. The few politicians who did join in were careful to keep a low profile. They were terrified they might be seen to be trying to exploit public outrage for political ends and they were well aware that any such attempt would attract ruthless retribution. Even the Flemish and French-speaking extreme right-wing parties – who hoped to capitalise on the anger of the people – lay low for fear of public humiliation.

On 20 October 1996 it became clear that the classic Belgian model had

had its day. The traditional political formulae for channelling social unrest would no longer suffice. The Belgian model had arrived at a crossroads: either it could follow the Italian example and sink ingloriously, or it could ring the changes with all the uncertainty which that involved. Clearly there was no longer a place for the classic Belgian crisis management.

The old Belgian consensus model

Compromise and consensus are an innate part of Belgian political society. Even before Belgian independence in 1830, the two political parties of the day, liberals and Catholics, had joined forces against the authoritarian rule of the Dutch King. In the early years after 1830, the two parties continued working together; and when they went their separate ways in 1857, there was not so much as a whiff of revolution. Even the socialist movement, whose popularity began to soar at the end of the nineteenth century, was soon drawn into the system. 1893 brought an all-out strike in support of universal suffrage, but before that the socialist leaders had already struck a deal with King and government. According to the historian Lode Wils, the strike served only '*to let off steam and as a chance to present the compromise as*

James Ensor, *The Just Judges.* 1891. Canvas, 38 x 46 cm. Private collection.

a hard-won victory'. During the First World War the socialists had no reservations about joining a government of national unity.

The three main political movements – Catholics, socialists and liberals – worked even more closely together after the introduction of universal manhood suffrage following the First World War. From then on coalition governments were the norm in Belgian politics. The days when a single party could determine policy were well and truly numbered. The three coalition groups were built on the existing fracture lines in Belgian society: between workers and capital (right versus left), between believers and free-thinkers and between Flanders and Wallonia. These three fracture lines dominated political life in Belgium until the 1980s; almost every issue had some connection with one or more of them. The situation only became explosive if the three fracture lines converged, and then there *was* a whiff of revolution in the air. Catholic, right-wing Flanders stood counter to free-thinking, left-wing Wallonia on the post-war Royal Question[1], as well as on the 'Schools War' (school funding controversy) of 1955-1958[2] and the strike against the Act of Unity of 1960-1961[3]. Consultation and consensus had to give way to confrontation and a full-scale power struggle. And yet even these rather revolutionary periods (in which a few lives were lost) did not go so far as to deal the deathblow to the Belgian consensus model. At the very last moment, just as the bomb was about to explode, the classic parties would succeed in defusing the crisis. When it came to the crunch, when the dike was at breaking point, the three main parties would close ranks to defend their position of power. Or, as the Leuven political scientist Luc Huyse put it, they formed *'collective border patrols and did deals, thereby fending off any possible competitors'*.

The favours of office

Taking over the machinery of government by means of political appointments proved a first-rate instrument. Not least it ensured a continuous flow of jobs and other advantages in the direction of the three parties reliant on each other to govern the country. Even the largest of the three – the Christian Democrats, who were almost permanently in power and could usually 'choose' their partner – had to take account of the others with whom they would have to form a coalition sooner or later. Agreements were made and appointments shared out accordingly. In other words, the whole apparatus of government was carved up and 'parcelled out'. Liberals and socialists could only take part in policy-making sporadically, but each time they came to power they demanded that their share of political appointments be stepped up.

Political appointments are the most spectacular expression of another Belgian practice, that of services rendered or back-scratching. Every politician looking to obtain votes organises an extensive network of 'meeting days', at which he / she meets hundreds and thousands of electors and 'arranges' all kinds of little matters on their behalf, ranging from a government post to planning permission or a pension. In the process, politician and citizen often actively seek ways of circumventing existing laws and regulations (previously approved by the politician). In return for a large number of

services, the grateful citizens repay the politician with a large number of preferential votes, thereby increasing his / her influence in political circles and bringing a ministerial post within closer reach. Consequently, the rendering of services on a massive scale is encouraged rather than denounced. The people have formed a picture of the 'politician-arranger', who is prepared to go to almost any lengths for a preferential vote. Competence or quality is not really a criterion for a political appointment. All that counts is the party card and allegiance to the political group. The practice of party political 'parcelling out' also characterises the sociocultural world. One of the (unintentional?) consequences of the Cultural Pact of 1973[4] was that the entire political spectrum had to be represented in the sociocultural institutions. The state broadcasting corporation, the BRTN, was the number-one victim here. A candidate's party colours were the prime consideration when it came to filling executive posts in radio or television. The number of offices the various parties had a right to was weighed up in apothecaries' scales and if there were not enough posts to go round, then another one was created. Slowly but surely the whole apparatus of government was peopled by political appointees. Not a single institution escaped: neither the judicial authorities, nor the army, nor the police. In Belgium the political allegiance of every high-ranking magistrate is crystal-clear, and when a socialist Procurator-General retires then he is replaced by a fellow party member. Following several recent appointments, the State Police is now regarded as being socialist in its allegiances, while the Christian Democrats have very considerable influence within the judicial authorities and the criminal investigation service. The Dutroux affair painfully disclosed the extent of these party political allegiances during revelations about the police 'war'.

The budgetary catastrophe

One reason the power of the political parties in Belgium has become so great is because those parties are only a part of a huge social organisation. Each of the three main parties is closely allied with other mass organisations: trade unions, national health insurance companies, sociocultural associations, etc. Even education has close links with the political parties. The 'free' Catholic schools are assured of the support of the Christian Democrats, while the state schools rely on the free-thinkers among the liberals and socialists to promote their interests. The network of both Catholic and socialist organisations was already very extensive at the end of the last century, and this complex developed in depth as well as in breadth. Flanders saw the emergence of a powerful Catholic pillar; Wallonia an equally powerful socialist organisation. The one balanced the other and ensured that the bulk of public money earmarked for the welfare state was channelled in their direction. Together with the friendly political parties, they negotiated the distribution of political powers, subsidies and appointments. Ministerial cabinets were made up of people concerned chiefly with defending the interests of their organisations. They quite often put pen to paper to write laws and decrees that were tailor-made for their 'client'. But consensus and consultation also meant that advantages for the one had to be extended to the others.

In the eighties – after the shock of the two oil crises of 1973 and 1979 – the disadvantages of the classic Belgian politics of compromise came painfully to light: public finances were in a catastrophic state. The national debt was sky-high. Belgium, along with Italy, had the biggest government debt in Europe. At the time of the Reagan and Thatcher neo-liberalism, when pressure was put on the whole of Europe to take firm action to reduce government expenditure, the Belgian model was creaking at the joints and seemed no longer affordable. Up until then, all pacts had literally and figuratively been bought with government money. The examples are legion: the Schools Pact of 1958[5] glossed over the ideological differences on the subject of education between Catholics and free-thinkers, but only at the expense of the government budget. Flemish-Walloon conflicts were settled at the cost of government expenditure: for instance, the new Autoroute de Wallonie was built by way of compensation for the enlarging of the Flemish seaport of Zeebrugge, and so forth. The reorganisation of government finances, closely followed by further steps towards European unification, the linking of the Belgian frank to the Deutsche mark and the impending introduction of the Single European Currency all served to shift the power centre away from the Belgian government and towards the European institutions. At the same time, the power of the Belgian government was further eroded by federalisation (see *The Low Countries* 1993-94: 118-123), whereby Flanders, Wallonia and Brussels were assigned extensive powers and resources at the expense of the central – Belgian – government.

The gap between citizen and government

Social discontent could no longer be bought off with jobs in the government sector, subsidies to organisations or interest groups and similar traditional Belgian formulae. In the eighties there was a growing disparity between the agendas of politicians and citizens. Pressure from European and finan-

The White March in Brussels on 20 October 1996 (Photo by Filip Claus).

cial-economic imperatives served to aggravate the problems of the people. Government was engrossed in making savings in expenditure and in any case showed itself incapable of taking efficient action to tackle social insecurity, poverty, the degeneration of urban areas, etc. The problems were such that the classic pressure groups, on which the Belgian consensus model was founded, were now out of their depth. Like the politicians, they too had concentrated almost exclusively on the traditional fracture lines in Belgian society. With a government which had no more money to buy (also literally) social peace, no more 'pacts' could be made. The former channels of communication with the people – trade unions, national health insurance companies, sociocultural organisations, etc. – were not in a position to give voice to the social discontent either.

Logically perhaps in a country where voting is compulsory, the first of the various authorities to pay the price for the growing gap between government and people were the politicians. Taking full advantage of the social changes, the extreme right-wing parties made great headway in the elections of 24 November 1991 and 21 May 1995. The people who voted for the extreme right were looking to register the fact that the politicians had ignored their concerns: unemployment, social insecurity, the problems created by the presence of large groups of immigrants, petty crime, the degeneration and decay of older parts of the cities, etc.

The Belgian disease

But it was not only the extreme right-wing voters who were discontented. Large numbers of those voters were victims of the government's socio-economic and financial policy, and in the past they had had no reservations about voting for left-wing and even extreme left-wing parties.

Other groups in society also felt very strongly that politics and politicians were no longer capable of tackling social problems. An ever-increasing number of people found that the classic Belgian solutions did not work any more. Rather than providing a remedy, the vehemently enforced politicisation and attendant favours of office, the party-political 'parcelling out' of the machinery of government, etc. had proved to be the root cause of the problems.

A series of unsolved murders in which public opinion assumed – rightly – that even bigwigs were involved, served to foster distrust. The Belgian judiciary seemed to be incapable of finding the perpetrators of the bloody 'supermarket massacres' of the Nijvel Gang (twenty-eight dead in the mid-1980s), the murder of the socialist Minister André Cools, the murder of the anti-hormone veterinary surgeon Karel van Noppen, etc. It also transpired in the early nineties that leading politicians had taken bribes from arms manufacturers (the Italian Agusta and the French Dassault) in return for purchasing military equipment. But still the judiciary failed to come up with any hard evidence. The media was ruthless in its reporting of the party political tug-of-war between magistrates and police departments. Examining magistrates who belonged to the Christian Democrat family were accused of deriving pleasure from declaring open season on socialists, while socialist magistrates and ministers tried to protect their political friends. The large Walloon city of Liège was nicknamed 'Palermo on the Maas'.

It was in this climate that a number of young girls disappeared. Again the judiciary did not succeed in coming up with any real leads. In an endeavour to find the missing girls, action groups of different kinds emerged all over the country and organised meetings and poster campaigns. Confidence in the classic governmental bodies (judicial authorities and police) seemed to have dried up completely.

In August 1996 the bomb exploded: following the chance arrest of one Marc Dutroux, the truth soon emerged and the bodies of some of the abducted and murdered girls were found. But at the same time it became clear in the most appalling way possible just how sick and incompetent the machinery of government had become as a result of a system of party political appointments, back-scratching and the like.

On 20 October 1996, 300,000 Belgians voiced their discontent. Discontent also about a society that had gone totally off the rails. A society in which a child's life had been reduced to mere merchandise. A society which revolves around money and material gain to such an extent that nothing is sacred any more.

And yet the attitude of the White March demonstrators was not negative. They were practically down on their knees begging for the sort of structural intervention that would bring an end to the Belgian disease: for a justice system that would serve the people and not vice versa; for a non-politicised machinery of government; for a policy that would protect children, and so on.

The White March in Brussels on 20 October 1996 (Photo by Tim Dirven).

While in the eyes of the demonstrators the Belgian politicians had flunked their competence exam, they were nevertheless allowed a resit. So the White March was also a sign of hope : hope for a better society and for a new political system. The Belgian politicians are now faced with the monumental challenge of forsaking the classic paths for new ones that will restore the confidence of the people. A Parliamentary Commission, set up to enquire into what had gone wrong with the investigation of the girls' murders, aroused high expectations. The Commission was unanimous in its conclusions and – most un-Belgian, this – it did not mince its words. But old political habits reasserted themselves, and the conclusions were watered down until little of substance remained. The Belgian disease had too strong a hold. If the politicians do not succeed in meeting this challenge, an Italian scenario may await Belgium, with all the traditional parties swept aside.

JOS BOUVEROUX
July 1997
Translated by Alison Mouthaan-Gwillim.

NOTES

1. Right after the end of the Second World War, the Walloon community was critical of Leopold III for what they judged to be his collaboration and failure to give a lead to the Resistance. The Flemish community, on the other hand, supported the King's decision to remain in the country during the occupation and to seek to shield the people, as he saw it, from the worst excesses of the German occupier. It was finally decided, after a referendum in 1950, that Leopold should formally give up the throne in favour of his elder son, the late King Baudouin.

2. Catholic education felt itself discriminated against by the then government of (free-thinking) socialists and liberals. The Catholics tried to bring the government down by means of strikes and mass demonstrations. The campaign was particularly violent in Flanders.

3. Following the loss of its colony of the Congo the Belgian government of Prime Minister Gaston Eyskens sought to impose a drastic programme of economies. Through strikes and demonstrations the socialist opposition almost succeeded in bringing the country to its knees; two people were killed in skirmishes with the police. The protest sometimes assumed revolutionary forms, especially in Wallonia, where demands for economic federalism became more vehement.

4. Because of the Catholic majority in Flanders the free-thinking minority felt discriminated against, among other things in cultural policy. The Cultural Pact stipulated that all major ideological groups must be represented in every administrative body. In practice this meant that the political parties increased their hold over cultural policy.

5. The bitter 'Schools War' was resolved by the Schools Pact of 1958. Burying the hatchet, it was agreed that in every municipality a state school should be established as well as a free Catholic school, thus providing for freedom of education and freedom of choice. The government guaranteed to fund the various networks.

hree

Countries in One Kingdom

The Netherlands Antilles and the Paradox of Independence

'The Antilles are a sea'
M.F. Da Costa Gomez

If the Netherlands is my fatherland, then the Antilles are my motherland. Six Caribbean islands in the tropics, married to a European country which lies between the dikes. The Antilles, that means warmth, homesickness, a longing for far-off places, poverty, riches and security. I feel the confrontation between fatherland and motherland most keenly when I am touring the six islands with parliamentarians from the fatherland. I am continually standing up for my mother, even when she doesn't deserve it. Why does she want to stay with my strict Calvinistic fatherland? For the money? Or is it something more than money? Why does she not want to become independent? Why does she receive visitors from the fatherland with her customary hospitality? Because she is warm-hearted and has time for everyone. A sea.

The Antilles are a sea, and the sea is full of whispered pretexts. Pretexts sometimes learned from Father, but which, eight thousand miles across the ocean, across the Tropic of Cancer, are twisted somewhat, but that is what Father's words are for, isn't it? Indeed, the proverb says: *'Papiado di verdad no to hanja stoel pa sinta'* ('He who speaks the truth hath no stool on which to sit').

The Antilles, as referred to here, comprise the Lesser Antilles islands *('Benedenwindse eilanden')* of Curaçao (150,000 inhabitants), Bonaire (14,000) and, 800 kilometres further North, the Leeward Islands *('Bovenwindse eilanden')* of St Maarten (30,000), St Eustatius (1,900) and Saba (1,200). The five islands just named together form one country: the Netherlands Antilles. Until 1986 the island of Aruba (60,000 inhabitants) belonged to the territory of the Antilles, but from January 1986 Aruba has been a separate state, just like the Antilles, with its own parliament, its own ministers and its own governor. Aruba and the Netherlands Antilles together with the Netherlands (15 million inhabitants) form the Kingdom of the Netherlands. Three countries of very different nature and size in one kingdom.

The paradox of independence

Since 1954 the Antilles have been an autonomous country within the king-

The flags of the Netherlands Antilles, the Netherlands and Curaçao.

dom of the Netherlands, with their own budget, in which the Netherlands has no say. But from the end of the sixties up until 1990 Dutch politicians wanted to see the autonomy of the colonies, as they then were, changed to political independence, and harped continually on that theme. But the Antilles politicians continued to say *'manán'*, which means 'tomorrow' in Papiamento, but which really means 'never'.

For all the political misfortunes of many new states along the equator, this was an unheard-of situation: the ex-coloniser wanted the independence of the ex-colony, but the latter did not. My astute mother could see through this paradox of independence better than the dogmatic father: political independence really only makes small countries dependent, unstable and in most cases violent even. The empirical truth of this position can be seen all along the equator. But dogmatists do not look, they believe. Even the simplest observation, that of the number of inhabitants, could not shift the Dutch dominie from his belief. 250,000 inhabitants, spread across six islands, what can they achieve in the international transactions of the twentieth and twenty-first centuries? Six ready-to-eat morsels off the coast of South America, two hours flying time from North America, pearls for the Mafia, the moment they lay glistening in the blue Caribbean Sea without the protecting parasol of a serious state. The absurdity of such an independence can be summed up in one word: smallness. Each on its own, or all five together, the Antilles are simply too small for what the Netherlands wanted. For the smallest country, Aruba, that is even more the case.

Such a misunderstanding naturally results partly from differences in approach, which have their roots in Caribbean history, on the one hand, and, on the other, in the Calvinistic history of Dutch prosperity, a hard guilder with a confession of guilt round the rim. The Dutch are easily caught up in the psychology of guilt. A sense of sin and self-blame are practised with almost masochistic enjoyment. Such psalms echo well along the dikes, but they are lost on sunny islands where the pleasant north-easterly trade wind provokes quite a different sense of pleasure, a different rhythm, a different conception of time and thus of history. The marsh dweller versus the tropical islander. The marsh dweller has had to conquer and maintain his country in a centuries-long fight against the water. That implies: work, work, and more work. And prayer, naturally, praying that the water will not rise. *'Ora et labora'* ('Pray and work'). The tropical island dweller would go catching fish in the sea, and, when he had sufficient fish, he would lie under the tamarind tree and eat, and talk, and drink. That gives you a different outlook on life, a different relationship with God. That makes for a different culture.

But the Antilleans know how to exploit the post-colonial guilt feelings of the marsh dweller, brought up on work and prayer, particularly when it comes to money. In spite of all the stereotypes of Dutch frugality, the Netherlands pumps enormous sums of money every year into the Antilles in the form of development aid. Never before has one nation given so much to another nation on an annual basis. Whereas an inhabitant of India receives thirty-five cents per annum from the Netherlands, the Antillean or the Aruban, that is their governments, receive more than a thousand guilders per annum per inhabitant, that is three hundred million guilders per annum of development aid. Moreover, the Antilleans and Arubans have Dutch passports, and therefore enjoy all the privileges of Dutch citizenship. If people are out of a job, they go to the Netherlands for benefit; those who wish to study go to the Netherlands and receive a student grant. The standard of living in the six sunny parts of the kingdom is three to five times higher than that in the surrounding countries. For the inhabitants, the Netherlands means social security.

Such generous help and assistance did not lead to greater independence. On the contrary. The nature and level of the development projects increased the islands' dependence on technical aid and expertise from Europe. International airports, sea ports, an international monetary exchange, a regional university and an International Trade Centre were developed on Curaçao and Aruba, but these cannot be staffed from a population of two hundred thousand inhabitants. The Antillean and Aruban people may be highly talented – many tens of thousands have studied and are studying in the Netherlands – but, with a population of the size stated, it cannot be expected that the necessary expertise for such pretentious projects is to be found

The monument to commemorate Admiral Michiel Adriaensz. de Ruyter's stay on St Eustatius. Saba can be seen in the distance.

The Hooiberg ('Hay Mountain') on Aruba.

exclusively within their own frontiers. Yet an archaic immigration regulation of the Antillean and Aruban governments demands precisely this. The European Dutch do not have the same rights in the Antilles and Aruba as the Antilleans and Arubans have in the Netherlands. These European Dutch cannot work there without permission from the Antillean or Aruban governments. Even the spouses of Dutch citizens who are accorded permission are not allowed to find a job. This unjust and inappropriate immigration system is maintained by the Antillean and Aruban governments, in contravention of human rights, and in stark contrast with the generosity of the Netherlands, under the banner of 'Antilleanisation'.

Given the high-quality infrastructure, the Netherlands often harps on about simplifying the administrative structure in the Antilles. As well as the national parliament and the national government, each of the five islands of the Antilles also has its own elected island council, its own representatives and a lieutenant-governor to govern it. With all these parliaments for such small population groups, the Antilles probably have the highest density of politicians in the world. Moreover, the Antillean and Aruban politicians do not forget that their ministers (for 200,000 and 60,000 inhabitants respectively) expect to be treated and remunerated in the same way as the Dutch ministers (for 15 million inhabitants).

For years there has been talk of changing the administrative culture, and of better control of finances in the Antilles and Aruba, but as long as the Netherlands pays out so generously the Antilles and Aruba are in no hurry. Indeed that suits Caribbean culture. Not to be in a hurry is more comfortable than to be in a hurry. Western people often forget that. In a country that has won itself from the marsh and the sea, haste and hard work are inextricably linked. Being in time is a dire necessity. You must keep ahead of the water, the tide. The Antillean lives in the water, because the Antilles are a sea. It is not in the nature of the Antillean to be on time. The clock is an unnatural object. True time is elsewhere. Where? In the time spent together, under the tamarind tree, in the game of dominoes and in hospitality. An Antillean once said to me: *'You have a clock, but I have time.'*

Yet guests are kept at a distance. If hospitality is freedom, there is no 'revering' of guests. The hospitality of the Antilleans was amply enjoyed by the Dutch politicians, ministers and members of parliament who took the trouble to fly over. Not to be in a hurry seemed, after all, a very nice thing for a short while. A boat trip on the blue sea, champagne, a barbecue on the beach: that's easy, and, to be fair, it keeps the money flowing. The Dutch don't rock the boat, so a lot gets done, sometimes too much. Guarantees for hotels on Aruba with its beautiful beaches, but with so many high-rise hotels that the sea has a constantly increasing supply of sewage to deal with and is already not so blue any more...Things will run their course, but there will be a price to pay, in the tussle between ecology and economy. More and more roads are being built on Curaçao, and there are more and more cars. And more and more council houses, and more and more bungalows, some of them virtual palaces. Oh yes, it is land of riches and plenty in a developing country, on the receiving end of annual aid of several hundred million guilders. Marsh dwellers can certainly learn something in the tropics, and it is this: don't rock the boat. And indeed, that is simpler in a warm climate.

Island psychology

Antilleans prefer to be called by the name of their island: Curaçaoners, Bonairians, Statians and St Maarteners or Leewarders. *'The Antilles are a sea'*, said Dr Da Costa Gomez, founder of a Christian political party, half a century ago. *'The Antilles do not exist'*, people still say, and by that they mean that the Antilles do not exist as a country. Actually there are only islands.

An island is its own cosmos... *'How long are you staying?'* asks one's host. And by that he doesn't mean how long you are going to stay with him, but how long you intend to stay on the island. *'When are you leaving?'* refers to when you are leaving the island.

There is something like an island psychology. The island dweller laughs

The Queen Emma Bridge in Willemstad (Curaçao). The facades of the houses are typically Dutch.

in agreement when you say that to him, but if you have pretensions about
knowing anything more about the island he will contradict you. Anyone not
born on the island remains a stranger. I have been coming to these islands
for thirty years now, and I am still a *'macamba'*, that is, someone from over-
seas, someone from a far-away place. *'Macamba'* is a term of abuse for a
white person, but it is also simply a designation, a somewhat vague definition, just as most of the arrangements on the island are rather vague.

The island constantly evades your grasp, five islands evade you five times
over. Two autonomous countries, no matter how small, are an extra worry
for the government in The Hague. When, in 1995, the Netherlands offered
the Antilles and Aruba the support of the Dutch navy against the traffic in
drugs to and via the islands to the USA, the Antillean parliament opposed
this on account of their 'autonomy', whereupon President Clinton asked the
Dutch government what on earth was meant by that. I presume that the complicated administrative structure of two hundred thousand Caribbeans in the
Kingdom of the Netherlands is not the first priority of the President of the
United States...

For all their hospitality the islanders are united in a conspiracy against
strangers. On the island, everyone works on the assumption that everyone
knows everything about everybody. People talk readily, and tell each other
the gossip. To tell someone something in confidence is a fairly sure way of
making it generally known. It points to the closed character and secrecy of
the island community. They know all about each other.

The closeness of an island such as Curaçao, the village-like way of dealing with each other and the visitor, the 'stranger', sits most uneasily with the
international character of trade and traffic on the island. The same is true for
Aruba, with its sixty thousand inhabitants, for St Maarten (between thirty
and fifty thousand inhabitants, no one knows exactly how many because il-
legal workers are cheap labour and they can easily be got rid of, and, if it
comes to that, easily thrown off the island. This doesn't always work, because then they flee to the French part of St Maarten).

On Curaçao and Aruba people are fond of talking about the corruption on

The old Jewish graveyard of Beth Haïm (1668) on Curaçao, with an oil refinery in the background.

the Leeward Islands. Is that to distract from the many tales of corruption doing the rounds of Curaçao and Aruba? One could write a thick tome on that subject. It is a fact that the Antillean government granted a licence to an American-Arabian oil company to start up an oil-terminal on Statia, and that the island of St Eustatius receives 15 guilders (read: fifteen guilders) for a tanker visit (normally the price is around 30,000 dollars per day). No one looks for the source of the corruption – not even the Dutch government which pays development money to the autonomous Antillean government. As regular as clockwork tens of thousands of millions are disappearing. Forty million of development money for the building of an airport on St Maarten, forty million guilders for building a water tank (the so-called 'tankergate') on Curaçao, and the name of the representative who diverted the forty million is known, and forty million guilders for building an hotel on Aruba, also to an Italian entrepreneur, the same entrepreneur as for the airport on St Maarten. But the rest is just tittle-tattle. Nothing is proved, but everyone knows the truth. And on the Leeward Islands they have a proverb that I gladly draw to the attention of all gossip-mongers: '*When somebody is pointing at you, three fingers are pointing at himself.*' Let the reader take the trouble to point and then to look at the other three fingers. He will see the island double-speak.

It is a real headache for the Netherlands, all these islands with their right of self-determination, their own administration, representatives and an island council, and in addition to all this the Antillean States, the parliament, with its own Antillean ministers. And yet the Antilles don't exist, so people say.

The headache for the Netherlands increases when one considers Aruba. Traditionally Aruba has always had only one desire, to be free from Curaçao, that is to say, free from the central Antillean government which has its seat on Curaçao. In the seventies, the period when the Netherlands was pushing the islands towards independence, that strong desire was cleverly manipulated by the Aruban political leader of the time, the ex-teacher Betico Croes. Indeed, the Arubans are a completely different race from the

Curaçaoners, with a completely different history. Arubans stem from the Indians, massacred four hundred years ago by the Spaniards on Curaçao, or driven back to Aruba and Bonaire. Arubans are proud and business-like, but business-like in a manner totally different from the more commercial Creoles from Curaçao, whose forbears came as slaves. Even the language, Papiamento, is spoken slightly differently on Aruba and Bonaire from the way in which it is spoken on Curaçao, and the inhabitants of the island prefer to emphasise the differences between Aruba and Curaçao rather than the similarities.

While the Netherlands and Belgium (25 million inhabitants) are becoming a province of Europe, the two hundred thousand Antilleans speculate every now and then as to whether to divide themselves into five countries: Curaçao, Bonaire, St Maarten, St Eustatius and Saba. Each of the islands and islets prides itself on its own history, population and racial origin (differences of colour from very light-brown, light-brown to dark-brown, and very dark-brown and black, indistinguishable to a *'macamba'*, each have their own name in Papiamento), a separate culture, a separate language – Papiamento on Curaçao, Bonaire and Aruba, English on the Leeward Islands, and the Papiamento and the English vary from island to island. The linguistic and cultural differences are no greater than those between West and East Flanders, than between the various Departments (administrative subdivisions) in France or between the counties in Great Britain, but the island is its own microcosm, where people see the sun set over their own sea and rise out of it again. On an island one very readily speaks in terms of the universe. The European Dutchman, with terms such as 'greater administrative uniformity', cannot cope with this, and if he should think he can, he is a *'macamba'*, and *per se* someone who in principle cannot understand what happens there. Remarkably enough, such a breaking up into islands could probably enable the government of the kingdom to work more efficiently and advantageously than it can with the present complicated structure, in which the country hides behind the island, and the island behind the country.

Already in the sixties tourism was heavily promoted by the Netherlands Antilles.

FURTHER READING

BROWN, ENID, *Surinam and the Netherlands Antilles: An Annotated English-Language Bibliography*. Metuchen (NJ), 1992.

DERKX, JO, *Netherlands Antilles and Aruba: A Bibliography 1980-1995*. Leiden, 1996.

GOSLINGA, CORNELIS CH., *A Short History of the Netherlands Antilles and Surinam*. The Hague, 1979.

HARTOG, J., *Aruba: A Short History*. Aruba, 1980.

KOULEN, INGRID and GERT OOSTINDIE (with Peter Verton and Rosemarijn Hoefte), *The Netherlands Antilles and Aruba: A Research Guide*. Dordrecht, 1987.

NORD, MAX, 'The Netherlands Antilles and Surinam, Treasure-Chests of Dutch-Language Literature'. In: *The Low Countries. Arts and Society in Flanders and the Netherlands. A Yearbook 1995-96* (ed. Jozef Deleu *et al.*), Rekkem, 1994, pp.251-257.

Of course things can't go on like this, and the Netherlands would very much like to see fewer administrative layers. But then the Netherlands will have to think up all kinds of other structures, while the Antilleans are busy negotiating, because they are born negotiators. The Antilleans will want to retain a Dutch passport and the Antillean politicians will want Dutch development aid Antillean style, the delights of Europe and so much more besides that ties them to the kingdom. And how they can negotiate! It is in their blood. Dutchmen are talented salesmen, but Caribbean trade and negotiations are not their forte. Moreover, the Dutch dominie streak frequently gets in the way of the salesman. When it is a matter of cooperation for development or of differences in colour, the dominie bows his anti-discriminatory head in anticipation, sometimes so deeply that it looks like discrimination of another kind.

Dutch law

Everything can serve as food for complaint – and people do complain about everything – except the law. Dutch law prevails in the courts. Despite all the differences of opinion, everyone is absolutely agreed about one thing: people want law 'Made in the Netherlands'. Most judges come from the Netherlands: white, upright young men with a brisk authoritative style, who provide an element of certainty amid the capricious, sweltering, putrefying climate. The main security for people, trade and society is legal security. Legal transactions must take place in Dutch.

The reader will already have understood that in this essay it is not my concern to come up with political solutions, except that the Dutch in the Antilles must be given the same rights (to work and immigration) as are enjoyed by Antilleans in the Netherlands. I have used the political antics to illustrate the clash and conjunction of cultures. We have known for a long time what happens when one colonises a country. But what happens when one wants to get rid of the ex-colony, but can't, and yet wishes to deal with it in a proper manner? Post-colonialism is a thing of the past, you are stuck with each other, a bit of Europe and a bit of the Caribbean. It is a unique process of decolonisation there in the Dutch Antilles and Aruba, without violence, without loss of life, but with all the multicultural problems of the living. Since the Netherlands finally accepted in 1990 that the Antilles and Aruba are to remain with the Netherlands, Curaçao and Aruba are, thanks to Gorbachov, closer to Russia than ever before. The Caribbean connected to Europe, that is a fine global thought.

PETER HOEFNAGELS
Translated by Sheila M. Dale.

The

Low Countries on the Road

Travel Writing in Flanders and the Netherlands

Katsushika Hokusai,
Dutchmen at the
Nagasakiya Inn in Edo.
1802. Wood engraving, 26
x 17.1 cm. Rijksmuseum
voor Volkenkunde, Leiden.

'*Travel is my private form of reflection*', the author Cees Nooteboom once said. '*You are transported, carried along, and that gives you time in which to look around. And if you look carefully, you start thinking. Travel sharpens your gaze*'. This pioneer of Dutch travel writing breathed new life into the genre in the 1980s. He picked the right time.

The Low Countries had gone through a period of considerable austerity in the years after the Second World War, but now there was once again money for enjoyable things such as travel. And the events of May 1968 had made the Dutch more aware of events in the rest of the world, such as America, Eastern Europe and Vietnam. The hippies had long since departed to trek across India and Pakistan, and the floodgates of mass tourism had not yet fully opened. For a writer, there were still a great many unspoiled spots to discover. Cees Nooteboom (see *The Low Countries* 1993-94: 137-152) was one of the first to undertake genuinely distant journeys, journeys about which he wrote very fine accounts. The fact that those early travel stories have stood the test of time is demonstrated by a recent reissue. It contains accounts of Nooteboom's journeys through lands such as Persia, Burma, Malaysia, Thailand and, above all, Japan, and every one of these accounts reveals the greatness of a literary traveller. Self-reflection, philosophical ponderings and an elegant style go hand in hand with an unerring feeling for important detail. And it is this same combination of qualities which made his latest major book *Roads to Santiago* (De omweg naar Santiago, 1992) one of the best books ever written about Spain. Even the Spaniards themselves share this view; the Spanish edition is already in its third print run there.

Cees Nooteboom opened the way for a flood of Dutch travel writing. Serious anthropologists, well-read mountaineers, inspired journalists, seasoned men and women of letters and even poets: they all threw themselves into the literary travelogue. The boundaries between literature and journalism became blurred; or more accurately, the two fields began to merge. Writers ventured into factual observation, while journalists began to produce finer sentences with more introspection than they had ever been allowed to write for a newspaper. Nonetheless, the genre remains fluid, without strictly defined boundaries. Some authors oscillate between novel and travel story; others have opted clearly for the novel. An example is Adriaan van Dis, whose *The Promised Land* (Het beloofde land, 1990) and *In Africa* (In Afrika, 1991) contain magnificent accounts of reunions with old friends in South Africa, a country to which, as a friend of Breyten Breytenbach, Van Dis was long denied access. But he has also reported on the terrible civil wars going on in the neighbouring countries, and on the chaos and dreadful upheaval in that great Africa. Van Dis demonstrates an unequalled talent for bridging the gap between travel and writing: '*Language is acupuncture for me; it removes my fear. And while the bullets are flying around me, I hesitate over the position of a comma.*'

Jan Brokken too appears to have gone back to the novel for good. His travel stories always were interwoven with literary precursors, in whose footsteps he travelled. In *The Rainbird* (De regenvogel, 1991) for example, he unravelled some of the mystifications surrounding the Belgian author Georges Simenon, as well as some of the characters portrayed in the latter's novels set in the African interior. And in *Good Evening Mrs Rhys* (Goedenavond Mrs Rhys, 1992), set on the island of Dominica, he attempted to solve the riddle of the author of *Wide Sargasso Sea*, struck as he was by certain phrases in that book: '*Too much blue, too much purple, too much green. The flowers too red, the mountains too high, the hills too close by.*'

While some authors have abandoned the travel story, however, others have stuck with it and grown into world-class travel writers. Not only that, but in recent years excellent new travel writers have emerged – most notably the two Great Ladies of Dutch-language travel writing, Lieve Joris and Carolijn Visser. Both continue to write remarkable travel stories; both are writers who have succeeded in elevating the genre to literary status: their books contain dialogues which could just as easily have been taken from a novel, and both writers have a gift for raising the tension at just the right moment. In short, they use all the techniques of the novel to reach the reader with their story, to lure him into their (travel) world.

It was Carolijn Visser who, like Cees Nooteboom, gave a completely new impetus to travel writing in the 1980s with her book *Grey China* (Grijs China, 1982). In contrast to the well-intentioned stories about the blessings of the Cultural Revolution, seen through the rose-coloured spectacles of the manipulated group tourist, to which readers had been treated up to that point, Carolijn Visser introduced the New Dutch Travel Writer: critical, inquisitive, analytical, fearless and accepting nothing she had not seen with her own eyes. Here were no outrageous adventures à la Redmond O'Hanlon, or the unseemly arrogance of Paul Theroux; instead, the reader was presented with an open spirit with a great hankering for the truth behind the apparent reality. Just as a novel provides insight into the soul or into human existence, so a good travel story creates a window into a country or another person's existence. Naturally, even the travel writer himself harbours doubts as to whether he, a passing stranger, can ever really discover the true soul of the country through which he is travelling. Carolijn Visser expresses this poignantly in *Voices and Visions. A Journey through Vietnam Today* (Hoge bomen in Hanoi, 1993) when at a certain point, after visiting the cities of Saigon and Hanoi, she decides that she might after all have more chance of finding the core of Vietnamese history in the countryside and thus sets off to visit a farming family: '*Well, I think, here I am sitting in an isolated mountain hut surrounded by a Muong family with a glass of rice wine in front of me. It's just that the soul of Vietnam is not really becoming much clearer to me*'. And yet she was able as no other to get through to the 'ordinary' people thanks to her disarming approach. Full of confidence – which is not the same as naivety – she marches up to somebody who catches her attention and then she sees how it turns out. Usually it turns out well. The result is that she quickly feels at home with people, wherever she may be in the world, and becomes involved in their daily activities or family outings. This is what makes her travel stories about China, Mongolia, Haiti, Estonia, India and Vietnam high points in Dutch travel writing.

Similar things can be said of Lieve Joris. She proved in *Back to the Congo* (Terug naar de Kongo, 1987; see *The Low Countries* 1993-94: 284-285) and *The Melancholy Revolution* (De melancholieke revolutie, 1990), which deals with the collapse of socialism in Hungary, that she had the ability to write atmospheric, intriguing and tongue-in-cheek travel stories, a trend which she continued with *The Gates of Damascus* (De poorten van Damascus, 1993), a penetrating account of her stay with a friend in Syria. And recent-

Jan Brokken (1949-)
(Photo by Klaas Koppe).

VOICES & VISIONS

A Journey through Vietnam Today

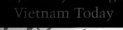

Carolijn Visser

ly she surprised everyone with her latest work, *Mali Blues* (1996).

Lieve Joris, too, intuitively pursues people during her travels whom she suspects of having a tale to tell. For example, she is on her way to Mali, but no sooner has she met a clever Mauretanian sociologist, than she immediately changes her plans and embarks on a fantastic journey with him through the country of his birth. The long title story is the best in this collection. In it, Joris describes the meeting and her weeks spent with the famous 'blues man' Boubacar Traoré, who bears the nickname Kar Kar. She senses that he carries a sad story within him, and that is above all the story she wants to hear. At first she distrusts her own motives: '*Am I perhaps in search of a noble wild savage?*' But Kar Kar promises her: '*One day I'll tell you a story. You may have travelled much in Africa, but the story I will tell is one you have never heard; no man can bear so much sadness. You will weep, and all those who hear your story will also weep.*' When he finally tells his story, it is not only Lieve Joris who is brought to tears, but the reader with her. After *The Gulf* (De Golf, 1986), in which she travelled alone through the oil states of Saudi Arabia, the Arab Emirates and Kuwait, writing a book which has become a classic about those countries, and after *The Gates of Damascus*, Lieve Joris has come up with a top-ranking performance yet again with *Mali Blues*. Together with Carolijn Visser and Cees Nooteboom, she makes up the Golden Trio of Dutch-language travel writing.

But new talents are also emerging. For example, there is Marcel Kurpershoek with his *Deep in Arabia* (Diep in Arabië, 1992) and *The Last Bedouin* (De laatste bedoeïen, 1995). He is an Arabist and diplomat who has spent much time with bedouin tribes in the desert and spoken with descendants of poets, simple shepherds and even with women, who are not supposed to talk to a Westerner at all. These are marvellous books which provide a deeper insight than any anthropologist could give of an ostensibly impenetrable culture. His recent work, *Reunion in Jerusalem* (Weerzien in Jerusalem, 1996), is also an interesting mix of history and topicality: only now does the background to the conflict surrounding the notorious tunnel, which in 1996 almost brought the Arabs and Jews to the brink of war again, become clear. Harm Botje, who spent twelve years in Cairo as a foreign correspondent, had already written an excellent book about that period, *Under the Spell of the Nile* (In de ban van de Nijl, 1991), but surpassed himself with *The Devil's House* (Het duivelshuis, 1994). It is a compelling and often hilarious account of Algeria in the 1990s. He pokes fun at the blustering leaders of the country, whilst at the same time presenting a serious picture of the excesses of Islamic fundamentalism. But he also presents the views of the Berber minority, who often have little time for fundamentalism, and travels to the Algerian hinterland, with the snow-capped mountains of Kabylia and the vast mass of the Sahara desert.

Lieve Joris (1953-)
(Photo by Klaas Koppe).

Sjon Hauser, by contrast, is more of a city rat: in *Thailand: Soft as Silk, Flexible as Bamboo* (Thailand, zacht als zijde, buigzaam als bamboe, 1990), he throws himself into the exciting world of lovers of the seamy side of life, of small-time hucksters. The Flemish poet Herman de Coninck also regularly ventured into the wide world in response to invitations to read from his own work; he wrote fine accounts of his experiences in *The Cowboy Chaps of Mary Magdalene* (De cowboybroek van Maria Magdalena, 1996), a book with a pleasant sense of self-reflection: '*I am not a true traveller. Travellers like to depart. I prefer to arrive*'. He travels through Israel, America ('*America is not a land in which to live, but a land to be passing through*'), South Africa and Ireland, but is fascinated above all by Africa, because '*here you occasionally still obtain a glimpse of how the world would be without civilisation. At least without what we term civilisation. Me, without myself*'.

It was a very different, and unexpected, land through which the Dutch writer Benno Barnard travelled in *Begotten by God on Europe* (Door God bij Europa verwekt, 1996). He opted for the country which held him in thrall: Belgium, '*a bastard begotten by God on Europe, a tangle of languages, borders and corridors, the cherished battlefield of the Great Powers*'. He criss-crossed the country, beginning in that area right in the east where most people still speak German because until 1918 they were subjects of the Kaiser. It is a fascinating story, particularly because of the linguistic confusion which arises in his every encounter with a Belgian. Later he goes to Antwerp, among other places, where he gives a splendid account of Jewish life today, rooted as it is in a long history. Barnard has a fascination with historical events, wars especially. But he talks a great deal with 'ordinary' Belgians too, for as he – a Dutchman born, but now a '*Belgicist*' – writes: '*Every journey in Belgium, however short, however long, ends in a café.*' A journey with many stopovers, then, but many conversations as well, for as befits the true traveller he travels alone and therefore *has* to talk to people.

Another writer who travelled alone, but who through anxiety was not able to penetrate to the true heart of the country, was Ellen Ombre in *He Who Means Well* (Wie goed bedoelt, 1996). Her chief aim in this book was to highlight the failure of development aid in Benin, with which the Netherlands has a cooperation treaty; in order to achieve this she loads her little Renault aboard the cargo boat which is taking her to Benin. There, everything goes wrong: the authorities refuse to release her car, she does not get on with the family she is lodging with and she has virtually no success in getting hold of aid workers. Of the latter she says: '*They came and went, were relieved by other do-gooders with a lucrative charter for a better life in the tropics. They lived in the finest houses in the most expensive districts.*' Nevertheless, her book remains suspended somewhere between an indictment and a travelogue.

Former colonies offer the Dutch-language travel writer a constant supply of interesting material: for Belgians there is the Congo, and for the Dutch there is Indonesia. The 'grand old lady' of Dutch travel writing, Aya Zikken, talks wistfully about the land of her birth in books such as *Return to the Atlas Moth* (Terug naar de atlasvlinder, 1981). In *The Spines of the Pig* (De stekels van het varken, 1993) Duco van Weerlee created a sharp but loving portrait of Bali, where he lives and where he sometimes encounters difficulties ('*All those cultural misunderstandings, you get fed up to the teeth with them*'), as well as an extraordinarily interesting journey in Irian Jaya, the former New Guinea, where he stays in the Baliem valley with the Dani tribe, who have a reputation as head hunters and cannibals. After many wanderings and conversations he comes to the conclusion that he is opposed to the old struggle of the Papuans for independence from Indonesia: '*More than 250 languages are spoken in Irian, and the same number of tribes distrust each other. There are so many scores to settle that, should the Indonesians ever leave, more*

Aya Zikken (1917-)
(Photo by Klaas Koppe).

arrows would fly above the island than cockatoos.' Wiecher Hulst, who had already written brilliantly about Indonesia in *From Sabang to Merauke* (Van Sabang tot Merauke, 1988), has also produced one of the best literary travel stories about the former Dutch colony with his recent work *A Friend on Lake Toba* (Een vriend aan het Tobameer, 1995). He starts and finishes at his favourite spot, the Danau Toba, the holy lake of the Bataks in Northern Sumatra. Between start and finish he travels to Medan, takes the old Deli railway, treks to Padang or to the as yet undiscovered (by tourists at any rate) island of Siberut. The common theme running through his account, however, remains the problem faced by everyone who travels and is in search of undiscovered regions or self-supporting tribes: either they have to adapt to the changes caused by tourism and other economic inputs, or they die out. Hulst writes in a very witty and ironic style, encapsulated in splendid dialogues, about development aid workers, religious fanatics, European drop-outs and other moronic tourists, about government officials who do not like his questions ('*YOU ARE WRRRONG!!*'); but his concern about developments in the new Indonesia, where the gulf between rich and poor is becoming ever wider and frustration at the lack of liberty and equality is increasing, is sincere. Elsewhere in this book there is an interesting interview on this subject with the renowned author Pramoedya Ananta Toer, who is censored in Indonesia.

Alongside all these exotic adventures, then, Cees Nooteboom may appear somewhat tame. But that is mere semblance, because in *Roads to Santiago* he expresses in the best possible way the motives and motivations of the true travel writer: '*I am about to undertake the journey one more time, and even now I know that I will be side-tracked, a tour being synonymous with a detour in my experience, the eternal, self-contrived labyrinth of the travellers who cannot resist the temptation of side roads and country lanes, of a branch road off a main road, of the sign pointing to a village with a name you have never heard before, of the silhouette of a castle in the distance with only a track leading to it, of the vistas that may lie in store for you on the other side of that hill or mountain range.*'

RUDI WESTER
Translated by Julian Ross.

LIST OF TRANSLATIONS

BENNO BARNARD: 'An Autumn Day in Bohemia' (Tr. David Colmer). In: *Leopard III: Frontiers*. London, 1994.
JAN BROKKEN: 'The Last Judgement' (Tr. Tony Briggs). In: *Vengeance! A Passport Anthology: no. 6*. Huntington (Cambs), 1993.
                         The Rainbird (Tr. Sam Garrett). Melbourne / Oakland / London, 1997.
LIEVE JORIS: *Back to the Congo* (Tr. Stacey Knecht). London, 1992 / New York, 1992.
                         The Gates of Damascus (Tr. Sam Garrett). Melbourne / Oakland / London, 1996.
MARCEL KURPERSHOEK: 'The Ghost of a Bedouin knight' (Tr. Sam Garrett). In: *Icarus 10*. New York, 1993.
CEES NOOTEBOOM: *Roads to Santiago* (Tr. Ina Rilke). London, 1997 / New York, 1997.
CAROLIJN VISSER: *Voices and Visions. A Journey through Vietnam Today* (Tr. Susan Massotty), Boulder (CO), 1994.

The

Low Countries through British Eyes

in Ages Past

In 1749, almost two-and-a-half centuries ago, the prolific and polyglot antiquarian Thomas Nugent published in four tiny volumes his immensely successful guidebook *The Grand Tour*. To define what his contemporaries could expect to learn, he wrote in the Preface: '*Travelling is a custom, visibly tending to enrich the Mind with knowledge, to rectify the Judgement, to remove the prejudices of Education, to compose the outward Manners, and in a word, to form the complete Gentleman*' (p.xi).

Archibald Skirving, *British Tourists*. 1792. Pencil. Private collection.

J.M.W. Turner, *Dutch Costumes.* Pencil, *Dordt Sketchbook*, f.17 recto, 1817 (Clore Gallery, London).

Robert Hills, *Tower of the Oude Kercke at Delft.* 1816. Watercolour (Photo by Sydney W. Newbery).

This edifying text referred to travel as the educational no less than plea-surable finishing-exercise for the sons of the great and good in eighteenth-century Britain. Traditional categories of travellers had always been diplomats and soldiers, merchants, scholars and artists. Earlier, a special incentive had also been piety – which meant laborious pilgrimages. True, Chaucer's exhilarating *Canterbury Tales* of the fourteenth century demon-strated that, as long as journeys remained inland, they could also be fun. But if a pilgrim's destination was abroad it was a different matter and required much preparation. This meant above all collecting lists of stages, recommended accommodation, rivers to cross, shrines to revere along the road – and instruction about the natives.

Originally, such information was based on personal experience. But in due course, as its market expanded and the genre proved adaptable for the use of other travellers, equally serious but with greater leisure, more resources and different interests, it changed in emphasis. Instead of shrines and relics, soon urban residences, castles and stately homes were included. In fact, by the seventeenth century, culture had quite superseded professional or pious motives for travelling. And by the eighteenth, going on a 'Grand Tour' of the continent with Rome as its ultimate target had become enough of a national institution for Nugent to pen his lofty principles.

These principles were much to the point and as late as 1815 they were still used as a motto for Thomas Campbell's *The Traveller's Complete Guide through Belgium, Holland and Germany*, which was defined by the astute printer as *Containing full Directions for Gentlemen, Lovers of the Fine Arts, and Travellers in General*. And in 1817, when the new 'battlefield tourism' had come to stay, this was updated and reprinted with an entire chapter on 'A Walk over the Field of Battle at Waterloo' (pp.62-74).

But then, both Nugent and Campbell could only fully come into their own on the strength of pages and pages of geographical and historical data to mentally arm the Grand Tourist on his way to Italy, via either France or Germany, with the Low Countries regularly as part of the outward leg – an itinerary that produced *The Traveller's Guide through the Netherlands* as Nugent's opening volume!

In all this, there was an obvious evolution in the European travel of Britain's upper-class youth. In the sixteenth century the poet-diplomat Sir Philip Sidney – fated to die in Holland in 1586 – warned his brother Robert when he wanted to join him that '*a great nombre of us never thought in our selves whie (= why) wee went, but onlie of a certain tickling humour to doe as an other man hath done*' (*Works*, III, pp.12-25).

At the same time Lord Burghley reminded the customary tutor accompanying his son – a functionary popularly referred to as 'bear-leader' – that he meant '*not to have him scholarly learned but civilly trained*' (Van Strien, p.7).

In actual fact, going on the Grand Tour to the Cradle of European Civilisation developed into a kind of 'invisible' or rather 'virtual' academy, not least because of the moral obligation to put the experience into writing in the form of a diary, a journal, or a series of letters, often printed afterwards.

For a pre-Grand Tour example, here is an English traveller who after arriving at the town of Gorcum in 1608 noted: '*The sweetness of the situation, the elegancy of their buildings, the beauty of their streets, and all things whatsoever in this town, did wonderfully delight me, insomuch that as soon as I entered into one of the longer streets, methought I was suddenly arrived in the Thessalian Tempe!*' (Coryat, p.639). The writer also happened to be something of an eccentric who had earlier returned all the way from Venice on foot to hang his worn-out shoes in his parish church. Disarmingly capitalising on his experience, he published in 1611 *Coryats Crudities Hastily Gobbled up in Five Moneths Travells in France, Savoy, Italy (...) and the Netherlands*; it contained one of the first recordings of the Dutch as a people that daily scrubbed the cobbles in front of their houses and sprayed their windows with water, thereby justifying the fact that in their language the same word was used for clean as for beautiful, viz. '*schoon*'.

Praise came to alternate with blame, though. In contrast to Coryat's Thessaly from Antiquity, Grand Tourist William Beckford, the voluble son of the richest sugar-tycoon of England (who as a boy was taught music by Mozart

J.M.W. Turner, *Environs of Dordrecht*. Pencil, *Dordt Sketchbook*, f.86 recto, 1817 (Clore Gallery, London).

and drawing by Cozens) wrote from Ostend well over a century-and-a-half later: '*So unclassical a place! Nothing but preposterous Flemish roofs disgust your eyes when you cast them upwards; swaggering Dutchmen and mongrel barbers are the first objects they meet with below.*' (ed. Mavor, p.23). As he proceeded by coach to Ghent, he continued: '*All is still and peaceful in these fertile lands: the eye meets nothing but round unmeaning faces at every door, and harmless stupidity smiling at every window.*' (p.24) At Antwerp '*the silence which reigned*' was '*more awful*' and by the time he reached the Moerdijk he defined the inhabitants as '*the most uncouth bipeds in the universe*' (p.28).

Essentially in similar vein, the great eighteenth-century connoisseur and letter-writer Horace Walpole pontificated in his *Anecdotes of Painting in England* (1762): '*A flat country like Holland is incapable of landscape*' (vol. III, p.811). Of course, in his day and age the prevailing idea in aesthetics was that a proper landscape required the '*undulating line*' postu-lated by the painter William Hogarth in his *The Analysis of Beauty* of 1753 (p.38). Their measure, moreover, was the scenery of Italy – while blissfully unaware of the supreme irony that English 'landscape' was Dutch '*land-schap*', i.e. land '*geschapen*', ('created' or 'shaped'), by the brush of an artist on his canvas and that for several generations the term had happily been borrowed '*from a people that are no great lenders but upon good security*', as the painter Edward Norgate put it in 1620.[1]

Still, it was Holland's unfamiliar flatness that at first sight did appal many British visitors. Only in the next century did it move the poet-laureate Robert Southey to lure his friend Henry Tailor to join him on a Dutch trip by telling him that '*You do not expect enough from Holland. It is a marvel-lous country in itself, in its history, and in the men and works which it has produced. The very existence of the country is at once a natural and a moral phenomenon*' and then announcing fairly and squarely: '*Mountaineer as I am, I expect to FEEL more in Holland than in Switzerland. Instead of climbing mountains, we shall have to ascend church-towers*' (*Life and Correspondence*, vol. v, 1850, p. 211). Whether, in addition to unique panoramas, his sport yielded the climber some insight into Dutch religious toleration has alas remained undisclosed. But he had a point, if only a metaphorical one: Dutch freedom of conscience could indeed best be viewed from a certain elevation.

As regards the Dutch people, the earliest and most important testimony is no doubt that of Sir William Temple, twice Ambassador at The Hague between 1668 and 1674. His near-encyclopaedic *Observations upon the United Provinces of the Netherlands* states: '*The People of Holland may be divided into these several Classes: The clowns or Boors (as they call them) who cultivate the Land. The Mariners or Schippers who supply their Ships and Inland Boats. The Merchants or Traders who fill their Towns. The Renteneers or Men that live in all their chief Cities upon the Rents or Interest of Estates formerly acquir'd by their Families. And the Gentlemen and Officers of their Armies*' (*Works*, 1750, p.47). He does not leave it at that, moreover, but goes on to elaborate: '*The first are a Race of People diligent rather than laborious; dull and slow of Understanding, and so not dealt with by hasty Words but managed easily by soft and fair; and yielding to plain Reason, if you give them Time...*' (p.47). And of the middle and higher ranks he does not hesitate to say: '*They strive to imitate the French in their Mien, their Cloaths, their Way of Talk, of Eating, of Gallantry or Debauchery; and are, to my Mind, something worse than they would be by affecting to be better than they need, making sometimes but ill Copies whereas they might be good Originals*' (p.49). Finally, getting on to the relationship of the sexes, he snorts: '*In general, all Appetites and Passions seem to run lower and cooler here than in other Countries. Avarice may be excepted...Their Tempers are not airy enough for Joy, or any unusual Strains of pleasant Humour, nor warm enough for Love. This is talked of sometimes among the younger Men, but as of a Thing they have heard of rather than felt, and as a Discourse that becomes them rather than affects them. I have known some among them that impersonated Lovers well enough; but none that I ever thought were at heart in Love; nor any of the Women that seem'd at all to care whether they were so or no*' (p.50).

Sir William Temple.

It is worth contrasting such stylish superciliousness with Henry Peacham, an older countryman of his and author of *The Compleat Gentleman*, who in his *Minerva Britanna* of 1611 recalled: '*With what excellent Bodies and Motto's have the Netherlandes, especially Holland and Zealand, vpon sundry occasions... commended their Invention to the world?*' (p.A3)

'*Their Invention*' clearly meant 'their having been invented' or 'shaped', and the attractiveness of this 'shaping' appeared so constant that nearly two centuries later the author of *The Belgian Traveller...* (etc.) would still confess: '*Should I choose a Dutchwoman for my wife, I should prefer one born or educated at Rotterdam. Either from the frequent intercourse with England, or from the many intermarriages with English families, the ladies of this city have in their looks, in their dress, and in their whole character, traits of great resemblance to the fair ones of Great-Britain.*'[2]

It is passages such as these that reveal what must be a central issue to any conclusions, viz. the quest for a secure identity. Foreigners have always instinctively been judged by English travellers in terms of prejudice and stereotype, their yardstick being the self and nothing but the self. The average seventeenth- and eighteenth-century Briton meeting 'the natives' found it almost impossible to free himself from preconceived ideas: confrontation with 'the other' subconsciously implied potential loss of 'selfhood' as a result of potential psychological 'invasion'– particularly so when a sense of kinship was also perceived (Spiering, ch.i). This lends a special overtone even to word-games like Temple's: '*Holland is a Country where the Earth is better than the Air and Profit more in request than Honour; where there is more Sense than Wit; more good Nature than good Humour; and more Wealth than Pleasure; where a Man would choose rather to Travel than to Live, shall find more Things to observe than desire; and more Persons to esteem than to love...*' (p.54).

It runs parallel to what the essayist Owen Feltham had to offer in *A Brief Character of the Low Countries under the States* of 1652 after three weeks observation of the 'Vices and Virtues of the Inhabitants', viz.: '*The Elements are here at variance, the subtile overswaying the grosser. The fire consumes the earth, and the air the water, they burn Turffs and drain their grounds with Windmills*' (p.13). What is typical in such writing is the frequent back-handed compliment. Here is Owen Feltham again, sneering: '*The people are generally Boorish, yet none but may be bred to a Statesman, they having all this gift not to be so nice-conscienced but that they can turn out Religion to let in Policy*' (p.26). Evidently, deep down, there was much envy of the Dutch Republic's success-story – which lasted until the end of the seventeenth century when the decline set in and Britain was proving her true heiress. As C.C. Barfoot has spelled it out in his fine study under the Temple-derived title of 'Envy, Fear and Wonder': until then the Dutch Republic embodied '*a living laboratory*' of a future, entrepreneurial state. (*Emporium*, pp. 223 and 231)[3]

Thus, on the eve of the well-known nasty sayings about the Dutch coined in the context of the four trade-wars fought between them, we find James Howell declaring in his *Instructions for Forreine Travel* of 1642 that the United Provinces were '*accounted the surest confederates of England and her fastest friends, for interest of religion, for community of danger and consequently of reciprocal preservation*' (*English Reprints*, 1869, p.59).

John Evelyn's voluminous *Diary* of the period not only contains fascinating observations on the social function of the art-trade, noting that farmers and artisans bought pictures for investment since there was not enough land to go round. He also remarks of the strikingly few beggars in Holland, '*so well are they provided for in workhouses and hospitals, worthy to be imitated*' (ed. E.S. de Beer, *The Diary*, 1955, II, p. 45), observations corroborated by Feltham when stating about Dutch houses: '*Their lining is yet more rich than our side; not in hangings but pictures, which even the poorest are furnish'd with. Not a cobbler but has his toyes for ornament*' (p.19). At the same time, numerous British visitors agree that the way charity, in order to fund orphanages and the care for the poor, was worked via taxes on fairs, theatrical performances, and lotteries, was admirable.

It was to take another 100 years before James Boswell (see *The Low Countries* 1996-97: 280), the future biographer of the great Dr Johnson,

J.M.W. Turner, *Amsterdam, Royal Palace*. Pencil, *Holland Sketchbook*, f.98 verso, 1825 (Clore Gallery, London).

would complain from Utrecht that his worst grouse was the coldness, dampness and fogginess of the climate which are held responsible for the chief characteristics of the people – to the inclusion of their drinking and smoking and lack of elegance (*Boswell in Holland*, 1952, p. 209).

To return to Temple, his *Observations* were never meant to be read as a guidebook, but Nugent was very much Temple-inspired, as was Campbell in whose very first chapter the reader is told: '*As a Dutchman is often a miller, a merchant, or a sailor, he always wishes to know which way the wind blows*' (p.26). Almost inevitably, then, judgements of the Dutch were mostly ambiguous. James Boswell came to Holland at his father's bidding in order to study Roman Law. A former contemporary of his at Cambridge, having been to Holland himself, wrote in reply to a sombre letter: '*The Dutch are so happy in their own dullness that I fear they can but make small allowance for your dissatisfaction....don't give too much way to your sensibility. ...Remember how much all pleasures depend on the mind and then, pray, try to Dutchify your soul*' (*Boswell in Holland*, p.12). Boswell gradually came indeed to feel at home at Utrecht where he had what he describes as '*excellent opportunity to study and at the same time to see foreign company*'. Like many a fellow-visitor he gives glowing reports of Amsterdam, The Hague, Leiden and beyond. He sees houses of correction, called '*spinhuizen*' for women and '*rasphuizen*' for men, and goes to popular houses of ill-fame, euphemistically called '*speelhuizen*'. He also frequents a so-called 'English Society' at The Hague and all the time practises his French – while incidentally falling in love with Belle van Zuylen...(see *The Low Countries* 1994-95: 125-130).

Now, in the Introduction to his *Complete Guide*, Campbell states especially that: '*As to the phlegmatic character of the Dutch, nothing can afford strangers a more lively picture of it than the coolness and silence with which even the sailors manoeuvre. You may see them working their ships up to a*

Robert Hills, *Flengatte near Brussels on the Road to Waterloo.* 1816. Watercolour (Photo by Sydney W. Newbery).

Robert Hills, Title page of *Sketches from Flanders and Holland* (1816).

Robert Hills, *In Amsterdam. Rembrandt's House.* 1816. Watercolour (Photo by Sydney W. Newbery).

shore or a quay amidst the most provoking obstacles and incumbrances without uttering a syllable!' (p.26-27).

This quiet of everyday life is constantly remarked upon by British travellers. The Gothic novelist Ann Radcliffe, in a fascinating passage on Dutch boats from her charming *Journey, made in the Summer of 1794 through Holland* (etc.) observes that: '*neither their number, nor their neatness, is so remarkable as the ease and stillness, with which they traverse the city; and indeed ease and stillness are much the characteristics of all efforts of Dutch industry. The noise and agitation, usual wherever many persons are employed together, in other countries, are unknown here*' (p.15). Even in 1833 her Scottish colleague Leitch Ritchie in *Travelling Sketches on the Rhine and in Belgium and Holland*, is still astonished that '*There is here also the same absence of the usuall noises of a city...: the very people appear to have a talent for holding their tongues; and the vessels that glide among the waterstreets, and stop at their own ware-house doors, are discharged in solemn silence*'.[2]

SKETCHES
IN
FLANDERS AND HOLLAND;
WITH SOME ACCOUNT OF
A TOUR
THROUGH PARTS OF THOSE COUNTRIES,
SHORTLY AFTER
THE BATTLE OF WATERLOO;
IN A SERIES OF LETTERS TO A FRIEND:
BY ROBERT HILLS.

LONDON:
PRINTED BY J. HAINES AND J. TURNER,
Margaret Street, Cavendish Square.
AND SOLD BY JOHN BOOTH, DUKE STREET, PORTLAND PLACE;
R. ACKERMAN, 101, STRAND; AND W. H. PYNE,
No. 9, NASSAU STREET, SOHO.
1816.

Charles Martin, *Turner Sketching.* 1844. Pencil. National Gallery, London.

Of course, it takes an artist to comment on the pictorial impression that this silent Holland made on British visitors beyond quaintness of costume and curiousness of living style. But even non-artists record again and again *déja-vu* feelings originating in memories of the Dutch land- and townscapes and above all the 'drolleries' that had been flooding into Britain, especially after the French Revolution. And it was becoming a commonplace that if there was one foreign countryside familiar to English eyes by proxy, it was that of Holland; by the time they saw the original, a hundred mornings and afternoons in museums, picture galleries, and country houses had done their work. (*A Time of Gifts*, p. 27)

British artists started touring Holland in force after the end of the Napoleonic wars. And from then on they came in large numbers. They singled out for praise the reliability and convenience of public transport by cheap and punctual towing barge ('*treckschuyt*') and waggon, by hired yacht or by chaise ('*sjees*'). Interestingly, in the eighteenth century, Holland was primarily seen as a country of towns and inland waterways, not of 'picturesque' rural scenery. As to works of art, travellers saw far more in Flanders, particularly in Antwerp, than in the North because of their prevalence in Roman Catholic churches. But that is a different story.

From before these wars there were Joshua Reynolds with *Journey to Flanders and Holland* of 1781 and Samuel Ireland with *Picturesque Tour through Holland, Brabant and part of France* of 1789, the first fully illustrated book on the Netherlands in English. Robert Hills' *Sketches in Flanders and Holland* of 1816 was keenly studied by J.M.W. Turner (see *The Low Countries* 1995-96: 198-207) whose first of five visits dates from 1817.

Amstirdam

Inn. the Arms of Amsterdam corner of ; Rusland table d'hote 3 oClock 2 florins with a Pint of Bourdx Pictures. the Surgeon Theater de Anatomie Stad House Rembrandt Corp de Garde over the Mesuem. gratuity a florin

OLIX – 10

J.M.W. Turner, *Amsterdam. Inn, the Arms of Amsterdam corner of ye Rusland / table d'hote 3 oclock 2 florins with a pint of Bourdx / Pictures. the Surgeon's Theater de Anatomie / Rembrandt Corps de Garde over the Museum / gratuity 1 florin.* (travel notes, copied from Hills). *Rhine-tour Sketchbook,* f.10 recto, 1817 (Clore Gallery, London).

Turner's over 600 Dutch sketches up to 1841 form an unequalled pictorial record, while his Cuyp-inspired *Dort or Dordrecht. The Packet-Boat from Rotterdam becalmed* of 1818 was the first oil of a Dutch scene on the basis of on the spot drawings by a British artist; his *Entrance of the Meuse, Orange Merchant ... on the Bar* of 1819 as well as *Antwerp. Van Goyen looking out for a Subject* of 1830 and *Helvoetsluys, the City of Utrecht, 64, going to Sea* of 1832 were compositions of the imagination, although in their details again based on observation (Bachrach, *Turner's Holland,* 1994).

Augustus Wall Callcott, Turner's colleague and rival, visited Holland in 1818 for his painting of *Rotterdam Harbour* and in 1826 for *The Quay of Antwerp*. Clarkson Stanfield produced several Dutch sea pieces, as did in the mid-nineteenth century E.W.Cooke who went to Holland eight times, specialising in beach-scenes at Katwijk and Scheveningen.[4]

Of course, the most striking aspect of British nineteenth-century landscape and marine painting was its reflecting of the general nostalgia for traditional ways of life and unwillingness to see the post-Industrial Revolution reflected in art. The steadily increasing number of visiting artists demonstrated their being profoundly influenced either by the Dutch Golden age or by the new Impressionism that introduced working-class women and children into their scenes.

So, long before the advent of mass-tourism, the British were already the most numerous foreign travellers in the Low Countries. Yet it was John Ruskin, that great eccentric artist-writer who, maddening though he often was even in his grand *Modern Painters* (1841-1860), never tired to repeat that '*We never see anything clearly... Everything we look at is only seeing enough of it to make out what it is*' (vol. I, Part II, p.145). Such, at any rate, is certainly one lesson applicable to the description of the Low Countries in so many English travelogues. Perhaps it is also a principle that even Thomas Nugent might well, if not have added, certainly have kept at the back of his mind when compiling the opening volume on the Low Countries in his pioneering *Grand Tour* manual.

FRED G.H. BACHRACH

1. NORGATE, EDWARD, *Miniatura, or the art of Limning*. London, 1620, p.42. The term 'land-scape' was introduced into English in 1598 by Richard Haydock in his Lomazzo-translation *Tracte containing the Artes of Curious Paintinge, Carvinge, and Buildinge* for the Italian '*paese*'.

2. GOLDSMITH, L.L., *The Belgian Traveller, or a Tour through Holland, France and Switzerland during the Years 1804 and 1805*, as in A.G.H. Bachrach, *Turner and Rotterdam*. London, 1974, p.114.

3. BARFOOT, C.C., '"Envy, Fear, and Wonder": English Views of Holland and the Dutch 1673-1764'. In: *The Great Emporium*. Amsterdam, 1993, pp.223 and 231.

4. KITSON, MICHAEL, *Katwijk in de Schilderkunst*. Haarlem, 1995, pp.56-78. This is one of the most illuminating essays on the subject.

FURTHER READING

BACHRACH, FRED G.H., *Turner's Holland*. London, 1994.

BARFOOT, C.C. and R. TODD, *The Great Emporium*. Amsterdam, 1992.

BARFOOT, C.C. and K.J. BOSTOEN (ed.), *Een Beytie Hollandsche. James Boswell's Dutch Compositions*. Leiden, 1995.

CAMPBELL, CHARLES, *The Traveller's Complete Guide through Belgium, Holland and Germany*. 1815; *The Traveller's Complete Guide containing full Directions for Gentlemen, Lovers of the Fine Arts and Travellers in General. with a Sketch of a Tour in Germany*. London, 1817.

CORYAT, THOMAS, *Coryats Crudities Hastily Gobbled Up in Five Moneths Travells in France, Savoy, Italy (...) and the Netherlands*. London, 1611.

LEIGH-FERMOR, PATRICK, *A Time of Gifts*. London, 1977.

MAVOR, ELIZABETH (ed.), *The Grand Tour of William Beckford*. London, 1986.

NUGENT, THOMAS, *The Grand Tour. Containing an Exact DESCRIPTION of most of the Cities, Towns, and Remarkable Places of EUROPE. Together with A Distinct Account of the Post-Roads and Stages, with their respective Distances...LIKEWISE Directions relating to the Manner and Expence of Travelling from one Place and Country to another. As also Occasional Remarks on the Present State of Trade, as well as of the Liberal Arts and Sciences in each respective Country*. London, 1749.

POTTLE, F.A. (ed.), *Boswell in Holland*. London, 1952.

SIDNEY, PHILIP, *Complete Works*, vol. III. London, 1923.

SPIERING, M., *Englishness. Foreigners and Images of National Identity in Postwar Literature*. London, 1993.

STRIEN, C.D. VAN, *British Travellers in Holland during the Stuart Period*. Leiden, 1993.

TEMPLE, WILLIAM, *The Works of Sir William Temple, Bart. To which is prefixed The Life and Character of Sir William Temple Written by a particular Friend*. London, 1750.

aps

for Eternity

Sixteenth- and Seventeenth-Century Cartography

in the Low Countries

Early maps   Mankind has been making maps since prehistoric times. Unfortunately, most of them were on wood, bark, skins, or some other material which disappeared over the years, so we have no record of them. Only a few, those carved in stone or metal, have endured the centuries. One of the earliest to survive is an Egyptian map carved in about 2000 BC on the side of a sarcophagus, or stone coffin; it shows the Valley of the River Nile and points the way to the empire of the dead. Another ancient specimen is a Babylonian map of the world as it was known at about 500 BC: a symbolic representation carved on stone, it depicted the world in a circle, surrounded by the ocean.

The Greeks of the sixth to the fourth centuries BC made an outstanding contribution to scientific cartography. Most of the Greek philosophers, such as Pythagoras and Aristotle, knew that the earth was round. Eratosthenes of Cyrene even came close to figuring out how large the earth was. He arranged to have two sticks pushed into the ground at two spots 800 miles apart – but on the same day and at the same time. He then had people measure the angles of the sticks' shadows. By comparing those measurements Eratosthenes came up with his estimate.

Another giant of cartography was Claudius Ptolemaeus, also known as Ptolemy, a scholar from Alexandria who lived in the second century AD. His *Geographia* contains the essential directions for the drawing of maps and the construction of globes, along with tables giving the latitudinal and longitudinal coordinates of some 8,000 cities and other important sites.

When most of this Greek knowledge was buried by the Dark Ages, cartography in Western Europe came to a virtual standstill. It was only some twelve centuries later – when refugees brought the *Geographia* from Constantinople to Rome and the Italians rediscovered it – that western mapmaking unfolded in the amazing development of the fifteenth and sixteenth centuries.

The Italians became modern civilisation's best link with ancient cartography and so were the early leaders in the new science. There were a number of flourishing cartographic centres in Italy even before the invention of the printing press. As early as the fourteenth century artisans in Genoa were making portolan charts – parchment navigation charts indicating coastlines and ports. But by the approach of the fifteenth century, the Italian mapmaking centres in Rome and Venice were being overshadowed in the international market by specialists from northern Europe. Their work had a stronger scientific basis and was presented in a more coherent and systematic manner than Italian maps. It was at Augsburg in Germany in 1472 that the first printed map appeared. Ten years later a man named Nicolaus Germanus of Ulm printed Ptolemy's maps along with a new map of Scandinavia called *Tabula Moderna*.

Flemish cartography

At the University of Leuven, founded in 1425, the brilliant mathematician and geographer Gemma Frisius described the principles of triangulation in his manual *Libellus de locorum describendorum ratione* (about the way in which 'to describe places'), published in 1533. Another Leuven student, Jacob van Deventer, acquired the practical knowledge to compile a series of maps of the different principalities, based on original surveys. From 1559 on the government commissioned him to make surveys and plans of most of the towns of the Low Countries. Since this assignment had a strong military import, the maps were not to be published, but sent to the court in Madrid. Nevertheless, copies were soon to be used by Braun and Hogenberg for their town-books.

In the middle of the sixteenth century Antwerp was the busiest port in the West. Merchants living and working there had an interest in the geography not only of their own country, but of the world as a whole. Moreover, it was an expanding world in which they lived. Every year new countries, islands, straits and sea routes were added to the widening horizon of the Westerners' environment. This curiosity about the world in which they lived brought forth the extraordinary scientific accomplishments of a few brilliant cartographers in the southern Low Countries, among whom two names stand out: the great scholar Mercator and the more commercially minded Ortelius.

Abraham Ortels, or Ortelius, born in 1527 in Antwerp, was an '*afsetter van caerten*' (a person who colours maps) who started a business in books, maps and antiquities on the side. Soon he was travelling to trade fairs in Frankfurt and Italy, where he met prominent scholars, among them Mercator. Ortelius had always cherished an interest in travel, geography and history; by the time he was 40 he had earned enough money to devote himself to geography and, more specifically, cartography.

Ortelius' oldest maps, from the period 1564-1567, are not exactly examples of mathematical precision or artistic finish, but a single brilliant innovation has guaranteed his place in the mapmakers' Hall of Fame: his design of the first map book or 'atlas'. Up until then, maps had been published in bound form; such collections are called 'Lafreri-atlases', after the Roman cartographer Antonio Lafreri. But their contents varied considerably and there was no unity of format or style from map to map.

Ortelius changed all that. First he drew up a plan of the contents; all maps would be approximately equal in size and not exceed normal book format. For some years Ortelius laboured until he had obtained 70 maps that covered all the then-known countries and regions of the world. These maps were uniformly engraved in copper and published in Antwerp in 1570 under the title *Theatrum Orbis Terrarum*. The maps were arranged as follows: one

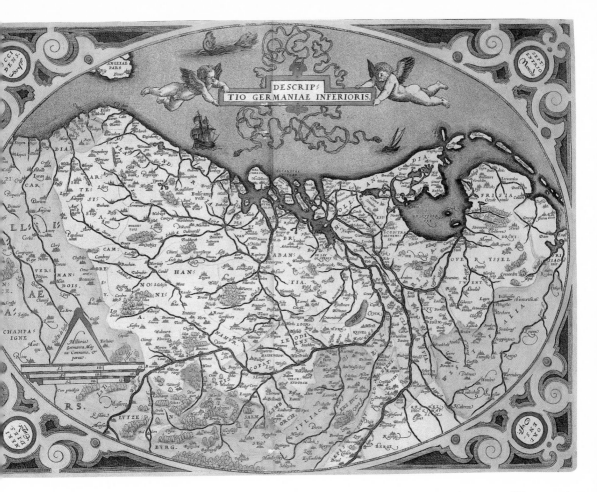

Abraham Ortelius, Map of the Low Countries (detail (1:1) from *Theatrum Orbis Terrarum*, 1570).

map of the world, four maps of the continents, fifty-six maps of Europe, six maps of Asia and three maps of Africa.

All the maps are about the same size and all share a similar decoration, lettering and symbolism. On the reverse of each map Ortelius printed a short text about the area concerned. He prefaced the atlas with a list of the map-makers, travellers and scientists in whose work he had sought inspiration. This list contains the names of 87 cartographers, and together with Ortelius' maps, which were engraved by Francis Hogenberg, it enables us to accord many sixteenth-century cartographers, whose original work has not survived, their rightful place among the masters of mapmaking.

The *Theatrum Orbis Terrarum* was regularly reissued and augmented over 42 years; the last edition dates from 1612 and contains 135 maps. From 1579 the atlas appeared with an appendix, the *Parergon,* a set of maps of the ancient world under the motto '*Historiae oculus geographia*' ('Geography is the eye of history'). After Ortelius' death in 1598 the famous '*Tabula Peutingeriana*', a copy of a Roman road map, was also included in the *Parergon.*

Gerard Cremer (Mercator; see *The Low Countries* 1994-95: 281-282), born at Rupelmonde in Flanders in 1512, is rightly called the most impor-tant cartographer after Ptolemy. The young Mercator's parents died when he

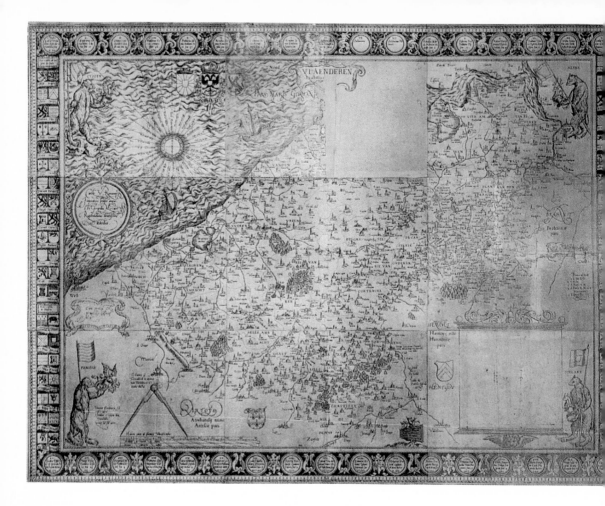

Gerard Mercator, Map of the County of Flanders (1540).

was a teenager and an uncle sent him to the University of Leuven, then still the only university in the Low Countries. His education there was primarily philosophical, but his studies left him unsatisfied: the Biblical version of the Creation taught at Leuven was clearly irreconcilable with Aristotelian physics. Mercator decided to undertake a truly independent study of the structure and genesis of the universe, the disposition of the heavenly bodies and the earth's surface, and the history of man.

This grand plan was thwarted, though, by the oldest of reasons – lack of money; so Mercator settled in Leuven as a surveyor and mathematics tutor. He was also a maker of scientific instruments such as astrolabes and armillary spheres, both of which were used to determine the position of the stars. He prospered and his clients soon included Archbishop Granvelle of Mechelen and the Emperor Charles v.

Commercial success gave Mercator time for the study of geography, which led him to cartography. His first map, dated 1537, was of Palestine. He followed this the next year with a world map using a double heart-shaped projection, then a map of the county of Flanders (1540), a terrestrial globe (1541), and a celestial globe (1551).

But Mercator grew increasingly unhappy in Leuven. Among other things, the Catholic government jailed him for several months on suspicion of heresy, which at that time implied Lutheran sympathies. So he moved to Duisburg in Germany. It was there, in 1585, that he brought several separate maps together to form the first part of his atlas. Thus he was about 15 years behind Ortelius, but the delay was due mainly to Mercator's more thorough and more critical approach.

Part I of Mercator's atlas contains 51 maps: 16 of France, 9 of the Netherlands, and 26 of Germany. Part II appeared in 1589 with 22 maps of Italy and the Balkan countries. Part III was prepared under his supervision, but was published a year after his death in 1594 by his son Rumold.

The term 'atlas' actually derives from a collection of all Mercator's works that he published under the title *Atlas sive cosmographicae meditationes de fabrica mundi et fabricati figura* (Atlas or cosmographic considerations about the construction of the world and its manifestations). The title page shows the mythological figure Atlas with a celestial sphere on his knee and a terrestrial globe at his feet: an allegorical presentation of astronomy and geography. In his preface, Mercator lauded the legendary wise prince Atlas of Libya as an example and symbol of the humanist scholar of heaven and earth. This Atlas is in fact a figure from the Greek author Diodorus of Sicily – and not the titan from Homer's *Odyssey* who carries the world on his shoulders. However, later cartographers confused the two figures and used Homer's legendary figure on their title pages. In any event, ever since Mercator 'atlas' has remained the common name for a book of maps.

Other famous names from this age include Gerard de Jode and his son Cornelis, whose *Speculum orbis terrarum*, published in 1578, is nowadays a very rare atlas; Jodocus Hondius; Petrus Kaerius; Petrus Plancius, whose materials were very extensively used by other cartographers; and Lucas Janszoon Waghenaer, who was the most famous Dutch author and publisher of sea charts of the sixteenth century. From 1572 to 1622 Georg Braun, a canon from Cologne, and Francis Hogenberg, a cartographer and engraver from Mechelen, published a six-volume townbook, called *Civitates orbis terrarum*. The six volumes contain views of the major European and non-European cities, arranged in a relatively arbitrary sequence. Each engraving is printed on a double page, with a brief Latin explanation on the back (in all some 360 illustrations).

Shift to the North When Antwerp was taken by the Spanish army in 1585, the harbour remained to a large extent closed to international traffic. Together with economic activity, cartography shifted to the Dutch port of Amsterdam, while the university of Leiden superseded Leuven as a centre of scholarship. Most of the outstanding cartographers who had strong pro-Reformation sympathies emigrated to Holland.

In the seventeenth century the most celebrated follower of Ortelius and Mercator was the Dutchman Willem Janszoon, known under the nickname 'Blaeu' ('blue'). In the winter of 1595-1596 he spent six months at the observatory of the renowned astronomer Tycho Brahe, on the isle of Ven in the sound between Denmark and Sweden. There Blaeu copied his mentor's star catalogue and so obtained the information he needed to make his own celestial globe. Returning to Holland, he moved to Amsterdam, at the time the most important port in the world, where there was a constant demand for new maps and up-to-date geographical information.

Blaeu's earliest work is a set of globes produced in 1599. The celestial one is based on Tycho Brahe's catalogue of some 1,000 stars and thus broke with the Ptolemaic representation of the heavens. Blaeu later brought out a nautical atlas, *Light of Navigation* (Licht der Zeevaert), which would remain the only work of its kind for more than 20 years.

Blaeu's first terrestrial atlases were modestly called *Appendix Theatri A. Ortelii et Atlantis G. Mercatoris,* an appendix which supplemented the atlases of his predecessors Ortelius and Mercator. In 1634, he published a complete atlas of his own, *Theatrum Orbis Terrarum sive Atlas Novus,* which contained 161 maps. Originally published in German, it was later brought out in Latin, Dutch and French. The atlas was also frequently augmented; all in all, Blaeu's *Theatrum* encompassed six volumes and 404 maps. His son Johan continued his work and in 1662 brought out a twelve-volume *Atlas Major* with 581 maps. Together with the eleven-volume *Atlas Major* of Johannes Janssonius, the son-in-law of Jodocus Hondius, it formed the summit of Dutch cartography. By the end of the seventeenth century the initiative in international cartography was taken over by the French. The ambitious King Louis XIV regarded cartography as an instrument of his expansionist policies; maps and atlases had to glorify his campaigns and conquests, and confirm France's leading role in the world. Louis granted promising cartographers an annuity, allowing them to pursue their research.

The appeal of old maps

What is the secret of these old maps, which, although outdated and obsolete, still attract a more than superficial interest from those who look at them today? I think it is the unique mixture of scientific knowledge from long ago and their artistic and decorative finishing. Although much of the geographical information on these maps may seem archaic and sometimes even slightly ridiculous (e.g. the belief in the existence of a continent at the north pole, which is apparent in many maps), their aspect still offers a great deal of intellectual satisfaction to a twentieth-century scholar with an interest in historical geography and exploration. Nevertheless, in order to interpret these maps correctly, one has to take into account a few basic skills concerning scale, orientation, projection, signs and symbols.

A map's scale gives a sense of the dimensions of the area shown on a map. Usually today the scale appears as a line divided into segments which are used to represent much larger distances, like one inch to 100 miles. Cartographers like the scale bar system because it is simple and direct, and it remains in use today.

Curiously, the bars were first used in nautical maps in the Mediterranean during the fourteenth century. Since each European country – often each principality – then had its own method of measuring distance, most maps of the period contain different scale bars. Understanding these is no easy task for the modern map reader, who must contend with countless obsolete systems.

The orientation of modern maps puts north at the top, but this was not always the case. Arab cartographers in the Middle Ages, for example, decided that south belonged at the top of their maps. Medieval Christian maps placed east at the top. In fact, the term 'orientation' comes from this practice, which permitted Christian mapmakers to venerate Jerusalem and other holy sites in the Orient.

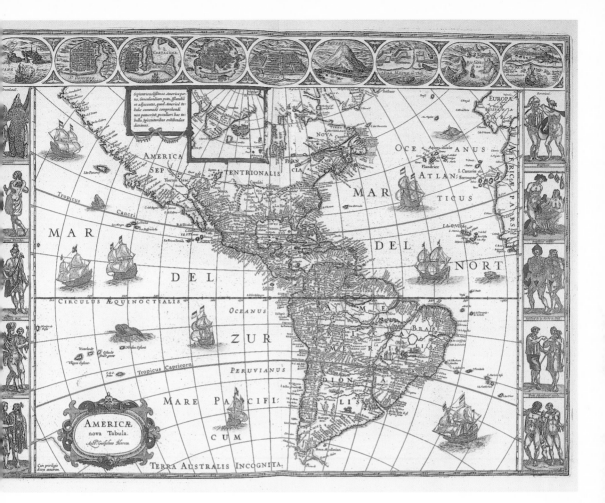

Willem Blaeu, Map of the Americas (1630).

During the Renaissance, cartographers invented a grid system, or graticule, of meridians and parallels to determine and describe the location of every place on the earth's surface. An area's latitude was always shown in relation to the equator. But the position of the prime meridian has been hotly contested throughout mapmaking history. In fact, it wasn't until 1884 that Greenwich, England, was defined as the prime meridian.

Spanish, Portuguese, Flemish, French and Dutch cartographers in the sixteenth century preferred certain points in the Canaries or the Azores, or the dividing line between Spanish and Portuguese spheres of interest after the Treaty of Tordesillas (1494), for their prime meridian.

Abraham Ortelius had the prime meridian running through the Azores in his world map of 1570. He numbered the meridians from zero to 360°, instead of 180' East and 180' West as is done today. Willem Blaeu chose Pico de Teide on the island of Tenerife as his prime meridian.

One of the toughest challenges for cartographers is map projection. It is impossible to transfer the earth's curve onto a flat sheet of map paper, but that has not prevented cartographers from trying. Since the sixteenth century, different solutions have surfaced: *conformal* projections for reproducing a small area shape, *equidistant* projections indicating accurate distances,

Johannes Baptista Vrients, Map of Great Britain (late 16th century).

and *equivalent* projections showing distinct surfaces. Actually, three kinds of projections stand out as the most useful to cartographers. Cylindrical projections put parallels and meridians onto an imaginary cylinder of paper wrapped around the globe. Plane or azimuthal projections use the same procedure on a plane surface tangential to the globe at any point. Conical projections project the globe onto a cone that touches the globe along a parallel. The Mercator projection is the best known of cylindrical projections. All latitudes are made equal in length to the equator, thereby stretching the earth's surface at the north and the south. This visual distortion has given generations of people an inaccurate view of the world.

But no map can ever be completely accurate, and cartographers know that. In fact, generalisation and selection are two key principles of cartography. The professional mapmaker uses a collection of signs and symbols which make up his cartographical alphabet. These are not used at random, however: the mapmaker sticks as closely as possible to what he wants to depict. For instance, before the eighteenth century, relief was depicted by tiny hills drawn on the map. By the end of the century, European cartographers changed these to hachure lines – those short lines which indicate slopes and also their degree and direction. To separate the sea from land masses, older maps used a wide line. Colour, of course, was an excellent way to distin-

Abraham Ortelius, Map of
Northern Europe (from
Theatrum Orbis Terrarum,
1570). Detail (1:1).

guish land from sea. Water was also indicated by closely spaced dots, wavy
patterns, outshore hatching and with form lines. These are a series of lines,
closely spaced and parallel with the coastline, which give an impression of
waves touching the shore.

Whenever the cartographer wanted to represent vegetation on a map,
which was rare, he used small tree symbols or other sketches of appropriate
flora. Often the mapmaker included miniature drawings of animals, birds
and reptiles to brighten up unknown regions that would otherwise be empty.
Even human activities were portrayed once in a while.

Since the Middle Ages, clusters of buildings were drawn to represent
towns and villages. Clever cartographers highlighted more important places
by varying the size of the symbols. Circles became the more abstract symbol for human settlements; bigger circles with the addition of other symbols
– like crosses or small flags – meant larger or more important towns. By the
sixteenth century a legend, or descriptive caption, often explained these
symbols.

The endearing charm of old maps is largely due to the artistic and decorative touches given them by gifted cartographers. Mapmakers embellished
their work with titles engraved in gracefully flowing script; map borders and
less detailed areas were rich with imaginative sketches of local life.

Lettering had to be both legible and artistic, and old cartographers made every effort to meet this ideal in their maps. Abraham Ortelius' map of the world, drawn in 1570, offers a splendid example. In a copperplate engraving that measured less than 14 x 20 inches, he used more than ten different types of lettering.

Like Nature, the cartographers abhorred a vacuum. They were reluctant to admit that there were regions of which they knew little or nothing. Abraham Ortelius is an exception: on his map of the world he devotes half the southern hemisphere to an as-yet-unknown southern continent ('*Terra Australis nondum cognita*'). Usually the gaps were filled in with elegant *cartouches* containing the title and author's name, the name of the patron to whom the map was dedicated, or the scale bar. The gracefully elaborate compass roses, too, could serve to disguise the lack of accurate knowledge of an area. Within the map itself the cartographer skilfully deployed an astonishing arsenal of eye-catching visual features which made its study into a fascinating journey of discovery for the contemporary, not only the modern, observer. Ships of every conceivable kind sail the seas, accompanied by fish and sea monsters. Exotic lands are populated with 'typical' native peoples and animals. Maps of Africa are adorned with elephants, lions, ostriches and dromedaries. Some went even further, with decorative borders incorporating depictions of typical costumes, towns and trading posts. Heraldry too provided welcome material for illustrations, both in the map itself and in the borders. Sometimes we find the family trees of ruling houses, and occasionally even small scenes from history.

A quite specific and original Dutch invention was the '*Leo Belgicus*': a map of the Dutch principalities in the form of a lion. The first of these was designed by the Austrian Michael von Eitzing in 1583 for his book *De Leone Belgico*, a historical and geographical description of the Low Countries published by Frans Hogenberg. The lion made its appearance during the revolt of the Northern Provinces, at a time of strong patriotic feelings coupled with a growing historical awareness. Between 1583 and 1815 more that thirty 'lion maps' appeared in four different versions.

The oldest, most classical version shows a lion rampant, facing to the right. Its head is made up of Friesland and Groningen. The back extends along the North Sea coasts of Holland as far as Boulogne. Its left forefoot is in Luxembourg, its raised right forefoot rests on the Rhine at Cologne. In 1611, during the Twelve Years' Truce when the war was dormant, a lion sejant (sitting) was derived from this archetype. In 1608 Hessel Gerritsz designed a whole new type of lion: he oriented his map to the west and drew a lion facing to the left. This lion's head is in Artois and it has all four feet on the ground, in Luxemburg, Limburg, Twente and East Friesland respectively. The final lion was '*Leo Hollandicus*': its background was the county of Holland, without Zeeland. This lion map was produced from 1612 until 1807. The lion invariably has a scimitar clasped in its right forepaw.

Although the lion features on the coats of arms of most Dutch principalities, it was not purely for heraldic reasons that Eitzing chose it as the symbol of the Low Countries. In the foreword to his book he tells us that the lion is the strongest of beasts and refers to Julius Caesar, who hailed the Belgae as the bravest of all tribes in Gallia. It was for exactly that reason that he felt justified in portraying the Netherlands in lion form.

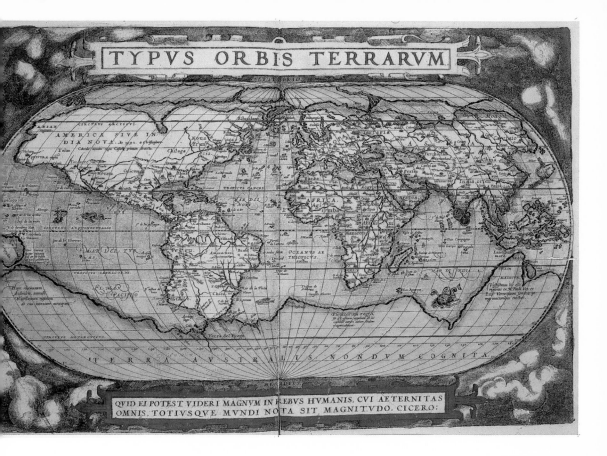

TYPVS ORBIS TERRARVM

QVID EI POTEST VIDERI MAGNVM IN REBVS HVMANIS, CVI AETERNITAS
OMNIS, TOTIVSQVE MVNDI NOTA SIT MAGNITVDO. CICERO:

Abraham Ortelius, Map of
the World (from *Theatrum
Orbis Terrarum*, 1570).

The popularity of the '*Leo Belgicus*' and its wide dissemination over
more than two centuries show that this symbolic map had not only a scientific and an artistic, but also an ideological dimension. At the precise
moment when the Dutch Revolt put an end to the region's brief political
unity, a type of map was produced which put a new emphasis on the coherence of the Seventeen Provinces. This being so, it seems no coincidence that
the last '*Leo Belgicus*' left the press in 1815, just when the partition of the
Low Countries was for a brief time revoked.

EDUARD VAN ERMEN

he

King is Dead, Long Live the King

The Uses of Reality in the Prose of Walter van den Broeck

When Baudouin, King of the Belgians, died suddenly on 31 July 1993, the media released a deluge of mournful prose, much of it maudlin kitsch, on their shattered readers. The writer Walter van den Broeck also reached for his pen, for if so much paper was to be expended on the king's death, then obviously literature too should have its say on the matter. And certainly Van den Broeck was in the ideal position for this. The character of the king had been a central motif in his writing since 1980, both in the novel *Letter to Baudouin* (Brief aan Boudewijn, 1980) and in the four volumes of *The Siege of Laken* (Het beleg van Laken, 1985-1992).

In his contribution on the event, published in a newspaper which is certainly not regarded as royalist, Van den Broeck wrote his final piece on a theme he had already developed in his novels. He had invented a fiction in which the very Catholic Baudouin, who in fact became king more out of a sense of duty than out of ambition, had secretly ceded the throne to his identical twin brother Gauthier (the French equivalent of Walter). The king then retired to a monastery. In his newspaper article, Van den Broeck made the 'real' king, now a monk, reflect on the passing away of his brother. Many readers were offended that Van den Broeck had chosen this literary approach and thus allowed his novel to merge somewhat with reality. They said that by doing so the writer had shown a lack of respect for the deceased sovereign. What they really meant was: a lack of respect for reality.

In itself the affair was no more than an anecdote, but it is characteristic of the common belief that a watertight seal should be maintained between literature and everyday reality. More specifically, it is held that, in the name of good taste, certain basic or delicate aspects of reality should be barred to the literary imagination. Taboo. Playing literary games with the recently deceased king was simply not done. But this is not at all the perspective from which Van den Broeck approaches literature. On the contrary, his iconoclasm derives not from a longing for destruction but from his ethics as a writer, and these are based on the conviction that if literature is to be meaningful then it should strive to develop a real social significance by participating in everyday reality. Van den Broeck had actually sent a copy of his novel *Letter to Baudouin* to the royal palace – after all, once a letter has been written you should post it.

Having been born in 1941, it is no accident that Van den Broeck's literary roots lie in the turbulent and innovative 1960s. In Flanders as elsewhere, many young writers were sensitive to the zeitgeist that held political commitment to be of vital importance and considered art as the ideal means of expressing it. That Van den Broeck opted for criticising the era in which he lived has a lot to do with his roots. He grew up in a so-called '*cité*', a working class district which was built around a factory. This factory was the be-all and end-all of existence for everyone living there. And the context was clear: the social segregation and inequality that went with life in a row of back-to-backs was clearly visible to them each day in the architecture of the very streets they lived in. The ultimate dream of every inhabitant was to get rich and move out of the *cité* towards a better future. The expansion of the welfare state in the fifties and sixties made this possible to a certain extent: it allowed talented young people like Walter van den Broeck to acquire an education, and thus escape working in the factory and being tied to the *cité*. So Van den Broeck became a teacher. His much older brother Jules, who turns up regularly as a character in Van den Broeck's work, did not have the same opportunities as a young man; he escaped by seeking his fortune in Mexico.

Those who got rich or had the chance to study escaped this predetermined future. Many young people who tried to do so ended up in an ambiguous state of alienation with respect to their roots. This ambiguity stemmed from the idea that they didn't have to be like their fathers and go and work like robots in the factory, though the brighter ones among them realised that once they left their neighbourhood they would end up in an equally conditioned environment, that of the middle class. The factory workers did manage to improve their lot with time, but paid the price in addiction to consumerism, ecological disaster and the decline of the spontaneous sense of solidarity.

Walter van den Broeck's awareness of all this led him to the profession of writing, with the dominant father figure as the symbol of his biological but also of his social origins. Consequently, his first novel, *Heir to the Throne* (De troonopvolger, 1967), written in a more or less traditional vein, was a story of symbolic patricide. To no avail, for his father would continue to haunt him throughout his whole work; Van den Broeck has never sought to deny his origins, quite the contrary.

In his second work, *A Long Weekend* (Lang weekend, 1968), an often hilarious slapstick novel, Van den Broeck raised the issue of his own work by appearing as a character in the book. In doing so, he extended his satire on the age he was living in to include himself: his character 'Walter van den Broeck', tormented by ennui, already embodied his first meditations on the meaning of being a writer. In retrospect, this doubting self-critical consciousness of his is certainly the reason why Walter van den Broeck has become one of the most important writers in Flanders today, unlike other members of his generation, many of whom have fallen into oblivion, and not unjustifiably so.

The few authors who escaped this fate, like Paul de Wispelaere and Daniël Robberechts, and continued to build an interesting oeuvre – though often without much public acclaim – distanced themselves from semi-naturalist and psychological novels. In their so-called 'opus literature', they

Walter van den Broeck (1941-)(Photo by Klaas Koppe).

combined social criticism with an extremely detailed critical analysis of language in which French Structuralism was often an important source of inspiration.

Like them, Walter van den Broeck, who is usually considered as belonging to this school of opus writers, never showed any sign of being one of those know-it-all do-gooders who wrote in that classical realistic style of prose which makes so much of the politically-active literature of the time so indigestible to present-day readers. When he subjected the comings and goings of his own time to critical analysis he did not forget to include himself in the proposition. It is characteristic of his work therefore that he allowed both himself and the other members of his family to become increasingly prominent characters in his novels. An indirect demonstration: his hastily written satire *Seized* (In beslag genomen, 1972), full of amusing and sometimes facile allusions to the cultural and political world of the day, is not without reason one of Van den Broeck's most dated novels, and technically perhaps his least successful work.

The desire for literary freedom in the 1960s provided Van den Broeck with the opportunity not only for innovation in the content of his prose but more particularly for a series of striking experiments with form. Unlike most of the other opus writers, in doing so he did not start from an existing concept of literary theory, but conducted an experimental search for ways of infusing a more powerful expression into the narrative tradition which had been handed down to him. These aims would change with the development of Van den Broeck's oeuvre. He no longer sought to provide a symbolic or satirical true-to-life image of reality. He became increasingly aware that reality seemed more and more problematic to him and so could not be known absolutely, let alone improved upon.

Again seen in retrospect, Van den Broeck's novel *362,880 x Jef Geys* (1970) was ahead of its time; as what he called a 'multiple' it was based on the principle of fragmented reality – though only developed in a rudimentary fashion. Postmodernism *avant la lettre* ! In the book, the character of the artist Jef Geys (a real person) is developed from the point of view of 9 non-hierarchical narrative agents in no specific sequence, as a result of which the novel is capable of 362,880 different readings, depending on the order one chooses to follow.

Doubts and insights gleaned from the fragmentary led Walter van den Broeck to a global analysis of the Self, to a complex all-inclusive *Identitätssuche*. In *Notes of a Genealogist* (Aantekeningen van een stambewaarder, 1977) he corrects idealistically and politically manipulated historiography by reconstructing his own family history. This was his first essay in giving literary form to a real experience, i.e. that of his grandparents, that flew in the face of deceit, canonised lies and official appearances. Van den Broeck completed this genealogical quest in his *Letter to Baudouin*, which provided a cross-sectional view of his childhood in the *cité*.

Though both novels are reconstructions commented upon by the author, and attempt to be as true to life as possible, Van den Broeck built an element of fiction into the second: he presented a snapshot in the form of a guided tour given by himself, as a nine-year-old child, to the recently crowned Baudouin. To the child, the king represented absolute power and unimaginable wealth, the antipode of the powerlessness and poverty of those living in the back-to-backs. But the king also stands for ritual and pomp, and as a result is only allowed to see a 'cleaned-up' version of 'his' people and country. This metaphor of kingship offered Van den Broeck the opportunity to draw our attention to the semblance and to the veil that always shrouds reality. By giving it a name, he succeeded in breaking through it.

These two novels set out a problem which had to be solved. The four volumes of *The Siege of Laken* which followed attempt to provide an answer, presented in narrative terms as a return visit by the character of Van den Broeck to the royal palace. Throughout this, Van den Broeck is on a quest for the cultural influences that determined his development as a person and as a writer. He quickly comes to the conclusion that a person can be peeled like an onion, layer by layer; in other words that an individual consists of nothing but cultural influences.

Formally, this four-part work with its complex structure consists of a long series of seemingly autobiographical fragments set within various narrative frameworks. But here the fictionalising process dominates – something which also can be seen from the striking intertextual character of these four volumes and the many mirror effects used in constructing the text. Throughout the four volumes, Van den Broeck projects reality upon literary fiction, creating a new literary reality in order to counterbalance the deceptive appearances that dominate everyday life. He turns the king who, blinded by semblance, stands on the other side of the mirror, into his ally in order to cancel out the contradiction between being and appearance and thereby eliminate alienation.

Using purely literary means, *The Siege of Laken* attempts to bring about a synthesis within the field of literature between a thesis bursting with sharp criticism of the period (power relations and human exploitation) and an equally critical antithesis (the illusory *petit bourgeois* dream of prosperity and cosy happiness). In striving for this synthesis Walter van den Broeck does not turn his back on reality. All reality is a construct, however. If people are to gain control of their own reality and take their fate into their own hands, they must commit themselves to living squarely and enthusiastically in their own 'banal' everyday world. He himself does it by writing, for what is a writer's task but to conquer reality and make it visible through literature?

MARC REYNEBEAU
Translated by Peter Flynn.

Extract from *Letter to Baudouin*

by Walter van den Broeck

Your Majesty,

You, who are wont to show a lively and uninterrupted interest in culture in general and Flemish letters in particular, you will not take it amiss that I do not provide you with a detailed account of myself. You already know me more closely and value my work more highly than those whose positions in the cultural sector should require that they devote serious consideration to such matters. This is more than obvious from the occasional modest allowances you extend to me by Royal Decree, which allow me to dedicate myself to *belles-lettres* without being subjected to too much material hardship.[1]

To enclose a curriculum vitae would, I fear, be but a demonstration of false modesty, and you know how I detest even ordinary modesty.

You should not regard the fact that I address you with a small 'y' as insolence. I am aware that your consort's secretary once declared in an interview given quite some years ago that you no longer insisted on the capital 'Y'.

I have always wished to write to you at length, ever since I was a child. I must tell you that this is typical of our family. My grandfather, you know who I mean, Peter Jules van den Broeck, corresponded for a considerable period during the 1950s with Lyndon B. Johnson, the Texan senator who, following the death of John Kennedy in 1963, was to become President of the United States. There was something the matter with my granddad's pension arrangements or some such. I will find out exactly what happened for you in due course.

My father, Robert Sidney van den Broeck, followed in his father's footsteps. He considered himself a socialist because he read the *Volksgazet* and was a loyal listener to the *Politieke Tribune* on the NIR, particularly when the socialist leader Jos van Eynde, with whom you are more than familiar, addressed the Flemish people so vociferously.

He was never a member of the Belgian Socialist Party, and only very briefly of the socialist trades union ABVV.

And every time we didn't finish our dinners he would say that they had better start another war right away.

He thought that the class struggle was an illusion. He knew working people too well, and was convinced that neither patient persuasion nor spontaneous reflex would make them cast off their yoke.

Someone who has been working hard for eight hours doesn't feel like preparing the revolution – he only wants to be left in peace.

He expected an awful lot more from the written word, though. If dark thunderclouds began to build up on the horizon – the Berlin Airlift, the Korean war, the Cuban crisis, the Vietnam war – he would reach for his pen and write, shrouded in a mist of silence and detachment, to the mighty ones of this earth.

We would automatically hold our breath far too long and walk on tiptoe all evening.

Eisenhower shouldn't be so spineless; he certainly knew the Russians from the war! He had to know what those Russkies had in mind for Western Europe!

Castro shouldn't slag off when it came to the United States like that; he would pay dearly for it one day. And then what would happen to all those world famous Havana cigars – three of which he would like to be sent in return for his good advice. Khrushchev should stop playing with fire. Hadn't his people suffered enough during the Second World War? It was the height of imprudence to so recklessly provoke America, which had the most powerful army in the whole world, by banging on conference tables with his shoes! And Lyndon Johnson should finally put an end to that business there in Vietnam. It could be done in a jiffy if he were only willing to take that top-secret laser gun they were talking about in the *Reader's Digest* out of the deep freeze. And so on.

This was clearly a substitute for taking real social action, but nobody would be able to reproach him later with having done nothing to try and improve the state of the world.

That my mother, fearing complications that might prove too much to bear for a working man's family, threw most of these letters in the fire is of little consequence.

I have briefly brought all this to your attention in order to prove to your majesty that my complaint is not based merely upon a whim[2].

And yet at the same time, I would like to make this distinction: it is not my intention to appeal to you to intervene personally in repairing an error of administration nor to provide you with any political or military advice.

1. On behalf of my wife, my two children and of course myself, I would like to take this opportunity of extending to you my heart-felt thanks.

2. This is, it seems to me, a real family trait. Five years ago my eldest boy, who was eight at the time, asked at dinner what the name of the mayor of Turnhout was – *Alfons Boone!* And where did he live? – *Look in the phone book!* An hour later he shoved a letter under my nose.

'Dear Mister Mayor, wouldn't it be possible to open a hall where poor people could get a square meal for three franks? Stefan van den Broeck, 18 Freedom Street, Turnhout.'

And could I post that for him in the morning.

A week later an envelope bearing the arms of the town of Turnhout dropped into my letter box.

'Dear Sir, In reply to your letter of 19.04.74 in which you requested that a hall be opened where poor people could be given a square meal for three franks, we hereby have the honour to inform you that we shall be forwarding your letter for further consideration to the Royal Benevolent Society for Social Charity which shares responsiblity for the affairs of the poor in our town.

With the highest regards,

On behalf of the Town Council

A. Goossens, Interim Secretary

A. Boone, Mayor'

From *Letter to Baudouin* (Brief aan Boudewijn. Antwerpen / Amsterdam: Elsevier Manteau, 1980, pp. 5-7).

Translated by Peter Flynn.

n

Search of Self

New Prose Writing in Dutch after 1985

Revisor Prose The wave of innovation which gave rise to the 'new' prose of the 1980s first made its appearance in the Netherlands with the publication in 1974 of the literary journal *De revisor*. The generation of young writers which it brought to the fore – Dirk Ayelt Kooiman, Frans Kellendonk, Nicolaas Matsier, Doeschka Meijsing and Patrizio Canaponi (A.F.Th. van der Heijden) – rapidly entered the literary canon as a group, thanks to the anthology of their work compiled by Carel Peeters (*Heart in Head* – Het hart in het hoofd, 1979), and to the attention they received in subsequent essays of his (collected in *Sustainable Illusions* – Houdbare illusies, 1984).

Form is paramount in *Revisor* prose: it excels in careful construction, in writing-as-craft. 'Pure' realism, a straightforward storyline (Jan Cremer), anecdotal and atmospheric writing (M. Biesheuvel, Maarten 't Hart), and direct political and social commitment (Harry Mulisch, *News for the Rat King* – Bericht aan de rattenkoning, 1966), all so characteristic of prose in the sixties and early seventies, have disappeared from the new writers' field of vision. The euphoric sixties were followed by an economic crisis which brought unemployment. As a result, a new inward-looking view of society emerged. From this point, the self and the individual imagination are central again; the new ego-age has begun.

In a typical *Revisor* story, the representation of reality is, in true post-modern fashion, questioned and the subjectivist ('idealist' in philosophical terms) position of the individual consciousness gives rise to a problematic relationship between literature and reality. The statement that '*the world is an idea in the minds of individuals*' applies to the work of Frans Kellendonk, Doeschka Meijsing, Nicolaas Matsier and Dirk Ayelt Kooiman as well as to that of Leon de Winter and, later on, of Oek de Jong. With his *Billowing Summer Dresses* (Opwaaiende zomerjurken, 1979), De Jong produced not only the book with which a younger generation of readers could identify, but also *the* epic of idealism and the ego-age, which marked the renewal of interest in the novel of ideas. The 1970s did indeed witness the return of intellectuality and erudition to Dutch literature. And it was this 'intellectual' and 'erudite' kind of novel which continued to dominate the literary scene in the 1980s, culminating in 1986 in *The Body Mystic* (Mystiek lichaam) by

Frans Kellendonk, whose work can be seen to have had a leading role in shaping the literary sensitivities of his generation.

In *The Body Mystic*, Kellendonk is first and foremost a critic of his own time and culture. The book caused something of a stir when the critics, condemning the antisemitic pronouncements of one of the characters, attributed them to the author himself. The novel opens in realist mode, constructed around a 'normal' family, but there is no obvious main character, and situations and statements – from the Easter story, the Song of Songs, and other biblical texts – are frequently mirrored and reversed. An ultra-conservative, aging father is confronted with the fact that his daughter is 'with child' by a Jewish doctor and his homosexual son infected with AIDS. This situation leads to provocative statements about sexuality and religion, and about human social and cultural relations in general. The novel can be read as a satire on the 'postmodern condition', but taken as a whole, it is formulated so ambiguously and ironically that a single interpretation is not really possible.

A breakthrough in Flanders The same development took place in Flanders, though somewhat later. After the euphoria of the 1960s with its belief in social change and involvement came disillusionment, self-reliance, the search for identity and an obsessive preoccupation with the nature of individual perception and the way it influences our knowledge of the world. This in essence neo-romantic tendency (which was also present in poetry) was, however, slow to appear in the South: the real breakthrough did not happen until the 1980s.

Around 1985 a remarkable double shift took place in Flemish literature. Monika van Paemel (see *The Low Countries* 1994-95: 131-138), known until then for several slim, fairly intimate neo-romantic novels, published her 'masterpiece' *The Accursed Fathers* (De vermaledijde vaders), a broadbrush epic which ensured her breakthrough in the Netherlands. At about the same time, in 1986 to be precise, the anthology *Beautiful Young Gods* (Mooie jonge goden) appeared, bearing the self-conscious subtitle '*Flemish Literary Talent*' (the subtext is *not* ironic). The book made it into the media spotlight, and although its contents were not representative of a group or generation, it had the advantage of focussing attention on a number of talented young writers like Tom Lanoye and Herman Brusselmans, as well as Stefan Hertmans and Guido van Heulendonk. *Beautiful Young Gods* was the precursor of what was soon to be known as the new wave of Flemish prose. It was quickly followed by a number of strong literary debuts which were not, however, presented to the public as forming a group: Kristien Hemmerechts (see *The Low Countries* 1995-96: 208-216), Rita Demeester, Patricia de Martelaere, Gie Bogaert, Eric de Kuyper. In fact, they were presented together as a group (without Gie Bogaert) retrospectively in the photographic exhibition *New Names. Twenty-one Newcomers in Flemish Literature 1980-1990* (Nieuwe namen. Over 21 nieuwkomers in de Vlaamse literatuur periode 1980-1990. With a catalogue by Paul Buekenhout bearing the same title, Palais des Beaux-Arts, Brussels, 1991), which actually highlighted the great differences between the 'twenty-one newcomers'.

Meanwhile, these authors have given new impetus to Flemish prose, and they have also taken steps to ensure that their books have received the critical attention due to them in the Netherlands. The fact that a number of them have found a home with publishing houses in the Netherlands may have created a favourable situation, though this is not to suggest a causal link. After all, it is not clear whether the quality of Flemish prose is improved by being published in the Netherlands or whether young writers from the South were attracted to and / or accepted by Dutch publishers because they were indeed producing better work. Be that as it may, the publishing house issue was apparently an important one in the eighties. It was in 1986 that Julien Weverbergh, a director of the Flemish publishing house Manteau, was removed by the board of Elseviers (up to this point, Manteau had had a virtual monopoly of literary publishing in Flanders) and started up a new publishing company (Houtekiet). This led not only to a great deal of movement of authors between the competing publishers, but also to a search for new writers which clearly bore fruit. But let us return to 1985 for a moment. *The Accursed Fathers* is the book in which Monika van Paemel found her own style, form and themes. But in the context of Flemish literature, the novel acquired a special bridging function. Both in form and substance, it occupies a position midway between the introverted, neo-romantic confessional prose of the previous 'quiet' generation on the one hand, and the sarcasm, bitterness and hard cynicism of the younger representatives of the 'no-future' generation on the other. Another striking feature is that, with Hugo Claus' *The Sorrow of Belgium* (Het verdriet van België), which appeared two years previously, *The Accursed Fathers* represents the Flemish variant of the 'roots' phenomenon which originated in the United States. In both cases, the authors go in search of their own past and background. This personal search is embedded in a larger world of social and political history. Such a combination of autobiographical and historical writing had been used earlier by Walter van den Broeck (in *Notes of a Genealogist –* Aantekeningen van een stambewaarder, 1977) and is also evident in *Disorder and misunderstanding* (Ontregeling en misverstand, 1983) by Greta Seghers and in *View of the World* (Het uitzicht van de wereld, 1984) by Alstein.

The gap between North and South was now bridged. All these novels are characterised by a narrative mode which is closely related to the 'crafted' Revisor-prose. They are novels which make liberal use of the arsenal of postmodern devices: careful construction, doubling or multiplying of temporal layers and perspectives, multiple mirror effects, the incorporation of internal cross-references and literary quotations. Perhaps even more remarkable is that this form of realism is also characteristic of the autobiographical documentary novel as realised by A.F.Th. van der Heijden (see *The Low Countries* 1993-94: 239-247) in his large-scale tetralogy *Toothless Time* (De tandeloze tijd) – a fictionalised self-portrait which, at the same time, chronicles a particular era. The first part of the cycle, *Parents Falling* (Vallende ouders), appeared in 1984; in 1996, the third part, consisting of two fat volumes, appeared and was immediately hailed as a literary monument.

The 'new' prose   The writers of 'new' prose in Dutch – the generation which made its debut in the 1980s – represent the many tendencies which had always been present on the literary scene without it being possible to single out any one of them as dominant or in the vanguard. Neither in the North nor in the South were there any groupings or magazines with clearly defined manifestos around which authors could come together. Where was the collective experience to draw them together or the collective idea for them to rail against? The new writers of the eighties had only themselves to look to in their search for and exploration of their identity and the world they lived in.

The growing diversity in North and South has also brought with it a broadening of themes. Beside the classic preoccupation of prose in Dutch – i.e. the description of the individual's world of experience – larger social problems and movements now come into focus: A.F.Th.van der Heijden and Joost Zwagerman write with their fingers on the pulse of time; Tom Lanoye, Herman Brusselmans and Kristien Hemmerechts, each with their own sharply differing personalities, express the wry sarcastic mood of their contemporaries. Even in the work of the newest writers, like Ronald Giphart, Arnon Grunberg and Paul Mennes, this cynical doom-laden *fin de siècle* thinking comes emphatically to the fore. There has even been talk of a '*nix generatie*' (a pun on Douglas Coupland's *Generation X*) which, in its own way, provides a picture of contemporary realities.

In his autobiographical first novel *Blue Mondays* (Blauwe maandagen, 1994), Arnon Grunberg gives a laconically narrated caricature of Jewish life. The family he portrays is marked by wartime trauma and a disastrous marriage, but the grotesque comedy which develops as the story unfolds also gains a wider dimension: it is ultimately a cynical, bitter and wryly drawn *comédie humaine* in tragic slapstick guise.

Alongside uncomplicated, small-scale realism we increasingly find writers looking beyond the confines of the self and problematising the relationship between reality and imagination. And these problems were already present in the prose of the many women writers who made their debut in the eighties. Marja Brouwers, Vonne van der Meer, Fleur Bourgonje, Margriet de Moor, Hermine de Graaf, Tessa de Loo, Nelly Heykamp, and, later, Charlotte Mutsaers – greeted by the (male) critics in the Netherlands with '*The new girls are on the march!*' – do not so much write a typically female kind of prose, but develop within a broad range of themes to which they, not surprisingly, add a 'feminine' sensitivity.

In this context, it is revealing to compare the two women writers who are most prominent in Flanders. There would seem to be a world of difference between the cynically observant realism of Kristien Hemmerechts and Patricia de Martelaere's hard portrayal of reality with its philosophical basis, but their central concern is the same: problematic relationships, the individual's vulnerability in an environment which offers no certainties.

It is also worth noting here that Patricia de Martelaere, with the emphatic philosophical interests which underpin her work, is representative of a tendency which had already come to the fore in the work of *Revisor* authors like Frans Kellendonk, Nicolaas Matsier and Doeschka Meijsing, and which was still noticeably present, if not prominent, in the work of writers making their debut at the end of the 1980s. Margriet de Moor (see *The Low Countries* 1995-96: 217-24) whose debut was in 1988, but who first attracted attention with *First Grey, Then White, Then Blue* (Eerst grijs dan wit dan blauw, 1991), which has already been translated into several languages, has much in common with the *Revisor* writers with her carefully thought-out prose (the sudden changes in perspective, for example) and thematising of the unknowability of reality.

The *Revisor* generation's novel of ideas could even be said to have grown into a philosophical novel when one considers *Mendel's Legacy* (Mendels erfenis, 1990) and *The Great Longing* (Het grote verlangen, 1992) by Marcel Möring (see *The Low Countries* 1994-95: 296-297), or *The Laws* (De wetten, 1991) and *Friendship* (De vriendschap, 1995) by Connie Palmen. They are, without exception, novels which '*are about something*', as Carel Peeters put it, and which have played a not inconsiderable part in changing the literary climate in the Netherlands, although there have been attempts to slate novels with a philosophical flavour as 'deadly boring'. But this kind of carping seems to be part and parcel of a change in climate.

If one tries to look at literature in Dutch in the last twenty years from a wider perspective and with a degree of detachment, it appears possible to discern, in the great diversity of form and theme, a common feature which literature in Dutch shares with literature elsewhere in Europe. For, after the experiment with the *nouveau roman* which coincided largely with the wave of protest movements (the new novel's formal innovation can be seen as a manifestation of the desire to undermine rigid fixed norms and forms), there was a return not only to 'ordinary' narration but also, strikingly, to autobiographical writing. What is quite remarkable is that Alain Robbe-Grillet and Nathalie Sarraute, the main practitioners of the *nouveau roman*, have in the meantime published their own autobiographical novels.

Viewed in this context, the ego-age which began in the Netherlands in the 1970s and which produced a novel with wider horizons in the eighties, does not look like an odd or excessive development. On the contrary. Interestingly, this autobiographical writing seemed at first to be concentrated around Southern authors whose work is, to a greater extent than that of writers north of the border, still shaped by a tradition influenced by the proximity to France and French literature.

In the idiosyncratic prose of Pol Hoste, which deserves to be better known, covert autobiography and social satire go hand in hand. Leo Pleysier (see *The Low Countries* 1996-97: 141-151), Eriek Verpaele and Eric de Kuyper, on the other hand, use a form of fragmented poetic autobiographical prose which seems only to have an equivalent in Jeroen Brouwers (see *The Low Countries* 1996-97: 97-109) in the Netherlands. Eric de Kuyper, author of a series of memoir novels initiated in 1989 with *Aunt Jeannot's Hat* (De hoed van Tante Jeannot) can be considered representative of this 'new' autobiographical writing. Delving into his own past gives him the opportunity for an evocative account of his social, cultural and family backgrounds. The pieces of the jigsaw puzzle which will eventually form the self-portrait are rearranged to give a wide kaleidoscopic picture of a time and of the cities where he lived. The confirmation that autobiographical writing in all its forms has developed into a genre in its own right was given by Stefan Hertmans, who in *To Merelbeke* (Naar Merelbeke, 1994) has not only described his youth with amused self-irony, but at the same time takes an ironic look at the genre itself by working numerous improbable or fantastic elements into the story.

In the Netherlands, too, the tradition of autobiographical writing has received new impetus, for example from the work of Adriaan van Dis. In the prize-winning memoir novel *My Father's War* (Indische duinen, 1994) the author goes in search of his roots in the former Dutch East Indies through

Connie Palmen (1955-) (Photo by Klaas Koppe).

fragmented and varied images of the past. This is more than a coincidence: when we consider how Van der Heijden takes his own autobiography as a starting-point for creating a general portrait of the period, and even considering all the differences in style and ideas between the two authors, we can safely say that what we are witnessing here is the revival of a tradition in the literature of the Low Countries.

ANNE MARIE MUSSCHOOT
Translated by Jane Fenoulhet.

LIST OF TRANSLATIONS

ADRIAAN VAN DIS:
My Father's War (Tr. Claire Nicholas White). New York, 1996.
ARNON GRUNBERG:
Blue Mondays (Tr. Arnold & Erica Pomerans). New York, 1997.
DIRK AYELT KOOIMAN:
A Lamb to the Slaughter (Tr. Adrienne Dixon). New York, 1986.
 MARGRIET DE MOOR
First Grey, Then White, Then Blue (Tr. Paul Vincent). London, 1994.
The Virtuoso (Tr. Ina Rilke). London, 1996.
MARCEL MÖRING:
The Great Longing (Tr. Stacey Knecht). London, 1995.
CONNIE PALMEN:
The Laws (Tr. Richard Huijing). New York, 1993.
LEON DE WINTER:
La Place de la Bastille (Tr. Scott Rollins). Haarlem, 1993.
Hoffman's Hunger (Tr. Arnold & Erica Pomerans). London, 1995.

'New Flemish Fiction' (guest editors: Hugo Bousset and Theo Hermans), *The Review of Contemporary Fiction*, Vol. XIV, no. 2 (Summer 1994). pp. 7-185. Normal (IL).

Five Extracts

Extract from *The Friendship*
by Connie Palmen

On the first day of school I saw her again, and a little while later we found ourselves in the same room. From the moment we crossed the threshold of the classroom our fate was sealed. It turned out just as I thought it would.

I'm used to things happening that way.

For years this would be the cornerstone of my experience: as soon as I was outside my parents' house, anything that I really wanted to happen would turn out that way. If something didn't turn out the way I wanted it, it meant that I hadn't wanted it enough.

Outside things go right or wrong.

Outside I play and have fun.

Not inside.

Inside I was powerless. Indoors I was at the mercy of a bewildering blend of security and fear, trust and betrayal, agitation and calm, care and neglect, cruelty and compassion, goodness and madness. Inside I ate and slept.

Inside I'm happy or unhappy.

Powerlessness, dependence and defencelessness will always be bound up in my mind with love and happiness, always.

Breaking that bond is unthinkable.

Every day when I leave the house, my stomach aches from love. On the way to school the pain lessens with every step and by the time I reach the playground it's gone.

Except now, on the very day I first find myself in the same class as Ara Callenbach, now my stomach is still hard and that touch of nausea hasn't disappeared.

It will be years before I learn to listen to the wisdom of my body, telling me with stubborn loyalty that it's there, trying repeatedly to tell me something that might be of use to me, if only I could understand.

But I didn't understand it, not yet. It was quite an effort for me to connect myself to my own flesh and blood. I was stone-deaf to the messages of my skin, heart and brain, of my liver, intestines and kidneys, and of those moaning, nagging female organs of mine.

The classroom was crammed full of desks and chairs. The fifth form of primary school was small, there were only twelve of us, but in the sixth there were all of twenty girls. I had eyes only for Ara Callenbach and ignored the calls of classmates asking me to sit next to them. I pretended not to hear anyone.

The fifth form was supposed to sit on the left side of the room, the sixth form on the right.

That is the hierarchy of the clock. Since we started imagining time as something that moves from left to right, more things go with the clock than just early and late, things like high and low, more and less, past and present. Everyone obeys this as though it were the most natural thing in the world.

Nothing's natural to me.

I often practise thinking against the clock.

Ara Callenbach headed for the last desk in the third row and I followed her automatically. She had a noisy way of walking. She stamped her feet forcefully on the ground and had to push all the desks slightly to the side to make room for herself. The other girls looked at her, enraged, but I was proud of the racket she made.

It was unseemly.

The third row was the row that divided and connected the fifth and sixth forms. I took my place at the desk next to hers. She didn't deign to look at me. I think she also took it for granted that I would sit there.

Not the teacher, though.

She had never been my teacher before, but because she was the headmistress she knew everything about all the children at school. She'd been there for less than five minutes and had surveyed the class without saying anything when she beckoned to me.

'I think it would be better if you and Mies switched places,' she said.

Mies was sitting almost at the front.

From *The Friendship*
(De vriendschap. Amsterdam, Prometheus, 1995, pp. 37-39)
Translated by Diane L. Webb.

Extract from *Blue Mondays*

by Arnon Grunberg

Arnon Grunberg
(1971-) (Photo by Klaas
Koppe).

After my vacation I took a job in a pharmacy owned by a man I knew from the synagogue. His name was Mr Hausmann and he collected Smurfs. My parents thought it was a good idea for me to have a job. So that I'd come to realise what time and money really meant, my father said. I had to deliver prescriptions to people who couldn't walk anymore or who could still walk but couldn't see.

They tipped me everywhere, especially in the old age home. One woman there gave me at least ten guilders. She wanted me to eat her food. I didn't have the slightest intention of eating her food, because it was all chopped up and mushy. All she had to do was to swallow it. Once she whispered in my ear, 'I don't want to eat ever again. I've eaten more than enough.' I absolutely did not want to be told that sort of thing.

'You must do what you think is best for you,' I said. Then I ate her custard anyway. I got twenty guilders for that, for that little bit of custard. 'Just have it', she said. 'I can't take it with me'. So I ate it and then I looked at the cold hamburger lying on her plate and I thought to myself, No, I'm not going to eat that, too, not for twenty guilders – it looks too greasy. They had warned me not to accept excessive tips, but I thought, I've worked for this one. So I thanked her and said, 'Enjoy your meal, ma'am.' And she said, 'God will reward you.'

A few days later Mr Hausmann told me to get a bicycle. My work was taking too long. Before me they had had a boy who did it three times as fast. It wasn't much quicker on the bicycle. There were always people who kept me. There was an old bald man with two birds in a cage. He had to be supplied with those large diapers for adults. He said, 'They can sing. Hang on there, boy, they'll sing in a minute.' I knew I couldn't leave until they'd sung something. Or rather I could leave, but then I'd have to go without a tip. I made five and a half guilders at the pharmacy, and if the birds sang the man gave me three times that. It took longer and longer before there was a peep out of the birds, and often I felt like picking them up and hissing, 'Sing or I'll squeeze the living daylights out of you.'

The worst thing was when he tried to lead the singing. He'd sing a few notes and then have a coughing fit that went on for half an hour. I'd have to slap him on the back and he'd fill the room with his spluttering. When he had one of those coughing fits he'd also mess his pants. The whole room would stink of it. When it was all over, he would start again from scratch. 'Let's give them a bit more of that mixed bird seed,' he'd say. Then I would have to look for the bird seed. Everything in the room was sticky – the closets, the doors, the floor, the cage, the chairs, the bird seed, the newspapers, even the money he gave me. The place always stank of urine. Even the light in the room was the color of urine.

When I finally got outside, I'd have to stop and catch my breath before doing anything else. Then one of the birds died. There was no more singing. The man just sat in his chair, a cloth over the cage. The dead bird still lay on the table. It began to stink. 'Shouldn't it be taken away?' I asked.

'Leave it alone,' he yelled. I no longer got my ten guilders. It was up to him if he wanted to rot away with that bird of his. When I rang the bell I would shove the diapers into his hand and take off.

Then there was old Mrs Cohn, who hated me. I always had to go right in-side when I went to her place in Roerstraat. I wasn't allowed to hang around on the doorstep in case she caught a cold. Even when it was almost ninety degrees out she could catch a cold at the door. Once inside, I had to sit down and eat a cookie. She only made me do that so that she could ask, 'And where is your *kippa*?' She wouldn't wait for an answer, because she knew what it would be. She would hurry to the closet, since she was much more spry than she let on, and pull one of her dead husband's skullcaps out of a drawer. I would have to put it on, a large black yarmulke, and then she'd say, 'Right, now we'll say the *beracha* together.' The two of us would say the blessing together and I would eat the cookie. With difficulty, because when you picked it up it crumbled, that's how old it was. Finally she would slip me a quarter. 'But,' she would say, 'that's not for you to keep. Put it in the blue box.' Then she would come hobbling up with her blue Jewish National Fund collection box. I'm sure she extracted that quarter from the box every time I left. It would have been a true act of charity if I'd bashed her brains in with that JNF collection box.

From *Blue Mondays* (Blauwe maandagen. Amsterdam: Nijgh & Van Ditmar, 1994, pp. 40-42)

Excerpted from *Blue Mondays* by Arnon Grunberg. Published by Farrar, Straus & Giroux. Translation © 1997 by Farrar, Straus and Giroux. All rights reserved. To be published by Secker & Warburg in Great Britain. Translated by Arnold and Erica Pomerans.

Extract from *Aunt Jeannot's Hat*
by Eric de Kuyper

The world of illusion or, as the English so aptly put it, of 'make believe', was his. Here the division between children and grownups imposed itself with much less force. Here the uncertainty about the many obstacles which daily life continually put in the way could be employed productively. Real and false: that was how the world fitted together, consisting of conventions and rules which you invent for your enjoyment and which you yourself can there-fore also adapt. You can believe in them or, if it comes to the crunch, stop believing in them. Take everything seriously, and nothing. Is there such a thing as a five-year old dandy?

He fitted much more snugly into the world of women than that of men. The men took everything so literally and seriously. Things were like this and not anything else. Of that they were convinced. But not him. To him things seemed to be a bit like this and at the same time like that. With women, everything was less definite and more unpredictable. There was more flexi-bility. Take Aunt Jeannot's hair, for instance. Of course, after years of jet black hair she couldn't switch to the red hair of Virginia Mayo or Maureen O'Hara just like that. 'Jeannot, that copper hair, isn't it a bit over the top?' But Jeannot herself thought it 'beautiful'. (The question 'what is beautiful' and particularly 'what is *more* beautiful' was constantly being asked.)

Eric de Kuyper (1942-) (Photo by Willy Dee).

His mother was more beautiful, wasn't she, when she put a bit of rouge out of the little round box on her cheeks with her finger and then ran the red finger over her lips. And she never went out without heating up the curling tongs over a gas flame and, after she had tested their temperature on a piece of newspaper, put a few curls in her hairstyle. Surely 'beautiful' was more beautiful than 'not beautiful'!

Aunt Jeannot's hats were surely unmistakably more beautiful than Aunt Emma's, which were brown or grey with a random dent here and another one there. It was a basic model that was then adapted to the new (?) fashion every few years by a milliner. '*J'ai encore fait une petite folie*', said Aunt Jeannot, whenever she was telling her Fons (Uncle Fons) that she had just bought another hat. Once, when she saw a seductive piece of millinery on a wooden head in a shop window, she exclaimed: '*Je vais encore faire une petite folie!*' It was a kind of oriental turban in grey-green, with two long veils of the same fabric which you could knot under your chin or tie behind your head depending on whether the weather was cold or mild. (The two veils were later cut off and given to him to play with.) Another time it might be a small toque of gleaming black silk, all draped and ruched, covered with fine mousseline and adorned with a splendid spray of '*aigrettes*'. An utterly '*coquin*' piece of millinery.

Back home, she put on the newly acquired hat, took it off again, and took up scissors and needle to give it a snip here and a snip there. She moved the aigrette from the left to the right-hand side, swapped the veil from the blue-silk-hat-with-assorted-fruit with the veil from the new 'toque', and was thrilled with her creation. 'A new 250-franc hat!', cried Fons shocked, 'and the first thing Jeannot does when she gets home is attack it with the scissors!' It wasn't primarily the 250 francs that he minded. It was his wife's creative urge, which he interpreted as a destructive urge, that alarmed him.

His mother did not share her sister's obsession with hats. As a three- and four-year old she had had to wear enormous hats with lace and feathers (like the grownups; there was a photo of the three sisters that bears witness to this), and she had thought it dreadful. Now, after the war, she was pleased and relieved that it was no longer considered absolutely necessary for women to wear hats in church. You still had to put something on your head if you went to mass, but it didn't have to be a hat, it could also be a scarf (a '*fichu* '). Furthermore, you could happily wear your hair down or with a hairpiece. The latter worked well, because her hair naturally formed a kind of 'beak' which was perfect for fitting on a full hairpiece on the front of her head. This was secured with a comb. All those years she looked much younger than her sister Jeannot, who was more the chic lady (although there was only three years' difference between them). Furthermore, as chance would have it, she even felt younger.

From *Aunt Jeannot's Hat* (De hoed van tante Jeannot. Nijmegen: Sun, 1991, pp. 61-62)
Translated by Jane Fenoulhet.

Extract from *To Merelbeke*

by Stefan Hertmans

How God amputated my right leg

At last – it was the longest day in the year, I lay dozing at the grassy edge of a forgotten old canal covered in duckweed – God alighted on my shirt. He first made his way laboriously as far as the fourth button and stopped to look around. He was a bright yellow colour, three millimetres long, in the shape of a kind of triangular insect, its body tapered towards its dark abdomen.

He was missing a leg. Back right.

A refreshing wind gusted through the poplars in the blueness. In the meadow behind me I heard the peewits calling, with their high, sucking whistle. Not far from me, a sheep was rooting around in the coarse grass along the bank.

When God had taken a good look at me, he made his way slowly and still as laboriously to the next button. His entire body swayed like a ship in a gale. He shut one of his green protuberant eyes tightly. Or rather: something slid across it like a steel shutter. I lay on my back and watched him with my eyeballs rolled down as far as they would go. I couldn't help sticking my chin and bottom lip out rather foolishly at the same time. I saw that he had noticed.

All around air rushed through air. The things in the world could only hold their own in the current with some difficulty.

I breathed carefully and looked at God's yellow, somewhat angular head with the big green eyes. He had something about him of an old devil, which didn't surprise me.

One-eyed Moenen...You are the devil out of hell.

With such a small creature you never know whether it can get out of breath. And yet I had the impression that God was panting. His head was tilted upwards towards me: a kind of living hammer with two big green nails driven into it. Hammer and anvil united in one head. Greetings. Unsightly head in which all secrets stretching beyond the furthest nebula are stored, welcome on the ground. The day is long, the night just a few hours of twinkling twilight. Take it easy.

I breathed a little harder, I don't know why. Sometimes, lying by a canal in the summer, you can feel such a strange excitement which comes from nowhere and is gone again just as fast. Usually, I lean over the water to look at my reflection. Then it seems to pass. My mother says it's to do with blood pressure. I think that it's caused by something else that I don't understand.

Somewhere in the distance I could hear someone hammering on something large, hollow and iron. The echo drifted across me. The sheep had turned to face the other way. I could still vaguely hear the tearing of grass between blunt, stumpy teeth. A black dropping had landed just within my field of smell. And still I watched the three millimetre long ruler of the universe. This calmed me; it was as though my brain was wafting away and the trees and shapes beyond the horizon were disappearing. I finally let my head drop back into the grass and slept.

A little later I awoke. A blackbird was standing by the water's edge on a kind

Stefan Hertmans
(1951-) (Photo by Klaas
Koppe).

of little beach. He pecked at fallen elderflowers, flung them above his head and began to peck at them again. God had approached my chin. To warn him about my terribly large and unwashed face, I opened my mouth as terrifyingly as I could and let my breath flow over him. This seemed to put him in ecstasy. There he sat, his angular yellow head raised, with his abdomen curling in the utterly revolting warm stream of air which emerged from my lips. He waited for me to stop, close my mouth again, and then moved his whole body from front to back as though about to make an obscene movement. Then, swaying, he climbed the last bit as far as my chin.

From *To Merelbeke* (Naar Merelbeke. Amsterdam: Meulenhoff, 1994: pp. 9-11)
Translated by Jane Fenoulhet.

Extract from *My Father's War*
by Adriaan van Dis

Adriaan van Dis
(1946-) (Photo by Klaas
Koppe).

Isn't that the way it was, Dad? That's how you told the story at our dinner table, with a touch more Malay; sorry, I've lost the words. You at the head, hidden behind streaming platters, spoon in hand and dishing up, the guests were served choice morsels. Now that you're dead, I dare to look you square in the face. With the years your eyes have grown lighter and less stern, as in the faded photograph behind glass. Our sun is stronger than you thought.

Let me put another helping on your plate, I'll color the rice with *sambal*, blood, and I'll inhale the aroma with delight.

Your stories kept changing quite a bit. Sometimes it wasn't a plank on which you floated but a raft, tied together with straps from the backpacks. Sometimes you were in the water longer, or the weather was different: a full moon and a sea strangely becalmed, so that the lamentations of the *romushas*, the Javanese coolies, could be heard far over the water. But your tale was always spellbinding, you wanted us to laugh, though we felt more like trembling.

The Javanese boy, remember? Suddenly it all comes back to me. He was hoisted up by one leg, the other one was bitten off by a shark. A medic wanted to tie up the bleeding stump with a rope, but the Japanese wouldn't allow it. A horizontal body took up as much room as three vertical ones, so he was thrown back in.

It didn't stop us from eating at all. If someone threatened to burst into sobs, or hands nervously fiddled with a napkin, you would suddenly summon up a stoker from Rotterdam, that joker who jumped overboard, right under the noses of the Japanese. 'Swimming home,' he cried, but he got no farther than a few hundred yards, for the Japanese fished him out and after a beating, threw him into the deepest hold. Did that stoker ever lay eyes on Rotterdam again?

Even though you couldn't pull my sled in winter and you didn't manage to climb up the dune when we were flying a kite, at the dinner table you were the toughest father in the whole village.

Let's order another glass of beer. Have a drink, man, throw all that anthroposophic nonsense overboard. Vegetables also ferment into alcohol in your gut; there's no doctor here to write prescriptions. Tonight I'm writing you back to health, my pen and I are master here.

Yes, I've become a writer. You used a ruler to drill the alphabet into me, and it has stayed with me, I thank you for that. I'm still a bad speller, but my sentences are fluent. You wanted me to be able to read and write at the age of four, and you succeeded. I had to pronounce long words without faltering. It was all about rhythm. I had to read the sentences to the beat of your ruler, one tap every two lines. *Robin the Giant* was the first book I read, and we finished it. Together we celebrated by going to the movies to see *Gulliver's Travels*, another giant, an excursion topped off with orangeade and coconut macaroons (baked on a thin wafer that made you joke about the Catholic's communion wafers). I could have skipped first grade. Robin is still my hero, a giant who could let people dance in the palm of his hand. I can do it too, just close your eyes... .

... I'll give you a pair of shoes – black, a gentleman never wears brown; I'll respect your good taste. You'll get a new suit, let the clothes from the trunk air out, and I'll set you down in Palembang, in the European quarter, in the street where my mother-to-be is living. You're holding a flower, give it to her, don't squeeze the stem, be gentle. Ask her to dance. You see what a giant I am? I can make you dance, in the street, a bit common, you didn't like that, without a jacket, the back of your shirt is damp with sweat, and don't pump your arm so much, sway, sway to the rhythm of my sentences... .

What? Too tired? You've had enough, your heart, even in those days? You can't rest until I let you, I'll keep you dancing, I'll let you die, but I've already done that. For the time being, you're right in the middle of your life.
I went in search of your past, Dad, and there's a lot that's different from what I expected. I asked the family, but I was told contradictory stories. Our mother wants so much to forget, and she's good at it. In the same way that our pale sun has faded your photograph, the years are wiping out her memories, and also I had to go to others for help.

About ten years ago I wrote a story about my early years by the sea, and at that time I had not heard about Pakanbaru, nor did I have any idea where and when you had been torpedoed. I wrote only about your raft, or your plank, and I can't remember how many days I let you drift – one, two or three? When I recount your life's story, I go right along with your lies.

From *My Father's War* (Indische duinen. Amsterdam: Meulenhoff, 1994, pp. 156-160)

Translated by Claire Nicholas White (English translation © 1996 The New Press).

Fresh

Food

Ten Young Poets from Flanders and the Netherlands

Henk van der Waal (1960-)

At that instant
stasis settles
with Swiss precision
among your small
hours of masturbation and
other delights,
for the rock's song weaves stones
in the mouth of those who come,
splitting beauty and unexpectedly
dispersing, like bales of linen,
the future

and so off we went
into the mist tapping our teeth
in wordless unknowing,
our tongue a fish stranded on a shingle
beach: tempora mutantur, nos et mutamur in illis –
while they simply take off the watch that
binds them to time, rinse their mouths, clear
their noses and shut their eyes so as to be completely
at one with laughter, sky and night, to
get rid of themselves – inadmissible

From *The Sphinx' Wrappings* (De windsels van de sfinx, 1995)
Translated by Paul Vincent.

Marc Reugebrink (1960-)
Heart

Deep inside the calyxes buzz
the ones I had to herd. A flower
is tried and tried again by bees
until a tongue uproots it

swallows it. That's how a lime-leaf
sometimes falls between your shoulderblades
a bull veers one last time
to face its slayer. I

lay my wreath of flowers round its horns
with care, till it raises hooves
and swims away across the sea.

From *Shroud* (Wade, 1991)
Translated by Marc Reugebrink.

Peter van Lier (1960-)

The Dove

A dove doesn't rest all curled up,
so it's definitely not ball-shaped
not at all. A dove at rest most definitely still has a neck,
a little curved even,
furled over, and a clearly perceivable beak as well pointing
downwards nicely.
It was yesterday I made this observation.

I was standing on the balcony,
there was no wind and it was sweltering hot,
and dark, but not quite pitch black. Because
when I looked up I saw above me at an angle its
silhouette.
I squinted into the darkness of the dingy streets, thinking I was alone
while right above my head (or almost) a
dove was resting.
Not that tears sprang to my eyes or anything, but I felt quite emotional, nevertheless.
Not like a ball, a dove at rest, I thought,
and more along the same lines,
later.

From *Slight Gesture* (Miniem gebaar, 1995)
Translated by Deborah ffoulkes.

Lucebert, *The Poet Feeds
Poetry.* 1952.
Water colour and ink,
42 x 56,5 cm. Stedelijk
Museum, Amsterdam.

René Huigen (1962-)
That which Is Irrefutable

To get a following
you must have theories
and those who have them
must refute them

Theoretically I'm a bird
and in reality a man
no-one 'd refute that

You have to have a bird's mind
to know what I know

And that's not a whole
lot because I acquire wings by flying

And a bird does not refute itself
it floats

From *Last Poems* (Laatste gedichten, 1994)
Translated by Deborah ffoulkes.

Peter Verhelst (1962-)
Knife-Throwing

She stands motionless, chalk-white, waiting.
Rigid with desire. When I look at her
she lies prone, bleeds from one breast.

She breathes hard, leaning half against me.
I hold sleep at bay so that I can feel her.
I kiss, I draw breath.

She puts her arms round my head, kisses me
again,
says from a dream *let me sleep with you,*
every night she will say it again out loud.

She gets up and lets her dress, her jewels fall,
selects the knives one by one
and winds her arms for a blindfold, laughs.

I feel her blood already streaming towards me.

From *Otto* (1989)
Translated by Tanis Guest.

Bernard Dewulf (1960-)
Coming Home

I love you, even though I cannot know it.
I think it when you come home from a day
in your life. But it's not a thought.
You stroke my cheek and who knows,
that gesture. It happens a thousand times
before it's real. Hang your coat on the hook,
a trivial thing, but tomorrow it won't happen
perhaps. Or shake the day from your hair.
What I then see in that is the start.
The house comes to be, the table takes its place,
we each cause the other. Surely it's not
conceivable that one should imagine all this.

From *Where the Hedgehog Goes* (Waar de egel gaat, 1995)
Translated by Tanis Guest.

Rogi Wieg (1962-)

Bacon

For beginners there are still gently swaying
lanterns, walks holding hands.
But advanced students
are required to go beyond that one love that
one sometimes finds; asphalt melts
under your feet, panting, you just make
your parents' end. And then you automatically become
a know-all in the face of beauty,
because beauty does exist.

I saw nothing special about the sky today,
you came home and scarcely kissed me,
I was washing cherries. Your hair curled
and despite your presence associations
were approaching of great sadness.

Whoever can manage to make a Sunday paper
on Saturday must get up
and embrace me. They can strip love
of tissue, remove the bacon from the flank
of the pig with a magic wand, reconcile
symbols with each other yet let them
remain real.

From *The Very Best Bacon* (Spek van mooie zijde, 1993)
Translated by Paul Vincent.

Peter Ghyssaert (1966-)

Fountains

Before day breaks the fountains
begin their daily task:
the casting up of thin
ethereal table-settings;

plait the effeminate shards
of the water together
to make a wineglass of them,
then a crystal wine-carafe,
from which they pour unstinting:
applause self-generated.

They flaunt themselves, hide in the mist;
they scold with drunken tinkling
and at last are silent,
calm from their boasting, waiting
for the fall of twilight

– a dark and perfumed woman
calling for all her eunuchs.

From *Cameo* (1993)
Translated by Tanis Guest.

Jo Govaerts (1972-)

What I'm aching for today
to wear a wisp of a summer dress
off-the-shoulder, with a low-cut
neck and back and above all
swishy around the hips

then go into the garden with it
the sun is shining warmly, but the wind
keeps it bearable and makes
the dress move and then

you're there too of course who
thinks the dress is beautiful as well and together
we take it off and hang it
on a branch

and lie in the grass looking at
this wisp of a summer dress in a tree, that's
what I'm aching for the most today.

From *What You Are Looking At* (Waar je naar zit te kijken, 1994)
Translated by Deborah ffoulkes.

Mustafa Stitou (1974-)
Grown Men

The Mosque in the shopping centre
is not doing well.
Berbers and mountain people hate each other's guts.
(A wise spokesman for the mountain people was actually
punched in the face.)
It is not about religion
but about who controls the local authority grants.
Rumour has it that the mountain people are going to found their own Mosque.
A hundred yards away, opposite Woolworth's.
(Get a move on, Ramadan's coming.)
The guys who had to attend the Mosque as children
had the Koran dished up to them as naturally as mother's milk
and drank it in with animal reluctance.
Abderzak and me for instance
are creased up.

From *My Forms* (Mijn vormen, 1994)
Translated by Paul Vincent.

All poems selected by Anton Korteweg and Frits Niessen.

Brief History of Dutch Tiles

Between the end of the sixteenth and the beginning of the twentieth centuries, hundreds of millions of majolica wall tiles were produced in the Netherlands. Tiles were the first items to be mass-produced for a growing Dutch middle class. These decorative tiles stemmed from a long history, starting in the Far East, then along the trade routes to the Middle East and the Mediterranean area, and finally flowering in Holland in the seventeenth century.

   The earliest use of wall tiles in the Low Countries in the late sixteenth

Floor tiles, 1500-1560,
red clay and buff slip (Gift
of Mrs Francis P. Garvan).*

century was for skirting boards – the bottom section of the walls that became dirty when the packed earth floors were swept. Skirting boards are always thirteen centimetres (five inches) high, the height of one tile. The tiles were both easy to clean and decorative. In addition, they kept the dampness caused by a high water table at bay, and prevented the whitewashed plaster walls from flaking. This proved especially useful since the small houses of the modest burghers were built close to waterways. Gradually other areas of the walls were panelled with tiles – first both sides of the hearth, and then the hallways. The best way to see how tiles were used is to study the genre paintings of seventeenth-century Dutch masters such as Pieter de Hooch and Johannes Vermeer.

At the beginning of the sixteenth century many Italian émigrés, including skilled potters, settled in the southern Netherlands, which under their influence became a centre for the arts. Many craftsmen fled further north, even before Antwerp fell to Spain in 1585. They settled along the rivers in the towns of Haarlem, Amsterdam, Delft and Rotterdam, where clay and transportation were readily available. These accomplished Italian potters revolutionised not only the aesthetics of tile making but methods of production as well. They refined the earlier roof and floor tiles, introduced new colours and designs, and influenced the direction of Dutch tile production for years to come.

The tiles were made of local clay, covered with finely powdered white tin glaze, and were decorated in colour. Both the motifs and the colours (ranging from yellow to orange and brown, green, and blue) were derived from the majolica produced in the workshops of Venice, Faenza and Urbino, where the Italian craftsmen had learned the techniques of preparing the clay, applying basic tin glaze, and adding painted decoration.

After shaping, drying and a preliminary firing in a 'biscuit' oven, a thin layer of white tin enamel (glaze) was applied and a *spons* (transfer pattern with the outline of a picture pricked with pinholes) was positioned above the tile and dusted with powdered charcoal. The charcoal outline was redrawn with a fine brush and the tile decorator filled in the picture with a heavier brush in the specified coloured glazes: cobalt blue, copper green, antimony yellow, and manganese-purple. Finally a clear glaze was applied. The tiles were fired again at a high temperature to produce a high gloss.[1]

When certain tile patterns proved particularly popular, other workshops would produce similar designs with minute changes in line and colour. Customers could place orders for specific patterns and shop around for the best prices. Because tiles were rarely signed, and because the tile painters continued to produce the same patterns over long periods of time in the same tradition, it is almost impossible to assign a specific artist and date to most tiles.

Style changes

The ornamental wall tiles of the late sixteenth and early seventeenth centuries bear little relationship to earlier Dutch floor tiles, which were decorated with geometric patterns or scrolls. Between 1580 and 1620 ornamental polychrome tiles show a configuration of interwoven vegetation

Ornamental fruit in quatre-foils, 1570-1600 (Gift of Edward W. Bok; gift of Mrs Francis P. Garvan).*

Animals and hunter in diamonds, 1580-1620 (Gift of Mrs Francis P. Garvan).*

Scenes from daily life,
1620-1650, corners
decorated with large leaf
motifs, possibly made in
Rotterdam (Gift of
Mrs Francis P. Garvan).*

connected by a design with white arabesques that were reserved to show up against the blue background. The overall pattern extends diagonally over four, sixteen or more tiles. This type, with endless combinations and variations, remained popular until the late 1620s. They were produced in some thirty workshops situated in neighbouring towns within a small geographical area. These colourful, ornamental polychrome tiles, produced in such large numbers, began to lose their popularity toward the end of the sixteenth century, although they remained in production until 1620.

Their place was taken by a different design of polychrome tiles, with diamond-shaped or circular frames encompassing human or animal figures. In the late sixteenth and seventeenth centuries, scenes of daily life were finding an ever-expanding market; favourite motifs included people dressed in the contemporary fashions, and figures engaged in games and pastimes of the period. Dutch patriotism and pride in the republic's hard-won independence from Spanish rule also inspired images of soldiers and militiamen. Throughout the seventeenth century, tiles depicting animals or flowers, especially tulips, were also favoured.

Tulips were first imported from China via Turkey (1555-1600) where they grew wild.[2] They became highly prized, especially the 'broken' or striped tulips (1600-1700) that had been attacked by a virus whose origin was unknown at the time. Tulips became one of the more enduring tile designs. The triple tulip pattern in polychrome or in blue was one of the most popular tile motifs; it was in production for well over two hundred years, from 1625 to 1850.

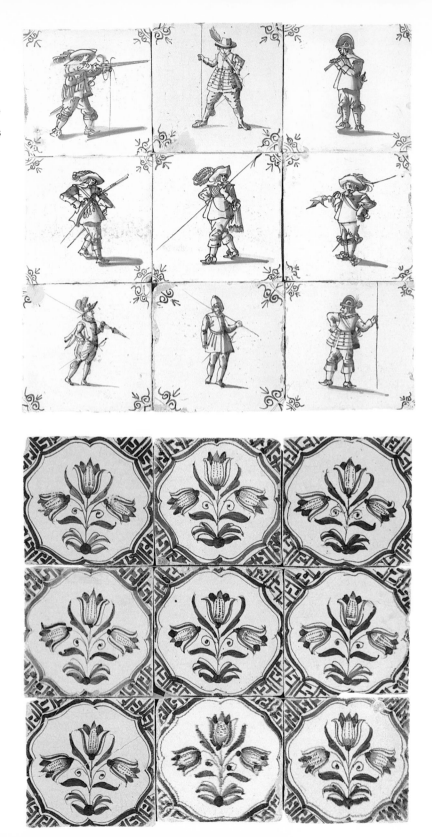

Pikemen and musketeers, 1625-1650, corners decorated with ox-heads, adapted from Jacob de Gheyn's *The Exercise of Armes* (The Hague, 1608; reprint New York, 1971), pike and musket sequences, pls. 1, 11 (Gift of Edward W. Bok; gift of Mrs Francis P. Garvan).*

Triple tulips in bracketed frames, 1630-1660, with mock-fret corner elements (Gift of Edward W. Bok).*

Shepherds and shepherdesses, c. 1700 (Funds contributed in memory of Adolf Schaap and anonymous donor).*

The rise of the Dutch Republic as a leading maritime and trading empire in the sixteenth and seventeenth centuries brought great prosperity and many foreign products. The influence of popular Chinese porcelain imported by the Dutch East India Company after 1625 led to a less colourful style of decoration than that seen heretofore. In response to the imports blue and white tiles became fashionable, and are still produced today. The Chinese influence also meant that special emphasis was placed on the figurative element. The decoration consisted of a central image and corner motifs that consist of the *Wan-Li* motif called mock-fret, the spiral ox-head ('*ossekop*'), the fleur-de-lis and their derivatives, and an endless range of variations.[3]

The Chinese influence was superseded circa 1685 when, as a result of the introduction of French fashions, the preferred colour glaze changed to manganese-purple. This stylistic change in Dutch tiles corresponded with the rapid expansion of cities in Holland, due to unparalleled economic prosperity. In the mid-seventeenth century, as the middle class became more and more prosperous, their houses became grander. The walls of the living quarters were covered with cut velvet or tooled leather, while plain blue and white tiles, which were cheaper to produce than the elaborately painted ones, were used to line the hallways and the kitchen walls. The trend away from polychrome products toward those with a simpler decoration led to a significant decrease in prices.[4] Also contributing to the price reduction was an improved clay mixture which enabled the production of thinner tiles.[5] Lower prices meant that tiles became available to a very wide public that

Men-of-war, frigates, flutes and a herring-buss, 1640-1660, Corners decorated with ox-heads, made in Harlingen (Gift of Mrs Francis P. Garvan; gift of Anthony N. B. Garvan).*

included a majority of urban dwellers and many of the well-to-do farmers.

Tile decorators took images from the ubiquitous prints of the day, which documented all the important events and were readily available. For the seafaring populations of the coastal towns the workshops produced well-known ships and sea creatures, whereas in rural areas biblical subjects drawn from the Old and New Testaments were the preferred wall decoration from circa

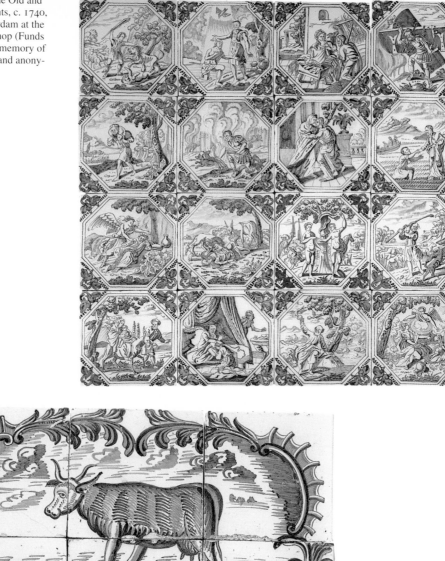

Scenes from the Old and New Testaments, c. 1740, made in Rotterdam at the Aelmis workshop (Funds contributed in memory of Adolf Schaap and anonymous donor).*

Horse and cow, 1760-1780, made in Makkum at Tichelaar's Koninklijke Makkumer Aardewerk- en Tegelfabriek, adapted from the 'wild horse'.*

1700 until well into the nineteenth century. These tiles, executed in either blue and white or manganese-purple, were produced in towns in Holland as well as in Makkum, Friesland.

The wealthy farmers preferred pictures of horses, cows, cats, or canaries, or floral tile pictures that fitted in the back of the fireplace or sometimes were set into a wall and framed by plain white tiles; this produced an effect similar to that of a painting hung on a white plastered wall in patrician homes. In agricultural Holland and Friesland it remained fashionable until late into the nineteenth century to decorate farmhouses, especially the kitchens, with such tile pictures; they are produced even today in Harlingen or in Makkum by the Royal Tichelaar firm, which has been in continuous operation since 1641. In a tile picture, each tile displays only a part of the overall composition, as opposed to tile panels that consist of an unlimited number of similar tiles. Tile pictures with flower vases were made in large numbers and in different sizes in Delft, Makkum and Harlingen. In Rotterdam tile painters like the Aelmis family (active from 1692 to 1787) created battle scenes, genre paintings, and floral still lifes reminiscent of Ambrosius Bosschaert the Elder and Roelant Savery or Jan van Huysum.

Export

Between the late seventeenth and the early nineteenth centuries, Dutch tileworks obtained important commissions to decorate churches, convents and monasteries in Spain and Portugal[6] with large scenes in blue or manganese-purple. Large tile pictures were also exported to chateaux in France such as Rambouillet (1715-1730), and the Trianon at Versailles (1670-1687), which were decorated with tiles throughout. In Germany, two castles at Nymphenburg near Munich (1716-1739) and others near Brühl (1729-1748)[7] were beautified with tile pictures. These large, polychrome tableaux of flower vases, used to cover the walls in the manner of French royal tapestries, were made in Rotterdam and Delft from circa 1700 to 1750.

Stimulated by the visit of Czar Peter I to Holland in 1697 (see *The Low Countries* 1996-97: 275), several palaces belonging to the Russian nobility were decorated with Dutch tiles. The most famous are Peter's Summer and Winter Palaces, and the Menshikov Palace in St Petersburg (1672-1729, extensively restored 1966-1984), now a branch of the Hermitage. The walls and ceilings of the staterooms as well as those of some bedrooms are covered from top to bottom with thousands of Dutch tiles, dating from 1710-1720s.[8] Several castles in Poland were extensively decorated with tiles in the mid-eighteenth century. These tiles served a different function than in the Netherlands. The architects who designed the new palaces adjusted the pictures to the dimensions of the walls, which were covered from top to bottom. The walls and ceiling of the grand staircase in Nieborów palace of the Radziwill princes were lined with tiles in 1774, as were the landing and an adjacent room.[9]

Nineteenth and twentieth centuries

In the late eighteenth and nineteenth centuries the tile industry in the Netherlands became less innovative and the era of outstanding tiles had come to a close. The product was revived by new designs for different types of decoration during the late nineteenth century. Influenced by the Arts and Crafts movement in England[10], Art Nouveau in France, Jugendstil in Germany, Nieuwe Kunst in the Netherlands, architects and designers commissioned tiles for specific locations: facades, porticoes, stations or other public buildings, and memorials. And as for the contemporary craft, some artists have received commissions for original tilework to embellish either interiors or facades, to be executed by the Porceleyne Fles in Delft or by the Tichelaar firm in Makkum.

In Europe, throughout five centuries, imaginative architects have used the wall tile to enhance their designs, either in blue and white or in polychrome, exploiting their unparalleled possibilities of colour and variety. Nonetheless, Dutch tiles have been taken for granted for far too long. Only recently have wall tiles been valued both as a form of decoration and as artefacts that can give us a great deal of information about daily life during the late sixteenth and early seventeenth centuries. The time has come for serious historical study of tiles as an important art form akin to the painting, drawing and print making of Holland's Golden Age.

ELLA B. SCHAAP

NOTES

1. TICHELAAR, PIETER JAN, 'The Production of Tiles'. In: *Dutch Tiles in the Philadelphia Museum of Art*. Philadelphia, 1984, pp. 37-41 and PAAPE, GERRIT, *De plateelbakker of Delftsch aardewerkmaaker*. Dordrecht, 1794 (reprint Amsterdam, 1978).

2. SCHAAP, ELLA B., *Bloemen op tegels in de Gouden Eeuw / Dutch Floral Tiles in the Golden Age*. Haarlem, 1984, p. 121.

3. Philadelphia Museum of Art, *Dutch Tiles*, pp. 174-177.

4. MONTIAS, JOHN MICHAEL, *Artists and Artisans in Delft: A Socio-Economic Study of the Seventeenth Century*. Princeton, 1982, pp. 312-313.

5. TICHELAAR, ' The Production of Tiles', p. 38

6. SIMÕES, J. M. DOS SANTOS, *Carreaux ceramiques hollandais au Portugal et en Espagne*. The Hague, 1959.

7. DE JONGE, C.H., *Dutch Tiles*. London, 1971, pp. 118-124, 128-129 and 135-136.

8. DOROFEËA, L.P., *The Menshikov Palace Museum in Leningrad*. Moscow, 1986, ills. 113-161 (English summary pp. 206, 214-217).

9. DE JONGE, *Dutch Tiles*, pp. 126-130, ills. 145-150.

10. LEMMEN, HANS VAN, 'De invloed van Willem Morris op laat negentiende eeuwse Nederlandse tegeldekors', *Tegel*, 12 (1984), pp. 31-34. Tegelmuseum It Noflik Sté, Otterlo.

Dutch Tiles Museum
Eikenzoom 12 / 6731 BH Otterlo / The Netherlands
tel. +31 318 591519
Opening hours:
10 a.m.-12 a.m. / 2 p.m.-5 p.m. (Tuesday to Saturday)
2 p.m.-4 p.m. (Sundays and Holidays)

* All tiles illustrated belong to the Philadelphia Museum of Art. Photographs by Eric Mitchell, Lynn Rosenthal and Graydon Wood.

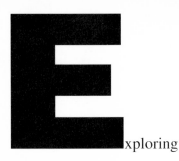xploring

the Limits of the Familiar

The Art of Guido Geelen

Some things only exist to be broken. After being designed, produced etc., they find their sole reason for existence in one brief action: crash, against the wall, bang, onto the floor, pieces, quick, into the dustbin with them. In Greek restaurants in Amsterdam, as elsewhere, waiters hand out plates to smash when things get lively. They are not the same plates as the food is served

Guido Geelen, *Untitled (Robbelien K 015, semi transparent glaze, décors Mulder Holland series no. 3780 and 4660).* 1988. 141 x 130 x 130 cm (34 parts). Collection PTT kunst en vormgeving, The Hague.

Guido Geelen, *Untitled (R.K. 015)*. 1992. Clay, 175 x 230 x 55 cm. De Pont stichting voor hedendaagse kunst, Tilburg.

on. Evidently this Greek tradition is so entrenched in the Netherlands that using the *dolmades* dishes would not be cost effective. Disposable dishes get eaten off at least once; the Greek variety has no other purpose than to be broken.

I once swiped one such Greek plate. Now it lives on as an anomalous beast in my kitchen, with no clear-cut function among all the paraphernalia that's supposed to be durable. Among the other crockery its presence is a relief. That plate, in its very wholeness, challenges the eternal immutability of what was meant to be.

In 1992 Guido Geelen made a sculpture that is a bit like such a plate, not before or after it's broken, but during the very act of breaking. The work consists of a red coloured wall into which are crushed everyday objects of use and common domestic ornaments. Standing before this structure, the eye picks out a vacuum cleaner, a computer, fruit dishes and table candelabra, lamps, doggies and other beasties that spent their days on chimney pieces. Geelen's work inspires the viewer with a deep sense of liberation. He has accomplished that which others, given the practical obstacles, can only dream of: he has wrested these objects from their fixed forms. They are still recognisable, but the TV is no longer a square, the tyre is no longer a circle, the little doggie's head is flattened, and the candelabra have subsided into themselves.

Geelen accomplished this by using the actual objects as moulds which he filled up with clay. The casts, still in a half-wet state, were then placed in a crate, which was fired in its entirety, to emerge as a block of a fierce flower-pot red, a rectangle of objects hurtling into collapse. You could call it destruction in motion, tempered by the rigour of pure linearity. Purchased by the De Pont Foundation in 1993, *Untitled (R.K. 015)* is housed in an ex-textile factory in Tilburg, Geelen's home city.

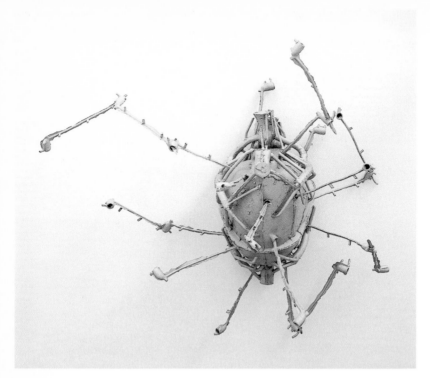

Guido Geelen, *Untitled
(Urinals).* 1994. Bronze,
c.120 x 120 x 100 cm.
De Pont stichting voor
hedendaagse kunst, Tilburg.

Although on the face of it Geelen's work is concerned with destruction, it is also about creation. Every one of his pieces is a meeting-ground for different kinds of creation: convergences between his own creation and what has been created already; between art and artefact, art and kitsch; between the hand-made and the mass-produced. His red wall he himself, for instance, describes as a good solution to the age-old sculptural dilemma of how to place an object in space. As it is, the wall is both sculpture and base.

Geelen often confines himself to simple shapes. As a result, from a distance many of his sculptures have a minimalist aspect, an impression reinforced by the fact that they are all in one colour. Only from close up do they show their capriciousness.

Geelen explored other classical sculptural objects – space, volume, material – in his statues with holes. When the clay is still wet, Geelen introduces hundreds of holes so that the still-malleable form almost caves into itself. This is then fired, and it's a matter of chance whether or not the clay tears when the heat makes it shrink. '*It's on the very brink of what can and what can't be sculpture,*' as Geelen puts it himself. The forms he chooses for these experiments are as mundane as they could be: a vacuum cleaner, a stove, or a urinal, often doubled back to back. Despite the holes, the shapes are clearly recognisable. The urinal gave Geelen the opportunity to smuggle in art history – he gives Duchamps' famous 'readymade' a lyrical twist.

It is not enough to call Geelen's mixes playful. Playful they always are, but often they are more than that. They speak of sadness and nostalgia and the will to overcome these. Geelen is never resigned to anything, his art testifies to a great optimism, to a faith in life.

Geelen was born in 1962 in Thorn, a white-painted village in Dutch Limburg. One of the first works he showed after completing his studies at the Tilburg Academy of Art was a porcelain egg resting on three porcelain feet. Critics commented that Geelen's egg had an aura of both fragility and pride.

In 1988 Geelen took part in the *First Blossom* Project, an initiative whereby a number of Amsterdam galleries each showed a new artist. *First Blossom* appropriately took place in spring and, in Geelen's case in any event, provided an incentive to celebrate themes of joy. In the Paul Andriesse Gallery he exhibited ceramic streamers which were heavily glazed to an outrageous brilliance. Beneath this teemed a vivacious mass of colour – lots of yellow, pink and green – which on closer inspection proved to consist of flower and shell shapes. Geelen had plastered his streamers with transfers used in the ceramics industry to decorate commercial vases and bowls. However, his intention was not to hold up an admonishing finger to the industry. We don't need him to point out how ugly the things with which we surround ourselves can be. What he was doing was, in short, to turn ugliness into beauty. '*I use the transfers purely for colour,*' Geelen explains, '*the motifs don't really bother me. If I need yellow, that's what I go for, never mind whether the shape happens to be a fish or a butterfly.*' A subsequent phase of experimentation involved dribbling red and white glazes and reflecting platinum over washing machines and other domestic appliances.

Even more baroque are the murals which predominated in his one-man exhibition of 1996 at the De Pont Institute in Tilburg. In these, the transfers still provide the colours, but a heavy top layer of glaze has taken on a life of its own, to the extent that the contours of the clay beneath are barely traceable. The reliefs are wall-mounted at eye level so that upon entering the viewer is immediately face-to-face with what appear to be huge shells from an unfamiliar sea. From closer up these change into landscapes, though the decorations do not in reality represent forests and hills but large-scale fruits. Seen from even closer up, hillocks and valleys with grazing cows emerge from beneath the glaze, forcing the viewer to narrow his focus. So enticing are the surfaces that one wonders how it would feel to skate or ski over them or, at any rate, to wait for the attendant to look away and rapidly glide a finger over their smoothness. A pig scurries over the bridge of a guitar, a small cow munches at an apple which in turn is surmounted by a bunch of grapes. According to Geelen, these murals represent collections of individual moments. You are not expected to take in the work as a whole, but to zoom in and out of the images. A unifying theme is that the base, or corbel, of each mural is formed by a ceramic tree trunk. That, in juxtaposition with whatever is atop, guides the viewer's imagination. '*If the tree trunk comes with books, you naturally think of paper which, of course, is made of wood,*' says Geelen. '*But in combination with fruit, you come to perceive it as a fruit tree, whereas a car tyre, for instance, would make you think of an accident – a car crashing into a tree.*'

Clay, Geelen's preferred medium, is an unusual choice for a sculptor to work in. Prominent in his huge and enormously high studio – a converted chapel right in the centre of Tilburg – is an ultra-modern computerised kiln. Geelen has been playing with clay for as long as he can remember. Thorn, his home village on the River Maas, is a traditional centre of brick and tile manufacture. As a boy, he would go round the factories asking for bits of

Guido Geelen, *Untitled (Washing Machine R.K. 015, R&S 63855, P.B.C. 'C')*. 1995. Clay, glaze, platinum lustre, wood, c.165 x 100 x 120 cm. The artist's collection.

Guido Geelen, *Untitled (Console with Fruit R.K. 015, R&S 63855, M.H. 329-5183, P.B.C. 'C')*. 1995. Clay, glaz, transfers, platinum lustre, 60 x 75 x 40 cm. Noordbrabants Museum, 's Hertogenbosch.

clay, and sometimes he would even be allowed to fire his pieces in the vast industrial kilns.

Geelen loves clay because it is more or less devoid of intrinsic qualities. Glass, for instance, is breakable, a property which can't help but conceptually determine your work if you use it. Clay is just earth. Formless.

Perhaps one reason why clay is an unusual and poorly regarded medium in the visual arts is because of its associations with arts and crafts and amateur pottery. Geelen shows that this reputation is unjustified. Often, when seeing his work, you can forget what substance it is made of – which is only reasonable, given that your mind isn't necessarily on paint when you see a painting. But in other of his works the material has a distinctive function. Moreover, he invariably stretches the possibilities of the material. In the sculpture with holes, for instance, the inner tension hinges on the relationship between the possibilities and the limitations of the clay. Sometimes he evokes a romantic mood. When the clay retains its natural red or grey, the works have an aura of antiquity about them. Thus the dusty brick red and friable consistency of the wall of televisions and candelabra conjure up the prehistoric age, and forgotten peoples who got their modern names from the way they shaped their pots.

At other times Geelen tries leaving not only the natural colour of the clay but also that of the glaze intact. He has made a series of vase-shaped sculptures in which clay and colour are completely divorced from one another. The clay is moulded into objects, such as a row of books or a couple of dogs, and the glaze set into it in the shape of a glass tube with tulips sticking out of it.

As evinced by his subversive use of commercial tranfers, Geelen is referring to the china industry. The titles of his work ridicule the pots and vases that are sold as applied art in galleries. According to Geelen, a lot of ceramicists think too highly of their material. A Geelen work is usually labelled *Untitled,* to which is appended a long list of letters and numbers which are taken straight from the trade catalogues and directories. An example of this is: *Untitled (R.K. 015, R&S 63855, M.H. 329-5183, P.C.B. 'C').*

When Geelen works in a medium other than clay, he is similarly anarchic. In a series on which he began in 1994 he again explores the limits of the familiar, but this time in bronze. The idiosyncrasy of a vacuum cleaner, urinal or tree trunk in putty-coloured metal is made odder still by anomalous antenna or rods which protrude from unexpected places. These are a by-product of the lost wax casting method in which the sides of the plaster mould are strategically honeycombed with fine drainage shafts and air vents, technically knows as runners and risers, to allow hot air to escape. Whereas by convention the extraneous, solidified tentacles are removed, Geelen treats them as an integral part of the sculpture. He elaborates this idea further, however. In one urinal-shaped piece, he has in part replaced this network of 'scaffolding' with casts of an object of a related shape: a traditional clay pipe. The end product is a conundrum, a maze of plumbing run amok. Smoke, metal and urine become materials with a great deal in common.

Guido Geelen revels in unlikely combinations and juxtapositions. For the Rode Poort group exhibition, held to celebrate the opening of director Jan Hoet's Museum of Modern Art in Ghent in 1996, he came up with yet another surprise. In place of traditional bases, his sculptures were on this occasion mounted on wooden storage racks. Slick and self-contained, the clay positively basked in the rough wood, as if inviting yet more elusive associations. Nothing needs to be disposed of.

BIANCA STIGTER
Translated by Sonja Prescod.

Guido Geelen, *Untitled (TV Vase Sculpture R.K. 015).* 1993. Clay, glass, fresh flowers, c.110 x 90 x 65 cm. Private collection.

The

DNA of Art

The Ceramic Work of Tjok Dessauvage

Tjok Dessauvage, *Writing*.

Great Britain is regarded internationally as the Mecca of ceramic art. Albion has a long tradition in this genre; there exist full courses of study and the artistic climate is extremely favourable to this art form. The specific attention devoted to it has even led to the growth of a separate ceramics circuit, with its own galleries, periodicals, critics and so forth. One of the consequences of this is that in Great Britain the art of ceramics has drifted a little away from the present-day world of the visual arts and is leading a life of its own. It is precisely this kind of segregation that the Belgian ceramicist Tjok Dessauvage intensely dislikes: he sees contemporary ceramics as just as essential and important as the 'major' arts of painting and sculpture.

Tjok Dessauvage, born in West Flanders in 1948, has reached exceptional heights as a ceramicist in his own country, and for ten years or so has also been gaining an international reputation with his intriguing pot structures. His ceramic sculptures are small, closed worlds, marked and scratched by the past, memory, emotion. His work is to be found in museum collections all over the world, from Ostend to Tokyo and from Finland to Italy. He has already won a whole series of prizes, including the INAX Design Prize in Japan in 1992, the 1993 Premio Faenza and the prize given by the town of Nyon at the 1995 Biennale de la Porcelaine. Tjok Dessauvage is an out-and-out ceramic artist whose intention is to rise above the debate between fine art and applied art. His conical, cylindrical and hemispherical pot structures are as austere as they are perfect in their finish, and the flat upper surface is the bearer of Dessauvage's message: the wonder of the organic life that can think in perfect abstract-geometrical terms.

Bronze, marble, even wood are 'noble' materials one may use to create Art. But not clay: that is immediately relegated to the category of Arts & Crafts, the applied arts. Tjok Dessauvage thinks this state of affairs is unjust, since the nature of the material should not be used as a criterion. The broad extent of clay's applications has ultimately worked to its disadvantage: its presence is overabundant, it can truly be used for anything; you can turn it, sculpt it, cast it, extrude it, you can produce extremely refined ceramics with it, but you can also use it to cast a toilet bowl. '*People sometimes talk of the porcelain syndrome: in the seventeenth century porcelain was as precious as gold, and yet even then there was a difference in the appreciation of its artistic value. In this century too, a scene made by Picasso in ceramic tiles is worth much less than one of his paintings*', says Dessauvage. He considers no material to be of inferior worth: as we know, great art can even be made from grease and from cows sawn in half.

Tjok Dessauvage does not produce any applied art in his studio in Sint-Eloois-Winkel. The techniques he has mastered are as essential as the painter's brush techniques or the sculptor's welding and carving techniques. Every technique and every material has its own riches and limitations. And

Tjok Dessauvage, *Return.*

the artist consciously accepts these limitations of the form: for example, a ceramicist cannot turn a square form. The basic forms in Dessauvage's work are the bowl, the cone and the cylinder. They are archetypal forms with which structures can be built, and are sufficiently neutral to be able to work on. '*A painter works in a square or rectangular frame. I use my specific forms to create miniature worlds.*' Dessauvage does not like to call them pots, because this makes too strong a reference to their traditional function. He talks of pot-structures and likes working with closed forms, whose flat upper surfaces provide the stage on which the essential element makes its appearance: a few scratched lines, a cast, a relief.

This marking gives substance to every work. A fine example is the pot-structure entitled *Diary of a Woodworm*. Dessauvage made a cast of the trail a woodworm left in a piece of wood and transferred this to the flat part of the pot. '*Every movement of the woodworm is recorded in this cast, and literally tells the story of its whole life: when the worm eats it moves. When it moves it eats. The image makes reference to a computer chip, and the structure of small channels is a superb condensation of "doing" and "living". It is structures like this that I look for. It might also be the print of a photo-finish, or an aerial photo of a village, with all those relationships and connections which are marked out by the culture, climate and agriculture. Or look at an electrician's wiring diagram, it's pure abstraction.*'

In the Sahara Dessauvage found Coke tins sand-blasted and discoloured by the sand and wind. '*The desert turns a garish can into an object that becomes completely integrated, in total harmony with nature. It is aesthetic recuperation.*' This is what Dessauvage also aspires to: he wants to create structures that retain a high degree of neutrality while at the same time having a penetrating voice. Not powerful or colourful images, but forms which put themselves in perspective and are highly abstracted so as to purge them of any anecdotalism.

The figurative pretext for another work may be a medieval crossbow or

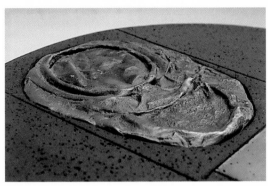

Tjok Dessauvage, *Sahara - Pop Art.*

the electrical diagrams already mentioned, up to and including what Dessauvage saw his neighbour doing in the garden: '*My neighbour was running fine wires across his little plot to stop the birds from taking the seeds. He studied it very precisely, looked from which angle the birds flew in and stretched the wires so as to keep them out of his vegetable patch. This resulted in a perfect geometric structure, the abstract result of empirical thought. I took some photos of it and incorporated the structure into my work. Without realising it, my neighbour had designed a marvellous geometric aesthetic work.*'

Many of the pot structures have double walls, since a single wall immediately leads to the theme of inside / outside, in which both sides are bound to influence each other. Dessauvage finds this too unequivocal: '*When you close the bowl you have a larger surface area on which to work and the formal presence is more pronounced. Its movement tends to go around it, rather than inside.*' Sometimes there is still a small cavity at the centre: this is the vital centre of each minimalist world, in which the movement is 'reversed'. And that leads to its growing completely still, becoming inert.

In his more recent work Dessauvage seems ingeniously to complete the circle of ceramic art: the pot is sublimated as a medium of information. '*Ceramics are the most important source of information about the past. When you go to an exhibition of any ancient culture, it is the shards of pots and clay that dominate. The drawings and figures on these shards teach us about important figures from history, and we learn things such as the way they dressed. This is pure chance, since clay is fire resistant while wood and textiles, for example, are not. So far fewer wood and textile relics have been preserved. Clay is both easy to work and found in abundance on every continent, so in fact it is the DNA of art. All the possible abstract and figurative forms from every possible culture have gradually evolved towards a synthesis.*'

It is this synthesis to which Dessauvage also aspires. Take a work like

Tjok Dessauvage,
Fragmentation.

Tjok Dessauvage, *Pinatubo*
(detail).

Window – Japanese Pottery Relic: sixteen closed pot structures standing rigidly in a row are topped with a framed photograph in the form of a window. It shows fragments of photos of old Japanese potsherds, plates and pots. This is 'new' art as a bearer of 'old' information, created from the same material.

The ceramicist must go through a long, hard process before he achieves the freedom to be able to work with the material without being held back by technical limitations. For example, Tjok Dessauvage studied countless glazing techniques, without putting them to practical use, because he hardly ever glazes his pieces. But he still learned the technique, because he does not want his creations to be hindered by any possible limitation. '*It is precisely that degree of difficulty that scares off a lot of artists. In some contemporary forms of artistic expression you can achieve a great deal with*

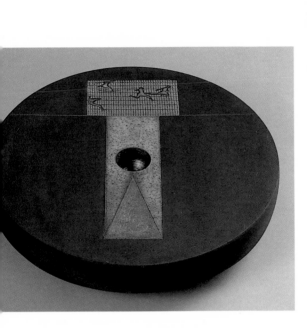

Tjok Dessauvage, *Photo Finish.*

much less craftsmanship or technical know-how.' Dessauvage is not bothered by this. The American artist Jeff Koons had some of his sculptures carved by Bavarian sculptors: Koons admired their virtuosity and he was quite honest about it. Dessauvage also sometimes works, within his discipline, for an artist who then integrates the ceramics into his own work, such as his fellow-countryman Wim Delvoye.

Ceramic art is currently experiencing a revival. But Dessauvage has his doubts about this: '*There is a double danger. On the one hand there are contemporary artists who work for a few weeks in a ceramics centre, after which they return to their original field and material. This makes little essential contribution to the development of ceramic art. And on the other hand there are the genuine ceramicists who are tempted into giving a repeat performance of contemporary art movements: laying ceramic shards on the floor of the museum, for example, just as Robert Long did twenty years ago in his Land Art. That does not add anything either, though most of the attention goes to these forms of ceramics. Ceramics should be able to develop as an independent art form.*'

In this respect, Dessauvage is a shining example: more than half his buyers are Belgian and international collectors who actually never buy ceramics. In this way they prove that the art of Dessauvage superbly transcends the material.

MARC RUYTERS
Translated by Gregory Ball.

From

Y Mañana? to *Manneken Pis*

Thirty Years of Flemish Filmmaking

Cinema as popular entertainment

In the 1930s Belgium boasted the largest number of cinema-goers in Europe. The enormous number of cinemas and the queues at the box office were not only important for the American distribution houses, which were slowly but surely catching up with their French competitors; the Flemish interest in the cinema as a form of entertainment also stimulated the production of a series of Flemish popular films. Filmmakers such as Jan Vanderheyden, Edith Kiel and, later, Jef Bruyninckx ultimately gave the cinema-going public what they wanted: comic films, and in their own language at that – usually a somewhat watered-down version of the Antwerp dialect. A Flemish classic from this period was *Whitey* (De Witte, 1934), based on the widely read novel of the same name by the regional writer Ernest Claes. The film owed its unequalled success above all to the acting performance of Jef Bruyninckx, who portrayed the pranks of a fourteen-year-old country boy in an uncannily natural way.

In 1952 the Belgian government began subsidising the domestic film industry for the first time. The subsidy took the form of the repayment of a percentage of the entertainment tax levied on commercial performances. This encouraged three young film freaks, Rik Kuypers, Roland Verhavert and Ivo Michiels, to work together to produce a 'different' film; inspired by the British Free Cinema, their psychological drama *Seagulls Die in the Harbour* (Meeuwen sterven in de haven, 1955) presented a stark contrast to the banality of the amateurish farce films of the day. Their efforts brought artistic success (including nomination in the Official Selection at the Cannes Film Festival), but were ignored by the public. The result was a stagnation in the development of a domestic film industry.

Eventually the government realised that the film industry needed more than the 'detaxation system' of 1952. After an unsuccessful attempt to establish a National Belgian Film Institute, Belgium's two language communities, which by now had become 'culturally' autonomous, each went their own way. On 10 November 1964 a Royal Decree was issued founding a Selection Committee for Dutch-language Cultural Films (Belgium).

Before this attempt to create some sort of film policy had any effect, however, the premiere took place in 1966 of *The Man Who Had his Hair Cut*

Emile Degelin, *Y Mañana?* (1966)(Photo by J.C. Boon).

Short (De man die zijn haar kort liet knippen), based on the novel of the same name by Johan Daisne. This production, which was made especially for television, gave André Delvaux a chance to demonstrate his talent for film. The filming of this important magic-realistic novel was initially heavily criticised in its own country but highly praised abroad. The renowned Parisian film journal *Les Cahiers du Cinéma* regarded Delvaux' film as quite simply a masterpiece. The modernist structure, with a well thought-out combination of sound and image and the magnificent performance of Senne Rouffaer in the role of the teacher-cum-lawyer who is destroyed by an impossible love, turned this into a film which still stands the test of time today. The lack of recognition at home, combined with the better production facilities in the French-speaking region of Belgium, caused Delvaux to turn his back on Flanders. He built up his film career with a number of more than serviceable French-language productions, including *Un soir, un train* (1967), *Rendez-vous à Bray* (1971), *Benvenuta* (1983), en *L'Oeuvre au noir* (1988). It was not until 1979 that he again completed a Flemish film, *A Woman in a Twilight Garden* (Een Vrouw tussen Hond en Wolf).

Underlying the subsidy policy which came into effect in 1965 was a desire to help the Flemish film industry out of the doldrums. The financial resources were minimal, however, and the government therefore sought to encourage co-productions with the Netherlands.

The first film produced with government support was *Y Mañana?* (Emile Degelin, 1966), a comic production full of visual gags in the Jacques Tati style. This story about a Flemish policeman (French actor Jacques Dufilho) who is prevented by all manner of complications from leaving the Spanish island where he has been spending a holiday, has three different 'endings', from which the cinema-goer him or herself has to choose. With *Cash? Cash!* (1967) Paul Collet and Pierre Drouot, both newly qualified producers, created a smoothly edited and cleverly portrayed thriller. Of these two films only the latter, which was aimed at young people, achieved box office success.

This was far from the case with the most important production of this early period. Harry Kümel's first full-length film *Monsieur Hawarden* (1968), based on the novel of that name by the Flemish author Filip de Pillecijn, was a genuinely remarkable work. Based on a script by the Dutchman Jan Blokker, who adapted the novel for the screen, the young Kümel managed to produce a film which is able to serve as a model for the artistically valid translation of literary work for the cinema. The dramatic story of transvestism, based on authentic details, about a noblewoman pursued for murder by the legal system, allowed the filmmaker to portray all manner of erotic relations in a subtle, ambiguous and highly stylised way. Initially cinema proprietors refused to show the film, and in the Netherlands the production also met with a negative response from the public. Finally, there was a repeat of what had happened with Delvaux' *The Man Who had his Hair Cut Short*: Kümel's debut won awards at the film festivals in Hyères, Chicago and Edinburgh and then returned to its own country where it found recognition, especially among film buffs.

And then, in 1971, the Dutch-Belgian co-production *Mira* suddenly burst into the cinema to great plaudits as a 'Flemish film'. At last filmmakers had succeeded, 37 years after Vanderheyden's *Whitey*, in bringing the masses back to the cinema. *Mira*, the film version of the well-known novel *The Demise of Waterhoek* (De teleurgang van de Waterhoek – written by Stijn Streuvels in 1927) by the Dutchman Fons Rademakers, did indeed have everything necessary to charm the public at large: a script with sufficient dramatic tension, a love story portrayed by popular actors such as Willeke van Amelrooy and Jan Decleir and the beautiful colour photography of Eddy van der Enden, who evoked the picturesque life and setting of 'poor Flanders' in the manner of a folklore dream. Within the story of a farming community which sets its face in vain against modernisation, a tragic love affair develops between a naive farmer's son and a promiscuous woman.

It seemed as if the commercial success of *Mira* had set the Flemish film industry on its way – especially since even the French-speaking cinema-going public of Brussels had been charmed by a Dutch-language 'Belgian' film. In retrospect, the success of *Mira* proved to be a mirage. The film did however start a trend which shaped a substantial section of the Flemish film industry. From then on, producers, filmmakers and the Selection Committee sought to appeal to the public through the filming of well-known literary works.

Following in the footsteps of *Mira*, two films appeared almost simultaneously in 1972; *Rolande – A Story of Passion* (Rolande met de bles) by Roland Verhavert, based on the novel by Herman Teirlinck, and *Louisa – A Word of Love* (Louisa – een woord van liefde) by the young, commercially-minded duo Paul Collet and Pierre Drouot. Neither film achieved the box-office success of their predecessor, though *Rolande*, in particular, was more interesting, both in terms of its theme and its structure. In addition to having

Fons Rademakers, *Mira*
(1971)(Photo Kunst &
Kino).

a girl's name in their titles, all three films had in common that their stories are set in the recent past (the start of the twentieth century for *Mira*, during and after the First World War for *Rolande* and *Louisa*), and therefore focus particular attention on the external beauty of the costumes and the emphatically aesthetic nature of the camerawork – a technique which cannot be entirely absolved of the charge of '*Schönfilmerei*', to which the carefully sought-out locations of castle grounds, rural settings and old urban neighbourhoods with their attractive merchant houses lend themselves. As with Rademakers, the dramatic tension in Verhavert's and Collet-Drouot's work is based on a conflict between the old rural mentality and the modern spirit with its new views on morals and values. In *Mira* the love story between the farmer's son Sander and the promiscuous Mira runs parallel with the struggle by the rural population against the building of a bridge which will link their hamlet to the town. In *Rolande* the country squire Renier (again Jan Decleir) falls victim to his passion for the unattainable, equally promiscuous Rolande. *Louisa*, based on an original script, recounts the collapse of an idyllic '*ménage à trois*', which is not tolerated by the hypocritical rural community. The weakness of Verhavert's highly stylised and technically very competent film lies chiefly in the overly literary treatment of Teirlinck's epistolary novel. The problem is compounded by the rather 'stagey' performance of many actors who were unable to shake off their theatrical origins.

Further along the literary path ... The preference for the filmed literature genre continued for years, explaining why many Flemish films bear the names of the often traditional literary works on which their scripts are based. These included, among others, the films *The Conscript* (De loteling) and *Pallieter* (Roland Verhavert, 1973 and 1975), *Whitey* (De Witte van Sichem, Robbe de Hert, 1980), *Flaxfield* (De Vlaschaard, Jan Gruyaert, 1983), *The Lion of Flanders* (De Leeuw van Vlaanderen, Hugo Claus, 1984), *The Van Paemel Family* (Het Gezin van Paemel, Paul Cammermans, 1986) and *Farmer's Song* (Boerenpsalm, Roland Verhavert, 1989).

Perfectly good films which looked back less nostalgically at the past included *Friday* (Vrijdag, 1980) and the non-subsidised film *The Sacrament* (Het sacrament, 1989), for which filmmaker Hugo Claus took his own literary work as a basis. The film *A Woman in a Twilight Garden* (1979) by André Delvaux, the maker of *The Man Who Had his Hair Cut Short*, was a striking instance of the relationship between film and literature..

In the mid-seventies the government encouraged collaboration between Flemish novelists and filmmakers. Funds were provided, for example, to enable the filmmaker André Delvaux to collaborate with the author and scriptwriter Ivo Michiels. Both set to work to create a story in which the central figure is Lieve (the French actress Marie-Christine Barrault), a petit-bourgeois woman who lives through the German occupation of Brussels during the Second World War, the Liberation and the ensuing repression, and who becomes worldly wise through her relationship with two men. This *tranche de vie* covering around fifteen years is made up of three parts: Lieve's marriage to Adriaan (Rutger Hauer), who later leaves for the Eastern Front in the service of the German occupier, her acquaintance with François (Roger Van Hool), a resistance fighter who hides in her home, and finally the return of Adriaan, from whom Lieve becomes increasingly alienated as he neurotically clings to his outmoded ideals. Finally, Lieve rejects both men and opts for an independent existence with her small son.

Michiels developed this plot in such a stylised manner that the script became a film novel in its own right. It appeared as a book in 1977 under the title *A Twilight Garden* (Een tuin tussen hond en wolf). In 1979 the film appeared in the cinema with the slightly amended title *A Woman in a Twilight Garden*; it is interesting not only because it was the first film about collaboration, resistance and repression in Belgium during and after the Second World War. As an intimate portrait of a woman, which depicts everyday, interiorised fascism within a man-woman relationship, it is also one of the best productions in thirty years of Flemish film history. Delvaux managed to structure his film and compose it both visually and musically in such a way that he immediately left his Flemish colleagues, who often worked in an overly illustrative way, far behind. This is due above all to his visual / pictorial style and his insight into the possibilities and functionality of the language of film. As a Belgo-French co-production, *A Woman in a Twilight Garden* was nominated in the Official Selection of the Cannes Film Festival, but was not a commercial success; it may have been too aesthetically constructed to engage the emotions of the public.

The engagement of Fugitive Cinema

A number of young film fanatics, such as Robbe de Hert, saw in the subsidies policy begun in 1964 opportunities for an original and personal film industry. The 22-year-old De Hert and a few friends founded the film collective *Fugitive Cinema* on 17 March 1966. This group of film freaks had no shortage of original film projects. They quickly set themselves apart with a series of short films and reportages, which brought in one international prize after another. Together with Guido Henderickx and Patrick Le Bon, De Hert was to give the Flemish film industry a new dimension.

The first full-length fictional film from Robbe de Hert was *Camera Sutra* (1970-1973), in which he deliberately broke through the classical narrative style. It is a typical montage film. The documentary fragments rant in polemic style against the Flanders of the time, where the establishment maintains 'order' and where 'culture' functions as a sweetener, among other things in the form of cycle racing and beer festivals. The lack of power to change this situation is reflected in the ironic / aloof filming of the fictional part, in which a group of young rebels unsuccessfully attempt to steal weapons from a munitions store. In essence the film is a post-1968 cry of despair by a powerless angry young man. Once again, the positive reception at domestic and foreign film festivals was in sharp contrast to the film's distribution and reception in domestic cinemas. After this, De Hert returned to documentaries with the long reportage *Le Filet Americain* (1978-1980).

Completing these two films had however brought Flanders' only film collective into severe financial difficulties. De Hert, Henderickx and Le Bon had no choice but to enter the commercial film industry if they wished to continue working as filmmakers. For De Hert this meant showing the film *Whitey* (1980) referred to earlier, a remake of Vanderheyden's cinema success from 1934. The box office success of the film led to a commission from the Belgian broadcaster BRTN – almost inevitably for the filming of a Flemish novel. De Hert accepted the proposition and created *Maria*

André Delvaux, *A Woman in a Twilight Garden* (Een Vrouw tussen Hond en Wolf, 1979)(Photo Elan Film).

Guido Henderickx, *Burnt Bridge* (Verbrande brug, 1975).

Danneels or the Life that We Dreamed (Maria Danneels of het leven dat wij droomden, 1982), based on the work of the same name by the traditional novelist Maurice Roelants, in which the author recounts how the close friendship between two women is disrupted by a smooth but superficial young man. De Hert placed the lesbian relationship, which Roelants merely hinted at in his novel, centre stage and relocated the story to the 1960s. In contrast to the novel, in which Maria (Karen van Parijs) exchanges her friendship for Irène (Arlette Weygers) for her love for Richard (Herman Gilis), in the film the lesbian love wins out over the heterosexual relationship. Filmmaker De Hert and scriptwriter Femand Auwera also added a framework story to their plot: a scriptwriter (De Hert's alter ego) treks to the TV station to negotiate on the filming of *Maria Danneels*. The process of creating the film itself was thus placed within the reworked Roelants story. The montage of image and sound, achieved among other things by inserting fragments from films such as *Casablanca, Psycho, Some Like It Hot* and *The Forty-First* (Sorok pervyl), forced the by now aging novel into oblivion. Originality, fantasy and ironising alienation, coupled with a talent for and knowledge of film, made *Maria Danneels* a unique viewing experience. It was to be the last film in which De Hert genuinely experimented with image and sound. He followed it up with a number of popular films such as *Rough Diamonds* (Zware jongens, 1984) with the Flemish comics Gaston Berghmans and Leo Martin in the main roles, *Blueberry Hill* (1989) a more or less autobiographical youth film containing a great deal of nostalgic music from the 1960s and, buoyed by the commercial success of this film, the sequel *Brylcream Boulevard* (1995). Guido Henderickx and Patrick Le Bon, too, ultimately had to comply with the laws of the film business.

In 1975, however, Guido Henderickx produced *Burnt Bridge* (Verbrande brug), which for years remained one of the most important Flemish films. Henderickx' debut in full-length films was important not only because the maker, with an aversion to the nostalgic Flemish film industry, placed the

story of a dramatic triangular relationship in a contemporary working class setting, but also because he followed American filmmakers in introducing a modern style, characterised by lingering shots – often recorded sequences – into Flemish film. With *Burnt Bridge* Henderickx confirmed the talent which he had been demonstrating since 1968 in a host of short Fugitive productions.

The work of Patrick Le Bon also initially had an authentic social dimension. This also applied to his first feature films, *Bye* (Salut en de kost, 1974) and *Hellhole* (Hellegat, 1980), which in addition to the necessary love story, dealt respectively with the themes of the exploitation of migrant labourers and damage to the environment through the dumping of chemical waste.

The fantastic cinema of Harry Kümel

With *Monsieur Hawarden* (1968) Harry Kümel had demonstrated the mannerist style which was to typify all his later films. In early 1970 he produced a commercial vampire film in a French and an English version, *Les lèvres rouges / Daughters of Darkness*, 'full of sex, blood and violence'. The four characters, a Hungarian countess, her female companion and a newly-married couple, once again have to deal with existential relationship problems. Once again semblance masks reality and once again the filmmaker plays with genres and styles, quoting among other things from Von Sternberg's *Shanghai Express* (1933) and even from his own *Monsieur Hawarden*. His extremely low-budget film not only enjoyed world-wide distribution, but developed into a genuine cult film in the United States. More important, however, was *Malpertuis* (1973), based on the fantastic novel of the same title by the Ghent author Jean Ray. It is the story of the young seaman Yann (Mathieu Carrière), whose imagination becomes reality: in a building in a port city, Malpertuis, he is confronted with the demi-god Cassavius (Orson Welles), who holds gods who have been degraded to petit-bourgeois citizens in his spell. The international cast which, in addition to the names already mentioned, included Susan Hamp-

Harry Kümel, *Malpertuis*
(1973) (Photo United
Artists).

Harry Kümel, *Eline Vere* (1991).

shire, Michel Bouquet, Jean Pierre Cassel and others and enjoyed a very high budget for Flemish standards of the time – though actually a mere $ 1000,000 / £ 60,000 – meant that the release of this production was awaited with great excitement. In fact making the film proved a difficult road for Kümel: there were the whims of Orson Welles, the limited acting ability of Mathieu Carrière, the Selection Committee which demanded a Dutch-language film and the cutting-room editor Richard Marden, who was no match for Kümel's vision, but who was imposed on the production by United Artists. The result was that *Malpertuis* never became what its maker had expected of it, in spite of the strong direction, luxurious scenery and splendid camerawork of Gerry Fisher. The film made it to the Cannes Film Festival, but only years later would it receive recognition.

In 1978 Kümel succeeded in completing another full-length feature film, *Paradise Lost* (Het verloren paradijs). As a result of this controversial production, it was years before Kümel again attracted interest. With *The Secrets of Love* (1985), an amusing erotic popular film, however, he once more gained the confidence of the financial backers for one of his long-cherished projects, the filming of Louis Couperus' novel *Eline Vere*, a masterpiece of Dutch naturalism.

Eline Vere (1991) meant a grandiose comeback for Harry Kümel. The title character (the French-speaking actress Marianne Basler) is a young woman suffocating in the mediocrity of the strict conventions and external pseudo-well-being of her bourgeois environment. The psycho-dramatic plot, which ends with Eline's suicide, gave Kümel an opportunity to evoke the *fin de siècle* life of The Hague and Brussels in all its semblance of glory. The perfectionist *mise en scène* with its splendid sets, interiors and locations, the first-class direction of the international cast, the wonderful camerawork of Eduard van der Enden and the strongly romantic music create an impressive piece of theatre, in which the mask of glitter and glamour hides the development of the existential tragedy of the lonely Eline Vere. The operatic style *à la* Visconti gives this luxuriant costume drama an added and individual dimension.

A new generation   In 1979, seminars in film scriptwriting were organised for the first time; they were taught by experts from the American Film Institute. One of the first participants was Marc Didden, a former journalist who in 1980 hit the heights with his script *Brussels by Night*. In 1983 the film appeared in the cinema. It seemed as if the Flemish film industry had acquired a new elan; for the first time, cinema-goers were introduced to a dynamic and authentic picture of life in the European capital. Max (François Beukelaers) leaves his house after a failed suicide attempt. Whilst wandering aimlessly through contemporary Brussels he meets a succession of characters: his retired workmate Louis (Michel Mentens), the barmaid Alice (Ingrid Devos) and her boyfriend, the Moroccan Abdel (Amid Chakir). The group cling to each other like outcasts. Max, however, drags the other three along on a purposeless journey which leads inexorably to a dramatic finale. A highly original script, a universal contemporary problem, an atmospheric *mise en scène*, multilingual dialogue, brilliant acting performances and direction all combined to make Didden's film debut a milestone in the history of Flemish film production. *Brussels by Night* was widely distributed and appealed in particular to young people. Didden's second film, *Istanbul* (1985), like his later films also based on an original script, was not quite able to live up to his brilliant debut.

Following in the footsteps of Marc Didden, two young filmmakers unexpectedly gave the Flemish film industry an international dimension: Dominique Deruddere (see *The Low Countries* 1995-96: 276) and Stijn Coninx (see *The Low Countries* 1993-94: 275). The latter won an Oscar nomination with his film *Daens* (1992), based on the novel *Pieter Daens* (1971) by the Flemish author Louis Paul Boon. The film recounts a dramatic period in the life of the socially committed priest Adolf Daens (once again played by a brilliant Jan Decleir), who at the end of the nineteenth century took up the cause of the exploited working classes in Aalst. The priest, after whom the *Christian Peoples' Party* founded in 1893 was named, was later forced to give up his political career. In 1899 he was even forbidden to wear the priestly cloth.

Marc Didden, *Brussels by Night* (1983).

Daens had a well-structured plot. The almost documentary sequences showing the working and living conditions of the working classes in late nineteenth-century Flanders, the central plot about the emotionally loaded conflict between Daens and his astute reactionary opponent Charles Woeste, Chairman of the Catholic Party, and the confrontation of spirituality with the 'case' that was Daens were skilfully combined by Ludo Troch. The film was further enhanced by the controlled colour photography of the highly regarded Walther vanden Ende. Above all, however, it was the masterly direction of the actors by Stijn Coninx which made *Daens* such a gripping popular film. He found suitable locations in Poland and inspired the entire film crew to turn in exceptional performances. Jan Decleir, for years one of the most important stage and film actors, put in a more than convincing performance as the rebellious priest. The same also goes for the French actor Gérard Desarthe (Charles Woeste), Julien Schoenaerts (Mgr. Stillemans, Bishop of Ghent), the debutante Antje de Boeck and the more experienced, young and talented Michael Pas, who as the young 'daensist' and the Ghent socialist, respectively, portray the 'love story' within the drama which is *Daens*.

International ambitions

The work of Dominique Deruddere is of a very different ilk. Deruddere belongs to a new generation of young people who identify with the Western counter-culture with which they came into contact through Anglo-Saxon pop and rock music and literature. It is therefore no coincidence that Dominique Deruddere's first full-length feature film *Crazy Love* (1987) was inspired by the work of the American poet and novelist Charles Bukowski. *Crazy Love* consists of three short films which portray the life of the same main character, Harry Voss, a man who hankers after love and affection. With the help of a striking musical backdrop, Deruddere transformed the raw Bukowskian world into an intimist poetic event.

In reading Bukowski, Deruddere came into contact with the work of another American author, John Fante. In this author's first novel *Wait Until Spring, Bandini*, Deruddere saw possibilities for a new film project. International acclaim for *Crazy Love* and the Fante revival which Bukowski had set in motion enabled Deruddere, in collaboration with Francis Ford Coppola's Zoetrope Studios, to mount a major international co-production between Belgium, France and Italy. Never before had a Flemish filmmaker been given such an opportunity.

Wait Until Spring, Bandini (1989) is a melodramatic chronicle of an

Dominique Deruddere,
Crazy Love (1987).

Dominique Deruddere,
Wait until Spring, Bandini
(1989).

Frank van Passel,
Manneken Pis (1995).

Italian family which goes through a particularly hard time during the severe winter of 1925. It is a Christmas tale of poverty, love and disloyalty, portrayed by actors such as Ornella Mutti, Joe Mantegna and Faye Dunaway. Deruddere adeptly breaks through the sentimentality of the melodrama by incorporating a lightly ironic undertone. The authentic interpretation by all the actors, particularly the three children, once again proved his talent as a director. Moreover, all the technical resources such as camerawork, sets and sound are so effectively used that what is a fairly unremarkable story in terms of content makes a deep impression on the viewer. In short Deruddere, with his taste for perfection and his talent, succeeded in creating a film which fitted in perfectly with American norms. The same can be said of the technical aspects, the aestheticising of poverty and the Hollywood preference for the traditional, melodramatic happy ending.

In contrast to its success in Deruddere's home country, where the work of this 'miracle child of Flemish film' received praise from all quarters, *Bandini* failed to make the commercial cinema circuit in the United States. It may be that its penetrating, subtle characterisation and controlled plot movement made the film too European for the American market.

It was to be five years before this talented filmmaker was again able to create a feature film. Deruddere became fascinated by a script by Charles Highson and Lise Mayer, both of whom worked for British television. Again, Deruddere opted for an international co-production involving Belgium, the Netherlands, Great Britain and France. The result, *Suite 16* (1994) was a Pinterian '*Kammerspiel*' with two central characters: a young Dutchman, Chris (Anthonie Kamerling), who is seeking his fortune as a gigolo on the French Riviera (Nice) and an older, rich, handicapped intellectual, Glover (the English actor Peter Postlethwaite). The power struggle between these two characters is merciless, with first one and then the other appearing to gain the edge. *Suite 16* is a contemporary English-language European film, which in addition to the ubiquitous commercial ingredients contains a penetrating, merciless – and thus not particularly cheering – analysis of the human condition. Its psychological message, embedded in a brilliant cinematic style, indisputably confirms the talent of a new generation.

The artistic and commercial success of Manneken Pis

Frank van Passel also displayed a talent for film in his first full-length feature film *Manneken Pis* (1995), an extremely low-budget production (see *The Low Countries* 1996-97: 273). It is an unpretentious love story about the naive and honest orphan Harry (Frank Vercruyssen), who earns his living as a dishwasher in a big city, and the tram-driver Jeanne (the ex-*Daens* actress Antje de Boeck), who is not lacking in erotic experience and is a little too passionate for Harry. When, after a great many hesitations on the part of Harry and several provocations by the girl, the two find each other, fate takes over. More important than the slightly simplistic plot is the way in which the director is able to push his actors into remarkably spontaneous performances whilst engaging the viewer with a modern suggestive, sometimes slightly poetic / nostalgic and slightly surreal film style. Van Passel's little film achieved surprising success among the cinema-going public and received plaudits at a host of international festivals (First Prize from 'La Semaine de la Critique' and 'Prix Jeunesse' at the Cannes Film Festival in 1995, as well as in Montreal, Chicago, Valladolid and Geneva).

The artistic and commercial success of the unpretentious *Manneken Pis* is indirectly the result of 30 years of subsidies policy. However imperfect, however limited and however bureaucratic this film policy was, it still offered a great many producers and filmmakers the opportunity to create films. This does not alter the fact, however, that right up to today there is still no continuous film production. If there is any continuity at all, then it lies much more in the fact that, until Marc Didden's *Brussels by Night*, the same directors' names cropped up time and again. Until 1983, the image of Flemish film was shaped above all by Roland Verhavert, Harry Kümel, Robbe de Hert, Guido Henderickx, Patrick Le Bon and Hugo Claus. Their personality and vision led to four genres: the pastoral film based on a well-known novel from Flemish literature; the socially aware contemporary 'working class film'; the surreal poetic film, to which the recent *Manneken Pis* belongs; and the comic popular film, which serious filmmakers had to produce in order to put food in their mouths.

Through all the setbacks and obstacles, Flanders continued to produce films, driven by the praiseworthy determination of the filmmakers who developed their talent in spite of the limited production and distribution opportunities. Often with an aversion to commercial considerations, they managed to produce a number of striking productions which, if there is any justice, will be able to count on growing appreciation in the future.

WIM DE POORTER
Translated by Julian Ross.

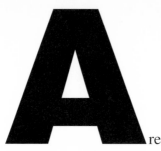

the Programmes Really Doing It?

Television in the Low Countries

The country renowned for being one of the most orderly in the world, where rules are made *not* to be broken, of which it is said that thought and action are ruled by a Calvinist past – that same country's broadcasting system is one of the most chaotic anywhere. The Dutch broadcasting system is, and always has been, so complex that it took a foreigner – the Fleming Herman van Pelt – to explain it. His 1974 study earned him a Doctorate at the University of Leuven. Since then, the situation has only become more complex.

Basically, the establishment of public-service broadcasting in the Netherlands dates from the 1920s, when radio was still a brand new medium. While in other countries the government justifiably claimed broadcasting rights, resulting in a single broadcasting licensee, in the Netherlands each of the various ideologies wanted to broadcast its own message. So that within a few years the strongly pillarised country could boast a liberal broadcasting organisation (AVRO), a socialist broadcasting organisation (VARA), a Catholic organisation (KRO) and an orthodox Protestant organisation (NCRV). A smaller, liberal Protestant organisation (VPRO) also joined the ranks. All these organisations established themselves in Hilversum.

At the beginning of the 1930s the government formally recognised this development: four larger organisations plus one smaller organisation, which transmitted their programmes via two radio channels. They were in such fierce competition with each other that, for example, during a national meeting of the socialist broadcasting organisation VARA, liberal opponents from the AVRO spread nails over the road to prevent further progress by car or bicycle. During the Second World War the Germans forcibly brought all the organisations together, but after liberation in 1945 the old system returned as if nothing had happened. As late as 1954, the Dutch bishops forbade Catholics to listen to the socialist station. But their ban was in vain: Catholic listeners refused to be deprived of the light entertainment programme *Showboat* on Saturday evenings; neither would they miss the famous orchestra The Ramblers, or other forms of amusement.

The pillarised broadcasting system was a reflection of Dutch society, where political parties, trade unions, daily newspapers and even sports organisations were separated according to ideology. During the war years of

1940-1945, when the loathing of the German occupier was at its strongest, mutual understanding increased, but it took years for the walls to give way. In almost every field except broadcasting, organisations merged. Even today, when commercial competition constitutes a good reason to cooperate, and even the politicians are urging cooperation, the broadcasting organisations still want to retain their separate identities.

The pillarisation of the old days was oriented towards emancipation, particularly for Catholics and socialists, and their own broadcasting organisations made a valuable contribution. However, this emancipation only related to groups, while individual emancipation was slow to follow. Today the viewer is little – if at all – interested in the ideological standpoint of those who have made the programme he is watching: the viewer's preference lies in the sphere of amusement, including quizzes, sport or entertaining films. Viewers rarely watch their 'own' programmes which reflect their own beliefs.

The 1970s heralded a new phase. Two organisations without an ideological following (TROS and Veronica) fought to establish themselves next to the older organisations. Although it was thought that they stood no chance, both organisations managed – in record time – to attract enough subscribers to allow them not only to catch up with but to overtake the large organisations. Veronica, which began as a pirate radio station, even went on to become the largest broadcasting organisation in the Netherlands, with more than a million subscribers. This station, geared to the tastes of the young, was so optimistic about its future that it went commercial in 1995, thereby giving up the last scrap of culture required by the Broadcasting Act. Veronica miscalculated, because within the context of cooperation with RTL (part of the powerful Luxembourg-German concern CTL-UFA) the once wealthy broadcasting organisation became a troubled newcomer, whose programmes attracted few viewers and in whom advertisers lost interest. A drastic revision of its programmes led to some improvement, but so far not enough.

Another candidate arrived on the scene in the seventies – the Evangelical Broadcasting Organisation (EO) to represent orthodox Christianity. In the opinion of many the NCRV, established for the purpose in 1925, had become too modern, however principled its standpoint. In order to ensure the production of certain types of programme such as documentaries, art and regional programmes, the national umbrella organisation NOS (Netherlands Broadcasting Authority) was established. The NOS also has the broadcasting rights to the most important sporting events.

Even after the departure of Veronica, there are still seven broadcasting organisations – plus the NOS – in the Netherlands, all claiming their share of time on one of the three public-service television channels. The number of subscribers determines not only allocated air time, but also contributions from radio and television licence fees and from advertising revenue. And this in turn is linked to the number of subscriptions to the various television and radio guides. It is, then, not surprising that the broadcasting organisations fight to maintain the exclusivity of their programme details. In contrast to Belgium and other countries, where radio and television programmes are published not by the broadcasting organisations but in the daily and weekly press, Dutch newspapers have to be content with scanty details. Only a ruling at European level could change this situation.

Flemish broadcasting and the language division

Belgium was one of the first countries in the world to experiment with radio. Even before the First World War, King Albert I had a transmitter mast set up in his palace gardens in order to discover the possibilities of the new medium. The war was an obstacle to further progress. During the 1920s a bilingual broadcasting organisation began transmitting programmes. It was not until 1935 that the organisation was divided into two directorates: one for Dutch-language programmes and one for French-language programmes. From this the organisation developed into the public-service broadcasting system we know today, under the names BRTN (for Flanders) and RTBF (for Wallonia). The small German-speaking part of the country has BRF – in fact no more than a regional broadcasting organisation. The Belgian Broadcasting Act of 18 May 1960 can be seen as a milestone. The Act, which formalised the division into two independent bodies, was seen as a recognition of the autonomy of the language communities. Since that time there has only been occasional cooperation between the two.

For years public-service broadcasting in Belgium has been a political football. Directors were appointed by parliament, whose members felt slighted if a programme was considered insufficiently sympathetic or even too critical. Managing public-service broadcasting in Belgium is certainly a daunting task, particularly since national or regional ministers determine the size of annual contributions to the broadcasting organisations. Restrictive rules still apply, for example in television advertising, which nevertheless provides much-needed revenue.

As early as March 1981, the fourth Martens cabinet in Belgium reached agreement on allowing advertising on television and radio. At that time, however, this concerned only public-service broadcasting. However, one week later the cabinet fell and matters were postponed. Three years later the governing parties reached a new accord, but it was not put into practice.

And so the situation continued for some time. Until, in September 1987, the Luxembourg concern RTL, together with a number of publishers in Wallonia, was able to begin transmitting French-language programmes.

Flanders had a different structure with VTM, with the participation of all publishers in Flanders except the *Standaard* group, whose management did not believe that commercial television could pay. Their judgement has since proved very far from correct..

In the Netherlands as well as in Flanders, 1989 was a crucial year for broadcasting. In both language areas, public-service broadcasting lost its monopoly following the advent of the commercial stations RTL-Véronique (shortly afterwards renamed RTL-4) and VTM respectively. This was preceded by years of internal strife, in the Netherlands because most broadcasting organisations had links with one or other political party and had therefore been able successfully to defend themselves for a long time, and in Flanders because not only politicians but also the publishers of daily and weekly newspapers set themselves up as interested parties who understandably feared a decrease in their advertising revenue.

Not until the 1990s did the realisation dawn that public-service broadcasting in Flanders – two television channels and six radio channels – would have to change its structure in order to survive. Under the pressure of commercial competition, viewing figures plummeted and many talented employees left. In October 1995 the Flemish regional government decided to make the BRTN into an independent company. A crisis manager was appointed from the business world and quickly took radical steps such as abolishing the civil servant status of employees and appointing new staff on contract. The company's name will be changed to VRT (with the 'V' of 'Vlaams' – 'Flemish' – instead of the 'B' of 'Belgian').

The Flemish BRTN thought for a long time that its commercial rival could not survive. But when VTM began to attract famous television personalities away from its public rival, and viewers as well as advertisers deserted in hordes, BRTN began to experience problems: BRTN's commercial broadcasting was heavily regulated, promised government subsidy did not materialise and the management reacted ponderously. It thus took some three years for public-service broadcasting to adapt its programming – and by then viewers had already switched to the commercial rival.

In the Netherlands the breakthrough came not from the politicians, who were after all constrained by the ideology of public-service broadcasting, but from business. In 1989 programme maker Joop van den Ende petitioned for a licence to run a commercial channel (to be called TV 10). At the same time, RTL announced from Luxembourg that it had similar plans. Farcical situations ensued. Van den Ende enticed away all the popular personalities from public-service broadcasting, engaged in costly advertising campaigns and won the sympathy of one or two national dailies. It seemed that RTL did not stand a chance. However, Dutch law prohibited any such broadcasting organisation as TV 10, while under European law the Luxembourg broadcasting organisation (RTL) could not be prevented. It was not until several years later that the Dutch government removed the obstacles to commercial television.

By this time, the number of commercial channels in Flanders had increased to three with the advent of Ka2 (linked to VTM) and VT4 (controlled by the Scandinavian SBS, with capital from the American giant ABC / Disney). VT4 has a unique structure: Dutch-language programmes are broadcast from London. SBS also began to transmit television programmes in the

Netherlands. The underdog won the sympathy of many viewers with its Dutch-oriented programming and substantial coverage of 'small news items'. A second RTL channel was less successful. After the mammoth alliance with Veronica, the European Commission in Brussels decided to close down one of the broadcasting organisations, and RTL's second channel was first in line. On 1 January 1997 the struggle for survival began, with reduced air time and above all increased coverage of news and background. As if 'zapping' Dutch viewers didn't have enough choice, the new channel Europa-7 arrived, in which a TV evangelist from the United States had a share, as well as two television channels belonging to the record company Arcade, one showing mainly repeats of old American series, and one with video clips.

From a political point of view, it is no longer so difficult to begin commercial broadcasting; it *is,* however, becoming increasingly difficult to reach audiences. While public-service broadcasting is conveyed into the viewer's home via the airwaves, the commercial channels are dependent on satellite links plus cable and, increasingly, this involves a subscription and a decoder. The cable companies have few new opportunities open to them, so that for each new candidate an old one must be dropped, often a valued foreign channel. In addition, beyond a certain point the overwhelming choice begins to have an adverse effect. The profusion of channels has even led to a situation in which three competitors broadcast the same American series such as *Star Trek* and *Married with Children*, though, fortunately, not the same episodes. Also, thanks to cable television, viewers in the Netherlands and Flanders have much greater access to European channels – a choice of 20 is the rule rather than the exception.

Average viewing time in the Netherlands is falling, say researchers. Each day the Dutch viewer watches an average of 2 hours 31 minutes of television – 16 minutes more than his Flemish counterpart. Compared with the Unites States (some 7 hours) and the United Kingdom (3 hours 20 minutes), viewing habits in the Low Countries are modest. The greater the choice of programmes, the harder it is to choose, and the sooner the viewer will switch off or over.

More and more advertising

However idealistically it is sometimes presented, the original philosophy behind broadcasting was not only to reach people at home, or to portray an ideal, but also to advertise. Even the first radio broadcasts in the Netherlands in 1919 contained commercials. This situation did not change for several years, until the government began to control broadcasting licences. After this it was to remain unchanged for almost 45 years: radio, and later television, without any form of advertising whatsoever. After the advent of television in 1951, advertising was discussed but never taken seriously. Five large Dutch daily newspapers joined forces to launch a commercial television channel in order to be ahead of the competition, but this was a failure. The listeners-turned-viewers and, in turn, the government, were not ready for it.

The breakthrough came in the mid-sixties. Wages and prices spiralled, broadcasting time was increased, and the public-service broadcasting organisations watched with horror as their precious reserves dwindled. Because of pillarisation, every large broadcasting licencee had links with a political party, so the decision was taken remarkably quickly. On 2 January 1967, the first (public-service) television commercial was transmitted: the Nederlands Dagbladpers (Dutch Daily Press Association), whose members felt threatened by the prospect of decreasing revenue from advertising, exhorted viewers to read newspapers. Some time later, radio advertising began. In order to compensate for lost revenue, the printed press receives a share of the revenue from radio and television advertising. Advertising in the dailies and a number of weeklies has indeed decreased, particularly in the case of major brand names, but they remain important media for advertisers. In the Netherlands 20% of advertising expenditure goes on television advertising; the corresponding figure for Belgium is 30% (Italy 50%, Great Britain 40%).

Originally, the amount of broadcasting time in minutes was modest – approximately 15 minutes per day – with all manner of restrictions relating, for example, to Sundays and public holidays. However, as broadcasting time increased, so did advertising. Nevertheless, after 1971, the 30-minutes-per-day limit remained in force for a further 10 years.

In the Netherlands, cable television has brought foreign channels into the home. Before cable television, only those who lived in the south near the Belgian border could watch Flemish programmes. This, and the less universal introduction of satellite dishes providing an even greater choice of viewing, caused the government to increase advertising time. There was, however, no subsequent explosive growth in advertising until RTL-4 (from the very same Luxembourg of the early years of radio) geared its production exclusively towards the Netherlands. At that moment the dike, guarded so conscientiously for 60 years, gave way. So that today more broadcasting time is devoted to advertising than to children's programmes or to art programmes. On 13 December 1995 the Second Chamber of the Dutch parliament approved a new law under which advertising via public-service broadcasting was increased to a maximum of 10% of broadcasting time, with a maximum of 12 minutes per hour. The legislator also allowed 'floating blocks' between all manner of programmes, plus commercials during breaks in, for example, football matches.

The latter is a bone of contention. While in Flanders half-time in a football match is still devoted to highlights and expert opinion, the Dutch viewer must be content with commercials. Sometimes things go wrong. During an important match between Ajax and Bayern Munich, which took the Amsterdam team into the final of the Europa Cup, viewers had to miss the beginning of the second half. But German viewers were worse off: they even missed one of the goals...

Such occurrences do nothing to enhance the reputation of advertising, despite the appearance of television personalities in commercials and a calculated dose of humour. At best, this ensures that advertising is not rejected out of hand. It does not alter the fact that the Dutch viewer, who in the 1980s was confronted with 40 television commercials per day, can now expect more than 14 times that number: 561 per day on average. It is no surprise that opponents are campaigning for a non-commercial channel in the Netherlands. However, the government is none too happy with the idea because it would mean a loss of revenue.

The bugbear of every advertiser is the remote-control device in the viewer's hand. It has therefore become commonplace for advertisers to repeat their message – and repeat it again. This causes yet more irritation. In recent years the manufacturers of sanitary towels and nappies have been battling it out on television – with commercials being repeated 100 times or more. Large concerns in particular, such as Procter & Gamble or Unilever, advertise heavily on television. And the situation is no different in Belgium where, in one year, Dash washing powder was advertised during 50 of the 52 weeks.

In Flanders, however, the situation is different. There is a sharper distinction between public-service and commercial broadcasting organisations because very little advertising is allowed to the public-service broadcasting organisation BRTN, and most advertising goes to the commercial broadcasting organisation VTM. Such a distinction does not exist in the Netherlands and the consequence of superabundant advertising is general anger, as pointed out – albeit out of self-interest – by the largest newspaper *De Telegraaf* (circulation 800,000). A survey revealed that 62% of all Dutch people regard advertising as a necessary evil, but that more than half the viewers feel they are being patronised through what they call false information, exaggeration, repetition and pushiness. In order to reduce viewers' frustration, interested parties have set up a foundation to promote the positive side of advertising.

As in the United States, large European countries have so-called cross-ownership, whereby one individual gains control of various types of media (Murdoch in the United Kingdom, Berlusconi in Italy, Bertelsmann in Germany). In the Low Countries this phenomenon used to be largely unknown, but is now becoming more widespread. The daily newspaper *De Telegraaf*, mentioned above, has an interest in SBS. The Dutch publishing concern Wegener has an interest in one of the two Arcade channels, and Flemish daily newspaper groups in VTM. The most active is the large Dutch group VNU (Netherlands Publishers' Association), which controls all the popular weeklies plus a significant share of the regional daily press. The VNU has not only substantial interests in the programme guides of a number of Dutch public-service broadcasting organisations, but also in the RTL channels. In Flanders, where the concern also publishes, it has acquired a substantial share of the channel VTM. When VTM's profits fell as a result of competition, that share was transferred to CLT-UFA. In contrast to the United States, where legislation is strict, cross-ownership is more loosely regulated in the Low Countries.

The power of sport

Sport – and football in particular – is the most important element in programming schedules. While 'cost-cutting' is the watchword everywhere, particularly with regard to documentaries, cultural programmes and programmes for the young, sport is allowed to expand almost without limit. In the battle for broadcasting rights, the sports unions push up the prices. In 1960 the television rights to the Olympic Games in Rome amounted to a million dollars. In 1996 the figure for Atlanta was one thousand times higher. In 1994, public-service broadcasters in Flanders were furious when television rights to the national football competitions went to the commercial rival. In the Netherlands, the Luxembourg channel RTL snatched away the rights to international matches from under its rivals' noses. Football is the draw *par excellence*: 25 of the 30 broadcasts with the highest viewing figures were football matches.

The real war broke out in 1996. The Dutch football union concluded an agreement with a number of large concerns, including Philips, to set up a new channel – Sport-7. It acquired the exclusive television rights to matches of the national competition, which until that time had – automatically as it were – gone to public-service broadcasting. The football union wanted to introduce a censorship of sorts, in the sense that production would be football-friendly, and incidents on and off the pitch would not be given excessive coverage. In addition, Sport-7 wanted to acquire the rights to other major events. The broadcasts would be transmitted on cable television, and every viewer would have to pay a monthly subscription.

The channel was launched on 18 August 1996, but immediately encountered fierce opposition. Cable companies refused to collect the subscription fees and, in large cities such as Amsterdam and Eindhoven, even refused to transmit Sport-7. Where the cable companies refused to transmit, viewers had to buy a decoder and subscribe to a costly package which included a Chinese channel and a porn channel. The Netherlands thus acquired an eleventh channel with the most popular programming, but unfortunately no-one really wanted it. The owners noticed this too: after 4 months Sport-7 had to cease transmission.

In order to attract viewers, one of the seven Dutch public-service broadcasting organisations uses the phrase '*It's the programmes that do it!*'. However encouraging this may sound, it is rarely true in reality. In the Low Countries today, television itself has become news. Television is no longer about the programmes, but about the struggle for survival of numerous competing broadcasting organisations, public as well as commercial. So that any sketch of the situation can be no more than a snapshot.

FRANS OUDEJANS
May 1997
Translated by Yvette Mead.

D avid

v. Goliath

Fashion from Flanders

What's that ? Flemish fashion ? Is there such a thing ? And is it up with the big boys ? About a decade ago it would indeed have been inconceivable, but today there is no doubt about it. Flemish fashion does exist. Though it took some time to get used to.

It must have been about ten years ago. I had just spent a day at a trade fair and was outside Olympia in London waving for a taxi. A Japanese man was quick to take up my invitation to share the cab to the city centre. What was my involvement with fashion? Journalist? Did I know the Belgian designers ? '*Ann Dee Meulemeester*' (sic)?? I was already nodding, and the Japanese was smiling to his back teeth: yes, he had seen their collection too, and immediately bought it. Those Belgians were very good. But oh dear, how did you pronounce those names ?

Today, barely ten years later, anyone who is seriously involved in fashion can spell their names backwards: Ann Demeulemeester, Walter van Beirendonck, Martin Margiela, Dries van Noten, Dirk van Saene and Dirk Bikkembergs. They had all graduated from the now highly-reputed fashion department of the Antwerp Academy of Fine Arts, and tried their fortunes in Paris – since time immemorial the centre of fashion *par excellence*. How they did that is a story in its own right. Geert Bruloot, proprietor of the Louis shop in Antwerp, where Demeulemeester and Margiela sell their collections, remembers it as if it were yesterday: '*So much talent assembled together is bound to rise to the top. It was an exceptional group, and that's also why the foreign press called them the Antwerp Six. Not because they made more or less the same clothes, but because together they attracted attention. As it happened they had rented a truck together to go to the trade fair in London, to save expense.*'

The Six had a lot in common: they were daring, provoking the spectators, going to extremes, and turning the world of fashion upside down. But their collections were markedly different from each other. Even at that time. '*Oh, they were extremely talented*,' said Marthe van Leemput, who taught in the fashion department for many years and knows 'her designers' as if they were her children. '*Walter was always working on a design until the last moment, while Ann was able to sleep peacefully that last night. Others – do*

An outfit by Ann Demeulemeester, shown in London in March 1988. This show included designs by all members of the Six.

Walter van Beirendonck: Summer 1997.

Puk-Puk, the guiding star from outer space for Walter van Beirendonck's W&LT project.

I have to say who ? – could not draw so marvellously, but their ideas were right, we had seen that immediately...' Sometimes Marthe helped with the stitching or sewing, at peak times, but she also did some washing-up here and there, if things became too sordid in one of her student's kitchens.

The Six made their breakthrough, each in their own way. Soon after graduating, Martin Margiela exchanged Antwerp for Paris: he was able to train under that French *enfant terrible*, Jean-Paul Gaultier. '*I phoned every day,*' said Margiela, '*Without result. Until one day I got an appointment. I met Gaultier and was allowed to stay. In the end I stayed for three years.*' After that he made a start on a collection of his own. With shows and his own studio as well. Ann Demeulemeester and Walter van Beirendonck saw things slightly differently: they accepted several commercial commissions from renowned textile companies in Belgium and in the meantime dreamed on paper of a collection of their own. Ann went to Paris only much later and there showed her own line in an art gallery, the Galerie Marquardt on Place des Vosges. It was only in the early nineties that she started on fashion shows. She made very personal, sometimes extremely delicate designs in her favourite colours of black and white, with an impeccable cut and superb materials. She was noted almost immediately by the international fashion press. She has now been right at the top for several years. The fact that she has been called simply 'Queen Ann', or 'rock 'n roll Ann' on the covers of illustrious fashion magazines like Women's Wear Daily (America's top fashion trade paper), can only give an indication of her status. And after all, Patti Smith and Linda McCartney are just two of her regular clients.

Van Beirendonck did crazy things. First there was his commercial work, commissions which he is still accepting even today, and then there was W&LT, a lunatic fashion project in which Puk-Puk, some kind of alien creature, guided us through outer space. Walter van Beirendonck is W&LT and vice versa – the master is the best advertisement for his own collection. When he walks through Antwerp on any weekday, passers-by turn round to look at him: with his flamboyant style of dress, his angular beard and the many rings on his fingers, he immediately stands out amongst the grey masses. He started very modestly in Paris, with a collection of sweaters which were, it's true, expensive but were also beautiful, and which he presented to the press and potential buyers in a quiet gallery. There was not yet any talk of shows. But that could not remain so for long. When W&LT went into business with Mustang, the giant jeans manufacturers, the light turned to green. The peak was his fashion parade in the Lido in Paris, where the dancers (and particularly their legs) were simply integrated into the fashion spectacular. The audience, sitting at luxury tables (that's how it is at the Lido) went berserk, and screamed itself hoarse. The clothes? Those livid colour combinations, dungarees, tight T-shirts, in other words contemporary work and home wear, which could only be a step in the right direction. Just as Van Beirendonck claims: kiss the future, that's the only slogan that works.

Ann Demeulemeester is sometimes called the most thorough, Walter van Beirendonck the craziest, Dirk 'long-legs' Bikkembergs the loudest and Martin Margiela the most intellectual. Dries van Noten was once reproached for having too much commercial talent under his cap, partly due to his family connections (his father was a tailor too). (One has to remember, by the way, that in fashion, just as in the other arts, the word 'commercial' has a highly negative ring to it). The quiet Dries van Noten tackled everything with the talent of the shrewdest manager: every fashion parade was a miniature spectacular that made everyone happy, and every collection was a step in the right direction. Van Noten sat everyone on benches next to each other – no reserved places like the other designers. Everyone equal before the law – those who wanted to sit at the front just had to get there on time. There was always a 'gag': in the summer Van Noten gave everyone a cool beer, or a fan; in the winter we got a blanket or a cup of hot soup. He was soon approached by the Japanese, and was quick to sign a contract with them. Yes, they could make his clothes in Japan, but only using his fabrics and his patterns, and, it goes without saying, his kind of atmosphere. The Japanese even came and copied the Christmas tree in the Modepaleis, his shop in Nationalestraat in Antwerp. Apparently his clothes are selling there like hot cakes. '*I just work by feel*', says Van Noten, '*Am I commercial ? And anyway, what's wrong with being commercial ? I simply make things I find beautiful. And that's that.*'

Dirk van Saene is a case of trial and error. Several years ago he started with a fully-fledged line in couture, a superb collection for people who fully appreciate such fine materials and a perfect cut. I often saw him sitting in his studio in Henri van Heurckstraat in Antwerp, cutting out a few ensembles with his assistant. He always turned out a dashing result. Recently, in October 1996, Van Saene gave his first full fashion parade in Paris. It was an amalgam of fine fabrics and deep colours, a comfortable range for today's women. The journalist from the *Journal du Textile*, who by chance was sitting next to me, had to gulp: was this yet another Belgian ?

Jan Welvaert: Summer 1997.

How is it that all these Flemish designers have made a name for themselves abroad, while my thirty-year-old cousin is totally unaware of their existence ? Does it have something to do with that typical Flemish perseverance ? That desire to see things through to the end – until you drop ? Ann Demeulemeester says, '*Speaking for myself, I just pushed on through all those years, doing my own thing, making my collection the way I thought it should be. Of course you are aware of it when you see that the big boys are getting interested. Vogue, Elle, and all those. You have to get used to it, but I did not dwell on it too much. Naomi Campbell called me up one day to ask me if she could take part in my show. I said no. Not because I do not think she is charming, but simply because she did not fit in my show. As I have already said, I do things my own way.*'

Martin Margiela says the same. His collections and shows break new ground. It was Margiela who substituted for his show a session of 'window shopping' in six great cities: Paris, Bonn, Tokyo, New York, London and Milan. It was Margiela who sent his models out onto the catwalk blindfold, at the time when the whole to-do about supermodels was being hotly debated in even the most local of papers. '*My concern was of course the clothes, not the models*', he said at the time, '*I think we had better forget all those side-issues. We might lose the point of the whole business - the cut, materials, colour, the idea.*' And there was definitely an idea, when in October 1996 we went to have a peep at his studio in Paris. Margiela had, for the occasion, revealed a sample of his capabilities to the world's press. His collection consisted chiefly of one colour: yellow. And all the clothes were

Raf Simons: Summer 1997.

Sarah Corynen: Summer 1997.

halves, no more, no less. Halves you could pin onto a basic garment, a so-called 'stockman', the front part of a tailor's dummy in hard beige linen.

International attention for what behind the scenes is called the Antwerp Six (the label is gradually driving these designers mad) has even had unmistakable results in the rest of Flanders. Because whereas buyers at fashion fairs used to take a detour round the Belgian stands, the attention they now pay to them is phenomenal. Commercial Flemish labels like Chine, Andres, Long Island, College, Helena van Haeren, Anvers and countless others make no attempt to hide it: they owe part of their success to the Six. '*We go along for the ride, that's for sure,*' says Monique Low of College. It is also certain that they are working increasingly hard on image and creativity. About ten years ago labels barely existed. In the past, countless textile manufacturers in Flanders produced just one single garment: raincoats, jeans or blouses. Today things are rather different, partly due to the textile plan started up in the eighties by the then economics minister Willy Claes. Work was carried out on various levels: the manufacturers had CAD-CAM equipment put at their disposal, making the creation of patterns more efficient. The 'This is Belgian' label was introduced; so that everyone who bought clothes could see whether it was Belgian made. This worked very much to the advantage of brand awareness, not only among clients but also among the manufacturers, who increasingly transformed their one-product policy into a complete, fully-fledged collection. Money was made available to support foreign projects: this is what enabled us to go to Japan six years ago, among other things. On top of this there was the Golden Spindle: a fashion competition that was to be a match for any international counterpart. The Golden Spindle has been awarded to Ann Demeulemeester, Dirk van Saene, Pieter Coene, Véronique Leroy and Christophe Charon.

As you can see, here are more names from the small world of Flemish fashion that deserve a mention. After all, the story did not end with the generation that graduated around 1980. Numerous others had at that time just started, or were to arrive much later, but stayed far away from Antwerp and its academy (by chance or otherwise). There are Kaat Tilley and Carine Lauwers from Brussels, and Chris Mestdagh, Jan Welvaert and Ingrid vande Wiele from Ghent. After the Six, even more promising young designers graduated from the academy in Antwerp. Anyone talking about Flemish fashion today has to learn yet more new names: Raf Simons, Jurgi Persoons, Sarah Corynen, Anna Heylen, Stephan Schneider and Olivier Waelkens. Simons, the only one who did not study fashion, but industrial design, has in the meantime become fantastically popular in Japan, with a collection that balances between the atmosphere of Andy Warhol's Factory and the video clips by the Smashing Pumpkins, of which he is in fact a tremendous fan. Simons worked his way to the top by means of videos whose production was planned down to the last detail. He held a fashion parade in Paris which was an enormous success. Persoons has only just started, two seasons ago to be precise, and he shows his 'chic trash' collection in a gallery in the Marais district of Paris every six months. And not without result. The last four made an impression at the fashion fair in Paris, and sold like mad to the Japanese, who clearly have a taste for this style. Sarah Corynen says, '*I don't know why, but we seem to be in great demand in Japan. We have never sold so well.*' Schneider and Heylen offer their silent assent. One can hardly call their styles similar, but they do discuss together which fair is the most important and which clients can best be avoided (due to late payment). Just the same as back then, among the first Six.

In the meantime, Demeulemeester, Margiela, Van Beirendonck, Van Noten, Bikkembergs and Van Saene are setting the fashion. They do not follow trends, they set them. Each season they set out markers for others to follow. Margiela's deconstruction was a subject that had remained totally unknown in the fashion world: he turned seams inside out, opened up an old pair of jeans and made a new skirt out of it, hung around fleamarkets, and most importantly, made a statement: fashion has to live. Years ago, when Van Noten came up with his first collection inspired by Asia, it appeared bizarre at a time when couture was being revived. Now everything is going in that direction. Ethnic is back. And while we are on the subject of couture, while every self-respecting designer was still totally submerged in the grunge period, and unfinished seams and a rather faded atmosphere prevailed, Dirk van Saene originated a return to elegance. His Jackie O' suits were innovative, and indisputably ahead of the trends. Ann Demeulemeester's asymmetry, which she had already shown in 1996, now became an absolute must for the summer. And then there is Walter van Beirendonck, who has been experimenting for years with technological mixes of materials, and colour combinations. Flemish designers may not have a style in common, but they do have the punch. Just like David when faced with Goliath, long ago. The difference is, this struggle never ends.

VEERLE WINDELS
Translated by Gregory Ball.

Jurgi Persoons: Summer 1997 (Photo by Ronald Stoops).

Stephan Schneider: Summer 1997.

Lieve van Gorp: Summer 1997.

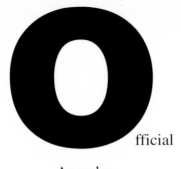fficial

Anarchy

Dutch Graphic Design

Amsterdam-based designer Shigeru Watano once remarked: '*Analytical and rational design principles govern Dutch design.*' He was right. Dutch graphic design has emerged from an essentially typographic tradition, and this analytical background has resulted in a clear and well organised typography – a management of the page – that is deeply concerned with visualising the hierarchies and the construction of texts.

With this as the point of departure, very different styles are possible: the 'classic' typographic style is a continuing, rich and living tradition in the Netherlands, but it is another style for which Dutch graphic design has been internationally recognised and applauded: a style that allows for a great variety of often rather complex images. A style that consists not only of a 'management of information', but is also the carrier of explicit personal interpretations and commentaries by the designer.

Although I maintain that a typographical approach underlies most of Dutch graphic design, the designers that I want to introduce here are generally aiming at an image. Organising information is only the beginning. On top of that the design must be evocative, emotional – and personal. Dutch graphic design is concerned with two – apparently conflicting – goals: to order information so that it becomes generally recognisable, but at the same time to be recognisably individual: the designer, the carrier of messages, wants to assert himself as well.

Dutch graphic design is constantly reconciling opposites: tradition and experiment, typography and image, institutions and individuality, rules and anarchy, and ultimately, art and application, function and expression. This merging of expressionist and functionalist approaches has become a Dutch design tradition in itself, from the 1920s onward – in the work of expressive functionalists like Paul Schuitema and Piet Zwart and more painterly designers such as Jan Sluyters and Dick Elffers.

The strength of today A few years ago, an exhibition of Dutch state-supported art and design was entitled: *The Strength of Today* (De kracht van heden). For the exhibition poster the young designers Mevis & Van Deursen proposed an image that is as powerful as it is unconventional: a blurred detail of one of the icons of

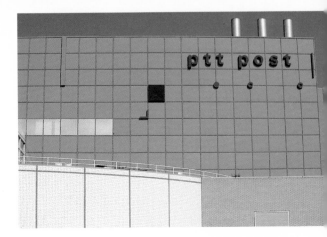

Dutch culture, a girl's portrait by Vermeer. From the famous girl's high-lighted eye, two boldly drawn arrows point outward: *'the strength / of today'*.

What is meant by this poster (apart from the message that there is an exhibition) is not explicit, only suggested. It can be read in very different ways: that the strength of today's art and design rests on a glorious past, or: that tradition only strengthens us if we keep an eye on it, and at the same time try to forget it, or: from what we know – now – we must keep an eye on the future, or: we may have only one past, but there are many ways to interpret it and to go forward.

Mevis & Van Deursen,
The Strength of Today
exhibition poster (1993).

Studio Dumbar, Decoration of the PTT building in The Hague (1989) (Photo by Lex van Pieterson).

This image also has something of a '*knipoog*', a 'blink-of-the-eye', something a little 'tongue-in-cheek', as the English say. The use of a time-honoured and revered image of Dutch painting to announce an exhibition of current Dutch art and design contains an ironic play on the tensions and rivalries between past and present – and a sidelong warning against pretentiousness.

I chose to analyse this poster at some length, because it comprises some of the main themes of Dutch graphic design: the search for bold and unconventional images, an intricate linking of image, typography and content, the use of equivocal imagery to provoke an interpretation by the viewer, and an ironic approach to both content and context of the subject, an irony that reflects the designer's personal point of view.

Irony and seriousness – another pair of opposing aspects that can be seen as characterising Dutch design culture. And one that can be traced even in the most prestigious printwork the Netherlands has to offer: its money. When the Dutch National Bank, in 1982, introduced its new fifty-guilder banknote, designed by Ootje Oxenaar, visitors to the Netherlands were frequently convinced that they were being cheated by their change-offices: these playful and brightly coloured slips of paper could hardly represent serious cash!

But in spite of Oxenaar's expressed appreciation for 'toy money' and informal imagery, these notes were instantly – and internationally – recognised as being of the highest design- and printing quality, and therefore posing almost insurmountable problems for forgers! The unconventionality and irrationality of the image conceal an utterly rational security-programme that explores the boundaries of the available printing processes. It is this combination of analytical professionalism and artistic freedom, that has led to a nickname for Dutch graphic design: 'official anarchy'.

The word 'official' also points to another remarkable aspect of Dutch graphic design, and one of the conditions for its flourishing: the traditional support for experimental design by large institutional clients. This support started in the 1920s, when the Dutch telecommunications company PTT employed the leading avant-gardists of those days, and it has been an important stimulant to renewal ever since.

A case in point is the reworking by Studio Gert Dumbar of the house style of the Dutch PTT, privatised as Royal Dutch Telecommunications Company, in the early 1990s. The rather rigidly typographical logo (derived from the existing house style), designed in three precisely defined variants for the three divisions of the company, provides a severe order that stimulates a high degree of recognisability, while at the same time leaving surprisingly ample room for playful variations on the established theme. Dumbar has created a vast range of decorative possibilities by 'deconstructing' the basic elements of the logo into simple geometric forms. The strict and simple rules that govern this – at times anarchic – play of forms and primary colours result in an abstract imagery that reminds you of the company, even when the letterhead 'PTT-telecom' is left out. Again we see a merging of strict functionality and freedom of artistic invention.

When asked what appeals to them in Dutch graphic design, foreigners will often tell us that it is precisely this curious combination of opposites: the paradoxical linking of our traditional Calvinist-religious severity, sobriety and orderliness to a great feeling for free expression, associative imagery and irony. Associated with this 'Calvinism' is a sense of responsibility, both to the process of communication and to the expression of one's own point of view.

Ironic Calvinism

Therefore, when designers like Anthon Beeke, Wild Plakken, or Mevis & Van Deursen accept commissions to design posters for the National Opera, for theatre companies or a cultural manifestations company, their intention is not only (or even primarily) to communicate data, but to do so in a consciously subjective, even idiosyncratic, manner. They demand that their work should be read, not as neutral information, but as a personal message and a sign-of-the-times.

In assignments such as this the designer can claim great freedom of interpretation and artistic autonomy, on the argument that the posters are not the primary source of information for a potential audience. The exact data will also be communicated via press, advertising and other media. The poster is accessory to this media-mix, it functions as a 'teaser', as well as acting as a metaphorical extension of the artistic processes that are at work in the making of opera, theatre and exhibitions – the poster not only says: 'come and see this', but also: 'we create images and stories, so you can enjoy and interpret them – come and make your own story, as we do...'

Not surprisingly, it is in graphic design for the arts and the theatre that we find the most outspoken designer-personalities: Anthon Beeke, for instance, has gained world-wide attention with his corporeal and sometimes shockingly sexual interpretations of traditional and modern plays. Wild Plakken have made themselves a reputation by politically and socially commenting on art, theatre, opera, and recently, television. For twenty years now, starting from the revolutionary 1970s, this designers' collective has uncompromisingly criticised society through sometimes almost cynical, sometimes remarkably poetic images and posters. Lately they have ventured into television: Wild Plakken member Rob Schröder has made leaders and short clips of TV samples, that comment critically on the medium. Being an editorially inclined designer in the first place, Schröder is currently working for VPRO television as a programme maker as well as a designer. Another poet, be it in a more literary vein, is Marten Jongema, whose painterly posters for

Anthon Beeke, *Human Rights* poster (1989).

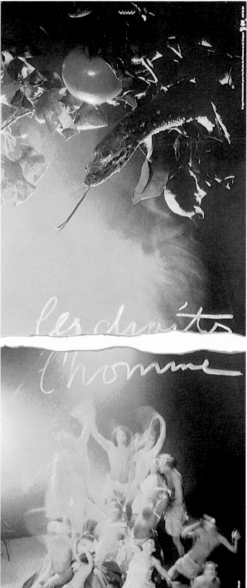

Marten Jongema, Caroussel poster (1991).

Wild Plakken, Poster for the twentieth birthday of Amnesty International (1991).

Jaap van Triest, Cover of *Vormberichten* (1992).

the Caroussel theatre group and for the Springdance Festival visualise an atmosphere, loosely associated with the subject and its interpreters, rather than illustrating a theme.

These designers, to name just a few, represent the strong tradition of artistic autonomy in Dutch graphic design. They 'accept' their clients, rather than being 'appointed' by them – a subtle but important nuance.

This artistic tradition resulted from the close relationship between artists, architects and designers of the avant-garde at the beginning of this century, and has since been strengthened by educational models derived from that same period: Dutch visual artists and designers share a common start to their education, and keep in close contact during the rest of their training at the academies of art. Given this background it is perhaps not surprising that Dutch designers – artistically trained as they are – tend to emphasise their conceptuality and compose their images on the basis of an artistic idea, rather than contenting themselves with executing a client's programme in a craftsmanlike way.

Perverted typefaces

On the other hand one shouldn't forget that there still is a strong tradition of Dutch typography. But even here, it will be noticed that contemporary typographers seek to do more than carefully balance texts and provide maximum readability – they often aim at a visual poetry of type as well. Type, as a more or less abstract repertoire of signs and forms, has been a major inspiration to such founding fathers of Dutch graphic design as Piet Zwart, Paul Schuitema and designer / printer Hendrik Nicolaas Werkman, and to later masters like Sandberg or Elffers.

Since the introduction of the computer in graphic design this abstract play with type has evolved in new directions. Manipulations of text and type

– sometimes beyond readability – give new energy to the tradition of dynamic typography. In Dutch design, more often than not the computer is used as a tool that facilitates typographical and image manipulation, and in the work of the more 'conservative' typographers only the professional eye will notice traces of this digital device. It is used as an extra tool that can combine fruitfully with the older techniques, as is suggested by Jaap van Triest in a cover for the design magazine *Vormberichten*, where a computer mouse seems to impregnate an ovum-like cogwheel.

However, since the large majority of young graphic designers world-wide start their professional careers by acquiring an Apple MacIntosh, the language of the computer becomes more and more visible in Dutch graphic design; though it hardly ever becomes a theme in itself, as in American, Japanese or English design.

Experimental typographers like Max Kisman, Erik van Blokland and Just van Rossum use the Mac to devise ad-hoc type and to combine amounts of type forms that would drive a phototypesetter crazy (not to mention the old lead-craftsman). They invent letter forms without fixed outlines, like the Beowolf by Van Blokland and Van Rossum, or mix types to an extent that would be considered obscene by 'classic' typographers. A programmatic perversion of this kind is the Fudoni by Max Kisman, one of the most prolific of digital type designers. This truly postmodern letter is, as you may have guessed, a contamination of the archetypal modern letter, the Futura, and the worthy old Bodoni. The combination of these two extremes of the typographical spectrum is all the more provocative in a country where users of serif and sans-serif type have cold-shouldered each other on ideological grounds for decades.

Erik van Blokland & Just van Rossum, Beowolf type (1990).

Kisman, who is now working in San Francisco for Wired television, has been internationally acknowledged for his experimental type design and for the expressive way in which he uses his letters in posters and magazines. His *Tegentonen* posters for Paradiso music centre in Amsterdam are in the best Dutch tradition of playing with type on the verge of a purely abstract composition of form. At the same time, these idiosyncratic variations on the letters of our alphabet do more than just reflect the individual aesthetics of one designer. Kisman also alludes to the fact that subcultural groups tend to

FF Beowolf

21 ABCDEFGHIJKLMNOPQR
abcdefhijklmnopqrstuvwxy
2 ABCDEFGHIJKLMNOPQR
abcdefhijklmnopqrstuvwxy
3 ABCDEFGHIJKLMNOPQR
abcdefhijklmnopqrstuvwxy

Max Kisman, MERGE poster in Linear Konstrukt type (1991).

Studio Dumbar, Dans Festival poster (Awarded with the Rotterdam Design Prize 1995). Designed by Bob van Dijk (Photo by Deen van Meer).

identify themselves through strict formal codes that set them apart from the crowd. In a poster for the experimental type magazine *Fuse*, he thematised this idea in Linear Konstrukt, an alphabet that is almost unreadable for those who 'are not into it'. Apart from the allusion to group identities, this typeface is playing with the postmodern notion of language as a set of signifiers that has only a temporal and unstable connection to fixed meanings. The signs could mean something, but then again, they could equally well be meaningless. This postmodern fascination with linguistic structures is aptly summarised in the six code words on the poster: Information, Communication, Modification, Recognition, Identification and of course in the embracing word MERGE.

Staged photography

As I have pointed out, dynamic typography, reconciling the opposites of expressionism and functionalism, characterises contemporary Dutch graphic design. Another important aspect here is the use of photography. Again, as in the abstract and decorative use of typography, photography is often employed in ways that seem to deny its documentary origin.

In many instances photographic images are treated as abstract formal elements that are constructed, together with the typeforms, into a composition. Again, Piet Zwart and Paul Schuitema are the great exemplars of the Dutch branch of this constructivist graphic design. Their use of photography has inspired generations of (not only) Dutch designers. Wild Plakken's technique of collage, for example, can be traced back to the 1920s, and from this experience with photography Wild Plakken have developed a highly personal way of expression through images. To them photos are signs, on a par with words or sentences. By combining them, by orchestrating a debate between images, they communicate a story that can be read as if it were written out.

Another designer who greatly influenced the use of photography in Dutch graphic design is Gert Dumbar. Together with photographer Lex van Pieterson he popularised a combination of three-dimensional typography and 'staged photography'. In posters for the Zeebelt cultural foundation and designs for the Netherlands Festival Dumbar and associates interpreted the flat print surface as a 'virtual space' in which letters and images seem to float about freely. With this photography-based technique, the Dumbar studio – without using computers – anticipated the possibilities for digitally reworking images and type.

Dumbar's techniques of three-dimensional typography, staged photography and his generous use of decorative elements like bent lines and dots (dubbed '*the measles*' by critics), have been copied to such an extent that his name has become a verb: 'to dumbar' means 'to be shamelessly decorative'.

Images and the ways in which they can be used and interpreted constitute an international language, the more so with every day that passes. The Studio Dumbar design team that worked on the Dutch PTT included members from many countries. And the originally Japanese designer Shigeru Watano has become a respected member of the Dutch design elite...

Global communication

These days, Dutch design is made by graphic designers who come from all over the world. 30 percent of the students at Dutch art academies come from outside the Netherlands. And they are being confronted with completely new tasks. In a symposium on Dutch and Japanese graphic design, Mitsuo Katsui stressed that '*we, as designers, are obliged to explore intensively the possibilities of the new electronic media, we should engage ourselves, and master this machine, so that it won't master us...*' I couldn't agree more, and I'm glad to say that in the Netherlands, as in Japan, there are young designers who are inquisitively and creatively exploring these new media.

The 'strength of today', in my view, lies in this creative influx into our well-established design tradition. New ways of communicating internationally, an explosively growing global network of electronic communication media and the exchange of the best that national traditions can contribute to each other's cultures and languages, all this is part of an exciting challenge to a new generation of designers: to serve a world that still suffers from mutual misunderstanding and crummy communications.

MAX BRUINSMA

Michael Samyn & Group Z,
part of the Love web site
(1996).

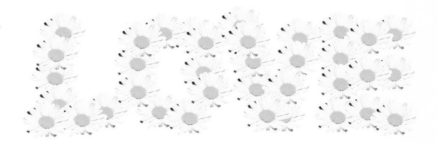

he

Vanitas Piece

in Dutch and Flemish Seventeenth-Century Painting

'Vanity of Vanities, all is Vanity'
Ecclesiastes I, v.2.

The *Vanitas* piece as an individual genre is an integral part of the richness and variety of Low Countries art. But while isolated works are much admired, the genre as a whole has attracted relatively little attention. There has been no exhibition devoted to the Dutch *Vanitas* piece since the *Vanity of Vanities* (IJdelheid der IJdelheden) held at Leiden in 1970 and there seems never to have been a show devoted to the Flemish *Vanitas* piece. This is in strong contrast to the enormous interest shown in still life as a whole, which has seen many different aspects explored both in exhibitions and individual studies.

Even though the historical Low Countries were irrevocably split into two by the beginning of the seventeenth century, the revived artistic tradition, recovering after the iconoclastic crisis of the previous century, maintained a surprising unity of subject matter. It was in emphasis and artistic style that North and South diverged so dramatically. For example, although religious subjects appeared much more often in the Catholic South, they were never absent in the dominantly Protestant North. Conversely, realistic landscape developed in the North, although Rubens in the South was able to produce masterpieces of realistic landscape as magisterial as any large-scale Dutch work.

Still life painting in general is far more homogeneous in its approach, and this is proved by the difficulty of working out whether a peripatetic artist such as Jan Davidsz. de Heem altered his style between Utrecht and Antwerp. Only occasionally did Catholic subject matter appear in still life painting in the Southern Netherlands.

Since the development of modern art history on a largely national basis there has been a tendency for Dutch writers to halt their enquiries at the modern Belgian border and for Belgian art historians and publishers to confine themselves to the historical provinces of Flanders and Brabant. Although this rigid division has often led to a deeper understanding of local traditions, ranging from the richness of the Antwerp tradition to the penchant for portraiture in remote Friesland, the unity of the whole has been underemphasised. This lack of general coverage has particularly harmed the study of still life painting, as there was a consistent still life tradition in almost every centre, great and small.

Still life itself fell into many distinct categories or sub-categories defined by subject matter rather than style. The range here was enormously wide. On the simplest level we have shell paintings as found in the work of the Dutchmen, Balthasar van der Ast and Adriaen Coorte. At the other end of the scale we have the magnificent banquet pieces of the Dutch Abraham van Beyeren and the equally grand kitchen and larder scenes of the Flemish Frans Snyders. Most still life painting falls between these two extremes, but even such a humble area as fish painting ranges from fish indoors – the Flemish Alexander Adriaenssen – to fish outside on the beach – the Dutch Willem Ormea.

There has long been an interest in the origins of still life painting in the Netherlands, and its course in the sixteenth century is now fairly well charted, expecially with such seminal figures as Pieter Aertsen and Joachim Beuckelaer whose influence ranges from Antwerp to Amsterdam, there being no political or religious boundary in their time. Many modern writers have emphasised the divergency of artistic style, resulting in distinctly 'Flemish' and 'Dutch' entities. When we turn to such areas as the fish painters we find it very much harder to work out whether the painting is from the North or the South, for the simple reason that the painters were observing exactly the same visual phenomena.

It is not surprising, therefore, that *Vanitas* painting has this unity of the subject matter between North and South. The message was the same and the depiction of the various warning devices required the same skill. It was not easy to paint flowers, wilting or fresh, nor to paint the human skull convincingly – not to mention the great difficulty of integrating each element into an agreeable composition.

The *Vanitas* piece by its very nature has a specific meaning – an arrangement of objects which warn the spectator either of the brevity of human life (the skull, the watch, the extinguished candle etc.) or of the uselessness of things of high monetary value when life itself is threatened. The luxurious vanities of the world – jewels, musical instruments, silver and gold objects – were a perfect excuse for the painter to display his skill in their depiction, and it was for the spectator to delight in that very clarity of observation. The moral became clear enough when *memento mori* such as the skull were included.

A good deal of writing on Low Countries *Vanitas* painting, especially the Dutch, has been concerned with its 'hidden' meaning. It has become a delightful intellectual game for scholars, and the general public has often been invited to join in by intriguing museum labels, exhibition catalogues, and books destined for general readership.

The *Vanitas* painter had nothing to hide. He wanted to depict each object as clearly as possible, at the same time allowing them to accumulate into an easily defined whole. It may be that some modern spectators are not used to soap bubbles because they are no longer a popular pastime with children. At the same time, modern urban living has virtually eliminated 'bugs' and so the bluebottle flies, which so often appear, may not so easily conjure up the idea of the maggots which are their larvae. We no longer have hour glasses in our drawing rooms and terrestrial globes in our studies, and we are tempted to regard these obvious symbols as merely quaint.

In spite of the attempts of so many writers, it is otiose to search for deeper

Nicolaes van Veerendael,
Vanitas. Panel, 34 x 45 cm
Musée des Beaux-Arts,
Caen (Photo by Martine
Seyve).

meanings in the *Vanitas* piece beyond the obvious symbolism of each lovingly depicted object. These deceptions of ordered reality were not intellectual puzzles but a gentle and usually decorative reminder of the human condition. Even religious symbolism is usually absent from the average *Vanitas* piece. Reminders of the possibility of Redemption were left to priest or preacher.

In his recent book on *The Cheerfulness of Dutch Art,* Oscar Mandel has written a short chapter on the *Vanitas* piece claiming, quite rightly, that the *Vanitas* piece falls into line with the rest of Dutch art – that it was essentially cheerful and was concerned on the simplest of levels with both story-telling and delight in the visual world. Mandel cites, albeit briefly, the contrast with Southern European art in the depiction of the same essential message – the brevity of human life.

In Southern Europe, still life was used much more rarely. It was easier to make the point with the depiction of the physical decay of the flesh: to the more decorous Northerners the message itself is identical. One of the most celebrated examples is the group of paintings in the Hospital de la Caridad, Seville. Here the normally sober Baroque artist Valdes Leal depicted the decay of the flesh with dramatic reality; his subjects were a full-robed bishop and a fully-clothed knight. Such an approach is nowhere found in the North, where the skull itself usually suffices to remind the spectator that the *Vanitas* is human.

The hardest task for the modern viewer in coming to terms with the astonishing variety of the *Vanitas* piece in the seventeenth century is to understand that these paintings were intended to delight as well as moralise. They seem much more sinister today, especially as the juxtapositions are, to modern taste, bizarre. The *Still Life with Two Skulls* by Nicolaes van

Veerendael still shocks on account of the lovingly crafted garlands of flowers which adorn the skulls. Veerendael was indeed a flower specialist and the skulls are truly unexpected in his art. There is an obvious delight in the painting of both the skulls and the flowers, and they are given equal emphasis by the artist.

Explanation of this juxtaposition does not come easily, but there is a clue in Shakespeare. 'Krantzes' are referred to by Ophelia: these were funeral garlands, and the tradition survived in England until the eighteenth century of weaving a garland of paper flowers to be hung over a virgin's pew in church after she had died. Here we may have a lost symbolism – the flower garland on the skull may tell us that the dead were virgins or lovers: on the other hand, if we follow Mandel, we may conclude that the picture is nothing more than an obvious display of skill with a *Vanitas* theme.

Veerendael's masterpiece raises further questions. We do not know whether this unusual picture was painted to order for a particular patron or whether it was painted for the open market in Antwerp. If the latter was the case, the artist would hardly have troubled to keep repeating a subject for which the demand was obviously limited.

The theme of the skulls as a specific emblem was taken to an amazing

Abraham van der Schoor,
Still Life with Skulls.
Canvas, 63.5 x 73 cm.
Rijksmuseum, Amsterdam

extreme by the obscure Dutch artist Abraham van der Schoor. The symbolism remains obvious but the artist has demonstrated his uncanny ability by painting it from numerous different angles and arranging the result pell-mell as in a charnel house. Again, for the seventeenth-century spectator it would have been the sheer skill which overrode the melancholia of the subject. The other *Vanitas* elements in the picture are decorative adjuncts which bring some limited colour to an otherwise monochrome composition. The books fill in the background, while the lit candle, rose and hour-glass fill the awkward spaces remaining at the sides. It would be hard indeed to find a hidden meaning in so uncompromising an image, depicting our collective deaths rather than the more usual solitary one.

The *Vanitas* work of Van der Schoor and Veerendael is essentially intimate in scale and purpose and it is this aspect of intimacy which is so often and wrongly seen as the essence of Low Countries art of the seventeenth century. Writers and museum curators have often concentrated on the small-scale works which are so much easier for study and contemplation.

Perhaps the masterpiece of the large-scale *Vanitas* akin to the banquet piece is Pieter Boel's *Allegory of the Vanities of the World*. It is dated 1663 and is therefore exactly contemporary with the late work of Rembrandt and the mature work of Jacob van Ruisdael and Meindert Hobbema. In the local Antwerp context, however, it comes rather late in the day, as the output of large-scale work was already in decline after the death of Rubens in 1640.

Boel adopts all the conceits of the banquet piece, piling up familiar objects in unlikely and unusual juxtaposition. In most banquet pieces the artist rarely depicted a table, as it would have been laid for eating: instead the idea was to pile up the objects in order to enhance the magnificence of

Pieter Boel,
Allegory of the Vanities of the World. 1663.
Canvas, 207 x 260 cm.
Musée des Beaux-Arts, Lille.

Salvator Rosa,
L'umana fragilità.
Canvas, 199 x 133.1 cm
Fitzwilliam Museum,
Cambridge.

the composition. Here the effect is overwhelming. There are few elements of wealth as valued at the time. The arts, the sciences and war are given equal emphasis. The main element in the centre of the composition is the bishop's mitre – ecclesiastical vanity was just as worldly as that of the arrogant militiaman. The whole is held together by an elaborate compositional device: the tableau is set in a ruined gallery piled up beside and over a solemn sarcophagus. When we search the picture for symbolism we find none. Each element speaks for itself as an object of earthly status and wealth, showing pride in ownership, pride in status, monarch and church, and (gentle reminder to the writer) pride in learning and creativity, with the globe, artist's palette and books.

The contrast between the Low Countries and Southern Europe has already been noted. Boel's approach can be seen in its true context of a delight in the physical object when we consider Salvator Rosa's *L'umana fragilità*. The image itself may be familiar enough to many people: it depicts an event and is not strictly a still life as this was not the Italian way of making the same point as the Low Countries painters. The winged figure of death swoops down on the figures of a woman and a child. It is only when we examine the numerous still life elements in the picture that the fundamental difference between North and South appears, adding further proof to Mandel's hypothesis. The still life elements are included as symbols and are not painted with any delight in their physical appearance. The owl (symbol of death) lurks in the right-hand corner, the soap bubbles, symbolising transience, blown by the child on the left, are difficult to see. The barely visible obelisk in the left background contains arcane symbols of death and discord which would have been understood only by the learned. In such a picture the artist has denied himself the sensuality which he could bring to bear when painting his large landscapes.

When we search in Low Countries art for parallels to Rosa's approach we still find a much more literal or matter-of-fact approach. This is seen in Leonaert Bramer's *Allegory of Transience* which takes an almost humorous approach. We see this in the seated skeleton, holding in its hands another skull, staring each other out with mock grimaces. The other objects are

Leonaert Bramer,
Allegory of Transience.
Panel, 80 x 61.3 cm.
Kunsthistorisches Museum,
Vienna.

varied enough but the emphasis is generally military, and a discarded pile of military accoutrements dominates the centre. The near light-heartedness of Bramer's approach is entirely in keeping with his temperament. Ultimately the picture speaks for amusement, and is entirely lacking in the searing and profound quality of Rosa's work.

One of the extremes of object-based observation in the *Vanitas* piece is Adriaen van Nieulandt's *Vanitas* of 1636. As usual, we are left in no doubt about the object or its meaning, from the fly on the skull to the butterfly perched on the ledge. The inscriptions are unusually explicit. *'Mourir pour vivre'* sticks out of the pile of books and *'Ecquid sunt aliud, quam breve gaudium'* ('Are there other things than a brief joy?'). The element of delight in the picture is emphasised by its small scale. The artist's skill can be marvelled at, even when, as in this instance, he was not a specialist in still life.

A question often asked concerns the ownership of these *Vanitas* pictures. Were they handed down in families as moral talismans, or were they traded in common with the other genres? The short answer is that we still do not know enough about collecting at the time. As with a high proportion of Low Countries art, the pictures discussed here – except, of course, the Rosa – do not have unbroken histories going back to the seventeenth century.

After a long absence, the *Vanitas* piece has come full circle in the late twentieth century. The seventeenth-century ones are appreciated at a safe distance; but once a living painter tries to bring the genre up to date, there are serious protests, as it is believed that the modern *Vanitas* offends against decorum. Damian Hirst has taken the old theme and changed it stylistically by exhibiting dead animals or parts of them preserved in formaldehyde. The reminder is exactly the same: the mortality of the animal is emphasised and sometimes physical decay is allowed to happen in the shocked presence of the gallery visitor.

It is a paradox of our times that so many people can find themselves in tune with the meaning and emotion of a Rembrandt, or uplifted by the Baroque ecstasy of a Rubens, but they still cannot take the homespun moral of the simple *Vanitas* piece.

CHRISTOPHER WRIGHT

A

Museum of Museums

The Story of the Teyler Museum

With the opening of its new wing last year, visitors to the Teyler Museum in Haarlem are now better able than ever before to enjoy the treasures of this oldest (1784) public museum in the Netherlands. For more than two centuries art and science have been exhibited side by side in this unique museum with its exclusively natural lighting and its outstanding exhibits in many fields.

The Teyler Museum is named after Pieter Teyler van der Hulst, a wealthy eighteenth-century Haarlem cloth and silk merchant. His family came

Wybrand Hendriks,
*Portrait of Pieter Teyler
van der Hulst.* 1787.
Canvas. Teyler Museum,
Haarlem.

originally from England (Taylor), but had to leave the country for religious reasons at the end of the sixteenth century and settled in Haarlem. Pieter Teyler later added the name of his late mother, Maria van der Hulst, to his own.

In 1756 Pieter Teyler made his will, possibly prompted by the death of his wife in 1754 and the fact that they had no children. In it he laid down with great precision what was to be done with his estate. First of all, a foundation was to be set up, with a board of five 'Directors'. This foundation was to establish two societies: the First or Theological Society, for the promotion of religion, and the Second Society, for the encouragement of the arts and sciences. Both these societies still exist today.

It is evident from his will that Pieter Teyler was a man of his own time, the Enlightenment. In those days it was taken for granted that knowledge and science elevated mankind. At his home Teyler had a collection which included coins and medals, drawings, stuffed birds, animals preserved in formalin, and a library. At set times – and by invitation – one could go and admire this collection at his house at 21 Damstraat in Haarlem.

After Pieter Teyler's death in 1778 his home became the Foundation House, the seat of the Teyler Foundation. By now the collection no longer amounted to very much. Consequently, the original executors decided to dispose of much of it, even though this was contrary to the terms of the will. They put a modern interpretation on Teyler's provision that his estate was to be used *for the encouragement of the arts and sciences, and for the public good*.

When he drew up his will in 1756, the wealthy and socially concerned Pieter Teyler will not have had in mind a museum such as we know today, but something more like a scientific institute. The decision to build a 'Hall of Books and Art' behind Pieter Teyler's house was taken by the Directors of the Teyler Foundation in 1779. In this 'hall' they planned to exhibit artistic and scientific objects, accessible to everyone ('*for the public good*'). Only when the foundation stone had been laid did they begin to form a collection.

The Amsterdam architect Leendert Viervant designed an oval room in classical style, with rich ornamentation. The layout and furnishings of the Oval Room have remained virtually unchanged since it opened in 1784, as one can see from an 1810 painting by Wybrand Hendriks.

The museum's first Director, Martinus van Marum, was a great collector with a particular interest in the sciences. He also made substantial purchases for the library. Very soon the museum was in need of expansion.

Between 1824 and 1826 two rooms were built next to the Oval Room, one above the other: a reading room for the library on the first floor and a lecture room on the ground floor. The latter was never used for this purpose. At first paintings by contemporary artists were exhibited there, later on drawings and water-colours. Subsequently the 'Water-Colour Room' was used for 75 years as a study room for the Art Department. Since the completion of the new wing in 1996 it has reverted to its old function as a gallery for exhibiting drawings and prints.

For the paintings the so-called First Picture Gallery was built in 1838; it now houses pictures by Dutch painters of the second half of the nineteenth century. It was followed in 1893 by the Second Picture Gallery, for Dutch painting between 1780 and 1860.

Meanwhile, the steadily growing science collections were seriously short of space. On the occasion of the Foundation's centenary the Directors decided to expand in the direction of the River Spaarne. They organised an international competition, but the entries failed to satisfy them. Ultimately they chose only a facade, a classicist design by the Viennese architect Christian Ulrich – who never saw his own project. The rooms behind the facade were the work of the Haarlem architect A. van der Steur Jr. The facade is adorned with an appropriate sculpture group, *Fame Crowning Art and Science*, by Bart van Hove.

This 'New Museum', opened in 1885, holds three new museum galleries, a large and a small lecture room and additional library space. The (present) entrance consists of a magnificent rotunda under a dome, with statues and stucco ornamentation indicating the wide range of the collections. It affords a view right through to the hub of the museum: the Oval Room. On the way to this central point the visitor first passes the paleontological collection, in which the fossils are still arranged according to the sites where they were found. Next comes the collection of physics and chemistry instruments and the 'Large Electrostatic Generator', about which more later.

The first floor of the New Museum is not always open to the public. Beyond a small anteroom lies the large auditorium, with its chairs upholstered with horsehair and a large workbench which reminds the visitor of the demonstrations given there in the past. Lectures are still held here, on subjects connected with the arts and sciences.

The so-called 'Mezzanine Room' of the library, which leads off the auditorium, is one of the most attractive areas in the Teyler Museum. Guided tours have recently been introduced during which visitors are shown some of the rare books. This room opens onto the first floor of the Oval Room, where the twelve built-in bookcases still hold many books.

Since 1885 scarcely anything has changed in the museum's eighteenth- and nineteenth-century interior, mainly because of the lack of money. What was

The Teyler Museum library, designed by A. van der Steur Jr. (c.1880).

once seen as a mark of poverty is now cherished as 'a museological museum'. As a model of museum construction, in 1983 the Teyler Museum was designated a 'museum of national importance'. The resultant government aid meant that work could begin on the backlog of maintenance, administration and cataloguing.

By the end of the eighties it was evident that the Teyler Museum needed to be extended, in particular to cater for the areas just mentioned. Well-equipped workshops and air-conditioned storerooms were non-existent. Special exhibitions always meant that part of the permanent collection of paintings had to be moved elsewhere. The preservation of the museum and its collections was at stake.

In 1989 the Zegelwaarden building was purchased from the PTT to provide accommodation for the staff and storage facilities. This building stood on land owned by the Teyler Foundation, and had been used by the long-established printers Joh. Enschede & Sons, next door to the museum, to store the postage stamps they printed. The following year a competition was organised among architects for an extension to the museum. One important requirement was to retain as much as possible of the old enclosed garden. Hubert Jan Henket produced the winning design.

The architect's plan demonstrates his respect for the Teyler Museum. His extension does not seek to dominate. As with the previous large-scale expansion of 1880, the Oval Room has been kept as the focal point. Henket has created a new visual axis (widthwise) from the new building to the Oval Room. A striking feature is the view from the new wing to the observatory (1784) on the roof of the Oval Room.

The Teyler Museum now has at its disposal a large exhibition hall, set slightly apart from the museum so that it does not block the latter's daylight. For the first time it has the space to display books and receive school groups, and for a museum restaurant with a view over the enclosed garden. The 'Water-Colour Room' has also been restored to its former glory as an exhibition gallery for drawings and prints.

The Teyler Museum is remarkable not only for its unique museological building history, but also because it exhibits objects from both the arts and the sciences. Many museums founded at the time of the Enlightenment have over the years come to concentrate either on art or on the sciences. The Teyler Museum still does both.

The museum has five themed collections or Cabinets, which may be considered as more or less self-contained: the Art Collections, the Paleontological and Mineralogical Cabinet, the Natural Science Cabinet, the Numismatic Cabinet and the Library. A brief account of each now follows.

Pieter Teyler stipulated in his will that his house should be occupied by a 'painter' or other devotee of the arts and sciences. This person was to be responsible for the drawings and prints cabinet. The first curator did not stay long; he did not get on very well with director Van Marum.

The second, Wybrand Hendriks, left a distinct mark on the Art Collections. The most important acquisition in his time (the beginning of the nineteenth century) was 1,600 drawings, mainly Italian, which had originally formed part of the collection of Queen Christina of Sweden. Among the items acquired were twenty-five pages of sketches by Michelangelo, as well as drawings by Raphael and the Haarlem artist Hendrick Goltzius. Apart from these, the drawings collection provides an almost complete picture of Dutch drawing between 1580 and 1900. Since 1983 the museum is once more collecting the work of contemporary artists.

The *Art Collections* of the Teyler Museum also contain some 25,000 prints, including almost the complete etchings of Rembrandt and Van Ostade, as well as copper engravings by Dürer and an exceptional collection of portraits of Dutch writers and poets. Since 1988, moreover, the museum has administered the art collection of the Haarlem banker Jonkheer Hendrik Teding van Berkhout, comprising some 800 drawings and 5,000 prints.

The small collection of paintings gives an – incomplete – overview of Dutch painting between 1780 and 1900. A number of the paintings were acquired as pairs, particularly in the early days. Thus, in 1825 the museum purchased *Storm at Sea* by J.C. Schotel; a few years later it commissioned his *Calm Sea*. B.C. Koekkoek is represented by a *Summer Landscape* and a *Winter Landscape*.

The *Paleontological and Mineralogical Cabinet* of the Teyler Museum is world famous, especially as a study collection. Almost everything displayed there is still lying just as it was placed in the New Museum a hundred years ago. Among its showpieces are the jaws of the *Mosasaurus* (a giant marine lizard) and the *Archaeopteryx lithographica*, the primeval bird. Only six other specimens of the latter are known. Acquired in 1860, it was only 'discovered' in 1970.

Part of the mineral collection is displayed in the central showcase in the Oval Room. Most of the exhibits were acquired by Martinus van Marum. In 1799 he bought the scale-model of Mont Blanc showing the first (scientific) ascent by Horace Bénedict de Saussure in 1787. This model is in the Oval Room. Later on, Van Marum also bought pictures and records of this expedition and even the very tip of Mont Blanc, which the climbers had brought away with them.

The most important acquisitions of Martinus van Marum, the first Director of the Teyler Museum, were for the *Natural Science Cabinet*. In 1783 he had

Michelangelo's *Study of a Male Nude for the Battle of Cascina* (black crayon, 40.4 x 22.4 cm), one of the many drawings in the Teyler Museum collection which originally formed part of the collection of Queen Christina of Sweden.

already had an '*uncommonly large Electrostatic Generator*' built, for experiments with static electricity. In 1784 this was placed in the Oval Room. Part of the central display case could be rolled away to make room for demonstrations. In 1885, owing to shortage of space, the electrostatic generator was moved to the New Museum. The piece was made in the same style as the Oval Room, a delight to the eye.

The approximately 1,250 physics and chemistry instruments of the Natural Science Cabinet were in no case bought as museum exhibits, but for research and demonstrations. The nineteenth-century instruments are in the New Museum, those from the eighteenth century in the Oval Room. In the past the instruments were taken out of the cabinets to demonstrate their use, but this is no longer done.

The nucleus of the *Numismatic Cabinet* probably comes from Teyler's own collection. However, it was not until the last century that the collection grew to its present size, thanks to two major bequests. The Teyler Museum now possesses the second largest collection of coins and medals in the Netherlands, with the emphasis on Dutch medals from the seventeenth, eighteenth and nineteenth centuries.

The science *Library* contains magnificent hand-coloured illustrated works including, among other things, flora and fauna, voyages of exploration and atlasses. Periodicals form an important part of the collection; of special interest are those of the Royal Society in London and the Académie des Sciences in Paris which go back to 1665.

A copy of the *Encyclopédie* of Diderot and d'Alembert was purchased almost as soon as it was completed in 1780. The library is one of the few places where a complete copy of John James Audubon's *The Birds of America* (1826-1840), with its life-size illustrations of the birds, can still be found. The library can only be visited on request.

For more than two centuries the combination of art and science, natural light and a magnificent interior has made the Teyler Museum unique. Those who have no interest in art, but come for the minerals, are nevertheless confronted with Art. Those who are only interested in art and do not care for physics are nevertheless fascinated by the large electrostatic generator and other treasures from the worlds of nature and technology to be discovered in the museum. The view of the testator Pieter Teyler that art, knowledge and science enrich mankind, still holds good today.

The facade of the Teyler Museum.

ANNEKE WERTHEIM
Translated by Rachel van der Wilden.

ADDRESS
Teyler Museum
Spaarne 16 / 2011 CH Haarlem / The Netherlands
tel. +31 23 5319010 / fax +31 23 5542004
Opening hours:
10 a.m. – 5 p.m. (Tuesday to Saturday)
1 p.m. – 5 p.m. (Sundays and Holidays)

ridging

Two Cultures

The Story of the Huygens Family

The Dutch Golden Age in the seventeenth century was a period which saw a quite extraordinary convergence of talent, not just in society as a whole, but also within the confines of a single family. There is no doubt that on the international stage Christian Huygens (1629-1695) has become the best known member of this family. The language of mathematics and physics is international by nature and knowledge of Christians's observations on light *(Traité de la lumière,* 1690) and his invention of the pendulum clock spread all over the world. But within the Netherlands it could well be that Christian's father Constantine (1596-1687) is better known than his son. Constantine used his mother tongue rather than the international language of Latin for his poetry, and as a result sacrificed fame throughout Europe to his love of his own country. He did this quite deliberately, judging that his own mission and that of his generation was to raise the quality of Dutch literature to match European standards. He became an important Dutch poet – but this only made him a big fish in a small pond.

So father and son united science and literature in one family. But there was much more to come. Constantine was a keen musician, playing a number of instruments. He was also a composer. His *Pathodia sacra et profana* (1647), moving settings of psalms and love songs, have been rediscovered in our own time and have been recorded on discs and CDs by well-known artists. The collection of scores in this book is, however, only a small fraction of what Huygens actually wrote. When he died he left more than 800 compositions to his son Christian. These, however, have disappeared without trace.

The Huygens family were also interested in the plastic arts. Constantine liked to sketch and was a connoisseur of painting. He commissioned a number of artists to paint portraits of himself and his family. In the autobiography in Latin about his early years, dating from 1629-1631, he wrote an interesting essay comparing the respective talents of Jan Lievens and Rembrandt, at that stage both still young men. He singled out for praise the precise and vivid way in which Rembrandt portrayed emotion. At the same time he criticised both painters for their conceit; why wouldn't they go to Italy to polish their genius? One of Rembrandt's rare remaining letters was

written to Constantine Huygens. Rembrandt informed him in this letter (of 12 January 1639) that he had just finished two paintings – of the Entombment and of the Resurrection of Christ – and commends them for the way in which they express *'the greatest and most natural emotion'*.

Constantine Huygens, the *uomo universale,* was also interested in architecture. He designed his own house on the Plein in The Hague, next door to the present day Mauritshuis (see *The Low Countries* (1993-94: 153-157) – albeit with the help of the famous architects Jacob van Campen and Peter Post. Unfortunately his palazzo was demolished in 1876 and there is now only a photograph to remind us of what it was like.

Constantine's sons inherited his talent for drawing. Christian, the scientist, was a creditable draughtsman. An engraving of a portrait of his father was used in 1658 to illustrate the first edition of *Cornflowers* (Korenbloemen), a collection of poems. We also have a copy he made of a head of an old man – by Rembrandt again. But Christian's eldest brother, called Constantine after his father, and who I will call Constantine junior, was an even better artist. During his travels at home and abroad he recorded his surroundings in hundreds of sketches and drawings, some of them very detailed.

Adriaan Hanneman, *Portrait of Constantine Huygens and his Children.* 1640. Mauritshuis, The Hague. Christian is in the upper left corner, Constantine Jr. in the upper right corner.

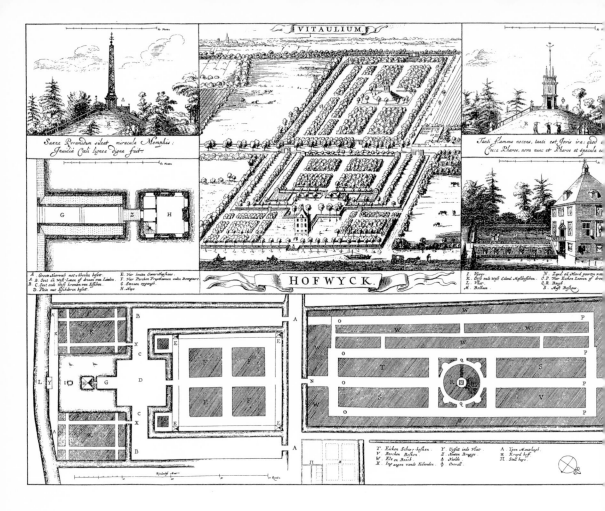

Saxea Pyramidum sileat miracula Memphis:
Inudiæ Cœli lignea digna fuit

VITAULIUM.

Tanti flamma nocens, tanti est Jovis ira: quod
Cocca Pharos, nova nunc et Pharos et specula es

HOFWYCK.

A. *Groen Sterweck met Abeelen beset.*
B. *Oost en West-Laen of dreun van Linden.*
C. *Oost ende West kromen van Elschen.*
D. *Plein met Elschdoren beset.*
E. *Vier houten Somer-huyskens.*
F. *Vier Percken Frygdommens ende Boomgaert.*
G. *Groen opgangh.*
H. *Huys.*

I. *Vyver.*
K. *Oost ende west Colnel. Mosthoffschen.*
L. *Vliet.*
M. *Boskan.*
N. *Lyst. en Noord poorten van*
O.P. *Vier Eicken Laenen of dreu*
Q.R. *Bergh.*
S. *Agt Boskens*

T. *Eicken Schar-bosken.*
V. *Bercken Bosken.*
W. *Els en Besch.*
X. *Inf. angen vande Eilanden.*
Y. *Usfut inde Vliet.*
Z. *Noten Brugge.*
Δ. *Nelde.*
φ. *Overall.*
Λ. *Yser Memelagh.*
Ξ. *Kruyd hof.*
Π. *Stall huys.*

The plan of Constantine Huygens' country seat Hofwijck, drawn by himself and included in the first publication of *Hofwijck* (The Hague, 1653).

Then after the generation of Constantine junior and Christian the link with art and science was abruptly broken. The rise, high tide and ebb, so often found in three generations of a family, applied just as much to the Huygens.

It all began in the Northern Netherlands with Christian Huygens senior (1551-1624), the grandfather of the physicist. He came from the Southern Netherlands, but had decided to become a Calvinist and was appointed Secretary to Prince William of Orange, the leader of the revolt against Spain – an event which ushered in the Eighty Years' War (1568-1648). It was his appointment to this post which brought Christian to Holland. After Prince William's death in 1584 he obtained another influential post as Secretary to the Council of State and then later Secretary to Maurice and Frederick Henry. In 1592 he married Susanna Hoefnagel, who came from Antwerp. She had a brother called Joris, who in exile made a living as a painter of miniatures and became quite well-known as an artist. So it was through the female line that the talent for the plastic arts came into the family.

The first Christian was always something of an outsider in The Hague, and for this reason he tried all the harder to pave the way for his sons.

Maurice, who was born in 1595, and his brother Constantine, born the following year, were given a first-class education which was clearly intended to prepare them for careers at court or as diplomats. The proud father wrote a short account of his sons' education. In it he wrote this about *'little Constantine'*, who was clearly destined for great things …: *'From the very first you could detect in him an outstanding genius and a devout disposition. He could walk without help before he was even 10 months old … While he was still very young he learned to recite his alphabet and to read and then to speak French and all with the same ease as his brother had done before him. I taught him music in the space of six weeks so that he could sing in perfect harmony with us before he was six years old.'*

And the delighted father went further still. Even before his seventh birthday, Constantine could play the violin *'with quite exceptional grace and perfection'* and a few months later he began lessons on the lute. He started Latin on his eighth birthday and by the time he was eleven or twelve he could even write poems in Latin. But he could also ride a horse well, to say nothing of his painting and modelling.

In his autobiography, mentioned above, Constantine gives an account of the education he received from the perspective of the grateful recipient, with some striking details and additional information. From these it seems that his father Christian used some original methods: *'It was winter and as is the custom we wore coats whose sleeves were adorned from the wrist to the shoulder with a single row of gold velvet buttons. Our father cleverly gave each of these buttons the name of a note of music. In this way we learned without any effort the correct sequence of notes, from top to bottom and back again.'*

We also learn from Constantine something about the dancing lessons which his father had given them despite advice to the contrary from a Calvinist clergyman. And he continued: *'Then we went on to learn how to put on and to doff your hat, how to offer your hand, how to embrace the knee of someone, how to bow your head and then raise it to look the recipient in the eye and how to genuflect.'* Like his proficiency in French, English, Latin and Italian, these were all indispensable skills for a courtier.

This kind of education worked just fine for Constantine, even though it was some time before his career took off. He tried the law first. Then he went as an attaché on a number of diplomatic missions: one in 1618 was to England. There he enjoyed some minor triumphs at the court of King James. Amongst other things he organised a lute concert for the King, who was gracious enough to break off his game of cards to listen to the young Dutchman. In 1622, on one of his later diplomatic missions, the King made him a knight and from then on he could call himself 'Sir Constantine'. But it was time for him to pursue a proper career. His time came in 1625, the year in which Prince Maurice died. He was succeeded by his brother Frederick Henry and this was Huygens' chance. He was appointed Secretary to the new Prince and went on to fill this function not just for Frederick Henry but later for William II and then for William III.

Meanwhile he had also made a name for himself as a poet. His first extensive collection of poems appeared in 1625. It was entitled *Otia*, 'Leisure Hours', something to do in one's spare time. In a curious way this collection of poems was a kind of letter of application. In the introduction

Thomas de Keyser, *Portrait of Constantine Huygens and his Assistant.* 1627. Canvas, 92.4 x 69.3 cm. National Gallery, London.

Huygens explained in detail that he considered his poems an act of service to his country, but that even so they were something which he had written in his spare time. He had never neglected his primary duties as a budding diplomat for them. But now that his youth was passing he hoped that he would soon be able to show fully what he could do for his native country. Just as these days one attaches a photograph and letters of recommendation to an application, so the young Huygens ensured that his book was embellished with a flattering engraving of himself and favourable quotations from prominent Dutchmen such as Daniel Heinsius, the internationally renowned professor of Greek and writer of neo-Latin and Dutch poetry.

Whether it was the result of this splendid book, or whether it was the forceful recommendations which had come from his father's contacts (his father had in fact died in the meantime), this time things worked out. As we have already noted, Constantine obtained a job for life. He wrote to his friends that his book was the last product of his free time. From then on he would no longer be able to '*otiari*'. As it happens this was by no means the whole truth. Like a true workaholic Huygens went on writing poetry whenever he had a minute or two to spare. He wrote when he lay sick, when he was travelling on horseback, when he was with the Prince in the field or in attendance at court. But the titles of his works made it clear that writing poetry could only be a secondary activity for him. His second major book was called *Cornflowers,* – beautiful, yes, but only weeds among the ears of corn. This was published in 1658 with a second impression in 1672. In his volume of compositions he added to the title *Pathodia* the word *'occupati'* – they were by a man who was very busy.

As well as his own original work he also did translations. It was Huygens who was responsible for introducing John Donne's poetry to the continent. There is some debate about the quality of the translations he did in the years 1630-1633. Huygens himself was modest about them: *'The translation of a poem is as different from the original as substance is from shadows.'*

In 1627 Huygens married Susanna van Baerle, a girl of musical and literary talents. They had sons and daughters and, as had happened to himself, Constantine in his turn set out in writing the way they were to be brought up. We learn from these details that Susanna had had a very anxious time when she was pregnant with Christian. She had been terribly shocked by an encounter in the street with a child with a horribly disfigured face. It was thought at that time that this could mean her own child would be similarly affected. But Christian was a fine child and although there were a few problems he developed quickly. He seems to have been a child who had a good memory and he was even heard to recite the Lord's Prayer in his sleep! His real forte, however, was arithmetic; in their lessons together he soon overtook his older brother. He was also good at music. But although Christian naturally received good tuition in French – and of course also in Latin – his father never succeeded in getting him to write poems or compositions in Latin; *'but on the other hand he quickly grasped anything to do with mechanics or other aspects of mathematics. He also knew immediately how to produce a model of something just as soon as he had read about it or heard me talk about it'.*

When there was nothing more the children could learn at home they went to the University of Leiden where Christian soon got the reputation of being *'the most learned mathematician of all the students at Leiden'.* But he did not neglect the fine arts. The brothers were interested in music and they took drawing lessons at Leiden. Their father spoke of his pride in the drawings his sons had done – and he particularly praised the quality of Christian's work.

Constantine senior may have viewed Christian's outstanding scientific ability with some astonishment, but never with antipathy. On the contrary; he was proud of his 'Archimedes', as he called him. He was in fact interested in science himself and corresponded with such European scholars as Marin Mersenne and Descartes. His poetry may not suggest any specific expertise in the field of science, but still he likes to display some scientific interest. He writes more as a researcher than as a mystic of what he reads in Nature, 'God's second book'. In the poem on his weekend home *Hof-wyck* he writes of nature: *'The clockwork's known to us, with every cog and spring.'*

The image actually comes from Kepler, but its use by the father of the inventor of the pendulum clock gives it a special effect. When Constantine senior used this particular quotation, Christian had in fact not yet invented his clock. But once he had done so, the poet wrote about it more than once – for example in a poem written for Christian:

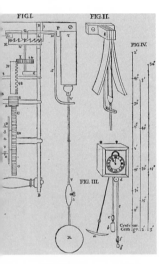

A pendulum clock and its mechanism, drawn by Christian Huygens in his *Horologium Oscillatorium* (1673).

Christian Huygens (1629-1695).

Son, who hast by God's guidance gloriously
Found out the unmoving motion of these movements,
Whatever the world's swings may bring you, good or ill,
Keep ever in your mind their constancy.

Just as Christian's invention made it possible to use an accurate chronometer at sea, so he himself, the master responsible for that work, should remain constant under all conditions.

These were lessons which Christian could well use in his own life, for he encountered both peaks and troughs. For quite a long time he was without a proper job and lived with his father. During this period he worked on problems in physics and mathematics. For example, using a telescope he had made himself, he discovered Saturn's moon Titan in March 1655. His brother, Constantine junior, helped him enthusiastically in building the telescope and in other similar activities. A visit to France resulted in him getting an honorary degree at Angers and, what was more important, a chance to make the acquaintance of fellow scientists in Paris. Back in The Hague again he began to publish his discoveries. One example was *Horologium* (1658), his dissertation on the pendulum clock. He sent copies of this to a number of French scholars, including Pascal. In 1660 he again travelled to Paris to extend his scientific contacts there. He was presented to Louis XIV and was given an honorarium for his work on the clock. Somewhat later he also visited London where he had discussions with Robert Boyle among others and in 1663 was elected to the Royal Society. But his future lay in Paris and in 1666 he achieved a leading position at the Académie Royale des Sciences.

Thus far he had prospered. But an unhappy love affair meant that his private life was less satisfactory. And life in Paris with all its intrigues and academic disputes brought on a deep depression which lasted for several months in 1670. Further problems followed in 1672 as Louis XIV invaded the Netherlands and Christian had to decide where his personal loyalty lay. The years in Paris passed, therefore, with a mixture of success, strife and sickness. In 1681 he was for a time at the family house in The Hague, but by then the beginning of the end was in sight. His return to Paris was no longer so eagerly sought-after, though he still remained in touch with all the great scholars of his age, like Leibniz and Isaac Newton. In fact Newton sent him a copy of his *Principia mathematica*. Huygens studied this with great attention and admiration and he met Newton in London when he was staying there in 1689 (see *The Low Countries* 1993-94: 186-192).

His last work, published posthumously in 1695, was *Kosmotheoros*, a thoughtful book in which among other things he answered – in the affirmative – the question as to whether the planets were inhabited by rational beings and discussed how their social organisation might look. On 8 July 1695 he died after a painful illness, unmarried and without children. His father Constantine had predeceased him in 1687.

Christian's older brother Constantine (1628-1697) had a much less eventful life. He had to wait even longer than his father for a suitable position. It was not until 1672, when he was already 45 years old, that he was finally appointed Secretary to Prince William III – the very post for which his father had been preparing him. He kept a diary of his travels with the Prince – with some risqué entries in it – and he illustrated this with sketches of what he

Constantine Huygens Jr.,
View of Maastricht.
Drawing, 1676. Teylers
Museum, Haarlem.

had seen on the way. These sketches have now been dispersed, alas, although in 1982-1983 a splendid exhibition was devoted to them entitled *With Huygens on his Travels* (Met Huygens op reis). Constantine junior died in The Hague in 1697, two years after his more famous brother, and his only son died in the same year. That brought an end to the halcyon days of the Huygens family. As writers, composers, artists and designers they had made the arts blossom, while Christian as the mathematician, physicist and inventor was responsible for the advancement of science. So that one house on the Plein in The Hague where Constantine and his two sons Christian and Constantine junior lived and worked was truly a 'bridge between two cultures'.

M.A. SCHENKEVELD-VAN DER DUSSEN
Translated by Michael Shaw.

FURTHER READING

ANDRIESSE, C.D., *Titan kan niet slapen. Een biografie van Christiaan Huygens.* Amsterdam / Antwerp, 1993 (an English translation of this biography of Christian Huygens is in preparation).

BACHRACH, A.G.H., *Sir Constantine Huygens and Britain* (Vol. 1, 1596-1619). Leiden / Londen, 1962.

BOS, H.J.M. *et al.* (ed.), *Studies on Christian Huygens.* Lisse, 1980.

DAVIDSON, PETER and ADRIAAN VAN DER WEEL (ed.), *A Selection of the Poems of Sir Constantijn Huygens.* Amsterdam, 1996.

Met Huygens op reis. Tekeningen en dagboeknotities van Constantijn Huygens Jr. (1628-1697), secretaris van stadhouder-koning Willem III. Zutphen, 1982.

SELECTIVE DISCOGRAPHY

ELLY AMELING / MAX VAN EGMOND, *Constantijn Huygens: Pathodia sacra et profana,* EMI, 165-25 634/35.

CAMERATA TRAJECTINA, *Muziek uit de Gouden Eeuw: Constantijn Huygens en Gerbrand Adriaensz. Bredero,* Globe, 6013.

A Poem by Constantine Huygens

On the Frontispiece of *Cornflowers*

He who sows corn hopes not for cornflowers too:
He works for food and need and profit from the grain.
But still the flower appears and mingles with the corn
Like uninvited guests, unbidden to the feast
Who enter in unasked and place themselves for show,
And look as happy, although lighter than the rest.
The others wish them gone, but if they, with their grace
Bring joy unto the feast, then they become accepted.
The cornflower in the field is profitless, but still
They lend, without denial, some beauty to the corn.
They stand amongst the stalks, like noble children seen
On Easter morning, clothed in blue and scarlet silk.
A weed, but of the best, most pleasing and most fine
And sweet and innocent, no poison in it lies.
 And for such merchandise I sell my cornflowers now,
My kitchen-herbs or weeds, my reader may decide
What name to give them. They were never sown
In the corn-acres where I sow and reap,
They are a gift of nature and the land; the corn,
Has nursed them into being. The good will gladly hear,
The bad must hear it now: amidst the restless press
Of Court's and Land's affairs, I have for many years
(As the Boat guides the Ship) being faithful in small things,
Helped to raise the heads of those who were bowed down:
And I for Church and Land have laboured *constantly*.
Have done what many know of, but not everyone;
Have done what few men, but not every man could do
(And thanks are still to come): I have put strenght and patience
Against great obstacles, being strengthened by God's hand,
Have broken through tough thorns, incurring no disgrace.
 These works I call my harvest, these are my best corn
Grown for the common good, and they therefore not lost,
And they therefore so spent, as every citizen
Still stands his country's debtor, in good years or in bad.
 What extra crop of flowers my cornfield has produced
If any one would know it, here is written down.
I place my cornflowers here, and stand their stems in ink,
My stratagem against untimely withering.
How they will seem, remote from fields, I cannot know,
The courteous praised them, when they grew amidst the corn,
And someone even owned, being kindly in his lies,
That weeds could be yet worse and these might please the eye.
Praise I my merchandise? No: freely censure them
So long as none accuse them of a poisoned taste.
For the rest I own and freely, reader, say
They are but cornflowers, they appear but blue.

The frontispiece of
Constantine Huygens'
Cornflowers (Koren-
bloemen, 1658)

From *Cornflowers* (Koren-bloemen, 1658)

Translated by Peter Davidson and Adriaan van der We

(in 'A Selection of the Poems of Constantijn Huygens',

Amsterdam, 1996).

**R**eality

and Art in the Work of

Jan Dibbets and Johannes Vermeer

When the camera obscura was invented, the seventeenth-century poet Constantine Huygens thought that the art of painting was finished. In the nineteenth century the introduction of photography gave people the same idea. Today, with the advent of virtual reality, the same predictions are being made. Every new technique which seems to reproduce reality flawlessly apparently offers yet another opportunity to proclaim the end of art. But art survives because its own truth stands alongside everyday reality. Art, even the most abstract, taps a deep-seated layer in us as if, as Plato once said, everything around us is merely a shadow of the real world far removed from ourselves.

The misunderstanding that still generally exists between the general public on the one hand and art historians, critics and gallery owners on the

Jan Dibbets, *Amsterdam-Düsseldorf.* 1996. Photo pasted on wall. The artist's collection.

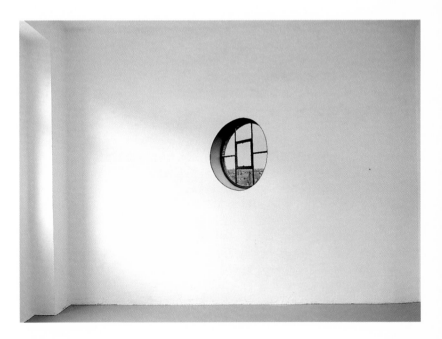

other is partly due to their different ways of judging a work of art. The professionals are involved with composition, colour and use of materials; they are only marginally interested in the story that a work of art tells. But the man in the street first looks for a story told by a painting. This impulse goes back a very long way, and is hardly surprising as the story is at the very root of Western art. For centuries the recognisability of the images gave a work of art both its didactic and its artistic right to exist. Although the story was often not realistic, the semblance of reality remained. For a long time the anecdote remained an important element in painting. It was only at the end of last century that some artists searching for a different reality began to work on two levels. To give an example: in 1896 the Dutch artist Johan Thorn Prikker drew in grease pencil a country lane in his Belgian vacation resort of Visé. Although it is a country lane, it is at the same time another composition: a work that we would now have no trouble calling abstract. In his 1968 standard work on the oeuvre of Piet Mondrian Cor Blok writes: '*But until various artists, virtually all at the same time in the period around 1910, began to paint non-representational art "the time was simply not ripe for it". That is to say, until then there were too many artists who felt that it just wasn't done (not to mention the attitude of the general public) for someone to venture that step alone. This does not mean that the world was impatiently waiting for abstract art around 1910, but that tolerance of unexpected changes – even if apparently fortuitous – had become an artistic habit. If someone made a discovery, he did not have to hide it in the attic for fear that the neighbours would see it.*'

The artist's eye

After a short but intensive scrutiny of the avenues open to him as a painter the Dutch artist Jan Dibbets (1941- ; see *The Low Countries* 1993-94: 311-312) opted for reality. But through his composition he transforms reality. Dibbets' photo collages, or photo fragments sometimes combined with pencil outlines or colour, are a reality that can only exist as a work of art. His art is determined by his view of reality as recorded by a camera. Memories of other works of art, sometimes fragments, sometimes compilations, but perhaps more often than not associations, are equally important components. The actual origin of each work is obvious as Dibbets names the places where the photos were taken. This adds an extra dimension to the artistic value of the work. Often familiar sites such as Soissons Cathedral, the Guggenheim Museum, or the Vondel Church in Amsterdam henceforth lead double lives as works of art and as churches or museums.

Dibbets' work is often said to have the clarity of Saenredam (see *The Low Countries* 1993-94: 231-238) and Mondrian (see *The Low Countries* 1993-94: 75-82) and the colours of Monet. But the work with which he may have the closest tie may be that of Johannes Vermeer (see *The Low Countries* 1994-95: 175-180). At all events, when I visited the major exhibition of Vermeer's work in the Mauritshuis in The Hague in the spring of 1996 Dibbets' work frequently sprang to mind. As the catalogue indicates, Vermeer's pictures, like Dibbets', are the product of an extremely painstaking and often time-consuming method of painting. In addition, the catalogue presents us with evidence that Vermeer's much vaunted 'reality' never in fact existed. If it is indeed the case that Johannes Vermeer's 'reality' is an artifice, then there is scant difference between his work of the seventeenth century and Dibbets' work of today.

Jan Dibbets, *Colour Study, H 1, 2, 3, 4*. 1976-1985. Photograph on board, 175 x 175 cm. Private collection.

Stage-set interiors Vermeer's early works were biblical or mythological in character; later he specialised in genre paintings, mainly interiors with one or two persons, or even only one woman. Street scenes and townscapes were both popular subjects for the Delft painters of the period. But in Vermeer's *Little Street* and *View of Delft* something transcendental has taken place: a moment has been frozen in time. It was long thought that he used a camera obscura. Research undertaken both in the United States and the Netherlands while the Vermeer exhibition was being organised has called this into question.

There is a difference of opinion on this point between Arthur Wheelock, curator of the Washington National Gallery, and Ben Broos and Jørgen Wadum of the Mauritshuis; it was thus not without significance that a camera obscura was on show at the exhibition in Washington, while in The Hague the pin-and-threads technique for studying the laws of perspective was graphically demonstrated by a photo of a painting with threads stretched out in front of it.

During the restoration of a number of the canvasses prior to the exhibition it became known that fifteen of the twenty-two paintings were shown to have a tiny hole where Vermeer had placed the pin to which a thread was attached to assist him with the foreshortening. But however carefully he built up his compositions according to the most up-to-date and complex rules of perspective, painting itself was always foremost in his mind, thus rebutting Huygens' claim that it was dead. Within a solid framework Vermeer took liberties: a chair catches the light despite being behind a curtain; the daylight that falls through two windows set in the same side wall throws different shadows; the reflection in the *View of Delft* of the city gates in the water of the River Schie has been enlarged so that it touches the other shore, where the viewer stands, to mention but a few examples.

The interiors Vermeer painted probably never existed in quite that form either. Research has shown that objects, even persons, have been moved

Johannes Vermeer, *Young Lady with a Water Pitcher*. c.1664. Canvas, 45.7 x 40.6 cm. Metropolitan Museum of Art, New York (Marquand Collection, gift of Henry G. Marquand).

about in compositions that now look particularly solid and true to life. Nowadays ingenious technical devices like infra-red cameras and computers can make these changes visible to us. For hundreds of years we thought that the woman in the *Young Lady with a Water Pitcher* from the Metropolitan Museum in New York had always stood against a whitewashed wall with a large map hanging on her right. An infra-red reflectogram has now clearly shown that the map was once further to the left, behind the woman's head. Furthermore, a chair with lion-head terminals, like the chair that is still partly to be seen, once stood between the woman and the window. Both elements disturbed the classic tranquillity of the scene; the large monochrome background gives the painting its serenity.

An examination of inventories of household effects carried out by the Leiden historian Thera Wijsenbeek-Olthuis and published at the time of the Vermeer exhibition in *Kunstschrift* (no. 1, 1996) indicated that the combination of valuable objects and relatively modest interiors was at best unlikely. She concludes: '*Summing up it may be said that Vermeer brought together an odd jumble of typical status symbols... which created an atmosphere that never existed in a Dutch interior...*'

Vermeer combined elements that would never have been seen together in

Perfect compositions

his own environment. Moreover, he changed the position of objects as he worked, moving things around until his compositions were perfect. *Young Lady with a Water Pitcher* is not the only painting to be changed; the *View of Delft* does not give an exact picture of Delft either. This way of working resembles that of Jan Dibbets more than three hundred years later. By around 1910 when the artist no longer '*had to hide in the attic*' (Blok) reality can still be the subject of a work of art, but for the avant-garde the difference between reality and art has become important. So while Vermeer's reality is in fact semblance, Dibbets' reality is legitimate as a work of art.

In the early twentieth century the work of art came to be accepted as its own reality. Jan Dibbets' work reflects this concept. Initially it was the conflict between the subject and its photographic image that interested him. Slowly but surely the parts of photos became nothing more than elements within the composition. At first Dibbets added a kind of clarification in pencil to the work. More recently, any lines there are, are on a par with the photos. Even more often colour plays just as important a role.

After an initial period of trial and error Jan Dibbets found his theme in 1969 when he photographed *Perspective Corrections*, first on the grass in Amsterdam's Vondel Park and later on his studio wall. In Vondel Park he laid a rope on the grass in an oval shape; when photographed this became a circle, while the trapezium on the studio wall became an almost free floating square on the photo. He tried out other possibilities in the series dealing with daylight and artificial light and the difference between them: *The Shadows in my Studio* (1969), *The Shortest Day at the Van Abbemuseum Eindhoven* (1970) originally planned as a series of slides, *Louvredrape,*

Jan Dibbets, *Perspective Correction, My Studio I, I: Square on Wall.* 1969. 110 x 110 cm.

Horizontal (1971) and *Daylight, Flashlight, Outside Light, Inside Light* (1971). These works are at the root of all subsequent developments, which take the form of a more and more sophisticated demonstration of the principle: what is there is not what you see, the artist determines what is shown. Just as Vermeer continued to move objects around until he arrived at an ideal composition, so too Dibbets continues to turn his subject matter until the form is achieved that gives us his vision in a nutshell. Ceilings or floors, the low Dutch horizon or the rich colour of the paint on a highly polished car; the detail and the whole are both on the cutting edge in relation to each other. Jan Dibbets succeeds in making his work logical within what is in fact the impossible framework of a work of art. Anyone who has seen his ceilings, windows and floors accepts that this is also a way of looking at them, that this flat interpretation exists alongside their three-dimensional reality. While Cézanne abandoned perspective in order to give his objects weight, Jan Dibbets cuts a space open with his camera. His lines and colour add that other dimension which artists like Thorn Prikker and Mondrian were searching for a century ago.

Jan Dibbets regularly uses windows both as a frame for the outside world and as a separation from it. An interior is never visible through a Dibbets window, but an outside view always is, even if it is 'only' the sky. The photos are always taken from inside even if the internal shutters of the windows

Jan Dibbets, *The Shortest Day at the Van Abbe-museum Eindhoven*. 1970. Photographs on board, 177 x 171 cm. Stedelijk Van Abbemuseum, Eindhoven.

The essence of the subject

sometimes seem to change into frivolous butterflies. The round windows have acquired the depth of their wall in the course of time because Dibbets now also photographs the stone dressing in which the window is set. The round window from Soissons, or Santes Creus or Vondel Church is photographed, enlarged, and cut cleanly from its surroundings. This circle is then glued to a square piece of paper which has been given a water-colour wash or otherwise painted in a single colour. To this background Dibbets sometimes adds lines in pencil or water-colour. Although through the windows the view into the distance remains permanently and compellingly present, at the same time these circles reflect the shape of the windows in the lines of their stone frames, or in the lines on the paper. The result is one of depth versus reflection, colour versus line, immobility versus movement. Johannes Vermeer painted the essence of his subjects with such fidelity that three hundred years later we are convinced that this is what Dutch interiors were like in Delft in the Golden Age. Even when conscientious scholars prove the reverse, Vermeer's vision is so strong that this recently gained knowledge does not affect our attitude towards his paintings. Dibbets' interpretation of striking architectural features is similar. In their endeavour to create compositions of great strength both Vermeer and Dibbets manipulate reality. The rules of their art defy reality, because their art exists independent of reality.

MICKY PILLER
Translated by Elizabeth Mollison.

Jan Dibbets, *Santes Creus Window*. 1990. Watercolour on paper and colour photograph, 73 x 73 cm, 68 x 68 cm, 73 x 73 cm. Private collection.

Master of Everyday Life

The Work of Constant Permeke

The Flemish painter and sculptor Constant Permeke (1886-1952) sought in his work to represent everyday reality. His subjects usually related to the geographical area in which he found himself at a given moment; he felt personally drawn to the simple, almost primitive way of life of fishermen and farmers, not only observing them but actually living among them. Whilst living on the coast (in Ostend) he painted mainly scenes from the life of the fishermen; during the time he spent near Ghent (in Sint-Martens-Latem), in the rural village of Astene and in Jabbeke (near Bruges), his work was inspired mainly by rural life. In addition to the simplicity and spontaneity of his subjects, Permeke was also struck by the eternal and universal values in their souls.

For Permeke, the essence of his expressionist vision lay in the artist's personal identification with his subject: in this way the creator of a work of art is able to reflect in his creation the essence of cosmic timelessness in his subject. For Permeke, the depiction of his subject became a recreation of reality. He did this with a sense both of monumentality and synthesis, disregarding the prevailing rules of form and style. By means of deformation, an effect achieved in part through the application of thick layers of paint, he attempted to accentuate reality in accordance with his own emotions and thus to strengthen the content of his work.

Permeke was born in 1886 in Antwerp, the son of the artist and restorer Henri-Louis Permeke. In 1892 the Permeke family moved to the seaside resort of Ostend, where Henri-Louis became the first curator of the museum in 1896. The young Constant received his first art lessons from his father, who allowed him to help with restoration work, and thus acquired great technical skill. He also got to know the work of James Ensor (see *The Low Countries* 1994-95: 156-168), who was a friend and regular visitor.

After leaving secondary school Constant Permeke went on to the Academy in Bruges (1903-1906), and then to the Royal Academy of Fine Arts in Ghent (1906-1908). Whilst in Ghent Permeke, like many Flemish artists of the time, was influenced mainly by Emiel Claus, a painter of luministic landscapes with an impressionist accent. As a result of this experience,

Permeke used the line and stipple technique of the Post-Impressionists in a number of early works, mainly landscapes. Permeke's compositions were less rigid, however, because of the more expressive and unpredictable approach which he had developed mainly through his familiarity with the work of Ensor. Other influences were the coloration of Theo van Rysselberghe (with lots of blue and violet) and the work of Vincent van Gogh.

The young Permeke also took part in the rich intellectual life of Ghent, and struck up friendships with the literary scholar P.G. van Hecke, the art historian André de Ridder and the artists Gust de Smet and Frits van den Berghe. In 1920 this close friendship led to the founding of the 'Sélection' Modern Art Group in Brussels, which was to set the tone for Expressionism in Flanders.

Permeke broke with the traditional views of his father, and before his studies in Ghent were complete he left the parental home; together with Gust de Smet he set himself up in the former studio of Léon Spilliaert in the Kaaistraat in Ostend. Through the work of the highly self-willed Spilliaert, with whom he had a rather troubled relationship, the symbolism and expressive force of Edvard Munch filtered through into Permeke's paintings.

In 1909 Permeke moved to the village of Sint-Martens-Latem, near Ghent. In this artists' village (see *The Low Countries* 1994-95: 148-156) he met Albert Servaes, whose work made a strong impression on him. Servaes' feel for symbolism and his religious-contemplative view of art quickly displaced the influence of Claus and offered Permeke the solution to his arduous struggle to externalise emotions. Servaes' painting *The Potato Planters* (1909) was of great importance here. This work contains no trace of luminism, which was felt to be inadequate for the expression of emotions; all that remains is the emotional depth in the depiction of the relationship between man and nature. This depth was brought out even more by Permeke through the thick layering of his technique and his use of deformation, which enhanced the strength of his compositions.

This new vision was clearly visible in his work from 1912, the year in which he married Maria Delaere and settled once again in Ostend. This time Permeke did not live in the centre of town, but in the fishermen's quarter. The sea and the life of fishermen became important themes, and the human figure assumed a prominent place in his work. Examples are the paintings *On the Quayside (Ostend women)* and *The Porter* from 1913: here, the impressionist vision has clearly made way for a more expressionistic approach: the portrayal is monumental and sober, lacking in any anecdotal element. The thickly applied paint also prevents any reproduction of detail. Only the essence is depicted, in a noticeably sober colour palette dominated by earth tones (brown, ochre and black). These tones are broken up here and there by a stroke of fiery red or heavenly blue, but in the main the sombre coloration reflects the hard reality with which his subjects (fishermen) were confronted daily. The paint texture thus became a determining factor for the content of Permeke's work, not least through the example of Van Gogh. In the same period he also became acquainted with the Futurism to be seen in the George Giroux gallery and in the work of Marinetti.

In the meantime Permeke had also become familiar, through journals and exhibitions, with other international movements in pictorial art, such as Fauvism, Expressionism and Cubism. Expressionist ideas gradually took

Constant Permeke,
The Porter. 1913. Pastel on
board, 66 x 40 cm.
Private Collection.

shape in Permeke's work between 1909 and 1912; he fell completely under the spell of the movement during his stay in England.

1914 brought the outbreak of the First World War. Permeke was called up and later seriously wounded, and taken to England, while Gust de Smet and Frits van den Berghe ended up in neutral Holland. For artists, the Netherlands was undoubtedly a better place to be in that period. De Smet and Van den Berghe came into contact with German Expressionism there (through the work of Dutch painters such as Jan Sluyters and Leo Gestel) as well as with Cubism (through the work of the Breton Henri Le Fauconnier, who had also ended up in the Netherlands). Permeke, by contrast, found himself literally and figuratively on an island. He remained in touch with what was happening in artistic centres in the Netherlands only indirectly – mainly through his correspondence with André de Ridder. When he was finally discharged from hospital he did take the opportunity to go and see Turner's paintings, and met other Belgians who introduced him to the London art scene. These contacts were short-lived, however, because Permeke quickly left the metropolis behind him in favour of stays in Wiltshire and, later, Devon. His first monumental works were created in the latter county, in Chardstock, Sidmouth and Sidford, and included works such as *The Butcher, The Cider Drinker* and *The Stranger*, all from 1916. Permeke's personal style came into its own in these paintings. The expressive element which had already reared its head was now given free rein; as a consequence, the simplified and synthesising representation of form was carried further. The colour palette became even more sober, with black, grey, brown and ochre hues beginning to dominate the image. The human figure once again moved to the foreground, being harmoniously embedded in the work.

Permeke spent most of 1917 in Sidmouth and Sidford, close to the sea. The works created during this period show a high degree of internalisation, which is expressed in the abstraction of reality. They are mostly landscapes in which the sun dominates, absorbing and abstracting the forms – works

Constant Permeke,
The Cider Drinker. 1916.
Canvas, 123 x 101 cm.
Sacher-Stehlin Collection,
Basle.

Constant Permeke, *Harvest in Devonshire*. 1917. Canvas, 121.5 x 126 cm. Provinciaal Museum voor Moderne Kunst, Ostend.

such as *Harvest in Devonshire* and *The Beach*. The superficial light treatment of Permeke's Post-Impressionist period has disappeared completely in these works; light is now represented atmospherically in a warm coloration of yellows, golds, ochres and reds. Both Ensor's use of colour and the cosmic dimension in Turner's work were important influences here. The perception of nature took on visionary characteristics and radiated an exuberant sense of the joy of life. Colour explosions such as these returned only sporadically in Permeke's later work.

On 20 April 1919 Permeke returned to Belgium and settled once again in the Vuurtorenwijk ('lighthouse district') of Ostend. His house had been partly destroyed and his financial situation was also anything but healthy. Confronted with the misery which war had caused, the *joie de vivre* he had experienced in Devon made way for an even greater internalisation and a deep-rooted empathy with his fellow human beings. In works such as *Evening in the Fishermen's Quarter*, the rounded contours of earlier works were replaced by straight, angular lines. The colours became hard and bright, with faded green tints evoking a controlled drama. Complex tangles in the background suggest the confused situation of the time. Fishing life was also the subject of a number of charcoal drawings from this period. Here again the monumental nature of the depiction is striking.

From 1920 Permeke, under the influence of French and Belgian Cubism, began to 'construct' his paintings more. An example is *Fair in Ostend* (1921). The human figure returns to the foreground, as it also did in a number of charcoal drawings of fishermen and women from the same period. In his monumental drawings Permeke linked realism and constructivism, the tall, sturdy figures exuding strength and temperament.

For another reason, too, 1920 was an important year for Permeke: it was the year in which he embarked on a friendship with the sculptor Oscar Jespers. Jespers introduced him to the African art of sculpture and awakened his interest in constructivism. Permeke began building a collection of African fetishes and images. Influenced by this 'primitive' art, he began representing the faces of his subjects schematically; the figures were depicted in a more 'wooden' way. *About Permeke* (1922) and *Friture Foraine* (1922) are masterpieces of constructivism. The influence of Cubism is abundantly clear here, although Permeke never allowed himself to be tempted into a doctrinaire Cubism: the analysis of form was always combined with a spontaneous interpretation of reality.

Constant Permeke, *About Permeke*. 1922. Canvas, 150 x 195 cm. Provinciaal Museum Constant Permeke, Jabbeke.

In the summer of 1922 Permeke was again in the vicinity of Ghent, this time in the rural village of Astene with his friends Frits van den Berghe and Gust de Smet. Gradually, farmers and country life took over as subjects in his work from the sea and fishermen, although Permeke still lived in Ostend. Examples are *The Porridge-Eater* (1922) and *The Black Bread* (1923). The highly structured nature of earlier works gives way here to a greater interplay between light and dark. In a painting such as *The Engaged Couple* (1923) – a very well-received work – the gigantic human figures dominate the composition in their serenity and monumental stature.

Permeke's work became stronger and stronger and from 1924 the painter gradually came to be seen as an established asset. In that same year he was even given his first retrospective in the Giroux gallery in Brussels.

Constant Permeke,
*The Engaged Couple.*1923.
Canvas, 151 x 130 cm.
Museum voor Moderne
Kunst, Brussels.

In spite of his interest in rural life, the sea never relinquished its hold on Permeke. Initially the seascapes from this period depicted stretches of beach, dunes or breakwaters, but the accent quickly shifted to the water mass in all its guises. In search of peace following his artistic success and a number of personal dramas – his little son Matheus died in 1923, followed in 1925 by his mother – Permeke spent some time sailing round in his yacht. He also tried to settle in the town of his birth, Antwerp, in the hope of finding peace there, but in 1926 he returned to Ostend.

From 1925 onwards Permeke was also regularly to be seen around Jabbeke, near Bruges, where he painted landscapes in the open air. All the seasons were depicted in these works with an intense use of colour and dynamic brush strokes. He also produced a number of nudes during this period. It is not so much the beauty of the female body which is central in these works, but rather its fertility.

Although farmers and the land they till had taken the place of fishermen and the sea, this shift of emphasis had virtually no effect on Permeke's theme of the primitive human being in his equally primitive environment. Between 1927 and 1930 he produced numerous monumental works which radiate this primitive life, reaching a high point with *The Sow* (1929), which was the cause of a considerable furore because of the choice of subject and its treatment.

In 1929 Permeke moved once and for all to Jabbeke, where he had had the large house known as *The Four Winds* built. In the same year a retrospective of his work – containing no less than 140 works! – was held in the exhibition gallery of Kunst van Heden ('Art of Today') in Antwerp. A year later it was the turn of Brussels, where a gigantic retrospective containing around 600 works was organised in the Palace of Fine Arts. Around that time Permeke was also already working on a number of large drawings, such as *Motherhood* (1929) and *The Farmer with the Shovel* (1930), in which the human figure shapes and dominates the entire composition. These monumental images marked the first step towards his later sculpture.

Things were going well for Permeke, both artistically and commercially. *The Engaged Couple* (1923), for example, was purchased by the Belgian State in 1930 for the sum of BF 60,000. The first monograph on Permeke, written by Achiel Stubbe, appeared in 1931. Apart from a number of large

Constant Permeke,
The Sow. 1929. Canvas,
165 x 180 cm. Private
Collection.

Constant Permeke,
Marie-Lou. 1938. Stone,
H 300 cm. Middelheim
Museum, Antwerp.

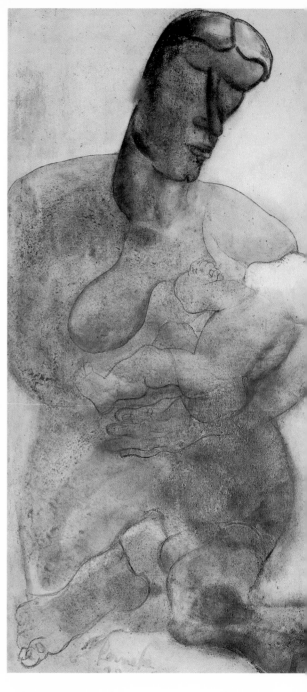

Constant Permeke,
Motherhood. 1929.
Crayon and oil on canvas,
180 x 90 cm. Museum voor
Schone Kunsten, Ostend.

paintings such as *The Weeder* and *The Three Farmers' Wives*, between 1932 and 1938 Permeke produced mainly landscapes. Where his landscapes in the years 1930 and 1931 were structured in an orderly way and dominated by rather pale colours, after 1931 they became highly colourful and temperamental. Other monumental works, too, such as *Well-Disposed* and *Farmer Lying*, bear witness to an enormous suggestive expressive power and imagination.

Between 1930 and 1940 Permeke continued to paint large landscapes, in which the figuration was reduced more and more. These paintings (such as *Golden Landscape,* 1935) are dominated by a monochromatic colour treatment, though usually accompanied by strong coloration. New seascapes were also produced, characterised by a lyrical and spontaneous representation of the subject. One such work is the large seascape painted by Permeke for the World Exhibition in Brussels in 1935. The lyrical informality of his new work attracted a good deal of criticism, particularly following the large Permeke exhibition of 1936 in Brussels; even his own circle of friends accused him of stagnation and a reactionary craving for traditional form. This reproach was unfounded, for Permeke took a visionary approach to these landscapes and added a cosmic dimension to them. In addition to the landscapes he also produced many impressive paintings of figures such as *The Potato Eater* (1935) and *The Coffee Drinker* (1928-1938).

Permeke was troubled by this criticism and decided resolutely to seek a new subject: the nude, and a new medium: sculpture, a choice inspired in part by his sense of the monumental. The period 1938-1939 became the most intensive phase of his career and culminated in a major retrospective in the Brussels Palais des Beaux-Arts in 1939, where his sculpture was exhibited for the first time. These works were received enthusiastically and Permeke was even compared to Aristide Maillol and Ossip Zadkine. Paul Haesaerts published a short study entitled *Permeke the Sculptor* (Permeke sculpteur). The artist had taken revenge on his critics.

In creating his sculptures Permeke started from scratch: because this discipline was totally new to him, he had to learn everything by experiment. He did this through his 'exercises in clay', which resulted in small statuettes whose primitive nature sometimes evokes memories of pre-historic art. The inspiration for them came in part from books on Hittite, Sardinian and Egyptian art which he had in his library.

His new love for sculpture meant that Permeke stopped painting for around two years. He did not give up drawing, however, and a number of grandiose works appeared in these years. They were all nudes, a genre in which Permeke gradually developed a mixed technique. By using charcoal and colour pigments, bonded with turpentine or water, he surpassed ordinary drawing: a strong plasticity was created, which is also found in monumental statues such as *Marie-Lou* (1938) and *The Sower* (1939).

1940 brought the outbreak of the Second World War in all its fury. This time, however, the fighting did not totally isolate Permeke from the world of art. Although Jabbeke, which lies in the coastal zone, became inaccessible, Permeke rented a house in Brussels in 1942. There was even time for artistic conflicts, with Permeke locking horns with the Haesaerts brothers, for example, when they classified him as an animist in their 1942 work *Le retour à l'humain*.

The world all around was in flames, but artistic life in Brussels carried on. 1943 was even a come-back year for Permeke; he was given an exhibition in the Bruegel gallery, while R.C. Delevoy, manager of the Apollo gallery, exhibited Permeke, Brusselmans, De Smet and Jespers together under the title 'Les Constructeurs'. Delevoy compared Permeke with Picasso and regarded him as the standard-bearer of Belgian art, a pioneer preparing the way for the later La Jeune Peinture Belgique group. By now Permeke's career was also socially established, with Gustave van Geluwe as his permanent patron.

Permeke was barred from painting or exhibiting by the German occupying force, but he ignored this ban, and in fact produced several nude drawings and a number of large landscapes in which he created a symbiosis between abstraction and figuration. In the ensuing years nude drawings played a key role in his production, sometimes as preliminary studies for his sculptures. A major exhibition of nude drawings and sculptures in the Palais des Beaux-Arts in 1944 caused Permeke some difficulties with the occupying Germans, but this only served to increase his energy. He threw himself into his work like a man possessed, produced several statuettes and maintained intensive contacts with sculptors such as Jespers and George Grard. He also made a start on new, large statues, though he destroyed many of them later. He was given technical assistance on these monumental sculptures by Pierre Devos, his future son-in-law, who helped to mould the figures. Permeke's typical 'experimental' technique, with which he sought to distance himself from other sculptors, consisted in moulding the image in plaster and then attacking it with a hammer and chisel. His technique was two-fold: modelling and hewing. He sometimes added pictorial elements as well by retaining the

Constant Permeke,
Nude Lying. 1938-1939.
Oil on paper, 90.5 x 149 cm.
Museum voor Schone
Kunsten, Ghent.

patinas created by the gum lacquer in the moulds. Permeke created only a small number of sculptures in a 'direct' fashion, such as his *Self-Portrait* (1940) in wood.

At the end of the 1940s he produced a number of surprising portraits of young women. In addition to *clair-obscur* effects, these images also sought to portray pictorial contrasts. In addition to a number of beach views, Permeke's work in the period between 1938 and 1950 produced mainly impressive nude drawings using the mixed technique described earlier. In a work such as *Nude with the Red Shoes* (1949), Permeke was able to combine his personal expressive method with a sense of feminine refinement. In this period he also produced a number of large charcoal drawings of the beautiful model Lea, of whom he also made a life-size statue. This work was dominated by a return to classical beauty. From 1938 onwards he also worked on the 'Niobe' theme, though this only assumed definitive form after the War, in a monumental statue. The Niobe myth – the petrification of a living form – symbolised the art of sculpture for Permeke.

Permeke's wife died in May 1948 after a long-drawn-out illness. In the previous year major retrospectives of his work had been held in Brussels,

Constant Permeke, *Farewell*. 1948. Canvas, 163 x 178.5 cm. Provinciaal Museum Constant Permeke, Jabbeke.

Amsterdam, Prague and Paris, but the artist himself withdrew more and more. In the sculpture for his wife's grave (*Naked Woman Lying*), all form of sensuality has disappeared, while the splendid painting *Farewell* (1948) is completely dominated by its mystical quality.

Eventually Permeke managed to shake off his troubles somewhat, and in 1950 he painted a number of striking works with a pure and clear coloration. In *Daily Bread* (1950) he reduced the colour treatment to a harmony of earth tints. The stark white backdrop to the figures means this work radiates an almost sacred atmosphere. *The Harvesters* (1950) and *The Yellow Nude* (1951) are paintings in which emotions are depicted at an abstract level in a flare of yellow and red. Bearing in mind that lyrical abstract art was to enjoy great success in the 1950s, these works show clearly that Permeke was not yet an exhausted talent.

In 1951 (barely one year before his death), urged on by a French friend, Permeke undertook a journey to Britanny. He stayed a few days and made only a few small sketches and drawings and one small painting. Once back in Jabbeke, however, in a burst of energy he painted seven pictures from memory. They are all Breton landscapes, mainly harbour views and coves. In a synthesising, almost monochromatic manner, he maintains his typical expressive language of imagery in these works, combined with a high degree of poetic sensitivity. As always, it was primarily the simplicity of the human figures and their bond with nature which fascinated him. This internationally renowned painter, this master of daily reality, took full part in the life of the people, even becoming a champion archer. In spite of his success Permeke, whose work had been consecrated by the retrospectives in Brussels and Paris in the period 1947-1948 as 'great art', always remained a man of the people.

Permeke's involvement with his immediate surroundings is idiosyncratic, but he transcends directly perceptible reality to arrive at a cosmic vision. It is precisely this quality that makes him a stubbornly individual and internationally significant expressionist. For it is not the case that Expressionism in Flanders emerged too late: it is a distinct movement that goes its own way, and while chronologically it may have lagged behind French Fauvism and German Expressionism, where quality is concerned it need bow its head to neither of them.

WILLY VAN DEN BUSSCHE
Translated by Julian Ross.

A

Race Apart ...

The Flandriens and the Golden Age of Flemish Cycling

Mac Bolle or Karel van Wijnendaele, pseudonyms of Karel Steyaert (1882-1961)

The Flandriens – weren't they those forced-labourers of road racing, from Flanders of course, members of that breed of racing cyclists who, particularly during the period between the wars, fired the imagination of the ordinary Dutch-speaking Belgian who was served up a constant, romanticised image of their almost incomprehensible feats of swaggering strength? A long sentence, that, rather in the style of the man who was godfather to the Flandriens and the heroic prose he wrote – namely Karel van Wijnendaele, or *'Koarele'* as he was universally known with a blend of familiarity and respect. He will be our guide as we seek out the origins of the 'Flandrien' concept and what it came to mean in later cycling history. In his masterpiece, *The Riches of Flemish Cycle Sport* (Het Rijke Vlaamsche Wielerleven), Van Wijnendaele takes us back to the early days and initiates us into what those Flandriens really meant. And we make a strange, rather bizarre discovery. Contrary to what we had always thought, the Flandriens were born on the cycle tracks of Brussels and Paris, and they celebrated their greatest triumphs in the Six-Day races in Chicago and New York; that is, in America. Strange though it may seem, they were track cyclists and not, as yet, giants of the open road.

To explain: it may be that their origins lay along Flemish roads, for Van Wijnendaele's book does mention quarrels and disputes following the Flemish Championship at Koolskamp in 1912. At the time this was a major event, more so than it is now; and with so much at stake it does happen that losers are reluctant to accept defeat. In this case the West Flemish cyclists accused the East Flemings of riding a concerted strategy against them. However, argument and mutual recrimination eventually led to some sort of reconciliation and understanding, and it was decided that they would all take to the cycle tracks and compete there as formidable two-man teams. What is at first hinted at is later set down in black and white: it was the young Van Wijnendaele himself whose bright idea this was. As a young hopeful he was not strong enough to make a racing cyclist, so he threw himself into the developing field of cycle journalism and as a privileged observer became also the constant companion of the Flemish cyclists he knew so well. Under the pseudonym Mac Bolle, for some ten years before and after the First

World War he accompanied those riders as they went in search of honour, fame and riches. From the Old World to the New and back again.

In those days it was mainly on the cycle tracks that fortunes were to be made, and the two-man events dominated everything else. Some famous pairs from the very early days: Marcel Buysse and Ritten van Lerberghe, Leon Buysse and De Pauw, Debaets and Persijn. They went out to win at any cost, first in Brussels, then in Berlin and after that in Paris. Right from the start, in Brussels, it was bull-at-a-gate stuff; the track director was greatly impressed by their competitiveness but intervened when things went too far, and the press at once split into two camps. The French-language papers wrote of *'near-savages'*, while the Flemish press lambasted the track officials for dishing out a few penalties. They complained of partisanship and unfair treatment of the *'Flandriens'*, as they were rather sneeringly called. They now had a label; before long they would wear it as a title of honour, though not without a fight. For the hostility they had aroused persisted for some time. For instance, on the final evening of the Brussels Six-Day race in 1913 actual fighting broke out. Riders, support teams, friends and supporters used their fists freely following mutual accusations as to who exactly had brought who down. For the whole commotion arose out of a number of falls, and it went on and on. Even after the lights were turned off, excited fans went on wrangling in the dark.

They had been scheduled to ride in Paris as well, but the management of the winter velodrome there heard such dreadful stories about *'those loutish Flemish cyclists'* that they decided *'not to accept any Flandriens at all, if only to avoid brawls and disturbances'*, according to chronicler Van Wijnendaele.

The First World War broke out, and even when it was over pro-Flemish sentiments were not, generally speaking, greatly esteemed in the higher French-speaking levels of Brussels society; they dared not ban the Flemish cyclists there, but in Paris they were still barred for a time as 'activists'. The war psychosis gradually faded, and in 1920 Mac Bolle and a couple of teams were able to take part in the famous six-Hour Race in Paris; though the French press went to town on the *'evil record of those Flemish bruisers'*. The three Flemish pairs took the first three places, however, and from then on the international road lay open before them. But once in America, and despite the successes they achieved there, they realised that sporting prowess was gradually being crowded out by show and spectacle. That was not so much their style; they became divided among themselves, personal conflicts arose and unity crumbled. At the same time the organisers thought there was still too much collaboration between them and often refused to accept more than one or two Flemish entries. In 1923, with track racing still in its heyday, the Flandriens were disbanded as a group. But their name was to outlive that relatively brief episode by many years.

Karel van Wijnendaele, a Fleming to the core, saw his Flandriens as the standard-bearers of a people struggling to emancipate itself and win equality of status with the French-speaking population. This is what he wrote on the subject: *'The Flandriens were more than sportsmen, for developments, events and circumstances were such that people began to regard them as having a great significance in the domain of the Flemish struggle, and in the end we had to accept this. The Flandriens, who carried the banner of victory*

Gerard Debaets (1899-1959): king of the cycle track, Flandrien and 'near-savage'.

Lucien Buysse (1893-1980), who won the 1926 Tour de France.

far beyond our borders, came in a sense to be our ambassadors, who showed people in foreign lands that we are not the inferior race that people in our own country would make us out: a race that has to make do with a dialect for want of a civilised tongue!'

Certainly, most of the riders did not race with these high-flown ideas of their mentor's in mind. They looked to the tracks to make their fortunes, but it was on the roads that they first made their name. Lucien Buysse, from a famous Flandrien family, won the Tour de France in 1926; the prize money was not that much, but he could demand and get 4,000 hard francs – then a fortune in itself – for riding in a first-class track race. The easy money to be made on the track did nothing to promote a serious approach to the sport or professional pride. Following in American footsteps there was too much show-business involved, and track racing soon, and for good, lost out to road racing. It was there, on the roads, that the legendary exploits took place, it was there that the fame of the Flandriens re-echoed once more, with the feats of Félicien Vervaecke, Sylveer Maes and many others; and especially in the Tour de France. The sheer hard work involved, the grinding slog on the Cols, the reports relayed to the people back home, all this had the home front in raptures. And in 1929 Maurits de Waele had actually won that same Tour de France, with Jef Demuysere in second place. Two names that became part of the growing legend surrounding the race of the Flandriens. And you know what patriarch Van Wijnendaele wrote of these and the other riders he so delighted in, almost as if they were his sons? *'Young riders, we adore you because you are beautiful, because you bear within you the power and fullness of life and can share it with all who come in contact with you. Share that power, yes, but also and above all share the forces for good that are in you. Be men, whole men, with ideas in your heads and marrow in your bones. Conduct yourselves in such a way that we can be proud of you, for you are the living, tangible image of our Race, of our people, of that tough, strong Flemish Race which "sought what was right, and won what it sought"!'*

Jef Demuysere (1907-1969) on the Tourmalet during the 1932 Tour de France.

The Flandriens as heralds of the battle for Flemish emancipation. Another romanticised image, of course, behind which reverberates the rhetoric of the time, the thirties, with that ecstatic note which drew other, greater nationalist movements into a march which led inexorably to war for God and Fatherland, and beside which the aspirations of our Flemish friend Van Wijnendaele went no further than a non-aggressive popular nationalism, preferably on two wheels.

The poor riders (rich, though, some of them) were probably not interested in all this. And it struck me, leafing back through the history books, that the 'Flandrien *avant la lettre*', Cyriel van Hauwaert, never got involved in all the to-do about the Flandriens. He was not there, or kept himself to himself, when Mac Bolle soared high and far with his Flandriens; this although he was the first Fleming to make a name for himself as a racing cyclist and the first to win both Milan-San Remo and Paris-Roubaix in the same year, 1908. Van Hauwaert went very much his own way; he later ended up in Brussels, living like a lord, a designer of cycles. A gentleman of standing, through his own efforts, who consequently saw no connection between his name and the Flemish Movement or anything concerned with it. A lost opportunity, really, for Cyriel van Hauwaert (Cyrille, rather, since he still spelt his first name the French way) actually came of good West Flemish stock, and could easily have become a more conscious pacemaker on the road to his people's emancipation. But he chose to head for Brussels, where he happily went on talking a bit of French – or even a whole lot.

Well, the burden of Flemishness loaded onto the Flandriens gradually diminished, particularly in the post-war period when Briek Schotte was the prototypical old-style cycling Flandrien. His slogging approach, his inelegant style, his distorted face, the whole navvy-like look of him – wasn't that why we called him the Last of the Flandriens? And for his results, too, for Briek was twice World Champion on the roads, and came second in the 1948 Tour de France behind Gino Bartali, the Italian legend, who in turn bore the weight of being the 'Catholic hope'. Briek Schotte then, with two inner tubes slung round his neck and water-bottles in his back pockets, was the typical Flandrien. And any Flemish cyclist who looked a bit uncouth, whose riding relied less on suppleness and more on brute strength, on pushing and stamping, would be labelled with the old Flandrien tag. For me Michel Pollentier was another such 'little Flandrien', a lightweight, but tough and powerful, bending low over the handlebars, and winning too, the Giro d'Italia, twice champion of Belgium, stage winner and yellow jersey in the Tour de France. The jersey looked rather grubby, it's true, when he was caught using dope up on the Alpe d'Huez, with that phial which contained someone else's urine under his arm. A dirty Flemish trick, that.

Any more Flandriens? Johan Museeuw, world champion in 1996, could have been one, with his background, his taciturn reserve, his determination to win. But a few years ago he got made over in the Italian style, polished up with sunglasses, hairpiece and multi-coloured attire. Rather over-modernised, the outfit at least. But where character and attitude are concerned, there's certainly still a Flandrien sleeping somewhere inside him.

Anyway, to sports fans from Brabant, Antwerp or Limburg the Flandriens were for a very long time simply the Flandersmen, the men from the two Flanders; we reckoned that if you came from East or West Flanders you were a Flandrien. The dividing line was the River Scheldt, and Flanders in its original sense, the old County of Flanders, lies on the other side of the Scheldt. They've been living there for centuries, the Flandersmen, the Flandriens if you're talking cyclists.

But I'll grant you this: Karel van Wijnendaele's Flandriens, they were a race apart.

JAN WAUTERS
Translated by Tanis Guest.

Jef Claerhout's *Le Flandrien* in Kanegem, a statue rendering homage to Briek Schotte (1919-).

‘Ah,

the comfort of a comparison’

The Poetry of Herman de Coninck

Herman de Coninck (1944-1997) was at the time of his death principal editor of the literary periodical *Nieuw Wereldtijdschrift*. As an essayist he wrote infectiously about poetry; but first and foremost he was, as he had been since his debut in 1969 with *Lithe Love* (De lenige liefde), the most popular poet in Flanders. The main reason for this success is that his poetry is so recognisable. De Coninck wrote about subjects close to home. And he did this in language of rare virtuosity which is at the same time accessible, which makes the reader think: I could do that too, if I knew how. And finally, he always took a balanced approach to his themes: humorous and playful, but without diminishing their underlying seriousness and tragic element.

The dominance of this playful tone, coupled with a typically adolescent love theme, seems to me to explain the public's continued preference for this first volume compared to his later work. Besides, the age-group to which this theme is calculated to appeal is precisely the one which still takes the most lively interest in poetry.

De Coninck's debut was in line with the atmosphere of New Realism which was coming to the fore in Flanders around 1970: a poetry grounded in the astonished observation of reality, expressed in simple, direct language. But right from the start he put his own stamp on it, as is evident from the way he formulated his approach in 1972: *'I write poetry because it is the one genre above all others in which by formal isolation one can give to a fragment of language a brilliance and intensity almost unknown in life, however close to real life the poem may be. It is that rare form of illusion that I am concerned with. I am a New Realist only in so far that I believe that one can make this illusion more subtle and more convincing by putting as much reality as possible into it. But however realistic a poem may seem, its intensity is always greater than that of real life, and in that sense it is also unreal.'*

This creed, in which the main concern of his poetry, for all its normality and comprehensibility, is for that subtle illusion, that poetic transformation, is also set down in a poem in which he confronts the miniature, imitation country of Madurodam (the poetic illusion) with the actual city of Amsterdam (reality):

just as one smiles:
'oh look, how real'
referring to, let's say, madurodam
– and never when referring to amsterdam –

I think that one should look on literary
realism in the same way, let it be
a likeness, certainly, but for God's sake
from time to time still let a woman
utter some shrill squeals of delight

The poems in *Lithe Love* bear witness to a great flexibility, a mental and stylistic suppleness, which can link such very dissimilar areas of experience as, for instance, nature and politics: *'water, sometimes it runs straight on / like an ideology (...)'*, or the experience of language and expression in language: *'in the word "armchair" I relax / as in an armchair'*.

De Coninck's sophisticated use of these and similar techniques, such as the play on set phrases, on literal and figurative meanings, makes this poetry seem spontaneous, fresh, almost improvised.

The second volume, *As Long as the Snow Lies* (Zolang er sneeuw ligt, 1975) has two parts. The first is called 'Oh look, how real', a title taken from the Madurodam poem quoted earlier. And this section is closest to the original volume: light-hearted observations, anecdotes, exercises in the playful and creative treatment of everyday things grown somewhat dull and dusty with familiarity. The techniques used are basically the same. A rhinoceros is described like this: *'He is as thick / as a thick neck'*; or, on the economy:

and again, zero economic growth must be
something like this: being on a motorway,
finding you've gone one kilometre too far,
and then having to drive another twenty
before you find an exit.

The volume's second part shifts the accent to a more personal lyric of feeling. Biographical circumstances probably have something to do with this: some years before, De Coninck had lost his wife in a tragic road accident. A good many of the poems deal with that fact or its consequences. But this never descends to biographical anecdotism. De Coninck's great technical mastery of his material enabled him to transform this drama in his personal life into objectivised images which the reader can fill in for himself. This increase in thematic depth, continued in subsequent volumes, automatically brought with it a reduction in the euphoric word-games. The humorous element is still there, but it becomes as it were calmer and more introverted, focused on dealing with feelings which in their raw state are so painful and unmanageable as to block all enterprise and initiative. Only by processing them can they again become the building-blocks of a flexible existence. And that is exactly what happens here. As one of the programmatic poems in a later volume puts it: *'The notion, so very useful in poetry, / that you can do things with emotions too.'*

Another way of formulating this change of direction is to say that the accent shifts from external to internal, from observable reality to one emotionally felt. Still better would be to say that the element of feeling, present from the beginning, now becomes more visible. Extratextual elements too, particularly the development of a neo-romantic youthful poetry in Flanders, focus attention more on this. No romantic nostalgia, though, in De Coninck; that is integrated into a plan for living that looks to the future:

and yet even the night is not
without hope, as long as the snow lies
it is never completely dark, no,
there's the light of a sort of faith
that it will never get utterly dark.
As long as there's snow, there is hope.

The volume *Sounding like an Oboe* (Met een klank van hobo, 1980) continued this movement towards acceptance of life and working with the emotions. The oboe (in Dutch, *'hobo'*) of the title is among the saddest-sounding of instruments; at the same time, with a play on the American word 'hobo', it is the *'tramp among instruments'*. It symbolises melancholy and homelessness in time and space. In these poems melancholy implies a tension between here and there, between now and then, in which both poles are equally important. The present gains in intensity because the past is still there, the absence of absolute happiness gives a deeper hue to the limited happiness which does exist:

Sadness is a photo from 20 years ago.
Family, still together, still in health,
is then. Surrounded by a frame of now.
The now it is that holds the past together.

The volume is constructed more or less as a series of love poems, describing the experience of love at different ages. It begins with the fresh eroticism of puberty, still *'full of dangers'* and ambiguous fears, and ends with the inexpressible tenderness surrounding a deathbed: *'he is not there now in as many ways / as once he was there'*

This chronological arrangement means that awareness of time becomes a central theme, and with that awareness of time the paradoxical sadness mentioned above. The poet's position in time is very hesitant, invariably ambiguous. The past is simultaneously remembered with nostalgia and kept at a distance. The losses inflicted by time are transmuted into gain. What time does with the past is compared to what it does with fruit: it makes preserves of them, a concentrate of summer. Or what it does with wine: intensifies the quality.

This paradoxality permeates the poet's whole experience of reality and feelings. Very many of these poems seem to be attempts at making the contradictions inseparable from life perceptible in language. It is as though he frames new definitions of love, happiness, grief, silence: *'Silence is the difference between saying nothing and having said it all already'*

Sometimes such paradoxical formulations are framed as aphoristic generalisations, sometimes they are embodied in brief stories, anecdotes: *'We walk, the two of us, through the autumn day. And in spring too I feel no different.'*

The contradictions do not disappear, but reach a wise and smiling reconciliation; no extreme, one-dimensional feelings here, quite the reverse: shadowy, ambiguous states of mind such as melancholy, tedium, pleasure and happiness too, but never in the form of delight or ecstasy. For happiness is, after all, *'knowing that it's something not for you. And being well content with that even so.'*

It is clear that De Coninck had gradually moved right away from neo-realism. The only thing in his later work that still recalls it is his concern to write comprehensible, reader-friendly poetry. With *Memory's Acres* (De hectaren van het geheugen, 1985) he went a step further, this time towards hardness and away from sentimentality.

There are four sections, with an opening poem, 'Genesis', as prologue. It is about Adam, ready and complete on the sixth day of Creation. From this starting position he sees the world, and it doesn't attract him much, all that silent hugeness: *'And then God said: now your turn. No, said Adam.'*

This sets the tone for the whole volume. It is not an easy tone to define. It has to do with being lost, with emptiness, awareness of time and death, a sense of being superfluous, of wandering in a disorganised confusion and longing for things to be clear. 'Mountains of Indifference' ('Bergen van onverschilligheid') is the title of the first, and longest, part. These are poems which draw most of their imagery from nature and the seasons, mainly in the densely wooded region of the Ardennes. Not the idyllic Ardennes of the tourist, but their desolation, their greyness, the indifference of everything there to the man among them. Nature here is both a mirror-image of the poet and the presence of that totally different Other that ignores the poet and his words, leading a life imperturbably its own.

There follows a series of emotion-based poems about his wife and daughter, everyday domestic life, which with their humorous sense of proportion and more anecdotal structure are the closest to his earlier work.

The third series, 'Broken Glass in the Sun' ('Glasscherven in de zon'), brings together poems on the death of his mother. These verses derive their force from the clash of tenderness and ruthless harshness, from a brutal kind of respect, which describes every last detail of the mother's disintegration so as to love what remains and be desolated when that too is gone:

Your skin translucent as a glass
that you have drunk to the last drop:
yourself. And I, not there alas

to let go of your hands, their fingers ten,
when you had got so far, so very far.
And to have held them tight, just before then.

The volume ends with 'On Foot across Lethe' ('Te voet over de Lethe'), poems inspired by Malcolm Lowry's *Under the Volcano* and Wolf Wondratschek's *Die Einsamkeit der Männer*. With these poems De Coninck bade a final farewell to the image that had pursued him since his debut with *Lithe Love*. That volume's light, playful eroticism of the imagination is now totally superseded by illusionless reality, tragedy and loneliness – the lone-liness of men with their pathetic bumbling. And the scornful superiority women feel for it. The first poem in this section ends like this:

For women have powerful sex-organs, high wounds,
mounts of Venus, caverns, creases
in which lost nights can never again be found.

and with them they play
like Mona Lisa with tourists and the moon with the sea,
breathtakingly, and with a touch of something like scorn.

These are the most pitiless poems De Coninck had yet written, shocking sometimes, devoid of illusions, about man in all his shabbiness, stripped bare, sucked dry, reduced to what he is: *'His prick shrivels. He hears his balls grating.'* In these poems De Coninck achieves a combination of tough-ness and clarity. The toughness necessary to write poetry about softness, doubt and yearning. The clarity that is essential in poems about the untidy moodiness of feelings.

In the later collections, *Singular* (Enkelvoud, 1991) and *Breast Stroke* (Schoolslag, 1994), a dual movement is perceptible: on the one hand towards poems whose inspiration is frankly autobiographical, about parents, children, marriage and love; on the other towards greater detachment and depersonalisation, in poems occasioned by photos and works of art and oth-ers which give greater prominence to the language itself. With hindsight this ambivalence was always there, but now it results in two quite distinct types of poetry. This is very noticeable in *Singular,* where the first series, 'The Plural of Happiness' ('Het meervoud van geluk') brings together almost bla-tantly sentimental verses about and for his children, while the poems in the second section, 'Without' ('Zonder'), could be termed exercises in self-less lyric, sometimes even formulated programmatically, as in the poem '44' which begins with the stanza: *'Without self, without subject. / Harp hung on willows. / Another instrument acquired.'*

At the end of the poem that other instrument which is to replace the harp turns out to be a rake, played like a violin with a saw for a bow: 'A Little Song'. But in this he is not entirely successful. For the strength and the lim-itation of Herman de Coninck's poetry lay in its personal voice, even if it sometimes sounds indirectly, through observations, comparisons, descrip-tions of scenes, photos or anecdotes.

After all, De Coninck's main stylistic weapon was always the startling comparison, explicit or implicit. His poetry is of a kind that makes connec-tions, which tries to put shattered reality back together again and in doing so offers comfort: not seeking to find a solution, but to make solitude more bearable by linking it to other solitudes. *Memory's Acres* already contained the following stanza:

Ah, the comfort of a comparison,
it almost helps. As soon as I hear the word 'like'
it all becomes less alone.

And the last poem in *Singular,* which deals with the search for concealment, ends like this:

So a comparison looks for
a poem for the night,
a man a woman,
a bookmark a fold.
Night claps the book shut.

This same division between biographical-anecdotal poems and exercises in detachment reappears in *Breast Stroke.* The first series, entitled 'The Spot' ('De plek'), contains verses on the indifferent vastness of nature and the quasi-superfluous presence within it of mankind: *'Life is lived between two sneers.'* Contrasting with this are the sections 'Mechelen' (De Coninck's birthplace), about crucial moments in the poet's life, and 'Pastorale', about his wife and children. Poems with a great deal of love, compassion and directly felt sentiment in them. They seem to be poems of intimate close-ness, akin in their playfulness to those of *Lithe Love.* But they were written with the wisdom of a fifty-year-old, they bask in the glow of autumnal plea-sure, of at once holding fast and letting go: *'I'm already busy remembering, but / it's still so much today, so gladly.'*

The whole volume thus becomes an exercise in detachment, in inertia, in presence. This paradoxical combination even comes to form the essence of De Coninck's poetry. The poem 'Poetry' ('Poëzie') says it plainly, and once again in the form of a comforting comparison: *'A picture needs a frame, / as happiness mortal fear.'*

HUGO BREMS
Translated by Tanis Guest.

Herman de Coninck's last collection, *Fingerprints* (Vingerafdrukken), was still in preparation when this yearbook went to press.

Herman de Coninck (1944-1997) (Photo by Klaas Koppe).

Five Poems by Herman de Coninck

Taarlo

We walk, the two of us, through the autumn day.
And in spring too I feel no different.
We walk through much brown tavern-brown of leaves
through much dark-red loss, *appellation controlée,*

that deepens in the cellar of the years.
We walk through the beiger-turning woods of Drente.
Hear the wind passing through the hennaed trees
sounding like an oboe, tramp among instruments.

33, and in the midst of the dark wood
of life. And with a sense of nowhere belonging,
at home in the woods and desolate at home.

Will we one day, maybe, ever?
The summer is past, the hay-making is over.
The here is nowhere, and the now is never.

From *Sounding like an Oboe* (Met een klank van hobo, 1980)
Translated by Tanis Guest.

Lithe Love (9)

your sweaters & your white & red
scarves & your stockings & your panties
(made with love, said the commercial)
& your bras (there's poetry in
such things, especially when *you* wear them) –
they're scattered around in this poem
the way they are in your room.

come on in, reader, make yourself
comfortable, don't trip over the
syntax & kicked-off shoes,
have a seat.

(meanwhile we kiss each other in this
sentence in brackets, that way
the reader won't see us.) what do you think of it,
this is a window to look at
reality, all that you see out there
exists, isn't it exactly
the way it is in a poem?

From *Lithe Love* (De lenige liefde, 1969)
Translated by James S Holmes (in 'Dremples', 7/8, Amsterdam

Envoi

If only she could see it, would see it. –
What is it that's still missing, God wondered, that sixth day.
Everything was too hard, Adam too, he'd had to do it
too fast. There should be less keen memory in it. And some smile.

Or was that the same thing? And what do you make it of?
Not of frivolity, but of knowing everything
and thinking it very bad, and not being put off.
And God invented compassion.

And after that two arms to put it in,
all kinds of things, coming, crying, being silly, superfluous.
Then He rested and thought: now what else do I need?

And then He made two eyes. –
So that she would see him as he died.
So that at last he'd be permitted to.

Memory's Acres (De hectaren van het geheugen, 1985)
Translated by Tanis Guest.

Birthday Verse

You never said anything. I always had to ask.
If you loved me. & you gave me a kiss.
If it was safe that first time,
& another kiss.
& a little later if I was doing it right
& a kiss, O.

You never said anything, always said it with your eyes.
Your eyes that stayed behind in your face
alone when I left you;
your eyes after crying:
you weren't there,
you looked at me like faraway places,
& I had to go there,

& once I had got that far,
the eyes that you used to say 'darling',
looking to see if it didn't change
on its way to me.

& when you lay by the road in the meadow,
O what all hadn't you broken,
your legs, your ribs, your eyes, me.
You never said anything, always said it with your eyes,
the way you lay there dying,
eyeing,

& your eyes that your son has in now,
that he uses to say: don't go –
you never said anything, he says it, & you look at me.

From *As Long as the Snow Lies* (Zolang er sneeuw ligt, 1975)
Translated by James S Holmes (in 'Poetry International', Rotterdam, 1983).

Yonder

I'm looking for a village.
And in it a house. And in that a
room, with a bed in, with a woman in.
And in that woman lips.

Outside the river broadens
to go farther, the silver-scaled,
fish-holding, boat-bearing,
sea-seeking, here-staying.

So a comparison looks for
a poem for the night,
a man a woman,
a bookmark a fold.
Night claps the book shut.

From *Singular* (Enkelvoud, 1991)
Translated by Tanis Guest.

order, within which there's room for chaos'

The Poetry of M. Vasalis

The poetic oeuvre of M. Vasalis (1909-) is admittedly modest in size (only around 100 poems in total, spread over three collections), but her poetry has nonetheless acquired a position all its own in Dutch-language literature of the twentieth century. It could even be argued that her poems were already classics when they appeared.

When she made her debut in 1936 with a number of verses in the journal *Groot Nederland*, there was general consensus among critics that here they were looking at a completely new and authentic talent. One of the most strikingly positive opinions came from Menno ter Braak, editor and figure-head of the influential journal *Forum* (1932-1936), which campaigned '*against the idolisation of form at the expense of human creativity*'. Vasalis' poems caused a '*poetic shock*' in Ter Braak because, as he put it in his own distinctive terminology, '*this poetry was something completely different from the murmuring of the innumerable epigonistic little volumes which slither gently down from the tops of the great glaciers*'.

When Vasalis' first collection *Parkland and Deserts* (Parken en woestijnen) appeared in December 1940, it caused something of a literary sensation, in spite of the extremely unfavourable political conditions of the time. Indeed, reactions were so enthusiastic that reprints followed each other in rapid tempo. The collection was also awarded the Van der Hoogt Prize in 1941, an important prize awarded by the Society for Dutch Literature as an encouragement to new literary talent. Within a year *Parkland and Deserts* had gone to its tenth impression, with a total print run extending to tens of thousands of copies – an unprecedented phenomenon in Dutch-language literature.

Above it all

The fascinating thing in all of this is that Vasalis remained above it all right from the very beginning. She could not easily be pigeonholed among others of her own generation – the poets of the 'Romantic Realism' school – because what intrigued her above all was the mystique of reality *in itself*. Within such an earthly metaphysical system, reality needs no romanticisation. This is perhaps expressed most strikingly in the poem 'The Idiot in the Bath' ('De idioot in het bad'; tr. James Brockway), in which Vasalis (who was a psychiatrist in daily life) created a spiritual X-ray, as it were:

His worried face grows handsome, blank, at ease,
his slender feet stand up like palest flowers,
his long and pallid legs, where aging lowers,
rise out of the green water like the trunks of trees.

In all this green he is as one unborn,
he does not yet know that some fruits are but rind,
he has not lost the wisdom of the body
and does not need the wisdom of the mind.

The penetrating directness of Vasalis' poetry also unintentionally caused a revolution in the world of literary criticism, in which the old dogmatic schisms simply no longer seemed important. Protestants, Catholics and Humanists alike had to abandon their own 'spiritual pigeonhole' in the face of Vasalis' unconditional surrender to the holiness of the everyday - *'reverence for the most ordinary things'* as she referred to it in 'Fanfare corps' ('Fanfare-corps'). In essence this ability of Vasalis' poetry to break down barriers always remained intact.

Although later – following the appearance of her second collection *The Phoenix* (De vogel Phoenix, 1947) – she did have to sustain an attack from the experimentalist Fifties' Movement, this attack was intended more to support the experimentalists' own manifesto and proved to have no effect whatsoever on general literary opinion. Later on, in a polemic essay, Rudy Kousbroek attempted to relegate Vasalis to the traditional gallery of a dusty past and, starting from that basis, posed the question of what standards the new poetry ought to meet. What follows is an extremely suggestive summary: *'That we no longer walk vaguely in parkland and deserts. That the flight of dreams is cast aside as unusable. That if it is necessary to fly, this flight takes place in reality. That the poet looks beyond the walls of his own attic. The heavenly verse in the earthly living room must make way for the very earthly verse in the very earthly world.'*

The paradox of this attack is that the poetry of Vasalis meets all these criteria. Vagueness has no place in her poetic idiom. The sound of crickets, for example, is portrayed in a very tangible, visually acute manner: *'the crickets' hoarse and creaking voices, / so many billion tiny brakes / scraping the night'.* And the dream, too – the number one trade mark of the romantic – functions in the poetry of Vasalis not as an escape route, but as a complex, shocking reality. The opening lines of the poem 'Time' ('Tijd'), for example, have since become a classic: *'I dreamed that I was living slowly, / slower than the oldest stone. / It was fearful, around me everything / I had known as still, shot up and shook.'* This is no romantic vision, but a dreamed, hallucinatory reality.

The collection *Vistas and Visages* (Vergezichten en gezichten, 1954) once again emphasised that Vasalis is the author of *'the very earthly verse in the very earthly world'.* She does, however, entirely in accordance with the advice of Rilke, try to avoid being misled by the appearance of things. She concentrates on the deeper layers, where other laws apply: *'Tracks of birds' feet in the snow, / an undertone of laughter in a voice. / Strange, that life should be coming back like this, / backwards, / in shadows, echoes, faintest traces.'*

In the ensuing years the majority of experimentalists from the Fifties' Movement also came to realise that there was no doubting the status, classical and vital in equal measure, of this poetry.

The breath of mystery

The poem 'Time' is an outstanding example of Vasalis' method of working: via a dream we are immediately placed in a different reality, where laws apply which we are normally unable to observe. It also becomes clear that Vasalis' fascination with time has everything to do with the relationship between dream and reality. Vasalis is not so concerned with the time-bound notion of mortality, but more with the question of what effect time has on our powers of observation.

Within our usual hierarchical order, in which stones are dead and the human eye is incapable of observing the growth of trees as *movement*, we lose sight of the cosmic turbulence which is constantly swirling around us. In the reality of the dream this safe perspective is abandoned, to make way for an inverted hierarchy: ' *I dreamed that I was living slowly, / slower than the oldest stone.*' This tilted perspective results in a totally different perception of reality, in which life and death alternate in a gigantic, accelerated tempo. The 'I'-figure, who is the only observer placed outside this dizzying scenario, only now sees '*The eloquence, the despairing will in the gestures of the very things*'. The effect of this personifying phraseology is that a sort of 'solidarity' arises between the 'I'-figure and the things, which after all are ultimately embroiled in the same '*breathless, (...) bitter fight*'.

The end of the poem implies that the dream may be at an end, but not the understanding which dawned within it: '*How am I ever to forget?*' For Vasalis, therefore, the dream does not function as a romantic escape mechanism; on the contrary, it results in an intensification of reality. The revelational nature of the dream has given things an inner dimension, as it were, so that the observer can no longer experience spring, for example, as a period of 'gentle dreaming' or 'silent blossoming'; in the vision of the world as corrected by the dream, we are henceforth confronted with '*vehement growth, / fine and passionate beginning, / starting up out of deep slumber, / dancing off without a thought.*'

In a letter to the writer Gerard Reve, Vasalis once declared her longing '*to hear (or feel) mystery breathing*'; this is in fact a *mystical* longing in which the boundaries between subject and object become blurred and there is no longer any past or future. The reverse side of this is a feeling of fragmentation. Both elements feature prominently in the poem 'The Sea Dike' ('Afsluitdijk'). The 'I'-figure, during a night-time bus journey over the long dike – through the sea – which joins the province of Friesland with the province of North Holland, is suddenly confronted with a double reality:

Then dreamily there drifts into my ken
The ghost of this bus, transparent glass
Riveted to ours, now clear, and then again
Half drowned in the misty sea. The grass
Cuts straight through the sailors. (...)

Briefly, a perspective is opened up of a reality in which land and water, spirit and substance, time and space coincide. The I-figure, too, is at once both subject and object: '(...) *Then I see pass / Myself as well. (...) / (...) a mermaid distressed.*'

Here, then, we are again dealing with an interaction between dream and reality, though now in the reverse direction, in which the instantaneous nature of time is extended: '*There is to this journey, I feel somehow, / Neither start nor finish, only at best / This strangely split unending Now.*' Vasalis expresses herself in similar terms in *The Phoenix*, in which she says: '*There was no clock, no time, only continuance.*'

Personal involvement

In 1935 the cultural historian Johan Huizinga published his study *In the Shadows of Tomorrow* (*In de schaduwen van morgen*), in which he presents a sombre analysis of the crisis in which West-European culture has landed. In his well-known opening passage he states: '*We live in a possessed world. And we know it. No-one would be surprised if the madness were suddenly to break out into a frenzy from which this poor European humanity would emerge diminished and bewildered, the motors still running and the flags still fluttering, but the spirit broken.*'

It is no surprise that the poet who has experienced this frenzy at first hand will leave traces of this in her work. Moreover, it is known that during the Second World War Vasalis used her profession as a psychiatrist to protect a number of Jews from deportation. And yet the word 'war' appears only once in *The Phoenix*, and even then it is in the context of a dream: '*During the war I dreamed that there was war.*' ('Phoenix I')

It is no coincidence that this poem is placed at the start of the collection. The Phoenix motif, the dying bird which arises in flames from its own ashes and thus becomes the symbol of vitality and creativity, is also a symbol of approval for the poet's work: '*And when I looked down at my own two hands, / I saw the finger that he clutched was blue / and while the bird was burning wrote a verse (...) / Then he looked round, as giving me his blessing.*' In the second Phoenix poem, Vasalis adds an extremely specific, personal dimension to this ancient myth. The motif of the burning bird turns out to be linked to the death in 1943 of her own small son, to whom the collection is also dedicated: '*Oh little phoenix, who possessed me for too short a time*'. This makes the following exhortation all the more poignant: '*Take your time, do not scream with pain, oh hand. / Write on till every finger is consumed.*'

For Vasalis, then, the point of writing lies primarily in a personal involvement with one's own fate. It is this, and only this, that makes possible a meaningful relationship with the outside world. In one of her talks Vasalis put it this way: '*The outside world is also inside us. For the most part, we are unknown, and certainly uncomprehended, even to ourselves. No theories, no introspection, no loving mothers can help this. We are constantly active, however, weaving in our innermost selves highly precise, transparent webs from the thinnest, toughest material, with which we create order and briefly tame the chaos over and over again, and in which we capture that which at such a moment can perhaps be called "meaning". An artist must also feel at home in regions unknown to him, whatever he may find there, whether he likes it or not, even if he is forced to accept that he doesn't feel at home there (...). In the moments of his creativity he is both his own Delphi and the mortal soul who visits the grotto.*'

It is this total honesty which makes the poetic landscape created by Vasalis so irresistible. In all the attempts to create enclaves of order *within* the poetry, there is still room for doubt and chaos. For example, the I-figure, confronted with stars, which exist '*guiltless and free*' (!) within their '*proud laws*', declares: '*I do not know what my true laws may be, / I seek a far, inhuman, certain sign / from out of this wilderness of pain.*' There is also doubt about the poet's own poetic powers: '*How strong reality, how weak / my instrument.*'

We can therefore conclude that in the second collection the poet has turned inwards to some extent. As a result, many of these poems have something of a *monologue intérieur*, in which the 'I'-figure subjects herself to a critical evaluation of her position as a person and as a poet. Vasalis is only too aware that this is a risky undertaking, and in the poem 'Cannes' causes the 'I'-figure to attain a sudden insight into '*the only true sin*': '*that I, scarce touched by what's most marvellous, / (...) and barely harmed by the most harmful things / have moved far distant from reality.*'

Poetic creation and reality

The collection *Vistas and Visages* can be seen as an attempt to restore the inspired contact with reality: '*for the first time I feel in all its fullness / in my own person what completeness is: an order, within which there's room for chaos.*' The vistas constantly derive their visionary power from the fact that they are embedded in day-to-day reality: the skeleton of a leaf, a waterside, an old woman. It is precisely these uncompromising realities which shape a person experiencing pain, separation and isolation: '*So many varieties of pain – / I'll name them not. / Just one: the letting go, the parting; / and not the severing but the state / of being severed chills the heart.*'

A poem like the one above makes clear that the attraction of Vasalis' poetry does not lie in her spectacular use of language, but in its totally pure composition. It is after all exceptionally difficult to express such basic emotions without ever resorting to cliché or rhetoric. Another Dutch poet, J.C. Bloem, – like Vasalis the creator of a small but unchallenged oeuvre – once referred to 'purity' as the only property which he wished to claim for his poetry. And he added immediately: '*This is by no means false modesty, because what I was seeking to achieve is no small thing. By purity I mean something which could perhaps also be termed personality (...): expressing a few essential things from life in a way that could be only mine, and no-one else's.*'

In his quest for purity, the poet sees himself confronted with a specific dilemma. Vasalis (in one of her rare reflections) once defined this dilemma as follows: '*Between conception and birth, the word loses so many of its potential forms, it becomes transformed from a heraldic bird into the familiar "domestic fowl", and only seldom do we see in the short, busy movements and in its staring, bright eye the flight, the gaze which was after all, so we thought, the intention. In this respect the poet lives his whole life between the devil and the deep blue sea, between the danger of stuttering immature, unrecognisable words or of expressing things too clearly in a language which has become an out and out jargon. In both cases his verse dies: either as an abortion or as a domestic fowl.*'

It is only from this tension that a poetry can arise in which the words – as the poet Martinus Nijhoff (see *The Low Countries* 1996-97: 213-219) put it

– '*sing themselves free from their meanings*'. There is yet another tension, however, which is even more unavoidable than the former, but much less palpable: the relationship between poetic creation and reality. Social changes can force a poet to re-evaluate his own position and poetics. Nijhoff experienced this in the 1930s, when he characterised the general crisis as a definitive bankruptcy of ideals. Nijhoff then went on to reappraise his autonomist poetics, in which the poem above all represented an *immanent* world of language. '*Poetry has to work for the future, in other words imagine that that future already exists and create quarters for the human soul there, as it were*', said Nijhoff. And thus, inspired by Huizinga's *In the Shadows of Tomorrow*, Nijhoff wrote his splendid sonnet cycle *Before Daybreak* (Voor dag en dauw, 1936).

Vasalis experienced something similar in the years following the Second World War, but her response to the spiritual crisis was totally different. When she was awarded the P.C. Hooft Prize (the Dutch State Prize for Literature) in 1982, she looked back on this period in her acceptance speech: '*I cannot possibly say that the 1940-45 War passed us, the elderly, by. But for us that War was an exceptional circumstance: we had already lived an entire life which still had much in common with that of the previous generation. We thought that, following that storm, we would be able to continue living much as before, though better, with greater insight. But what we gradually came to realise was that that storm had become a permanent climate, a climate in which we did not belong.*'

For Vasalis this resulted in a new dilemma: 'shouting' or 'remaining silent'. The former strategy would boil down to the creation of a 'domestic embryo', something which she observed in much experimental poetry after the Second World War and which in her view was even worse than the 'domestic fowl'. As a *poet* she decided to adopt a position of silence, though the term 'powerlessness' to escape from the impasse is perhaps a better description. Because the post-war climate brought about a mental sea-change in Vasalis. '*What happened to me after the War*', she said, '*comes down to the following: my own faith, my own happiness or unhappiness, my views, opinions, knowledge and commentary, were all rigorously put into perspective. I had a sense of futility, of my inability to apply that increase in scale (...). I was constantly forced to the conclusion that my commentary was completely superfluous and that there was no point in striking my match alongside the raging fire*'.

One can of course regret the poetic silence of Vasalis, and many readers and critics have done just that. And yet one can feel nothing but respect for the radical honesty of her position. A poet after all needs sustenance, something for which I can still find no better word than 'inspiration'. If this inspiring force is no longer active, then only artificiality remains. Vasalis was not willing to make this concession – in which she would have become an epigone of herself – and that does her credit. Her small oeuvre is a sparkling witness to the *condition humaine*: '*an order, within which there's room for chaos*'.

ANNEKE REITSMA
Translated by Julian Ross.

Time

Sometimes, silent, gazing through the open pane,
your beauty overwhelms me like despair,
despair no consolation can extinguish,
not by word, not by a kiss,
despair as big as me, as old, as vain.

That I can see you but cannot be you,
cut off from you, by my own eyes, my sight,
that you can sit there, created so separate,
it hurts as giving birth will do.

When you sit silent, gazing through the pane,
sometimes the wind will rise and stir your hair,
the fringe along your forehead, where it lies
like reed along the edges of a tarn.
At times a cloud comes sailing through the air,
I see the shadows move across your eyes.

And then it is as though you'll always be
but I may only live beside you for a while,
exiled by my temporality.
And then you turn your head, I see your smile.

From *Vistas and Visages* (Vergezichten en gezichten, 1954)
Translated by James Brockway in consultation with the poet.

I dreamed that I was living slowly,
slower than the oldest stone.
It was fearful, around me everything
I had known as still, shot up and shook.
I saw the urge with which the trees,
singing with hoarse and halting sound,
were writhing upward, out of the ground;
the seasons flying, changing hue
and fading fast as rainbows do…
I saw the tremor of the sea,
its welling up, its quick retreat,
like the swallowing of a giant throat.
And night and day, of brief duration,
flare and die, a flickering conflagration.
– The eloquence, the despairing will
in the gestures of the very things
that used to look so rigid, still,
their breathless, their bitter fight…
How could I not have known, not seen
it all before in earlier days?
How am I ever to forget?

From *Parkland and Deserts* (Parken en woestijnen, 1940)
Translated by James Brockway in consultation with the poet.

If there is music for it, I want to hear it:
I want music for the old, their strength reprieved,
who are ploughed with furrows deep and sheer,
and who don't believe. Who still know lust and pain.
Who loved, possessed, and lost again.
And if there is wisdom that is not fatigue,
clarity that is not death, decline,
that I want to see, that I want to hear.
If not, let foolishness and clouded thought be mine.

From *Vistas and Visages* (Vergezichten en gezichten, 1954)
Translated by James Brockway in consultation with the poet.

A portrait of M. Vasalis by
Paul Citroen (1960)
(Collection Letterkundig
Museum, The Hague).

The Sea Dike

The bus rides like a room across the night.
The road is straight, the dike is without end.
At left the sea, tamed but recalcitrant.
A little moon distils a delicate light.

In front of me the young, close-shaven necks
Of a couple of sailor boys. They do their best
To stifle yawns, they stretch their arms and legs,
And on each other's shoulders drop to rest.

Then dreamily there drifts into my ken
The ghost of this bus, transparent glass
Riveted to ours, now clear, and then again
Half drowned in the misty sea. The grass
Cuts straight through the sailors. Then I see pass
Myself as well. Only my face
Is drifting on top of the surface swell
And moves its mouth as if it would tell
A story and could not, a mermaid distressed.
There is to this journey, I feel somehow,
Neither start nor finish, only at best
This strangely split unending Now.

From *Parkland and Deserts* (Parken en woestijnen, 1940)
Translated by A.J. Barnouw.

Sotto Voce

So many varieties of pain –
I'll name them not.
Just one: the letting go, the parting;
and not the severing but the state
of being severed chills the heart.

Lovely still, the skeleton of a leaf,
light as a feather on the soil,
its only virtue now itself.
But between the arteries of grief
no joy left now to grant relief:
the meshes of your absence, framed
and held together now by pain,
grow ever wider still with time.

So poor, and for being poor, ashamed.

From *Vistas and Visages* (Vergezichten en gezichten, 1954)
Translated by James Brockway in consultation with the poet.

Phoenix II

This evening, when on a quiet visit,
where words, like bees, had formed a glistening
swarm,
nostalgia, – a bird out of a grassy thicket,
that had concealed him, kept him safe from harm
–

shot up, perpendicular, to the sky
with a cry I thought that everyone must hear.
And then I recognised who had flown out of me,
who, for his lofty nest, had sought my fire.

Oh little phoenix, who possessed me for too short
a time, I see the fires that are his eyes,
I feel the pressure on this hand where he has sat,
I hear the music of his wings as up he flies…

Take your time, do not scream with pain, oh hand.
Write on till every finger is consumed.

From *The Phoenix* (De vogel Phoenix, 1947)
Translated by James Brockway in consultation with the poet.

October

Tender, young, as though it were the eve
of spring, but lighter still now the fruit has gone,
with thinnest mist between the yellow leaves,
quietly autumn settles in.

I simply feel that, like a child,
I love. Something young, something old?
End or beginning? Something so dear,
so distant from all strife –
not as if the end of life,
but the spring of death were drawing near.

Naked the trunks, the crowns blown bare,
and this beset by silence, mist.

From *The Phoenix* (De vogel Phoenix, 1947)
Translated by James Brockway in consultation with the poet.

aintings

with an Inner Dislocation

Magic Realism in the Netherlands

**The aura
surrounding
Magic Realism**

The name of an art movement can be deceptive. It may be derived from a single work or an anecdote or it may only apply to a short period, and the artists thus lumped together may not regard it as a useful label. Carel Willink, one of the leading figures in Dutch Magic Realism, thought that 'Fantastic Realism' better described his work, and others liked the term 'Neo-Realism'. These alternatives prefer other adjectives to 'magic', so that they immediately sound less weighty. The word 'magic' suggests conjuring and associates the paintings with adroit tricks or belief in supernatural forces. To avoid this undesirable or incorrect connotation, the term 'mysterious' could be used to indicate the atmosphere emanating from these works.

In any case the point is to distinguish between 'ordinary' realism and Magic Realism, which differs from the former in combining elements that have nothing to do with each other but nonetheless form an entity in the painting. There are countless styles of painting that are more or less realistic. We shall not get involved in art-historical discussions as to the correct terminology, in which great importance is attached to the careful use of such terms as figurative, naturalistic, realistic and true to life. In defining Magic Realism, however, it is useful to make a broad distinction.

The many experiments at the beginning of this century, from Cubism and Futurism to Expressionism and Dadaism, led to increasingly abstract art. In the mid-twenties, however, many painters abandoned the purely abstract and began including figurative elements in their work once more. In the case of some artists this reassessment produced a specific form of realism which is often termed 'Magic Realism'. This term was first used in 1925 by the German art critic Franz Roh to characterise the work of several young painters who reacted against Expressionism by depicting their subjects with great precision and in a way that was almost true to life.

The Magic Realists opted for realistic depiction, but that did not mean that their subjects were also strictly realistic. As we shall see, they gave an unusual twist to their representation of reality. However, Dutch painters such as Willink and Koch never turned reality upside down in the manner of Surrealism, a movement which became prominent mainly in France (and in Belgium), but which had no significant following in the Netherlands.

Surrealism played with the level of reality in the depiction much more explicitly. It is usually obvious at first glance that we are not dealing with a 'real' event. In paintings described as Magic Realism, on the other hand, what is depicted is possible, but not very likely. Another difference is that the Magic Realists were much more inclined to see painting as a goal in itself; in this sense their work is technically more sophisticated than that of most Surrealists. It may be that this subtlety plays a role in the fluctuations in the public's appreciation of this art. In this century, after all, 'true art' is supposed to have an obvious shock effect, and a high level of technical skill may be thought of as a disqualification.

The choice of a realistic style of painting was often viewed in a political light even while Magic Realism was still in its heyday. This was because both Fascism and Communism favoured social realism. For many, particularly after the Liberation, this was reason enough to condemn or at least distrust Magic Realism; other realistic movements were also 'suspect'. This remained the situation for many years. During the Cold War realism in painting was again associated with political ideology. Appreciation of abstract art inevitably went with left-wing, progressive attitudes, and a taste for realism was seen as reflecting right-wing or conservative views.

Comparable but very different

This rather one-sided view of the matter becomes less tenable when we look at the work of the various Dutch artists grouped together as Magic Realists. Starting points for a different approach can be found in their development as individual painters. While they knew each other, they certainly never formed a movement or even a group. The last occasion on which the work of eight artists was brought together under the label of Magic Realism was in 1992 at the Gemeentemuseum in Arnhem. Between 1950 and 1970 two successive directors of this museum laid the basis of a substantial collection, buying work by Schuhmacher, Hynckes and Ket as well as Willink and Koch. These five artists are generally regarded as Magic Realists, but the differences between them are sometimes greater than the similarities.

Although this group is rather arbitrarily put together, it is interesting to consider the work of some of them to see what lies behind their objectionable realism and what emotions it evokes today. For these magic masters are far from forgotten, though they are all now dead. In 1995 a retrospective of the paintings of Pyke Koch was held at the Museum Boymans-van Beuningen in Rotterdam, which itself owns a number of his finest works.

The early Willink

The best known Magic Realist is undoubtedly Carel Willink. To find out what preceded the realistic and at the same time mysterious paintings for which he is celebrated, we must follow his development from the beginning. On the advice of his parents the young Carel Willink began studying architecture, but soon realised that he was more interested in painting. As a schoolboy he had gone to many museums with his father, who also taught him how to paint. While he was still an architecture student, the rather traditional style which he had learnt soon gave way to a more progressive approach. Although he decided in 1919 that he wanted to be a painter, it was his father who decided where he was to study: Berlin. During his Berlin years, from 1920 to 1923, Willink did not confine himself to painting. He followed developments in art closely but was also very interested in film.

All his impressions were immediately incorporated in his paintings. His sources during this period are sometimes immediately obvious, as in two collages which are closely related to the work of the German collage artist Kurt Schwitters. Willink is clearly searching for a style of his own, and he tries out the styles of painters he admires, particularly Paul Klee but also Georg Grosz and the Dadaist John Heartfield. Willink also saw the 'Pittura Metafisica' of the Italian Giorgio de Chirico in the Nationalgalerie in Berlin, but this influence only became important later on.

Willink tried out the various styles quite conscientiously and was evidently less concerned with the underlying theories than with the fact that they were all modern and new. Like his contemporaries he reacted against what was 'bourgeois', and thus perhaps against his own background. Berlin was a valuable experience for him, and he became more and more persuaded that the way to complete freedom was through pure abstraction. Not only what he saw around him, but much of his own work in 1922 and 1923 was almost entirely abstract.

Return to recognisability

In 1924 he went back to Amsterdam, where he was pleased to find that he soon attracted attention as an 'innovative' artist. He now became interested in developments in Paris, as well as in the art world in the Netherlands, and he followed them through exhibitions and magazines. In Paris purely abstract painting, which there much more clearly than in Berlin followed from Cubism, had for years been dominant. But at the time when Willink

Carel Willink,
Constructivist Composition.
1923. Canvas,
144 x 143 cm. Museum
Princessenhof, Leeuwarden.

Carel Willink, *Ariadne of Bolivia*. 1926. Canvas, 168.5 x 99 cm. Gemeentemuseum, Arnhem.

returned to Amsterdam and began to take an interest in events in the French capital the importance of abstraction was sharply declining. It continued to exist, of course, as a stylistic device, but it was no longer the automatic choice, and recognisable elements once more got a place in painting.

Willink's response to this was not immediately to abandon the Futurist and Constructivist principles which then played a role in his work. But his paintings from this period show that he too began to include figurative elements. In the paintings with abstract, geometrical forms more human figures gradually appear, though they look very unnatural because they too consist of cylinder-like shapes. Willink's return to realism thus begins with the inclusion in the composition of figurative and sometimes narrative elements, which have little or no relation to their abstract context. In her book on Willink's early painting Marja Bosma says that this phase was of

Carel Willink,
The Marabous. 1962.
Canvas, 97 x 102 cm.
Gemeentemuseum,
Arnhem.

great significance for his later work. Willink discovered, she says, that by
bringing in stylistically foreign elements you could produce bizarre compositions with a suggestion of an underlying narrative meaning. And this idea
developed into the basic principle of Willink's work. This thesis does indeed
seem convincing when we look at his later paintings, which often present an
unusual conjunction of elements.

That the ideals of abstract art were not sacred to Willink is also shown by
his use of photographs and even picture postcards as 'models' for his work.
Such an approach – drawing inspiration from trivial reality – was of course
far removed from the lofty ideals of more principled artists. In his search for
a style of his own Willink was evidently inclined to experiment with various ways of working and was not distracted by possible objections. With
hindsight it seems as if he was trying different methods of portraying 'reality', both literally and figuratively, and in ways ranging from the very con-
trived to the intuitive. Thus between 1925 and 1926 he produced both paintings based on the image on a picture postcard and works with surrealistic
overtones.

Here again his relation to the work of the Italian painter De Chirico comes
into the picture. Bosma argues plausibly that there is an affinity between
Willink's work and that of De Chirico. If we look at De Chirico's paintings
from between 1910 and 1920, with which Willink was familiar, we see a
collection of objects arranged in an unconventional way; objects such as
sculptures, parts of buildings, drawing instruments and bunches of fruit. The
spaces in which these elements are found are always deserted; there is no

trace of a human presence. This gives the paintings a still, but also slightly oppressive aura. The bringing together of heterogenous elements in one painting is also characteristic of Willink's work. Both artists combined the exalted – classical arcades and busts of scholars – with the ordinary or everyday. It is as if in De Chirico Willink not only recognised ideas of form that appealed to him but also saw correspondences in atmosphere and intensity.

In the autumn of 1926 Willink left for Paris, where he worked as a pupil in the studio of the painter Henri Le Fauconnier. Wim Schuhmacher, one of the Magical Realists considered below, was also working there at the time. The choice of this studio shows that what Willink was looking for in Paris was not the latest trends in painting but an opportunity to consolidate and deepen the knowledge he had already acquired. At Le Fauconnier's there was traditional drawing from a model and great attention was paid to the classical art of painting. As a result there was a greater emphasis than in the past on the study of painting techniques. De Chirico may again have been the inspiration for this more craftsmanlike approach, because after his metaphysical paintings he too switched to studying the masters of the Italian Renaissance and began making his own paint. In retrospect Willink's period in Paris marks the less than polished transition from modern art to more classical painting. For the artist himself this was not a sharp break; for him what has been called his 'retour à l'ordre' was a natural step in his development.

In the course of 1931, after a period of wide-ranging study, Willink achieved the style of his own for which he had been so diligently searching – a personal synthesis of the many influences through which he had worked his way. From the development he went through we can deduce that via abstract art he again arrived at figurative art. There is no question of any direct relationship with the realists of the nineteenth century: it was a new vision of reality which he shared with his contemporaries. Some critics saw this return to figurative art as a relapse into old norms and values. But in fact it was a forward movement. Thus the achievements of abstract art, such as the discovery of the separate strengths of form and colour, would remain in place. Much more importantly, however, the way in which artists depicted the reality around them changed. In nineteenth-century painting a 'view of reality' was presented on the basis of a positive, enquiring attitude. After the horrors of the First World War this idealistic mentality changed: faith in progress was shaken and the world came to be seen from a less clear-cut point of view. The modern painters could simply get no further with an outdated view of 'reality' and they sought out new ways.

If we look at Willink's mature paintings we can see at once that what he depicts is not taken from life. Instead, he constructs a realistic situation from separate fragments. An exotic animal in a European landscape, a naked lady running across a street or a present-day scholar in the ruins of a Greek temple. Yet because of the chilling perfection with which it is painted we almost believe it is real. Because of a louring sky or the heavy shadows on a deserted square we have the feeling that at any moment something may happen. We are briefly under the spell of the convincing *mise en scène*, the minutely finished details giving us something to go by, but then everything turns out to be an illusion. Only the painter has a grip on the situation: he has us in his

Between appearance, truth and enchantment

power and transports us to a reality stage-managed by him, a world in which the unities of time and place are ignored, so that there are no obstacles to creating encounters which are possible in theory but never happen in practice.

The remarkable world of Pyke Koch

Pyke Koch seems to have been even less interested than Willink in presenting a traditional view of reality. Koch was a self-taught artist who gave up his law studies in 1927 in order to paint. He did so very single-mindedly, although he only produced 85 paintings over 55 years. This limited output had to do with his labour-intensive painting technique, but above all with his views on art and its presentation. For Koch art was an intensely serious business, and he was extremely precise in working out his ideas on the canvas and in the arrangement of exhibitions. In comparison with artists like Willink, who learned to shape their own reality through studying existing art, the self-taught Koch was much freer in his attitude towards the depiction of reality. He had models and sources of inspiration in art, such as the Renaissance artist Piero della Francesca, but the historical development of styles and the theories that went with them were of no interest to him. This probably explains why his work is so distinctive and shows so few influences. Another characteristic, according to the art historian Carel Blotkamp, is that the paintings seem to show great sureness of touch despite being the result of a lengthy working process. In his book on Koch he remarks that however many hesitations and doubts had to be overcome during this process, in the end the paintings seem extraordinarily lucid and well thought out.

The origins of his subjects are diverse, writes Blotkamp. They sometimes derive from childhood memories, later events or dreams and sometimes from existing images, such as photographs and films. It is never a question of a literal 'translation': the different elements are joined and transformed before being given their place in a painting. In the course of his career Koch developed his own visual vocabulary with a highly symbolic character. Often the viewer is transported into a situation which seems to be taking place in a dream but is at the same time so realistically depicted that it rivals actual reality. In almost all his work there is a sensual, expectant atmosphere. The mysterious and sometimes disturbing details mean that it is not easy to decipher the paintings, and the protagonists Koch presents are hard to fathom.

Majestic portraits

A striking feature of Koch's oeuvre is the sometimes more than life-size female figures. *The Shooting Gallery* is an example, as is *Bertha of Antwerp* and the much later *Women in the Street*. Both the frontal pose and the direct gaze of the women give the works intense expressive power. A viewer who stands right in front of the painting literally feels himself to be in the vicinity of the figure and thus becomes involved in what is depicted. While Willink's figures are always well dressed and look elegant, almost chic, Koch's figures – especially in his early work – are unadorned and confrontational in their plain robustness. Indeed, he deals with a completely different side of society, just like German films of the twenties, which made a deep impression on him. The actress Asta Nielsen, who played leading roles in some of those films, was a source of inspiration when he was painting fantasy portraits such as *Bertha of Antwerp*. When these paintings were first

Pyke Koch, *The Shooting Gallery*. 1931. Canvas, 170 x 130 cm. Museum Boymans-van Beuningen, Rotterdam.

exhibited they caused a considerable stir – to the astonishment of the artist, who did not understand how the women could be seen as depraved creatures when he thought their kindliness was as plain as a pikestaff. Apparently these figures could not radiate charm because they did not have aesthetic and innocent, not to say virgin, faces: this was how he cynically described the hypocritical attitude of the public.

In contrast to a number of other painters, Koch accepted the term 'Magic Realism', which was introduced to the Netherlands in the early thirties. Although he did not write much about his work, he did give an elegant and clear description of Magic Realism. It was included in the book *Contemporary Artists* and reads as follows: *'The Surrealists created situations which are physically impossible; Magic Realism confronts us with situations that are possible, even commonplace, but contain an element of improbability, or are improbable tout court. Magic Realism exists by the grace of ambiguity, which is the source of a fascination on an entirely*

Pyke Koch, *Women in the Street*. 1962-1964. Canvas, 114.5 x 150 cm. Gemeentemuseum, Arnhem.

different level than that of beauty (or morality). It is brought about by the introduction of unobtrusive contradictory elements. Whereas the representations used by Surrealism are separated from reality as if by the stroke of an axe, the same is achieved in Magic Realism as if by a hardly perceptible, cautiously executed cut with a razor blade, leaving reality intact on the outside, but with an inner dislocation'.

As is again clear from this description, the Magic Realists attached great importance to painting the subject so perfectly that the 'inner dislocation' only becomes apparent later on. Koch and Willink both believed that in their day the technique of painting was being neglected and they investigated – each in his own way – old methods to find out how the physical qualities of objects were imitated in paint. They relied heavily on a book by Max Doerner, *Malmaterial und seine Verwendung im Bilde*, which described the methods of the Old Masters. The paintings of Hynckes, Ket and Schuhmacher also show a prodigious mastery of technique, apparent above all in the painting of objects such as a glass bottle or the coat of an animal. Their models in this craftsmanlike approach to art were the Dutch and Flemish Primitives, the painters of the Italian Renaissance already mentioned and the Dutch masters of the seventeenth century.

The light on things

Like Willink, the last three Magic Realists to be considered here were influenced by the great art movements of the beginning of the twentieth century, such as Cubism. This can be seen in the structure of the composition, which often consists of contrasting and sometimes distorted motifs, and in the choice of subject. In particular the still life is extremely popular, with traditional elements such as flowers and fruits, bottles and glasses and dead animals. As described above, the artists revelled in depicting the various materials on canvas.

In the early thirties, at about the time that Carel Willink was arriving at a synthesis of different styles, the Belgian-born Raoul Hynckes attracted attention with his still lifes. From as early as 1923 he had taken part in the group exhibitions by the Hollandse Kunstenaarskring at the Stedelijk Museum in Amsterdam, but he was then still working in an impressionist style. An exhibition at the same museum by artists such as Braque, Picasso, Metzinger and Severini had such an effect on him that he changed his style radically. The emphasis was now on 'fine painting', with careful attention paid to light effects. It is sometimes said that a ghostly light always shines in Hynckes' paintings, the effect of which is of course intensified by the somewhat macabre objects they present. Human skulls and dead animals do not exactly make the work cheerful, and the dark colours do not help either.

Pyke Koch, *Bertha of Antwerp*. 1931. Canvas, 95.5 x 81 cm. Gemeentemuseum, The Hague.

The transitory nature of things was his main theme in these years, and in this he followed the tradition of *Vanitas* still lifes. He did not, however, adopt the characteristic seventeenth-century symbolism, which was often rather moralistic. He approached his theme on the basis of his involvement with the content, but the form of a complicated object such as a skull could also represent a challenge to his painting technique. As a result the balance sometimes tilts towards a melancholy approach, as in the fine hunting still life *Undergrowth* of 1938, while other works are much more detached.

One of Hynckes' friends was Wim Schuhmacher. Compared with Hynckes' fairly intense *Vanitas* paintings, Schuhmacher's work is gentle and almost romantic. He painted objects meticulously in strikingly light, greyish tones. His still lifes and portraits are bathed in a diffuse light. Thus *Portrait of Mrs D.* has a strange, lucid glow which gives the woman depicted an unearthly presence. This is partly due to Mrs D.'s unnatural pose in the landscape, the result of the montage technique used in creating this painting. For in fact Schuhmacher painted her sitting not in a hollow in the dunes but on a bench in his holiday cottage; only later did he fill in the background landscape. Of

Raoul Hynckes,
Undergrowth. 1938.
Canvas, 99 x 109 cm.
Gemeentemuseum,
Arnhem.

the painters regarded as Magic Realists, Schuhmacher is undoubtedly the least provocative. He had great technical skill, but his oeuvre lacks paintings that cause a shock. They are sometimes alienating but they do not have the power to wrong-foot the viewer, to amaze him or make him shudder.

Also subdued but of a very different calibre are the paintings of Dick Ket. Articles on Ket always point out that his health was weak and that he was at home a great deal, so that he had to choose subjects close at hand. This does not seem to have prevented, and may indeed have been responsible for, his developing a trained eye for the life hidden behind everyday subjects. He painted portraits of his father, his wife and, most of all, himself. Not sparing himself in the least, he submits to his own penetrating painter's gaze. He also recorded the objects in his surroundings with precision. Ket was an absolute master of his craft, but his technical knowledge was not a goal in itself. There are few artists who could depict an ordinary enamel bowl so realistically and at the same time so movingly. But as with the artists considered above, we should not be tempted into making a comparison with a photographic image, because Ket's still lifes are also completely artificially constructed. An unusual combination of elements or a distorted perspective sometimes makes his paintings unreal. It was this alienating atmosphere that ensured that Ket was counted among the Magic Realists. He did not work from dreams or fantasies, yet with his penetrating view of ordinary objects and himself he gave his art an extraordinary intensity. The combined realistic and enigmatic aspects in the paintings of Willink, Koch and – to a lesser extent – Hynckes, Schuhmacher and Ket earned them the joint title of Magic Realism. Those paintings no longer seem so shocking as they did then; yet even today many people find them intense. However, realistic art has still not extricated itself from discussions about 'good taste'.

Wim Schuhmacher, *Portrait of Mrs D.* 1934. Canvas, 91 x 146 cm. Gemeentemuseum, Arnhem.

Self-portraits and still lifes

Dick Ket, *Self-Portrait*.
1933. Canvas, 39 x 27 cm.
Gemeentemuseum,
Arnhem.

Dutch Realism   Since the end of the eighties realism has made a comeback. A new generation of artists has unblushingly painted landscapes, portraits and even still
lifes. But these are no modern-day genre pieces. They do not show us everyday reality but an imaginary rendering of it, a do-it-yourself reality so to
speak. It would not seem exaggerated to see a historical link with the Magic
Realists. They share the realistic way of painting, combined with a free
approach to the nature of the subject's reality. Remarkably, the young artists
have encountered the same kind of criticism as the Magic Realists did in
their day. An exhibition organiser lamented in 1992 that he had to defend
the realistic artists he had selected against the so-called 'possessors of good
taste'. Many people still seem to hold the view that realism can only be
conservative. Yet realism is flourishing, and today it displays rather more

sense of proportion and humour than did Magic Realism, which with hind-sight is indeed enigmatic, but because of its seriousness can also sometimes be tedious.

The exhibition organiser cited above believes that stimulating, realistic painting is an indestructible phenomenon in the Netherlands. This is said to have to do with the rich seventeenth-century tradition, but also with geography. By this he means that the place where artists live influences their work. Deprived as we are in the Netherlands of dark forests and mountain tops shrouded in mist, we simply cannot surrender to mysterious and rarefied thoughts. The fact that everything is flat and thus visible is said to cause an irrepressible longing among Dutch artists for secrets. In the absence of a 'reality' that stirs the imagination, we create one for ourselves, so the theory runs.

It is indeed noteworthy that for some time now many artists have again seen a challenge in realism: from moving and almost sentimental kitsch, with a great deal of old-fashioned painting, to highly manipulated realism, which is more evident in photography. Some works do have similarities with Pyke Koch's eloquent description: *'leaving reality intact on the out-side, but with an inner dislocation'*. In linking the historical framework and the geography of the country, the author has been too much guided by the wish to come up with a fool-proof explanation. His theory, imaginative as it is, is like the images of the Magical Realists: it is indeed possible, but not probable.

INGEBORG WALINGA
Translated by John Rudge.

FURTHER READING

BLOTKAMP, C., *Pyke Koch.* Utrecht, 1982.

BOSMA, M., *De onbekende Willink: het vroege werk 1920-1930.* Utrecht, 1992.

BRAND, J. and K. BROOS (ed.), *Magisch Realisten en tijdgenoten in de verzameling van het Gemeentemuseum Arnhem.* Zwolle, 1992.

VAN VEELEN, IJ., 'Hollands realisme geeft toon aan', *Het Parool,* 1 August 1992.

he

Poetry of a Futuristic City

Object-Maker and Artist Jeroen Henneman

'I am whatever I paint'. For the Amsterdam artist Jeroen Henneman (1942-), houses or pianos are self-portraits. *'I want to express as strongly as possible on that flat surface what is in my head'*. Each painting is a portrait of the memory. He draws and paints objects, not just any old coffee pot or piano, but objects which take on a life of their own. It is an upside-down world: objects, not people, are the victors in the struggle. Henneman refers to painting as a homage to Pablo Picasso, the master of distortion. Objects have always been important in Picasso's work. They were given a soul. Henneman treats objects anarchistically. While drawing or painting a city he makes it explode; a piano shows its teeth. He greatly admires Max Beckmann, painter *par excellence* of the exploding cityscape. His admiration for Beckmann inspired him to paint. How does Henneman visualise an exploding cityscape? In an interview he once said: *'A whirl of houses is a good subject for composition'*. He wants the cluster of houses to lose its natural form so that we can no longer clearly see it, but sense, largely through the play of light, what it is about. *'It's not an urge to paint in an abstract form, but the question which continually springs to mind is: how far can something be distorted?'*

Henneman admires Magritte, Miró, De Chirico and Redon, but also Marcel Proust. He likens some of Proust's images to *'scratches on a slate with a slate-pencil'*. Equally, Henneman was deeply impressed by Jean Cocteau's film *Orpheus' Testament* (Le testament d'Orphée, 1960), and in particular by Cocteau's inventiveness: *'A man lifts his hand and there is a talking mouth in it, which he later kisses. Lots of mirrors and doors. You see an endless corridor of hotel rooms, but that corridor must be tilted because the men walking along it are pressed against the walls. The end of the corridor must slope away: you see them fly downwards, performing the strangest caprioles.'*

People rarely feature in Henneman's drawings. The images are clear: lighted windows, a house, a chair, everyday objects. Aggression and dynamism grow in his later work. White sails attack a villa as if they were sharks' teeth. Windows burst from a high building, and staircases float in space. Henneman calls himself an object-maker, referring to his three-dimensional objects which are often regarded as ingenious jokes. For happenings he arranged all manner of objects in a theatrical manner.

In 1988, commissioned by the Theatergroep Amsterdam, Henneman created the theatrical piece *Ambush* (Hinderlaag), an absurd production in which objects are the boss. They literally come to life on stage, and have human characteristics. *Ambush* is a horror story: tables and chairs are initially friendly towards the guest, but become increasingly hostile and even destructive. Henneman is making fun of the way we take things for granted in daily life.

Yet Henneman does not create arcimboldesque paintings, i.e. accumulations such as those by Giuseppe Arcimboldo, the Italian Renaissance painter of outlandish and fantastic portraits. Arcimboldo's librarian is composed of a stack of books, with hair of fluttering sheets of paper. Each of his paintings is, as it were, a museum, a sort of doll's house in which the hunter is the sum of animals, the sea the sum of fishes, the cook the sum of kitchen equipment.

Henneman's drawings and paintings, on the other hand, fly into pieces. They are joyful ballets in which the objects dance with each other. They compose unexpected and bizarre situations on the canvas. His work nonetheless looks very aesthetic, with correct proportions, precise colours, sometimes almost mathematical and angular.

Jeroen Henneman, *Still-Life* (1982).

Jeroen Henneman, *Eclipse* (1976).

Jeroen Henneman, *Goldfish* (1982).

Jeroen Henneman,
The Cosmos (1971).

In 1990, in a dummy (a book of blank pages) of Harry Mulisch's *The Composition of the World* (De compositie van de wereld, 1980), a marvellous book in which the author tackles the question of the octave, and the question why a note and its octave are simultaneously *the same* and *not the same,* Henneman made 600 sketches to accompany a cycle of poems by Mulisch, *Opus Gran.* In that thick book of blank pages Henneman created a city in hundreds of small drawings – notes in sketch form – with a square, a frieze, an owl, a mirror, an obelisk, a sphere, a woman, a staircase, a bow and a tree. A city such as Giorgio de Chirico created. And Mulisch writes: '*Clotting blood. Deserted terraces. / Flaking balustrades carry still / the warm impression of an ineffable ruler.*' Henneman has charted the city, sketch by sketch. He has transformed Mulisch's abstract cycle of poems into pictures. '*But only my breath now fills the city. / The city now breathes only in the pupils of my eyes / in that blackness.*' In the book *Henneman, Sketches and Drawings. Preliminary Studies for Opus Gran (Henneman, Schetsen en tekeningen. Voorstudies voor Opus Gran,* 1990), Renée Steenbergen compares the obelisk in one of the drawings with a '*gigantic pencil that props up the firmament*'. Henneman draws the city; he describes a city without people, in which architecture rules supreme. '*Henneman is an architect, his pencil is an obelisk.*'

Around the turn of the century, Baudelaire's '*cité fourmillante*' came into being, the '*bee-hive city, city of dreams where the ghost taps you on the*

Jeroen Henneman, *A Scene from the Lives of Things* (1972).

Jeroen Henneman, *Lake Returns Regards* (1979).

shoulder in broad daylight'. Cubists and futurists painted the metropolis, the bustle; the Eiffel Tower as the symbol of *'a new century'* and the cars on the boulevards. They depict what T.S. Eliot once called the *'unreal city'*. Henneman's city is just such a place: a collage of unreal and impossible things. It is a sort of poetry of the futuristic city. To a certain extent Henneman's world can be compared with what Filippo Tomaso Marinetti describes in his first futurist manifesto as *'the synthesis of a day in the life of the world':* a tableau of trains and motor bikes, airships and cars, of telegraphs and phonographs, cinemas and daily papers.

Is Henneman a joker? Not really. The pencil drawing *Back to Work from Home* (Terug naar het werk van huis) is *'a drawing of a lonely pencil in the foreground',* wrote one critic, *'which has drawn a graceful line, a couple of small houses in the distance, and the silhouette of a coffee pot and cup'.* Despite the apparent clarity, there is still something mysterious about it. With reference to an exhibition of Henneman's work, the Wansink Gallery in Roermond claimed that *'Henneman's work is difficult to describe'.* His art is often elusive. His characteristic themes are clear but at the same time surreal, ironic, puzzling and unequivocally melancholy: buildings, bridges, windows which radiate light into the darkness, objects which make weaving movements although normally considered incapable of this.

Perhaps it is a chaos, a jumble in Henneman's head. Yet strangely enough some of the paintings, and in particular the drawings, evoke Giorgio de

Jeroen Henneman,
The Crystal Piano (1977).

Chirico's famous tableau of an autumn afternoon on the Florentine piazza of Santa Croce: a beautiful square with a facade, an antique statue, two almost sculptural figures and their shadows. De Chirico's *pittura metafisica* and Marinetti's Futurism were the foundations of modern art, but they show two contrasting aspects: scepticism as opposed to the glorification of speed and aggression.

Henneman keeps his preliminary studies, sketches and drawings for many years, in meticulous order. Sketches are the memory of an artist. They are the direct reflection of his thought. They are usually much more fanciful and more subtle than the eventual work of art for which they are preliminary studies.

Drawings are also more intimate. They show the artist's deliberation, the hesitation and the searching. They are unconstrained experiments, often scribbles. Perhaps Henneman's cityscape for *Opus Gran* is not as impassive a tableau as De Chirico's piazzas. Each drawing is an invitation to draw yet another tableau, to tread the side-paths and to explore the city. '*I work like a chess player*', Henneman once said, '*move by move, and then I know how to win*'.

PAUL DEPONDT
Translated by Yvette Mead.

FURTHER READING   *Jeroen Henneman: een overzicht.* Groningen, 1989.
De stad. The Hague, 1989.
Schetsen en tekeningen: voorstudies voor Opus Gran. Amsterdam, 1990.

Comic Strips Today

Morris & Goscinny: *Lucky Luke.*

There are few places in the world where the comic strip is so closely inter-woven with daily life as it is in Flanders. Not only do newspapers and week-lies publish an unending stream of new episodes of cartoon series, there are also magazines devoted entirely to comic strips. Piles of new ones are to be found in every supermarket, and in the smallest of newsagents. For enthu-siasts there are also markets, festivals, exhibitions, special issues and so on. Various popular comic strip characters can be seen in streets and parks in the form of statues or in murals. But in the main it is youngsters who devour them most voraciously. In spite of the wide range of other forms of enter-tainment (TV, computer games, etc.), Flemish children are still very happy to read the adventures of their favourite cartoon characters. In fact most of these books are tailored to a juvenile readership.

While other areas of popular culture in Flanders, such as pop music and the cinema, are highly Americanised, comic strips from abroad play only a minor part in the whole. But popular as native-Flemish comic strips may be within the bounds of Flanders, there is little market for them in French-speaking Belgium and abroad. It must be remembered that the most popular Flemish series appear in advance in the daily papers. Newspaper cartoons from abroad rarely succeed on the international market in book form, with the exception of a few American comics like *Peanuts*, *Hagar* and *Casper and Hobbes*.

When Flemish work is brought out by a French-language Belgian publisher it has a much greater chance of achieving an international break-through. The best example of this is undoubtedly the humorous Western series called *Lucky Luke*, created by Morris, who was born in Kortrijk. This series started in *Spirou*, a comic strip weekly issued by the Walloon publisher Dupuis, and is heavily influenced by American animation films and the Westerns of the forties. Morris, who has worked for French-language publishers almost his whole life, has by now sold about 278 mil-lion books world-wide. The popularity of the comic books led to *Lucky Luke* being adapted for the silver screen, both as a cartoon film and as a feature film starring Terence Hill, and for television. In 1984 the big American animation studio Hanna & Barbera made a series of 26 cartoon films for TV, but the rogue cowboy did have to exchange his cigarette for a blade of grass, which also brought him a prize from the World Health Organisation. The author himself attributes part of the success of his cartoon to its international flavour. In *Lucky Luke* Morris parodies classic Western scenes and incorporates historical events from the Wild West. And since the mid-fifties Morris has also employed the services of foreign scenarists, such as the late Goscinny of *Asterix* fame.

Nowadays quite a number of Flemish artists collaborate with scenarists who speak another language: Vance with Van Hamme *(XIII)*, Jean-Pol with Cauvin *(Sammy)*, Johan de Moor with Stephen Desberg *(The Cow* – La Vache / Kobe de Koe), Griffo with Dufaux *(Giacomo C.)*, etc. They therefore also work with French-language publishers and their comic series are published in various languages. Comics produced by Flemish people alone appear to find it harder to cross the language border, with the exception of the phenomenal success of *Bob and Bobette* (Suske en Wiske; see *The Low Countries* 1995-96: 46-52) in the Netherlands and French-speaking Belgium. In addition to this there are a few comics such as *Tom Carbon* and *Cowboy Henk* that have appeared in several West European languages.

Flemish comics are currently almost always based on an 'original' scenario. They may, exceptionally, also be based on an existing story. Marvano has ventured into the adaptation of novels, such as the sci-fi *Forever War* by the American Joe Haldeman, about a war between the Earth and another planet at some time in the future. It is actually a metaphor for the crazy Vietnam War that Haldeman was sent to as a soldier. But Flemish cartoon artists generally write their scenarios themselves or work with a permanent comic strip scenarist; it is only exceptionally that someone from outside the profession is called upon. One example was Eric Joris, who engaged a number of Flemish writers and film-makers for *The Dangerous Cooks* (Les cuisiniers dangereux). Another striking fact is that, almost without exception, it is only men that earn their living from drawing cartoons; there are only a few female authors around, such as Erika Raven.

Willy Vandersteen: *Bob and Bobette* (Suske en Wiske).

The publication of strip cartoons

In Flanders the majority of publishing companies are in Dutch hands, including those marketing comic strips. This is true, for example, of the largest producer of Flemish comic strips, Standaard Uitgeverij, which has almost all the top comic series on its lists, including *Bob and Bobette* and *Red Knight* (De Rode Ridder), and also publishes its own weekly comic strip book for children. About five hundred Dutch-language books of comic strips appear every year. Though work by Flemish authors makes up only part of the total, in absolute figures it has the largest turnover!

At present, the three best-selling comic strips in Flanders are *Bob and Bobette*, *Jommeke* and *Jo & co* (Kiekeboe). These are all series which regularly appear in advance in newspapers or weeklies and of which three to five new books are published per year, in editions of about one hundred thousand. The books are printed in four colours, have a paper cover and a set number of pages (32 or 48). The average price of one of these books is about 130 BF (roughly $ 4 or £ 2.50), which is slightly more expensive than an American comic book but considerably cheaper than a French cartoon book with a hard cover. One-shots, self-contained books which do not form part of a series, are fairly rare in the Flemish comic strip world.

The way a comic strip is published may seem to be independent of its method of creation, but nothing could be further from the truth. To start with, authors of comic strips who have to provide a newspaper with two strips of cartoons every day are under a certain constant pressure year after year. Comic strips created in such circumstances are therefore both literally and figuratively serial products, usually being made by a small group of people with a fixed division of labour. Advance publication in a newspaper also influences the form and content of the comic strips. Since every page in a book has to be divided in two for the newspaper edition, the authors' page is composed of four rows of pictures. This also has implications for the story's continuity: it is preferable that each episode (consisting of two rows) in the newspaper should end on a note of suspense. By publishing in a news-paper, an author can at the same time make use of hot topics, as Marc Sleen has been doing for half a century in his *Nero* series. Comic strips of this sort have to be read in their context, if all the allusions and references are to be understood. For technical reasons with regard to printing, clear line drawing has become the dominant style in Flemish newspaper cartoons. In newspa-pers, of course, only the black ink drawing is used; colours are added for the book edition.

Marc Sleen: *Nero.*

Major genres

Any attempt to delineate clearly defined genres is condemned to make use of unfair generalisations. Even so, I shall try to distil a number of distin-guishing features from the multiplicity of Flemish comic strips. In the first place, most Flemish comic strips are made to be accessible to children, with simple chronological narrative structures, a clear and meticulous drawing style, a transparent use of language, and when there is humour it has to be fairly obvious; in other words these comic strips are highly readable and popular in style.

Jef Nys: *Jommeke.*

However varied the range of Flemish comic strips may currently be, there are certain genres that appear rarely or not at all; these include violent su-perhero comics, erotic and porno comics, documentary cartoons, biography and autobiography, experimental comic strips and religious comic strips. Genres that are popular are the family comic, the humorous comic and the adventure comic. These genres often merge into one another, since the Flemish family comic generally blends humour with elements of adventure; the latter is less commonly found in the American family comic, for exam-ple. The Flemish comic family (*Bob and Bobette, Nero, Jommeke, Jo & co* and *Urbanus*) is usually very varied in its make-up, both with regard to age and to appearance and character. These Flemish cartoon characters are everyday figures, not real heroes like Tintin and Tarzan. Take Nero, for example, an archetypical middle-aged 'Belgian', a hero in spite of himself, and in fact devoted to his armchair and slippers. Another interesting arche-type in the Flemish comic strip is the often unworldly 'professor / inventor', like Nero's son Adhemar or the absent-minded Gobelijn in *Jommeke*. Nys'

Jommeke is a boy of about ten with a very characteristic haircut (a 'thatch'). Together with his group of friends he has all kinds of highly imaginative and exciting adventures, in which there is not a trace of violence. All of Jommeke's adventures have a happy end. Though the happy ending may have become almost a permanent feature of Flemish family cartoons, a series like *Jo & co* sometimes risks a departure from this rule. Merho, its author, is apparently not very optimistic regarding certain present-day world problems (e.g. the democratisation of former dictatorships). The most daring family cartoon is undoubtedly the risqué *Urbanus*. Linthout's style of drawing is disarmingly naive, but there is a great deal of social criticism mixed in with the ruthless humour.

The humour in Flemish comic strips has come a long way since the Second World War, but it remains less varied than in other comics such as the French or American ones. One particularly strong trend in Flanders is nonsensical or absurd humour, the leaders here being Kamagurka & Herr Seele. By contrast, social satire, the chief genre in nineteenth-century European comic strips, appears very rarely. In *The Cow*, by Johan De Moor and Stephen Desberg, the satire is hidden beneath a form that is mischievous and playful. Kobe looks like an ordinary cow, but sometimes she goes out into the wide world as a secret agent and takes up the cudgels against pollution and other contemporary excrescences.

A separate trend is the humorous comic that focuses on a famous TV personality, such as a comedian, a pop singer, a politician, a sex symbol or a children's idol. The great majority of these merchandising comics are substandard and quite ephemeral. The only ones which have been successful in appealing to a broad readership for a longer period are *Urbanus* and *Samson & Gert* (based on a tremendously popular TV series for young children, centred on a fluffy dog called Samson).

Another widespread genre is the 'naughty boy' comic, about children who get up to mischief. The former 'cheerful rascals', conversant only with innocent pranks, have now given way to brash and independent cartoon children like Legendre's *Biebel*.

Whereas the Japanese manga and American comic books explode with action, in Flemish comic strips it's relatively peaceful. Flanders produces no pure action comics containing violence for violence's sake. Action is in most cases used in thrillers or crime stories. *XIII*, by William Vance, is a deftly drawn, exciting macho adventure series. The scenario is by one of Europe's most popular scenarists, the French-speaking Belgian Jean van Hamme, who likes to borrow ideas from novel writers and film scenarists. In the case of *XIII* he drew part of his inspiration from the books of Robert Ludlum.

The great majority of Flemish comic strips are set in the present day, but there are also those that are set in the past (e.g. *Bakelandt*, set during the eighteenth-century French occupation) or the future (e.g. *Forever War*). Generally speaking, Flemish comics are interested in only a limited number of historical periods and in specific locations. The Middle Ages in Europe remain popular. The stories are always fictional, though employing historical elements. The more fantastic genres such as science fiction, tales of heroes and sword & sorcery occur less frequently but do play a major part in *Red Knight*. It was started in 1959 by Willy Vandersteen as a Flemish version of the American *Prince Valiant* by Hal Foster. In the hands of Karel

Merho: *Jo & co* (Kiekeboe).

Karel Biddeloo: *The Red Knight* (De Rode Ridder).

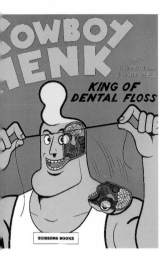

Herr Seele & Kamagurka:
Cowboy Henk.

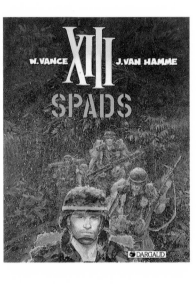

Vance & Van Hamme: *XIII.*

Linthout: *Urbanus.*

Biddeloo *Red Knight* evolved during the seventies into a baroque comic with an unlikely mixture of historical fact, myths, science fiction and fantasy. Biddeloo is also one of the first mainstream Flemish comic strip authors to have introduced numerous good-looking female characters. 'Good', for example, is personified in the blonde Galaxa, a pin-up with the proportions of Pamela Anderson, while 'Evil' is represented by her raven-haired counterpart Demoniah, who shares her rival's vital statistics. This comic series differs sharply from other Flemish newspaper cartoons in graphic terms too, by its use of found images (e.g. photocopies of photos of castles) and its almost psychedelic colouring.

On the fringes of these big commercial editions there are also a number of alternative and more experimental comics by younger people whose periodicals (*BILL, Verdomd Goed Tijdschrift,* etc.) and books they mainly publish themselves. These 'autarchic' or small press comics, so called because of their small scale and limited editions, are an international phenomenon, with a great deal of interchange between the various authors and collectives.

One might lament that adult comics are still in their infancy in Flanders, but the main aim of the vast majority of Flemish comic producers is to create unpretentious entertainment, since that is apparently the only thing that yields a profit. This popular cartoon culture does have a considerable economic value, not only in terms of turnover, but also in providing employment.

The authorities do not concern themselves with the comic strip industry. In contrast with their colleagues in the literary, visual and performing arts, the film world and radio and TV, the authors of comic strips cannot benefit from working grants or subsidies. In Flanders comic strips are still unjustly seen as purely consumer products. This, despite the fact that comic authors like Spiegelman, an American, Breccia, an Argentine, and Mattotti, an Italian, have already proven that the comic medium has other, artistic, strengths.

Sometimes mom is a bit absent-minded...but she makes great pancakes (by Steve Michiels in the second issue of *BILL*).

PASCAL LEFÈVRE
Translated by Gregory Ball.

LIST OF TRANSLATIONS

MARVANO and HALDEMAN, *Forever War*. NBM.
MERHO, *Jo & co: The White Blood*. Standaard.
MORRIS and GOSCINNY, *Lucky Luke: The Stagecoach*. Flight Publishing.
SEELE, HERR and KAMAGURKA, *Cowboy Henk: King of Dental Floss*. Scissors Books.
VANCE, WILLIAM and JEAN VAN HAMME, *XIII*. Catalan Communications.
VANDERSTEEN, WILLY and PAUL GEERTS, *Bob and Bobette*. Ravette Books.

Alternative work of the 'small press' can be found in:
BILL. Bill Productions (since 1993).
Formaline. Bronzen Adhemar Stichting (1995).

FURTHER INFORMATION

Belgian Centre for Comic Strip Art
Zandstraat 20 / 1000 Brussels / Belgium
tel. + 32 2 2191980 / fax +32 2 2192376

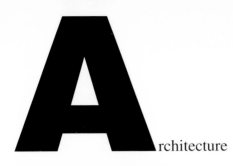

Architecture

without Qualities

The Designs of Stéphane Beel

Architecture may no longer be society's scapegoat, but that does not mean that it has been freed from the straitjacket of prejudices and obsessions that restricts its movement. Young architects trying to approach their discipline with an open mind confront an almost impossible task. Either they take refuge in a dream world where they can develop splendid architectural metaphors unhindered and occasionally see them actually built, or they shy away from all challenges and produce one nondescript building after another. The Flemish architect Stéphane Beel (1955-) rejects this dilemma out of hand. He wants to liberate architecture from its cultural isolation and make it an enrichment of everyday life in a very concrete fashion.

There is no better example of this approach than one of his recent projects, the regional offices of Christelijke Mutualiteiten in Eeklo in Belgium, which were first occupied in September 1996. The brief called for offices to be combined with various public areas. More importantly, the project involved re-using an industrial complex, a large dairy in the town centre. From the outset integrating the new with the old was a basic requirement, even if the architect decided to demolish the dairy. But Stéphane Beel was not in favour of that; he hardly touched the existing buildings.

The new plan was suggested by the urban situation. The dairy building was envisaged as a screen between two squares marking out two different neighbourhoods. An internal street running through that screen would connect them. From this first option everything else follows naturally. In the internal street are the public departments and the entrance to the private area with the offices and administration. The internal street broadens out to form a space that acts as a third square, enclosed between the two others. Using hardly anything, a whole district is transformed here, and interior and exterior spaces are related.

What is true of the urban space is also true of the interior. It has been completely transformed and internalised. Light now flows playfully from all sides into what used to be dark storerooms. The bright, cheerful interior leads to a fully glazed conference room, which is attached to the building like a soap bubble, supported only by tall pillars. This room marks one of the entrances and thus differentiates the two facades in relation to the two

Stéphane Beel: Regional offices of Christelijke Mutualiteiten in Eeklo (1996) (Photo by Jean Godecharle).

Stéphane Beel: Provincial offices of BACOB bank in Bruges (1992) (Photo by Klaus Kinold).

Stéphane Beel: Extension to the university building at Kortrijk (1993) (Photo by Reiner Lautwein).

squares. It also throws open the closed block and reveals a glimpse of the interior. Conversely, it turns the square onto which it opens into a kind of interior. It floats above what could have been a traditional water garden. But here the water has been replaced by irregularly scattered, glistening coal. In the autumn the fallen leaves turn it into a delightful symphony.

This continual interplay of diverse areas of meaning within an open framework linking them all together, like characters in a novel, has been typical of Stéphane Beel's approach from the beginning. The old is made new and the new old. The obvious seems unexpected and the unexpected obvious, the void is full and the fullness void, the commonplace becomes poetry. To the extent that there is a development, it is one of ever greater control of the means, of an increasing intensification of the work. There is less and less need to accentuate anything. The means employed become ever more direct, leaving behind any reference to 'style', universal and free.

Going back chronologically, the new building at Kortrijk for the Catholic University of Leuven (1993) provides an enlightening comparison with the transformation in Eeklo. This too was a project in an existing situation. Stéphane Beel was given the commission, as in Eeklo, as the result of a competition. Only two parts of the original master plan had been realised, at opposite ends of the site. Here again Beel began with a proposed urban design in which his architecture would be situated. He suggested that the existing buildings should be linked by a long gallery on two levels. New buildings could be plugged into this axis in phases. The main advantage of this intervention, however, was that, while preserving the landscape, it would give the university a clear identity and a presence.

The building for the economics department was the first addition designed by Beel; it also contains the new main entrance. As in Eeklo, the centre consists of an agora, which is partly covered and partly open. It is from there that one experiences the whole building. Sharp colour fields with spaces cut out for the windows govern the spatial arrangement. The architecture is relieved of its heaviness. Severity becomes light and playful. The pleasure lies not in the additions, but in the masterly freedom with which necessity is treated. This apparently lucid and simple building is full of subtle allusions. It remains a vital and surprising landscape that can be rediscovered time and again.

The provincial offices of BACOB bank beside the ring road in Bruges, completed in 1992, just before the Kortrijk project started, seem at first sight to lack the urban anchoring of the previous designs. But this impression is mistaken. For here too the whole building is a specific response to its context or, rather, turns its incoherent surroundings into a true context. These surroundings consisted of an extraordinary hotchpotch of derelict allotments, with a street coming to a dead end at the ring road, and a remnant of countryside with a wood. The building absorbs these very diverse components and makes of them a splendid entity. The architect's creed sounds convincing: there are no impossible situations; everything has a potential for life. With this project one is inclined to say: the more thankless the task, the greater the challenge and the more intense the solution. The motorway accompanies the building, presenting a taut volume on legs beneath which a fairly complex plan has been worked out and above which, like a ship's wheelhouse, the technical services form a gentle curve. The other long elevation, facing the allotments, presents a very different picture of staggered volumes, vertical accents and more homely materials. But here again, as in other cases, the miracle lies in the extraordinary unity in which these autonomous elements interact in an almost self-evident way. In contrast to the closed exterior, the interior is light and open.

These basic qualities can also be found in Stéphane Beel's other public buildings, such as the much talked-about offices of Spaarkrediet in Bruges of 1988. We recognise them too in several projects planned for 1997: the Raveelmuseum in Machelen / Zulte, the Tack tower in Kortrijk, the Central Museum in Utrecht. Again, these are cases where existing constructions are

Stéphane Beel: Design for the extension to the art centre deSingel in Antwerp (Photo by Stéphane Beel).

Stéphane Beel: The De Clerck residence in Kortrijk (Photo by Catherine Poels).

to be adapted and expanded. In the proposal for the extension to the art centre deSingel in Antwerp, the relationship between old and new once more provides the stimulus. Incidentally, this is not the first time that Stéphane Beel has worked on deSingel, a building by Léon Stynen. In his design for the Stynen exhibition at deSingel in 1990 and the addition of a door with Stynen motifs, he had already shown how refreshing the respectful treatment of an existing oeuvre could be.

Stéphane Beel made his debut in 1985 with a dwelling in Zoersel in which he brilliantly transformed all the factors in the surroundings into a surprising residence. He has repeated this feat several times since, in villas in Brasschaat and Rotselaar and in houses in urban settings. With the minimal extension to an old residence in Kortrijk he produced a masterpiece. But, finally, Villa M. in Zedelgem, completed in 1992, can serve as the most explicit example of his approach: an architecture that no longer proceeds from an existing image and, precisely because of that, proves able to generate new images. The point of departure is again the situation: the half-neglected

vegetable garden of a country house in woodland with fragments of a wall as the dominant element. The wall is so to speak the paradigm of Beel's architecture. In all his designs the wall surface is conspicuous. The existing garden wall indicates the orientation. Parallel to it a long beam is placed above ground level. And that's it! As with his other designs, the self-evident quality becomes extreme. The beam contains the dwelling functions and is largely closed on the side of the wall, thus creating a closed access route that leads to the centre of the house, the agora, where all the different dwelling and living functions merge. The middle section of the side facing the garden is completely open, so that one lives as it were in the garden and is shielded. It is impossible to imagine a more powerful image of what architecture today can be. Here architecture renounces itself in order to be itself again, an architecture without qualities.

GEERT BEKAERT
Translated by John Rudge.

Stéphane Beel: Villa M. in Zedelgem (1992) (Photos by Lieve Blancquaert).

rom

Dutch Student to London Schoolmaster

The Literary Work of Gerrit van de Linde

There was a time when the man who called himself 'The Schoolmaster' ('De Schoolmeester') was honoured as the colossus of Dutch popular verse. No schoolchild's induction into the muses was accounted complete without knowing an appropriate selection off by heart, while his more quotable lines were virtually common parlance. Particularly towards the end of the nineteenth century his collected poems, a single volume unambiguously entitled *Poems by The Schoolmaster* (Gedichten van den Schoolmeester), sold on a phenomenal scale. The tenth edition of 1886 alone, for instance, ran to 20,100 copies. In the early years of the present century, one Dutch manufacturer of confectionery was even distributing the book free in return for chocolate bar wrappers and proof of purchase. From this zenith his popularity gradually declined. Demand dwindled and dwindled until finally, after the Second World War, the complete edition dropped out of print altogether, relegating The Schoolmaster to virtual oblivion.

Then in 1975 a new edition, prefaced by an introduction revealing previously unknown information about the author, led to a renewed interest; and this was reinforced by the publication (1977) of further new material – The Schoolmaster's letters to Jacob van Lennep. These letters show The Schoolmaster to have been not only the creator of witty, bizarre poetry, but also a letter-writer of uncommon élan. Today The Schoolmaster stands acknowledged as a unique figure in Dutch nineteenth-century literature for his outspokenness, his clever and original use of language, his cavalier treatment of the canonised literary rules and genres, and his sardonic, subversive commentary on manners and mores.

So who is the man behind the pseudonymous Schoolmaster? A schoolmaster, indeed, but not one who originally aspired to that calling or ever practised it in the Netherlands. In fact, The Schoolmaster was the headmaster-proprietor of a London boarding school.

Gerrit van de Linde was born in 1808 in Rotterdam, where his father was a well-to-do tradesman. From an early age young Gerrit's literary gifts were already quite apparent. Even as a schoolboy he was regularly invited to present his poetry at literary fellowships. Such fellowships, a more self-conscious drawing-room version of the French-style literary *salon*, were an institutionalised part of Dutch nineteenth-century middle-class culture. In 1825 he entered the University of Leiden as a student of theology destined for the ministry. He quickly attracted many friends, and also made his mark in university literary circles as a talent to be watched. He read his verses at student literary gatherings and contributed to student literary almanacs. He also put on very popular puppet shows for his friends and family, in which his salacious and satirical bent came to the fore. Academically, he was content to take his studies at an easy pace. Towards the end of 1833, however, this pleasant mode of existence foundered abruptly on scandal. First a young lady, a musician's daughter with whom he had been conducting an affair, bore him an illegitimate son. At the same time word got about of a liaison with the young wife of a chemistry professor who, after years of childlessness, now likewise found herself in a delicate condition. The cuckolded professor retaliated by having his young rival sent down from the university, and his wife's extra-marital pregnancy terminated. Next, the Leiden fraternity of shopkeepers and purveyors, with whom he had enjoyed credit for years, learning of his disgrace, to a man called in his debts. Since they were also aware that Van de Linde senior had lost his fortune, these creditors became so pressing that Van de Linde had no option but to make himself scarce.

Thus in late January 1834 Gerrit van de Linde, debarred from the university, the ministry and, hence, from respectable society because of his overenergetic love life, and hounded by creditors because of his insolvency, took ship for England, where, as his friends impressed upon him, he would at

Portrait of Gerrit van de Linde as a student (Collection P.A.M. van de Linde, Wildridge, Australia).

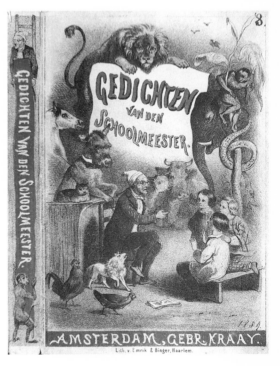

Cover of the first edition of *Poems by The Schoolmaster* (Gedichten van den Schoolmeester, 1859) (Collection Koninklijke Nederlandse Academie van Wetenschappen).

Students of the Minerva Fraternity in Leiden. The student with the curly hair behind the man on the chair is Gerrit van de Linde (Collection Atlas van Stolk, Rotterdam).

least be beyond the reach of litigious Leiden shopkeepers and vengeful Leiden academics. He disembarked in London not knowing the language, owning barely a change of clothes, and with just about enough in his wallet to pay his way for a week or two. Ahead lay a dark spell of dire penury, humiliation, sickness and loneliness. Of his numerous friends the only one to remain loyal to him was the by now already well-known novelist Jacob van Lennep. To him Van de Linde immediately began to address long, entertaining missives to dispel his solitude and to preserve this single friendship and link with the past.

The first difference between the Netherlands and his new island home to strike the youthful exile, was the relative merits of the whores. As he put it to Jacob van Lennep:

When fleshly ragings hammer 'n clamour for naught but prompt alleviation
'T were better to postpone need-I-say-more till Holland's parts for satiation
For in England there's not a whore worth recommending
They lay like monuments supine upon the bedding
In truth to screw a sign of life into an Anglo-Saxon tart
Requires a second with the hiccups bouncing underneath to make her start.

When Van Lennep visited his friend in June of 1834, the two of them marvelled to behold a prostitute plying her trade on crutches in Drury Lane. Van Lennep, goes the story, is supposed to have addressed her as follows: '*The devil my dear miss, left you fair of face, but our Lord gave you a couple of crutches*', upon which Van de Linde quickly rejoined: '*Nay, blessed, rather, the heifer sound upon four immaculate extremities, inclining to none but her own mate's bollocks' tender mercies.*'

Other aspects of the shadow-side of London life also became familiar to him. The theatres, he discovered, swarmed with pickpockets. The air of the metropolis was so foul that he developed a respiratory complaint and began to cough up blood. Writing to Van Lennep, he confided that he wished he were dead, even if that meant parting from the one and only fellow-being likely to notice his demise. A series of attempts to earn his living as a book dealer, a private tutor, and a schoolmaster, all ended in failure. He did, however, make the acquaintance of some notable and distinguished people, among them the Quaker doctor-philanthropist Thomas Hodgkin and Henry Philip Hope, a retired merchant banker and public benefactor. The latter in particular proved a generous patron to Van de Linde when he loaned him a considerable sum of money towards his first boarding school venture at the beginning of 1835. Van Lennep, meanwhile, canvassed his own friends and relations in the Netherlands for the remainder of the funds his banished friend required to set himself up in his new profession.

Keeping a boarding school was no sinecure, as Van de Linde soon discovered. Life was a constant struggle against shortage of money and unreliable staff. He learned to beware of bankrupts. Families on the financial way down were in the habit of boarding out their children; when the fees became due at the end of the quarter they would promptly remove them, and send them to another school for one term more of complimentary board, lodging and education.

Bit by bit he managed to surmount these obstacles. Especially after his marriage in 1837 to Caroline de Monteuuis, the pretty, young and accomplished daughter of the proprietor of a French residential school, life went more smoothly for him. By 1843 he was in a position to establish himself at Cromwell House, a grand house in Highgate, where his *'collège français'* gained an increasing reputation as time went by.

Van de Linde's success as an educator in England must have been due in great measure to his teaching methods, which were not only new to England but happened to be in tune with the times. He was, for instance, opposed to corporal punishment, and propagated a non-traditional curriculum with an emphasis on modern languages as well as mathematics and the sciences, for which there was an insatiable demand as the Industrial Revolution gained momentum. Most likely he had himself been educated at a modern Dutch *'Nutschool'*, where the prevailing principle was an enlightened, benevolent Rousseauean belief in the natural good of the child which, if properly nurtured, made the use of physical correction superfluous. It did not take all that much, Van de Linde concluded, to make one's mark as a pedagogue in England. '*I have already introduced numerous improvements here which I recollect from my own schooldays, as it appears to me that the system of education in Holland is a hundredfold better than in England,*' he told Van Lennep. Among these improvements was the abolition of the strap and cane, for which he substituted a scale of grades for conduct. One mother, though, he reported to his friend, complained about his disgraceful neglect of her son. Repeated examination of the young scholar's backside had revealed to her no hue other than that which nature intended, whereas formerly that self-same back was wont to display every colour of the rainbow as a testimony to his previous headmaster's ministrations.

Once established at Highgate, a prosperous village enclave on London's outskirts, Van de Linde transformed himself into a respectable and respected member of the community, with access to the very best circles. His

Interior of Cromwell House (Highgate), with Mrs Van de Linde and her eldest child (Collection P.A.M. van de Linde, Wildridge, Australia).

The backyard of Cromwell House (Highgate Literary and Scientific Institution).

intimates included leading critics, lawyers, antiquarians, educational re-formers and abolitionists. To fit into his new environment with such seam-less ease he must have thoroughly saturated himself in its rules and tenets. He also became a communicant of the Church of England, an absolute pre-requisite for social acceptability. Dissenters were at that time still excluded from official appointments, and it would have been inconceivable that he should be entrusted with the tutelage of the offspring of the well-to-do middle classes had he continued to profess the Dutch Reformed Protes-tantism of his origins. Furthermore, this theologian *manqué* from Leiden always presented himself in clerical garb, and styled himself The Reverend Gérard van de Linde Monteuuis.

Switching from his native Dutch to English caused Van de Linde no difficulties. Within a matter of months he had so thoroughly absorbed his new language that he was able to recite by heart entire passages from the key works of English literature, and was even writing home in English, report-ing to Van Lennep with relish on the annihilating critiques meted out by the English press to Dutch *literati*. Apart from Bilderdijk, he too did not hold the Dutch literary establishment in much esteem. He was dizzy with excite-ment on first encountering the works of Coleridge, Dickens and Lamb, declared himself '*well-nigh crazed with joy*' by one of Wordsworth's odes, and took Shakespeare for his '*bible*'. With reference to his own work, it is difficult to assess to what extent Van de Linde may have been influenced by English literature. Certainly a particular brand of Anglo-Saxon humorous writing was then in its heyday, and it would be unnatural if this had not provided him with at least one source of inspiration in penning The School-master's verse. We know that he was familiar with Byron's *Don Juan*, with *The Pickwick Papers*, and was a reader of *Punch*. Certainly there is an affin-ity between the sardonic humour of Byron's epic *Don Juan*, and the humour of The Schoolmaster's longer poems such as 'The Shipwreck' ('De schip-breuk'), and 'The Sandwich and the Gold Prospector' ('De boterham en de goudzoeker'). Whether he was also familiar with the nonsense verse of Richard Barham and Edward Lear, with both of whom he has been com-pared, is not known. He must certainly have been aware of Lear, however.

An engraving of Cromwell House (Highgate). The handwriting is Van de Linde's (Gemeentearchief, Amsterdam).

In 1848 the *Book of Nonsense* took England by storm, and Lear was also a contributor to *Punch*, of which Van de Linde was a reader. Be that as it may, Van de Linde was already writing absurdistic verse before quitting the Netherlands; long, that is, before he knew English, and long before Lear made his debut.

After his flight to England, it was many years before Van de Linde's work was seen in the Netherlands again. It is clear from the many scintillating verses and expressive utterances that animate his letters to Jacob van Lennep that he was constantly engaged in honing his skills. But he was so hurt by being banished from his own country, and so nervous of letting his name appear in print, that despite Van Lennep's repeated urging he resisted all pressure to publish his poems. In the event, the general public's introduction to The Schoolmaster dates from 1850, when Van Lennep persuaded his friend into contributing to *Holland*, his own new almanac; even then, he dared to publish only under a pseudonym.

The verse of The Schoolmaster is completely unlike that of his Dutch peers. He pulls the rug out from under every accepted canon of poetry, juggling and kneading the vocabulary to create a completely novel language of imagery, connotations and associations. Technically he is extremely adroit, displaying an equally masterly hand in prolonged rhyme sequences, in intricate passages of double-rhyme, and in complex internal rhyming patterns.

One feature that sets his work apart from contemporaries both in Holland and elsewhere, is a complete absence of metre. At a time when metric verse was *de rigeur,* The Schoolmaster disdains to cast his so-called '*knittelvers*', or non-verse, in the prescribed mould of stressed and unstressed syllables, set to fixed schemes of alternating shorter and longer lines. Often the end result looks like a hodgepodge on paper, with some lines so sustained that they overrun, and others comprising but a few syllables. Still, especially when read aloud, the result scans impeccably, and the lines balance out perfectly. Furthermore, his skilful manipulation of assonance, dissonance and alliteration permits individual lines and phrases to be drawn out or foreshortened at will, to allow for different interpretations. Despite the lack of formal metre, usually an indispensable aid to memorisation, his timing is so easy on the ear that a few readings will suffice to imprint them on the mind without too much conscious effort. Other instantly identifiable Schoolmaster hallmarks are his quirky metaphors and figures of speech, outlandish personifications, non-sequiturs, confusing word associations, hyperbole and over-the-top elaborations, which he heaps one upon the other in exuberant explosions of verbal animation which seem to spill over with elation at their own daring. He'll play with cliché, proverb and dictum, dissolving the boundaries between the metaphorical, the figurative and the literal so that nothing means what it says, and vice versa. He'll interpolate a sly word or two which suddenly exposes the underlying meaning of a common expression. He'll draw bizarre analogies and comparisons in which the larger concept is viewed, as it were, through the small end of the telescope: in the upside-down mental universe of The Schoolmaster you'll see the sun shine bright as a candle.

In keeping with his disdain for the received canons of his art, The Schoolmaster does not eschew to make short shrift of authority as represented by an ubiquitous officialdom, eternally on its dignity, eternally letting itself be waited on at its own convenience. Bourgeois society, with its predilection for cosy, domestic scenarios, equally comes in for a thorough drubbing from The Schoolmaster. He translates the grandiose *Leitmotifs* of Romanticism into homely *tableaux*: a violent shipwreck transforms itself into a mediocre print on a parlour wall, its savagery permanently becalmed. In short, it is the worthy little man, who thinks the world can be scaled down to his own perspectives, whom The Schoolmaster is out to reduce.

Whether Van de Linde ever appeared in the English press is difficult to establish, especially as authors' names were not invariably cited in the magazines and journals. That he was not a frequenter of literary circles we know, although he did number several publicists among his friends. He was particularly intimate with George Croly, a clergyman who enjoyed considerable renown as a critic and poet and was closely associated with the *Literary Gazette* and *Blackwood's Magazine*. It is therefore not inconceivable that Van de Linde too should have contributed to these or other journals, but even if he did, he could as well have published articles on education as verse. Our general impression is that his career was on the whole confined to education, although he does from time to time mention something to Jacob van Lennep about having contributed to the press, but without giving any particulars. He was, however, an active member of several societies for educational reform and may, perhaps, occasionally have represented these in writing.

The Schoolmaster had never enjoyed robust health, and in the autumn of 1857 he fell ill. Four months later, on 27 January 1858, aged not quite fifty, the Reverend G. van de Linde Monteuuis passed away at Cromwell House, Highgate, '*deeply regretted by his sorrowing family and a numerous circle of friends*', as the announcement in *The Times* deaths column records. His widow was left with four young children to raise and a school to run.

From the poet's personal archive and from the material already published in *Holland*, Jacob van Lennep now compiled the anthology which appeared in 1859 and would very quickly make The Schoolmaster a household name. The first edition of *Poems by The Schoolmaster* sold out inside three months;

Poster advertising the first illustrated edition of *Poems by The Schoolmaster* (Gedichten van den Schoolmeester, 1872) (Collection Koninklijke Nederlandse Academie van Wetenschappen).

second and third editions followed in 1860 and 1861. Even more successful was the sixth edition of 1872, the first to contain illustrations (by Anthony de Vries). The widow and her children, however, derived little benefit from all this; as was usual at the time, the publisher had bought the rights to the poems for the – as it turned out – paltry sum of 240 guilders.

In his introduction to *Poems by The Schoolmaster*, Van Lennep wrote that his friend had always remained a Hollander at heart. And indeed, as his verses testify, Gerrit van de Linde consistently cherished his roots in the field closest to his heart: his native language. Here, for all his demure exterior, he continued to permit himself the liberties he had enjoyed as a student. In his everyday life as a London schoolmaster, The Schoolmaster may have conformed exactly with what was expected of his clerical station and his profession, but in his verse and in his letters Gerrit van de Linde never ceased to be a rebel who challenged every literary canon and rule of grammar in his explorations of the Dutch language.

MARITA MATHIJSEN
Translated by Sonja Prescod.

Three Poems by The Schoolmaster

Schoolmasters

He who, *of his own free will*,
And in his garret's gloom,
With headache pounding doom,
And nose blocked up with chill,
With bladder over-full,
Libido like a bull,
And stiffness in his neck,
Five panes through which wind blows,
And doors that will not close,
And gout in legs and toes,
Becomes a crazy wreck;
Is a less sorry freak
Than he, who all the week,
Amid the schoolroom's hell,
The grime and noxious smell,
Brats' questions full of air,
Nails bitten till quicks are bare,
Scratching to give lice a scare,
The *filthy* collars everywhere,
And the teasing to despair
Of the young must bear.

From *The Schoolmaster's Letters* (De brieven van De Schoolmeester, 1987)

The Lion

A lion's the sort of fellow
Who's never, ever yellow.
  His eyes are bigger than those
Of a giant, as is his nose,
   And he gnaws
   With murderous jaws;
   His claws slash
   With a speed as quick as a flash;
   His tail's force
   Can unseat a trooper on horse:
   And with teeth bared
He'll very soon have the whole troop running scared.
To conclude, he has been, ever since days of yore,
   The world's fiercest carnivore.
   Just recently in London town,
   A lion gulped a lady down;
   No, I'm wrong, I confess –
It wasn't the lion, but the lioness.

   The lion is born as a quadruped:
   Two legs at the rear and two at the head;
Or, so others claim, two right-hand legs that fit,
   And the other two legs set opposite.

   The lion's companion in life
   Is the lioness, his wife,
And for the young ones, while they are still fed at their mother's breast,
   The name 'cubs' is commonest.

   Golden lions and wooden lions too,
   Dutch ones included, are a long-lived crew;
They can still be seen on pub signs and coats-of-arms, though in woods
they're seldom on view.
Should ever a real lion approach you one fine day,
You'd be well advised to retreat without further delay;
   Though if stuffed or dead he'll do you no harm;
   In that case it'll just be a false alarm.

From *Poems by The Schoolmaster* (De gedichten van den Schoolmeester, 1975)

The Wolf and the Lamb

A Fable

(After La Fontaine.)

'Tell me, curly head,' said a wolf to a lamb by a brook:
'Why are you standing there drinking, as if no one would ever look?
It's high time we got acquainted and had a good chat in this nook.
That will be very different from romping with rams in the grass.
Were you going to dirty the water? I can't let that pass.'
'But, dear sir,' said the lamb. 'What am I to do?
How could I dirty your water? I'm not nearly as high up as you.'

The wolf was outraged by this comment, or its ambiguous sense,
Since wolves are always rather quick to take offence,
And said, 'If that word is your last,
As it's so frequently been in the past,
A young thing like you are will never bamboozle me so.
Why, you hoodwinked me like that only six short months ago.'

'I assure you, sir,' said the lamb, 'it's no fib,
That I was an unweaned infant then and lay helpless in my crib.'
'Well, my lambkin,' cried the wolf, as he closed in on the lamb,
'Then it must have been your son's wife or else your father ram.'

'I've no father nor daughter-in-law neither, not me,'
Said the lamb, and trembled like a leaf on a tree,
For the moment forgetting its whole pedigree.

'If you're trying to fool me,' the wolf said , 'you'll soon realise
That you must not ever pull the wool over decent folk's eyes.'

Then he wolfed down whole, in his glutton's way,
Like an English oyster, his curly prey.
And took what was left home as a gift to appease his little cubs' cries.
The lamb, of course, thought this not a great treat,
But as for the wolf, it was right up his street.

You sheep, and you children! The moral's that, even by quiet brooks,
A prowling wolf's not nearly as friendly as he looks,
Unless your parents have first given you, at least,
A strapping young nanny, who's a match for the beast.

From *Poems by The Schoolmaster* (De gedichten van den Schoolmeester, 1975).

All poems translated by Paul Vincent.

hronicle

Architecture

Continuity and Change Herman Hertzberger's
Recent Architecture

The work of architect Herman Hertzberger (1932-) has, in recent years, exhibited rapid development, with its culmination to date in the Chassé Theatre in Breda (1992-1995). At first sight this theatre, in which all the performance spaces are brought together under one undulating roof, is far removed from the work Hertzberger has been producing from the early sixties, the most famous example of which is the offices for the insurance company Centraal Beheer in Apeldoorn (1968-1972). For many years, each new design was the logical outcome of its predecessor, so that a highly coherent oeuvre resulted. This coherence now seems to have disappeared, but that is not in fact so. Although Hertzberger has moved on from the structuralist idiom in which repetition and linking of like forms was the guiding principle, he is nevertheless still building on his earlier work with his noticeably freer forms and compositions.

Hertzberger set up his own office in 1958, directly after finishing his architectural studies at the Delft Polytechnic. As a student he had already won, in collaboration with his fellow student Tjakko Hazewinkel, a competition for a students' hall of residence in Amsterdam that was built between 1959 and 1966. In the interim, a factory extension in Amsterdam (1962-1964) had been completed. In this building, Hertzberger's typical idiom found its first expression. Its salient features are configurative forms and the use of cast concrete, concrete, glass bricks and glass as the principal materials. This personal style took shape during the period when Hertzberger was on the editorial board of the periodical *Forum*, on which Aldo van Eyck and Jaap Bakema were leading figures. For roughly four years between 1959 and 1964 *Forum* was the mouthpiece and platform for a group of architects with a similar humane outlook, a similar view of the social significance of architecture as an essential aspect of life and, in many respects, a similar method of design which has become known as structuralism. The first issue published by these editors had as its title *The Story of a New Idea*. This new idea was an alternative to functionalism, which was perceived as bleak and rigid. It was an appeal to the imagination of the architect to create an environment in which the individual could feel at ease. This has remained Hertzberger's aim. Only the outward form in which he has clothed it has been transformed in the course of time, as can be seen, for example, in the series of schools he has built over the past thirty-five years. Hertzberger began his first school, the Montessori Junior School in Delft, in

Herman Hertzberger: Chassé
Theatre, Breda (1992-1995)
(Photo by Sybolt Voeten).

1960 and designed four extensions to it between then and the early eighties. This school contains the essential elements of all the schools he has subsequently built: the arrangement of the classrooms around a central space, which takes the place of the corridor in conventional schools. This central area is not only the practical link between the various classrooms but is also the social cement of the school: the meeting place before and after school hours and the place for communal activities, such as the performance of school plays. In the Apollo Schools in Amsterdam South (1980-1983), which are two stories high, the staircase in the central space functions for the first time both as staircase and platform. This staircase-platform is found in almost all his later school buildings up to and including the recent Anne Frank School in Papendrecht (1992-1994). The connecting spaces in the office building built for Centraal Beheer in Apeldoorn between 1968 and 1972 have a similar function. This building is the second structuralist monument after Van Eyck's Orphanage in Amsterdam, built between 1955 and 1960. Here, the corridors are not simply conceived as the link between A and B but also as the place where employees can socialise. Hertzberger has institutionalised the informal relations which, since the seventies, have become customary in offices where the coffee machine functions as a modern village pump. Typical of this informal non-hierarchical office is the structuralist repetition of cube-shaped office islands, by means of which the large building is reduced in scale.

After Centraal Beheer, the next large building to be reduced in scale by repetition was the Vredenburg Music Centre in Utrecht (1973-1978). The last large building in this series is the monumental building for the Ministry of Social Security and Employment, built between 1979 and 1990 in The Hague. The building can be regarded as the culmination of a long period in which Hertzberger used the structuralist design method. In this phase concrete columns were the normative elements of the facades and interiors of the majority of his buildings.

In the period during which the Ministry was being built, a change came about in Hertzberger's work which has led, in the nineties, to a freer approach, more directed to the overall form. Examples are the theatre complex in The Hague (1986-1991), the library and music school in Breda (1991-1993), the office for the Benelux Trade Mark Office in The Hague (1990-1993) and the Chassé Theatre in Breda.

The freedom which Hertzberger has allowed himself in his recent work is in conformity with one of the principal trends in architecture over the past ten years. Everywhere in the Western world an increasing number of buildings shows a movement away from the strict order of square geometry. Anyone who consults the international architecture journals of recent years will be confronted above all by undulating, folded forms, irregular volumes, slanting lines, inclined planes and oblique angles. The increasing use of the computer in architectonic design has been a significant factor in this development. Not only does the imagination of many designers seem to have gained a new dimension; of at least equal importance is the fact that the great computational capacity of the computer makes complex structures possible.

Characteristic of Hertzberger's recent work is the dominance of the roof. The undulating and folded single-span roofs of the Chassé Theatre and the Anne Frank School may be regarded as the continuation, using other means, of a principle that has guided his work: the pursuit of coherence. Up to the end of the eighties, Herzberger sought this coherence in the warp and weft of architecture: repeating forms, the linking of identical modules and the continuity of the load-bearing elements, the architectural order, as Hertzberger himself calls it. The results are comparable with textiles: they have an undeniable coherence but not necessarily a selvage. Buildings such as the Centraal Beheer office and the Vredenburg Music Centre could in principle be extended in any direction. Nowadays Hertzberger's work has a more strictly delimited form. Sometimes architectural unity is achieved by the overarching roof. In addition, however, Hertzberger employs various other means. From the end of the eighties, for example, an emergence of the clear, rounded form can be detected: the drum, or sections of it. The drum is a motif that Hertzberger was already using in the sixties, as in his competition design for the Amsterdam town hall (1967) in which the assembly halls are housed in drums that run riot in the string of rectangular box shapes. At the beginning of the eighties he rediscovered the possibilities of the circular plan and since then drums and circles have been appearing in a variety of functions.

The recurring presence of the drum in Hertzberger's work is characteristic of the tenacity with which he explores the architectonic possibilities of a limited number of themes. One of these themes is the staircase. It would be interesting to place all the various staircases Hertzberger has produced over the previous decades next to one another, to see how many solutions are possible for the relatively simple straight and spiral staircase. Nothing demonstrates more clearly the consistency of his work than the continuing series of variations on staircases. Moreover, the staircase could be regarded as a metonym for Hertzberger's architecture. As a connecting element, the staircase is a preeminently cohesive feature. Its invariably eccentric siting illustrates his rejection of hierarchy. And the often multiple functions of the staircase, which also serves as a platform, meeting place or view-point, underlines his continuing devotion to architecture, not primarily for its own sake, but as a means to creating an environment in which human beings can develop as social beings.

HANS IBELINGS
Translated by Lesley Gilbert.

Strolling through Flanders, Past and Present

'*I have good news from Ghent. And better news still from Antwerp.*' In the second edition of his *Flemish Cities Explored*, Derek Blyth is enthusiastic about the successful restorations of neighbourhoods and buildings in the notable cities of Flanders. According to the author, many positive changes took place in the period between the appearance of the book's first edition in 1990 and the second updated edition in 1996. Care and attention for the ancestral legacy is growing; the cities of Flanders are becoming increasingly fashionable.

This opinion is at odds with the criticism of urban policy often voiced in Flanders itself, but Blyth's enthusiasm is contagious. One quickly develops enormous respect for his knowledge of a wide range of art forms and the wealth of information that he has up his sleeve about the six Flemish cities of Bruges, Ghent, Antwerp, Mechelen, Brussels and Louvain (Leuven). The author, who lives in the Brussels area, takes the reader along on a series of walks that are clearly marked on handy maps. In fact, there are several walks provided for each city, making it possible for visitors to reach remote and less familiar points of interest. Blyth does not limit himself to the traditional cathedrals, churches, castles and museums. A rustic beguinage on the edge of the city, a narrow, fashionable little alley or a jolly modern café all make their appearance. The medieval ambience from the age when most of the great Flemish cities were in their heyday is effortlessly evoked, but the Flanders of the 1990s is also aptly described.

Many will be surprised to see that Brussels is included in *Flemish Cities Explored*. Outside Belgium, the Belgian capital is chiefly known as a French-speaking locality. But it should not be forgotten that Brussels was originally Flemish and did not become heavily gallicised until the nineteenth century. With its more than 100,000 Dutch-speaking inhabitants, it remains, paradoxically enough, one of the larger 'Flemish' cities.

Derek Blyth has also provided an introductory general historical sketch of Flanders, from the Roman conquest in the first century BC to the present. This enables him to place the information about the six cities within a broader framework. There are several notable points of contact with Anglo-Saxon history. Military cemeteries close to the old First World War Front in West Flanders attract tens of thousands of visitors every year. A fascinating but confusing period was the late thirteenth and early fourteenth centuries: the Flemish aristocracy had feudal ties with France, but the city guilds, influential associations of craftsmen, reacted against the local rulers and chose the side of England. Only after several battles had been fought did the French succeed in settling the dispute in their own favour. It is a great pity that the author makes an unfortunate linguistic excursion in this introduction. In a few sentences he attempts to describe the current language situation in Belgium, which he expresses in such oversimplified statements as '*the Dutch spoken by the Flemings is old-fashioned compared to the Dutch spoken in the Netherlands*', and '*the French spoken by the Walloons is archaic and quaint*'.

One happy discovery is the supplement 'Flanders for Children'. Young people who don't care to be dragged along from museum to museum or from cathedral to belfry can take a bit of solace here. The author directs their attention to fun boat rides through old city centres, a zoo, splendid parks and child-sized museums. The other supplement contains mostly practical information such as museum opening hours, addresses of hotels, and tips concerning restaurants and cafés. The literary-minded are made aware of places that play

Jacques François Joseph Carabain, *The Grand' Place in Brussels c.1900.* La Maison du Cygne, Brussels.

an important role in English, French and Dutch novels.

Flemish Cities Explored is informative as well as practical. In such a successful combination of general cultural publication and tourist guide, one doesn't mind the presence of the occasional minor error.

HANS VANACKER
Translated by Nancy Forest-Flier.

Derek Blyth, *Flemish Cities Explored. Bruges, Ghent, Antwerp, Mechelen, Brussels & Louvain.* London: Pallas Athene, 1996; 380 pp. ISBN 1-873429-61-4.

Dutch Books in London Libraries

Dutch and Flemish paintings have fascinated the British for centuries, and London museums are justly famous for their collections of Low Countries art. Interestingly, much the same can be said for books from the Low Countries, and so we find, in more than 20 libraries across London, very important collections of Dutch and Flemish books. The presence in London of these collections, built up during centuries of cultural contact and exchange, casts a fascinating light on British intellectual and cultural history, and reflects the long-standing and abiding British interest in the culture and society of their neighbours across the North Sea.

Provision for the general public is basic, but adequate. In the Victoria Library in Westminster, for example, the on-line computer catalogue offers access to a modern collection of over 1,000 books, in Dutch as well as in English, covering a wide range of interests such as art, architecture, cinema, cities, the colonies, costume and design, gardening, history, language, literature, music, printing and publishing, the Second World War and tourism. Through the Interlibrary Loan system these books are available at any public library in the Greater London Area. Another general collection – but a far more extensive and comprehensive one – is that of the London Library, in its wonderful club-like building in St James's Square, off Pall Mall. Established in 1840, this library is especially strong in the fields of Dutch literature, art and history, including Dutch colonial history.

But London's true strength is in its specialist collections. In the field of history, first of all, the Institute of Historical Research of the University of London in Bloomsbury houses the 5,000 volumes of the Low Countries Collection, built up by Professor Pieter Geyl and his successors. It consists of two large rooms full of primary sources and scholarly publications concerning the history of the Netherlands and Belgium. In the same building, on the fifth floor of Senate House Library, the Goldsmiths' collection contains many Dutch materials in the history of trade and commerce. The Belgian Collection there holds another 5,000 volumes, both in French and in Dutch, on Belgian Art, History and Literature, on the Congo and South Africa, on the Monarchy and on Belgium during the Second World War. Around the corner, the library of the School of

Oriental and African Studies (SOAS) contains many more books, journals, maps and globes concerning the colonial exploits of the Belgians in the Congo and the Dutch in the Indonesian archipelago. The latter subject is also covered in the holdings of the Southeast Asia Department of the British Library, while the Dutch Seaborne Empire and Anglo-Dutch maritime rivalry are the subject of the Dutch books, manuscripts, prints and atlases held in the National Maritime Museum in Greenwich.

A second major field of interest is that of natural history, botany and gardening. In the beautiful old library of the Royal Horticultural Society in Vincent Square, a ten minute walk from Victoria Station, one may consult modern Dutch works on, for example, the garden designs of Mien Ruys, but also the seventeenth-century handbook by the gardener to the Prince of Orange, published in Dutch, French and English. This library also holds the magnificent eighteenth-century folio editions, gloriously illustrated, of the botanical works by Rumphius on the Indonesian Spice Islands, by Van Rheede tot Drakesteyn on India's Malabar coast, and by Maria Sybilla Merian on Surinam.

In the field of religion, excellent collections of Dutch and Flemish books are available in Lambeth Palace Library, in the Dutch Church in Austin Friars and in the Leo Baeck College of Jewish Studies. These libraries contain early editions of Plantijn, Elzevier, Blaeu and other famous sixteenth- and seventeenth-centuries printers and publishers from the Low Countries: Dutch Bible translations; multilingual Bible editions; early Dutch Judaica and Hebrew books printed in Amsterdam; the Protestant Church Fathers in Latin; the works of the Remonstrants and their Calvinist opponents; and fiery Reformation pamphlets such as Marnix van St Aldegonde's vitriolic *Beehive of the Roman Catholic Church* (De byencorf der H. Roomsche Kercke, 1569), published in English translation in London in 1636.

For publications on Low Countries art, a key resource is the National Art Library in the Victoria and Albert Museum in Kensington, while specialist research libraries are available in the Courtauld Institute (especially for the Dutch Golden Age) and the Tate Gallery (modern avant-garde art of the nineteenth and twentieth centuries), all with significant Dutch holdings.

The biggest concentration of Dutch book collections is to be found in Bloomsbury. In University College London the Dutch Library, established in 1919 and today housed in the beautiful Moccatta Room, holds some 10,000 volumes in the field of Dutch language and literature, covering all periods and areas of Dutch and Flemish literary history, including some 200 early printed editions. The Library of the University of London in Senate House holds much more than the collections mentioned earlier. Its Elzevier Collection, for example, consists of 700 early Elzevier editions plus a further 400 books from other seventeenth-century Dutch publishers. In addition, there is the archive of Professor Emile Cammaerts, who was involved in the public defence of the Belgian King Leopold III after the Second World War. But the jewel in the crown is the unrivalled Dutch collection in the British Library, which contains hundreds of thousands of Dutch books in the Humanities and Social Sciences, from the earliest days of printing to the present. This includes some 50,000 books published before 1800, more than a quarter of which are unknown and unavailable in the Netherlands. These holdings make a unique and invaluable contribution to the *Short Title Catalogue Netherlands* (STCN), while many other departments in the British Library also contain extensive Dutch materials such as newspapers, pamphlets, early editions, maps and atlases.

The Dutch and Flemish books in these London collections constitute a great resource, a cultural capital waiting to be discovered and explored. To celebrate these treasures from 500 years of printing and publishing in the Low Countries, an international and interdisciplinary exhibition-with-conference will be held in 1999 in the new British Library at St Pancras.

REINIER SALVERDA

A *Directory of Dutch and Flemish Book Collections in London Libraries* is in preparation at the Dept of Dutch at University College London.

Film and Theatre

'I always put my actors first' The Films of Frans Weisz

Anyone wishing to call Frans Weisz (1938-) an actor *manqué* can count on his wholehearted agreement. All the works of this Dutch feature-film director are imbued with the love of his life: the theatre and its actors. After being expelled from drama school for not exhibiting sufficient talent, Weisz auditioned with virtually every theatrical group in the Netherlands. In 1958, when the Dutch Film Academy was founded in Amsterdam, he enrolled as its first student – still determined to find a place for himself in the theatre, even via this circuitous route. But in the event, things turned out quite differently to what he had expected. After his spell at the Film Academy, Weisz had become just as fascinated by the camera as he had been by his beloved theatre. The seeds had now been sown of his small but well-respected oeuvre.

In the 1960s, at the Centro Sperimentale di Cinematografia in Rome, Frans Weisz improved his knowledge of the cinema. He could have chosen no better surroundings for his temperament and natural talent for things theatrical. He eagerly imbibed the works of both Visconti and Fellini. It was not only his short stature which earned him the nickname 'Mini-Fellini'; in 1965, early in his career as a film-maker, his poetical film *Sunday on Grand-Jatte Island* (Een zondag op het

eiland van de Grand-Jatte) was awarded the Dutch State Prize for Film Art (since discontinued).

In no time at all, he had managed to persuade his friend the writer Remco Campert to write a film script of one of his novels. *The Gangster's Moll* (Het Gangstermeisje, 1965) was made in the wake of the brand new Dutch *nouvelle vague* represented by such directors as Adriaan Ditvoorst, Wim Verstappen and Pim de la Parra. *The Gangster's Moll*, filmed in high-contrast black-and-white, was rather confused, but very much an art film. Unfortunately, the film suffered from the misapprehension of the critics that this was an attempt at the creation of a female James Bond. In reality, it was a fairly abstract piece of work about imagination and reality.

For a long while, Frans Weisz was the one and only film director to make a living by directing advertising films. His commercials for the *Drum* brand of tobacco became exceptionally popular, breaking the taboo on a serious film director being involved in advertising.

The 1970s can be characterised as an unsettled period for the Dutch film industry. The *nouvelle vague* had ebbed silently away because of a lack of public interest, and the industry now steered a course towards more commercial, mainstream cinema. Paul Verhoeven created a stir with his film version of Jan Wolkers' novel *Turkish Delight* (Turks fruit,1969) and, to everyone's surprise, Frans Weisz too was to be found in the ranks of those film directors seeking a larger audience. With *The Burglar* (De inbreker, 1972) and *Naked over the Fence* (Naakt over de schutting, 1973), both film versions of detective novels, Weisz proved he could be a skilful narrator of quick-fire, no-punches-pulled stories. And yet he was taking a risk. For the lead in both films he had chosen Rijk de Gooijer, known mainly as an entertainer, and as one half of a comic double-act. Weisz can be given the credit for having discovered in De Gooijer the great actor who would go on to play the role of his life in his latest film *Last Call* (Hoogste tijd, 1995).

Spurred on by the enthusiasm of the public-at-large, Frans Weisz moved on to direct two mass-audience films *Red Sien* (Rooie Sien, 1975) and *Jet, Have a Heart* (Heb medelij, Jet, 1976). With the exception of *One Sultry Summer's Evening* (Een zwoele zomeravond), which he made with the cooperative Het Werktheater, he now appeared to be concentrating on more seriously artistic cinema. After three TV adaptations of avant-garde musical plays, he made the film which was to establish his reputation as an almost unDutch director of theatre films.

Charlotte (1980) was based on the life of the Jewish artist Charlotte Salomon, murdered in Auschwitz in 1943. She left behind an entire autobiography consisting of a series of 769 gouaches and writings with the title *Leben oder Theater?*. This was the perfect subject for a film director who had made the theatre his life and who had quite often made his life into theatre. This international production, with Birgit Doll and Derek Jacobi in the lead roles, gained Weisz the artistic recognition that had so long eluded him. He began

Frans Weisz, *Last Call*
(Hoogste tijd, 1995) (Photo by
Pief Weijman).

more and more to specialise in theatrical films, with a penchant for fluent camera work round carefully constructed scenes and actions meticulously rehearsed by the actors.

Havinck (1987) proved to be a brilliantly acted play for the intimate theatre, while *Malicious Delight* (Leedvermaak, 1989) was an admirable demonstration of the work of one particular theatre group, being the award-winning film version of the long-running play of the same name by the poet and playwright Judith Herzberg.

Another taboo was now broken when Frans Weisz began to direct television productions without making any concessions that would damage filmic quality. Both the six-part series *On Closer Examination* (Bij nader inzien, 1991) which dealt with the lives of young students in post-war Amsterdam, and the three-part series *On Hire-Purchase* (Op afbetaling, 1992) were also produced in cinema versions. Once again, and especially in *On Closer Examination*, the cooperation of younger, up-and-coming actors made an impression on audiences. The series was awarded the Dutch film prize *Het Gouden Kalf* (The Golden Calf).

This now seemed to be a suitable moment for Weisz to attempt his *magnum opus*, the filming of Harry Mulisch's complex novel *Last Call* (Hoogste tijd, 1985). This book contained all the ingredients so dear to Weisz: the world of the theatre, multiple layers of meaning, and an opportunity for Baroque staging and design. Both the novel and the film deal with the old variety artist Willem Bouwmeester (a role cut out for Rijk de Gooijer), one of a prodigious family of actors. But he is also the black sheep of the family who never comes up to expectations, always makes the wrong decisions and forfeits his chances of success. During the Second World War, he had continued to work under the auspices of the German occupying forces, an unforgivable sin in Dutch eyes. Consequently, after

the war, he was reduced to acting in radio plays and working as an extra.

Willem Bouwmeester is given one last chance. He is asked to play the star role of an old actor making himself up in the year 1904 for his farewell performance. On account of the countless intrigues surrounding the person of this actor, this final performance becomes a fiasco. But during rehearsal Bouwmeester has had time to ponder on the vicissitudes of his existence and feels himself obliged to let several skeletons emerge from the cupboard. He has descended like Orpheus into the Underworld to rediscover his Eurydice, his soul.

Jan Blokker, who wrote the film script, successfully reduced the structural complexities of a novel about an actor playing an actor, in a play within a play, to a brilliantly clear tale, in which Weisz could make the most of his love of the theatre. He makes good use of the apron, the wings and the footlights, as well as of period costume. This is fully in accordance with Weisz' credo: '*I always put my actors first*', since the director tailors all the camera angles to the interplay between the subdued style of our day and the pomposity of acting of around 1904.

Last Call offers the audience some excellent performances in sumptuous surroundings and with an intriguing plot. The numerous parallel events and the emphasis on dress do, however, serve to prevent the film from ever attaining the psychological depth and emotional involvement expected by the audience. Weisz has therefore still not made his definitive film of the theatre; as the director himself always exclaims: '*The next one, that'll be my real masterpiece!*'

GERDIN LINTHORST
Translated by Eric Dickens.

The Netherlands Theatre Institute Restyled

The thin partitions have all been torn out of the building's stately rooms, and construction workers have removed the strip lighting that had been haphazardly screwed onto the ornamental ceilings. In June 1997, the five Amsterdam canalside houses that are home to the Netherlands Theatre Institute (officially: 'Theater Instituut Nederland') were restored to their former glory.

The renovation lasted about two years, forcing the Netherlands Theatre Institute staff to double up on more than one occasion. While the builders were working on the Bartolotti House, a seventeenth-century architectural *tour de force* on the left side of the complex, the whole institute was transferred to the right-hand part of the building.

But now the buildings are on display once again in all their grandeur. At the same time, the renovated structure satisfies every possible expectation of a modern art institute. The library has been greatly expanded, there is a large auditorium, and the entire complex is equipped with an advanced computer network so that video images can be shown throughout the whole building. The central house, another monumental building through which a splendid spiral staircase twists and turns, will once again serve as the entrance to such areas as the exhibition rooms.

The Theatre Institute began by displaying costumes and posters. In 1922, a private collection of theatre documents was placed in the hands of a single organisation. For years the Tooneelmuseum toured the city until it was given permanent accommodation on the Herengracht in 1958. Its collection is still growing. New scenery models from large companies are given a place in the archives and imaginative costumes are purchased. A few years ago, for instance, the costumes that were used in *Groosland* (1989) were acquired. In this National Ballet production, the dancers performed in vast, flesh-coloured outfits. Today the museum presents an overview of the heyday of Dutch popular theatre, from the establishment of the famous Amsterdam 'Salon des Variétés' in 1839 to the outbreak of the Second World War in 1940, in two of its large rooms. There is also plenty of space for temporary exhibitions.

In 1993, under the leadership of its current director, Dragan Klaic, the 'Nederlandse Theater Instituut', as it was then known, merged with other institutes dedicated to one of the performing arts. Since then, all the performing arts have been combined in the Netherlands Theatre Institute: drama, dance, mime, puppet and object theatre, young people's theatre, opera and theatrical entertainments such as musicals and circuses. From these six categories, one form of theatre is singled out each year. That subject is given special attention in all the Institute's various departments. When the attention turned to puppet and object theatre in 1996, workshops were organised at which foreign puppeteers and theatre professionals talked about their work. The Institute's publishing department, which issues about ten new publications annually, placed special emphasis that year on puppet and object theatre. Thus appeared a biographical portrait of Cilli Wang, the Austrian-Dutch artist who combined cabaret, dance and puppetry into a unique theatrical form. An exhibition of puppet and object theatre was also organised, but was forced to tour as a travelling exhibition because the Institute's museum rooms were still in the process of reconstruction.

Now that the renovation of the buildings on the Herengracht is completed, the focus has turned to the dance. The reason for this choice is that an international conference on dance is scheduled for November 1997.

The Netherlands Theatre Institute fills an important public function. Each year, 10,000 visitors make use of the library, which contains an extensive archive of clippings and a large collection of audio and video recordings, programme booklets and scenery photography. Information may also be requested by telephone about that theatre production fifty years ago of which someone still has such fond memories. For theatre buffs who would like to know more about a particular production that is currently running, the Netherlands Theatre Institute organises Theatre Encounters on a

The Netherlands Theatre Institute in Amsterdam (Photo by Roel Bogaerds).

regular basis. At these events, enthusiasts can come to the auditorium and listen to discussions between journalists and theatre professionals.

In addition, the Institute is eager to act as a forum for practitioners of the performing arts. In this capacity it convenes gatherings at which theatre professionals can share their experiences. The Amsterdam Summer University, for example, affords the Netherlands Theatre Institute a good opportunity to organise workshops for directors and choreographers.

The Institute also offers services in quite a different area. What are the fiscal snags that theatre companies ought to know about while touring abroad? It's a prosaic question, but theatre professionals have to face it sooner or later. For this reason the Institute, working with a tax consultancy, issues a brochure that contains an answer to this question. Next year the Netherlands Theatre Institute will be organising a symposium on the juridical aspects of the stage arts.

In 1996, St Petersburg celebrated Peter the Great's visit to the Netherlands three hundred years earlier (see *The Low Countries* 1996-97: 275-276). A huge cultural event was organised for the occasion in which the Netherlands Theatre Institute took responsibility for the theatre programme. An anthology of theatre plays was issued as well as a publication about the Dutch theatre. In addition, a number of companies travelled to the Russian seaport to present several productions. The Institute regularly takes advantage of such international cultural events in order to promote Dutch theatre abroad. Among those performing at the Expo in Seville in 1992, for instance, were Toneelgroep Amsterdam with a multi-lingual version of their collage-production *Ballet* and the company Dogtroep (see *The Low Countries* 1994-95: 274-275) with one of their spectacular performances.

The Netherlands Theatre Institute works intensively with the Flemish Theatre Institute. In fact, together they cover the whole of Dutch-speaking theatre. Four times a year the two institutes put out *Carnet*, a journal issued in both English and French that keeps foreign readers informed of goings-on in the Dutch-speaking theatre. A video is being prepared for the coming year which offers an impression of current tendencies in the theatre in the Netherlands and Flanders. The five monumental buildings may be located in the heart of Amsterdam, but the activities of the Netherlands Theatre Institute extend far beyond the country's borders.

PIETER BOTS
Translated by Nancy Forest-Flier.

ADDRESS
Netherlands Theatre Institute
Herengracht 168 / P.O. Box 19034 / 1000 GH Amsterdam /
The Netherlands
tel. +31 20 551 33 00 / fax +31 20 551 33 03

RECENT PUBLICATIONS
COULING, DELLA (ed.), *Dutch and Flemish Plays.* London / Amsterdam, 1997.
ROBSON, CHERYL (ed.), *A Touch of the Dutch. Plays by Women.* London / Amsterdam, 1997.

Dance in Flanders

During the eighties there has been a marked increase in interest in dance in a number of countries. Choreographers and dance companies from Flanders, too, have been the focus of international interest. But until recently anyone who wanted to learn more about this development had to delve into libraries and archives for a whole series of articles. The end of 1996, however, saw the publication of the first fairly detailed study of 'Dance in Flanders'. The starting-point of the book,

Anne Teresa de Keersmaeker,
Ottone, Ottone.

on which fifteen different authors have collaborated, is the glory years of the eighties and nineties. But to show just how successful these have been, it is necessary also to give the historical context.

In the first chapter, therefore, the authors seek out the roots of avant-garde dance, which they locate in the thirties. They go no further back in time, because in the nineteenth and early twentieth centuries dance was not regarded as an autonomous art form but as a subdivision of opera. After the Second World War a structural framework came into existence, with a school and a professional company. Here the book discusses the pioneering role of Jeanne Brabants, the driving force behind the Royal Flanders Ballet (see *The Low Countries* 1996-1997: 74-79). Due attention is also given, of course, to the importance of the Frenchman Maurice Béjart. He established himself and his *Ballet du Vingtième Siècle* in Brussels from 1960 on, where he founded Mudra, a dance school which also influenced developments in the eighties.

The present flourishing condition of dance (and theatre) in Flanders is due to a number of factors. Here it is important to stress the role of the arts centres. They were the first in Flanders to organise performances of dance for their public. Festivals devoted solely to dance, such as *Klapstuk* and *Beweeging*, were also held. Gerard Mortier, and the opera house De Munt which he successfully directed in the 1980s, provided a further stimulus to the performing arts. And of course there were foreign elements too which had an effect on Flemish avant-garde dance. Particularly influential were American modernism and postmodernism, which reached Belgium some twenty years down the line, and Pina Bausch. Bausch's work brought the contemporary Flemish dance world once more into contact with the expressionist tradition in dance and with the Central European school.

The book also gives a detailed account of the work of Anne Teresa de Keersmaeker (see *The Low Countries* 1994-95: 59-62), Wim Vandekeybus (see *The Low Countries* 1995-96: 274-275) and Jan Fabre (see *The Low Countries* 1995-96: 117-125), the three outstanding figures of the period. In addition to these three we are offered a whole string of other dancers. Here it becomes apparent that in fact 'Flemish dance' is hardly an accurate term. Nationality is of no great significance in the world of dance. The Frenchman Béjart was for years the leading spirit in dance in Belgium, the francophone Anne de Mey began her career in a Flemish company, the Mexican Besprosvany made his debut with the Flemish group 'Furioso', and so on. Only the American Mark Morris, Maurice Béjart's successor at the Munt Theatre, failed to achieve success. Béjart's legacy was too much for him; he was never accepted by public or press.

Finally, the book also discusses the relationship between dance and film, writing about dance and dance teaching.

In the last fifteen years dance in Flanders has gone through a remarkably swift and successful evolution. This book offers the reader a great many elements which explain how this success has come about. On top of that, it is abundantly provided with illustrations. Where the words fall short, the photos make everything clear.

DIRK VAN ASSCHE
Translated by Tanis Guest.

Dance in Flanders (ed. An-Marie Lambrechts, Marianne van Kerkhoven and Katie Verstockt). Bruges: Stichting Kunstboek, 1997; 245 p. ISBN 90-74377-40-8.

'Big black holes with the glittering of diamonds' Theatre according to Ivo van Hove

Just now Ivo van Hove (1958-), the Fleming who heads the Zuidelijk Toneel in Eindhoven, is one of the most important stage directors in the Netherlands. Van Hove brings new life to a sort of theatre that is considered by many as outmoded and old-fashioned, in a company whose task it is to produce repertory plays for their large theatre and then to take them on tour throughout the country. Ivo van Hove's productions are frequently selected by the jury of the Theatre Festival as being among the ten best of the season. The great public interest in this ' Renaissance' of repertory theatre is evidence of a need that is deeply rooted in Dutch culture.

Van Hove's productions, based on dramas by both classical and modern playwrights, are couched in a contemporary language that is not based on external elements, but establishes links with personal and more general themes. In addition to this, Van Hove is able to make creative use of the innovations introduced in recent decades in the Netherlands and Flanders (mainly in small theatres and experimental groups). He also continues to develop them, in close cooperation with Jan Versweyveld, his permanent set designer, and the actors, whom he forges into a close-knit ensemble.

After training as a stage director in Brussels, Van Hove contributed to the birth of several Flemish theatre companies (Akt Vertikaal and the Witte Kraai). By the time he began work on his first full-scale productions for De Tijd, he had already been experimenting for several years with his own scenarios, location projects and performance-like events.

One of his first classics, *The Bacchantes* (De Bacchanten, 1987), was a play of complex contrasts: both contemporary content and timeless significance were added to the ancient myth Euripides had incorporated into the play. In *Macbeth* (1987), Bertolt Brecht's statements on the tragedy provided the starting point. The personal theme and the politics were interwoven, not realistically but with a marked use of irony and melodrama. The director's approach sought to bring out the echo of and connections with our own time.

Van Hove was later to return both to the Greek classics and to Shakespeare. After directing several productions for Dutch companies like the Theater van het Oosten (Shakespeare's *Richard II* in 1990) and Toneelgroep Amsterdam (Wedekind's *Lulu* in 1989),

he staged an *Ajax / Antigone* double bill (1991) and *Hamlet* (1993) for Het Zuidelijk Toneel. Other names characteristic of his repertoire are James Green, Eugene O'Neill, Tennessee Williams and Edward Bond, playwrights who have most of the time enjoyed classic status. His approach is typified by respect for the writer and the pursuit of clarity: '*Each sentence of the text itself is analysed. In the end I want to be able to explain every one of a character's actions*', says the director.

O'Neill's *Desire under the Elms* (1985), *Mourning Becomes Electra* (1993) and *More Stately Mansions* (1994) all deal with the role of Fate in human existence, as do Edward Bond's *Saved* (1992) and *Hamlet*. The struggle with the metaphysical God or gods is often transposed on stage into the conflict between man and the power of his surroundings or, more psychologically, with aspects of his own character. In Ivo van Hove's eyes, dramas are either about families or about kings: the two fundamental structures around which the world is organised.

In certain productions, but especially in *Desire under the Elms*, a ritual and theatrical lyricism was created by means of dance elements and music. In this family drama, set on a farm, in which O'Neill tells a fragment of the social history of New England, the spotlight is on the actor and his two basic instruments: language and the body. The pursuit of authenticity in the acting had its counterpart in the stage setting, with a number of real cows on stage. The actors communicated in a language that came from being shackled together, from feeling each other wildly and bestially, from crawling towards each other jerkily and convul-

Ivo van Hove (1958-)(Photo by Geert van Kesteren).

sively, and finally from breaking through the silence of wordlessness with impotent screams.

Saved was dominated by contemporary visual culture. Van Hove treated this play by Edward Bond, set against a working-class background and in which a religious theme is secularised and attacked, as a scenario. The dialogue contains numerous references and symbols relating to dialogues, containing such concepts as mercy, tribulation and temptation, which are taken from the Bible and Christian teaching. In one particular scene a baby is stoned by a group of youngsters: verbal and physical violence here clearly stand for the mocking and crucifixion of Christ. This was the farthest he had yet gone in the field of the obliteration of realism. This obliteration takes place in many ways, both structural and in the incidental: in the design, the elimination of the characters' psychology, in the emancipation of the sounds, in the directing, which divides the action from the text, etc.

As a director on the one hand Van Hove operates within the boundaries of psychologically realistic theatre, while on the other he integrates anti-illusionist, alienating moments into his directing, or uses intensification and magnification. The influence of 'performance' makes itself felt very clearly here. When his directing is based on the personality of the actor, it signifies a quest for a moment at which the action on stage becomes almost authentic, almost reality. When the boundary between acting out the character and being oneself within the character disappears, then the body, subject to taboo, frustrated, longing and desiring, tells its own story. Bodies such as those of Sara and Simon in *More Stately Mansions*, one of O'Neill's less frequently performed plays.

His latest productions confirm this director's affinity with the English-language repertoire. Van Hove was also invited to direct *More Stately Mansions* for the New York Theater Workshop in September 1997. But discoveries have also been made in other literatures and texts, e.g. in the first version of Camus' play *Caligula*.

The story of the Roman emperor Caligula and his reign of terror is set in today's technological world, in which video images, recorded live and displayed simultaneously on several screens, are combined with live acting. Tight directing places the emphasis on the emperor's personality, at one and the same time an inconsolable child and a dangerous madman. In Van Hove's version, poetry and politics struggle with each other, as do nature and reason, emotion and intellect, word and image, while at the same time complementing each other. On his journey through the world of theatre, with its texts and meanings, Van Hove is creating a theatrical poetics of his own and building up a body of work in the same way as artists and poets do. In his work, things which cannot be united form a temporary symbiosis. '*I am a psychological play maker, but not one who thinks psychology is enough; it has to rise above reality. It must become poetry. After all, to me theatre is about paradise, lost or utopian perhaps, but nevertheless paradise. It is about a dream. Theatre should reveal big black holes, in which suddenly appears the glittering of a diamond.*'

HANA BOBKOVA
Translated by Gregory Ball.

St Anna's Chapel in Antwerp

Whenever one looks at a view of a city from the Ancien Régime, one is always struck by the way in which in those days the silhouettes of cities were determined by the large number of towers rising above the grey mass of dwellings. The greater part of these are the towers of the principal parish and monastic churches; but there are usually also some small towers to be seen, the towers of small chapels connected with convents, or almshouses, or which were maintained by a craft. In the seventeenth century the city of Antwerp had around fifty such public places of worship, in addition to the five parish churches, and one of the few small chapels to have survived is St Anna's Chapel. Its history is a fine example of the devotion of a few private individuals, just as it owes its present-day restoration entirely to private enterprise.

St Anna's Chapel (also known as the Dry-shearers' Chapel or Keizerskapel), in Keizerstraat, was built in the period 1512-1517 by the guild of dry-shearers. The dry-shearers were textile workers who clipped the dried cloth after it had been fulled; that is to say, they clipped off the threads of the nap which were too long. In the sixteenth century Antwerp was a major centre for the import of raw cloth which was then finished there. In this context, dry-shearing came to be an important craft, and the craftsmen could afford to build their own chapel. The chapel was under the control of the craft during the Ancien Régime. It was dedicated to Saint Anna, the patron saint of the guild.

The chapel is a fine example of Brabantine Flamboyant Gothic: a single-nave church of white limestone under a high slate roof with a spirelet. The interior is relatively simple, but none the less luxurious by virtue of a number of embellishments which were added in the seventeenth century.

From 1625-1648 the guild put its chapel at the disposal of the parish of St Willibrord, since the pastor of this parish had fled for safety within the city walls on account of the Eighty Years' War between the Low Countries and the Spanish Empire. He brought with him the statue of Our Lady, with its miraculous powers, and set it in St Anna's Chapel. Partly owing to the attraction of this statue, the chapel became an important place of worship for Antwerp and the surrounding area. Following the Peace of Münster (1648) parish and statue left the confines of the city walls again, but, at the request of the people living in the neighbourhood, a new statue was placed in the

Alexander II Casteels, *Interior
of St Anna's Chapel.* 1710.
Canvas. Keizerskapel, Antwerp.

chapel and mass continued to be celebrated there.

Because of the wealthy area in which it was situated, and its attraction as a place of worship, St Anna's flourished during this period. A new baroque framed altar with a canopy was added, as was a new organ-loft. Abraham Matthijssen's painting of the Assumption of the Virgin Mary was purchased for this altar. The beautiful black and white marble floor was laid in 1680, and a baroque outer porch was also added. The considerable collection of religious silver, which is still in the possession of the chapel, was built up in this period. The show-piece in all this is undoubtedly the huge sun monstrance of gilded silver, made in 1653 by Hendrik Corbion. In those days it cost the fabulous amount of 558 guilders. For the purpose of comparison: at that time the highest paid worker earned less than a guilder a day, and most people received barely half a guilder.

During the French period, after the abolition of the guilds and craft organisations and the closure of the churches, St Anna's came into private hands. A baker, Petrus Vingerhoets, quickly succeeded in hiring the chapel, and in 1880 it was re-opened for public worship. For a few years the chapel even had a parochial function. A collection among the parishioners raised enough for them to buy the chapel back. It became and remained the property of a tontine which always included the churchwardens, among others, among its members. In 1899 it came into the possession of the White Fathers (African Missionaries); nearly a hundred years later, in 1989, they sold it to Xavier Nierberding.

Mr Nierberding wanted to acquire the chapel for the European University in Antwerp and open it again for public worship, after years of closure and neglect.

To this end, and without any state input, a considerable restoration campaign was started under the leadership of Rutger Steenmeijer. The result is clearly to be seen. For instance, radical work was necessary to stabilise the West facade, while the valuable nineteenth-century leaded windows needed extensive repairs. The chapel's entire collection of moveable art objects was also refurbished. On 10 September 1994, after three years of restoration, St Anna's was opened to visitors. Since then it has been accessible every day to worshippers and art-lovers. In 1995 this magnificent restoration won first prize from the Royal Society for Historic Towns in Belgium.

Thus, the concern of individual people has been a constant in the chapel's history; in the sixteenth century it was raised by the dry-shearers, in the second half of the seventeenth century it flourished with the support of people in the surrounding neighbourhood, in the French period it was saved from demolition by a baker and other local residents, and recently the European University has succeeded in restoring it to its former glory.

MARIE JULIETTE MARINUS
Translated by Sheila M. Dale.

ADDRESS
St Anna's Chapel
Keizerstraat 23 / 2000 Antwerp / Belgium
Services in English on Sundays and Holidays (6 p.m.)

FURTHER READING
Jean-Pierre de Bruyn and Maurice Meul, *De Keizerskapel te
Antwerpen*. Antwerp, 1994.

Chivalric and Urban Culture in the Low Countries during the Late Middle Ages

The last few years have seen a growing interest within the international academic world in Medieval Dutch literature. One example of this is the collection *Medieval Dutch Literature in its European Context*, published fairly recently by Cambridge University Press. One striking aspect of medieval Dutch literature is the fact that, in contrast to the rest of Europe, the urban elite in the Low Countries was relatively late in producing its own literary fiction.

Towards the year 1300 the Flemish aristocracy was politically and socio-economically on the decline, and Flemish towns were reaching the culmination of a process of demographic, economic and political development which began around the year 1000. And yet, until the end of the fourteenth century, the urban elites appear to take no part in literary patronage: in the towns, too, the chivalric romance led the field.

Possible explanations for this paradoxical lack of a typical urban theme in the medieval fiction of the Low

Countries during this period could lie in the imitative behaviour of town-dwellers, a pseudo-aristocracy who revelled in chivalric literature and lifestyle. On the other hand, a contra-indication for this hypothesis is the emergence in the twelfth century of fiction in the vernacular, a phenomenon which implies the intellectual hunger of a new public which differed from the traditional nobility and clergy. Nor can it be claimed that the urban citizenry had no intellectual basis: as early as around 1200, Ghent already had town schools, typically catering for the needs of merchants. And in 1128 the Flemish towns were already so far emancipated that they could play a full part opposite the Count in the political decision-making processes.

Just to the south of Flanders, in Arras, a lively pattern of organised urban literary activity and patronage existed from the year 1200. Arras even had two types of urban literary community: on the one hand an elitist society club, Le Puy, comparable with the later Chambers of Rhetoric, and on the other hand a more popular *confrérie* for *jongleurs*, which was comparable with the later critical popular theatre. Some of the impulses for these clubs admittedly came from outside, from courtly circles. These clubs, to which every self-respecting citizen of Arras belonged, prove that town-dwellers of all social levels participated in this rich literary life of Arras. Adam de la Halle and other celebrities were paid both by the elitist and by the popular confrérie. We should not be surprised at this early bourgeois patronage: Arras housed well-to-do merchants and bankers. The fact that Adam de la Halle, for example, brought more shepherds and knights on to his stage than urban citizens in no way implies that he was writing for an aristocratic audience. Literary sociology demonstrates the existence of compensation literature, and here, too, imitative behaviour undoubtedly played a role, with well-to-do citizens aping aristocratic behaviour patterns in order to set themselves apart from the urban *hoi-polloi*.

In any case, the lighter Arras *Chansons* from the thirteenth century do often focus on the citizenry, both in admiration for economic success stories and in satirical reflections on the immorality of fraudulent businessmen or the sexual promiscuity of Arras' bourgeois females.

It is interesting to note here that the theatre productions and public festivals in Arras were organised by citizens for citizens, but that in the years 1258-1272 these same proud citizens also received noblemen from Artois during their lyrical evenings, and even welcomed the Count of Anjou, the English Prince Edward and Duke Henry III of Brabant. These occasions thus contributed to the image-building of the proud town. Above all, however, the phenomenon demonstrates that one and the same literary product was consumed by a very diverse public, though admittedly with an equally diverse decoding system. Adam de la Halle's *Jeu de Robin et Marion*, composed in Arras in around 1276, was written according to one researcher for an aristocratic public, and in the opinion of another researcher for the citizens of Arras. There is a simpler formula: could the work not have been written for a mixed public, for aristocrats, well-to-do patricians and less well-off craftsmen?

If there are no sharp divisions between aristocratic and bourgeois consumers of culture, and if we accept that the irony of a bourgeois story can appeal to courtly readers, and vice versa, then the dominance of the courtly theme and the relative lack of genuinely bourgeois subjects until well into the fourteenth century need no longer be seen as a symptom of a lack of a broad urban public for literature from the twelfth century onwards; this then removes a good deal of our initial paradox.

The Flemish Reynard epic (see *The Low Countries* 1995-96: 233-239) is a second case in point. We can hardly claim that the target group for this work was in the first place the nobility. The story existed in French before it was translated into Dutch and circulated in the Low Countries; nobles and clerics thus did not really need the Dutch version. This must therefore have been aimed at a new public, alongside and on top of the traditional audience.

Just as we cannot exclude the bourgeoisie as readers of courtly lyric, however, so aristocratic and clerical readers cannot be excluded from the readers of the Dutch version of the Reynard epic, despite the fact that the work is a highly critical parody of courtly life. Urban readers could have great fun with the cynical passage in which the author, with a specific wink towards those citizens, attacks the dog Courtois (= 'courtier'!) because he speaks French at every opportunity, an explicit allusion to the cultivation of French as the language of culture by the Flemish aristocracy from the twelfth to the fifteenth century. They were, it has to be said, eagerly copied by the bourgeois elite of Ghent and Ypres; thus they too, like the citizens of Arras, had free access to the French chivalric romances and courtly lyric.

There is yet another striking feature here. One might have expected that periods of flourishing culture at the courts of the Low Countries would have diminished

Detail of a miniature from the *Livre des tournois*, ordered by Gruuthuse, a bibliophile from Bruges (Paris, Bibliothèque Nationale, Ms. 7361, fr. 2692, f. 68).

urban culture in those same periods. This is not the case, however. On the contrary, there is a remarkable synchrony. The brilliant courtly culture of Philip of Alsace (mid-twelfth century) coincides with the first wave of political self-awareness in the Flemish towns. The same applied to Brabant at the end of the thirteenth century, Holland around 1400 and, above all, the Burgundian Netherlands under Philip the Good. One bearer of culture (noble ruler) challenged the other (the towns); each relied on the other. Finally, and typically, these successful periods occurred when the dialogue with other cultures was more intense: Philip of Alsace and his towns engaged in inspiring contacts with the rest of Europe, the former via the court in Troyes, the town merchants via the annual markets in the same Champagne region. This cosmopolitanism in no way hindered the original development of the *Ars Nova* of Jan van Eyck and Guillaume Dufay.

These issues are extensively discussed in *Medieval Dutch Literature in its European Context*. In some 15 essays, Frits van Oostrom, Herman Pleij, W.P. Gerritsen, *et al.*, provide in-depth analyses of the specificity of courtly and urban literature in the Low Countries, the chivalric romances, the presence of the Arthurian cycle in the Low Countries, Reynard the Fox, creations based around the theme of love, religious works, didactic literature, works on nutrition and cooking, and the theatre. Particularly useful is the English translation of a number of Medieval Dutch texts in the Appendix, as well as the exhaustive summary of existing published translations.

WALTER PREVENIER
Translated by Julian Ross.

FURTHER READING
E. Kooper (ed.), *Medieval Dutch Literature in its European Context*, Cambridge, 1994.

The Utrecht Psalter A Unique and Precious Ninth-Century Book

The Utrecht Psalter is referred to as a 'masterpiece', even, 'a wonder of the world'. It is a book made of vellum between 820 and 835, with 182 leaves on which are written in majestic Roman capitals the 150 psalms of the Bible and a number of canticles (Bible songs). Appropriate illustrations have been made for the psalms, and it is principally these drawings which give the book its special character.

The drawings were probably made by various artists, maybe eight in all. That does not alter the fact that the style is consistent. The content of the psalms is depicted as far as possible by means of concrete objects. The originators have sought these points of reference to a great extent in the reality with which they were familiar. For the monks in question that was not entirely a reality of their own direct observation. To a considerable extent their artistic activity is intertextual in nature. They have drawn on existing traditions

Detail from the Utrecht Psalter (c.820-835): '*Blessed is the man that walked not in the counsel of the ungodly.*' (Psalm 1, vs. 1).

with regard to the portrayal of historical and mythological scenes, from the early Middle Ages as well as from classical antiquity.

Whoever examines the illustrations in the Psalter is faced with a challenging puzzle. What has its roots in tradition and mythology? What has its roots in contemporary historical reality? An example is offered by the drawing relating to the first line of the first psalm: '*Blessed is the man that walked not in the counsel of the ungodly.*'

The blessed man is one who buries himself in a book. Let us suppose it is a Psalter, the book that was popularised by the Benedictines. Behind the man stands an angel making a gesture, one of protection perhaps from two babblers further away who are trying to distract him. His blessed state is shown not only by this angel borrowed from Christian tradition, but also by the place where the '*beatus vir*' is to be found: a temple. But the expression on his countenance, and his whole body attitude depict something that the illustrator has been able to observe in his immediate surroundings: attention and intellectual effort. The same is true for the equivocal attitude of the tempters, the ungodly. Thus the illustrations also provide a historical entry point to a universal psychological world. Every human person depicted is a 'fellow human being from the Middle Ages', with his recognisable general human, but also personal, traits. But there is also the specific historical conceptual universe of the Middle Ages, to be found in churches, buildings, implements, weaponry, but also in fantasies such as the representations of saints being torn apart by wild animals and birds flying away with hacked-off parts of bodies.

The illustrations are not only remarkable for their content. They have an undeniable artistic value: all 166 of them can be considered as products of what is called 'naïve art'. What is striking in this context is the attention devoted to action, to movement and to the expression of feelings, in countenance and body, even though the drawings are so extremely tiny. Could that be the reason why the illustrators did not make use of colours, as was customary for the miniatures with which manuscripts of the middle ages were illuminated? The drawings are done in dark ink, in a brownish colour (bistre) with shading achieved by the addition of water or white wine, or by not dipping the pen so deeply in the ink.

Anyone who takes the time to examine the drawings carefully will be rewarded with a very special aesthetic experience, because they invite one to share in the pleasure which the creators clearly took in their work. True, the drawings are on occasion rather vague, or seem to have been done in a hurry. But that can add to the suggestion of movement.

The Psalter was produced during the period of the Carolingian Renaissance initiated by Charlemagne, undoubtedly for a personage of high standing, quite possibly for his son, Louis the Pious. It comes from the scriptorium of the French monastery of Hautvillers, which was responsible for many famous manuscripts. It has been in Canterbury's Christ Church, and in private hands in England and Holland. Its travels came to an end when in 1716 William de Ridder, an official of the Utrecht Provincial Council, donated it to the Library of the University of Utrecht. Hence its name – the 'Utrecht Psalter.'

Utrecht is very proud of this unique and precious book, and very circumspect in its handling of it. It is kept in the University Library in a strong safe. The Catherijne Convent in Utrecht – the Dutch national museum for religious art – mounted a special exhibition in Autumn 1996, on which occasion the public were able to see the manuscript.

AART VAN ZOEST
Translated by Sheila M. Dale

FURTHER READING
Koert van der Horst et al. (ed.), *The Utrecht Psalter in Medieval Art. Picturing the Psalms of David.* 't Goy, 1996.

A CD-ROM about the Psalter can be ordered from the Utrecht University Library (Wittevrouwenstraat 7-11 / 3500 DA Utrecht / The Netherlands).

An Overview and a Remembering A New History of the Low Countries

Anyone setting out to write a history of the Low Countries immediately finds himself faced with one fundamental problem: how exactly to define the subject of that history? For, after all, in the past the Low Countries have assumed different forms at different times. They have included not just the present states of Belgium and the Netherlands, but also the Grand Duchy of Luxemburg and parts of Germany and France. While on several occasions in their history they have formed a single national or political entity, they have spent far more of their time as a group of autonomous principalities or as regions belonging to several different states. So just what are the Low Countries? That in the past this vague entity has been known by a variety of names (Flanders, the Netherlands, the Seventeen Provinces, Belgium) only adds to the complications.

The compilers of the latest general history of the Low Countries, published under the rather puzzling title *The Drama of the Low Countries,* were well aware of the problem. In the book's introduction they lament the fact that, sadly, the Low Countries are not among those *'countries with a simple, straightforward national history, where one language, one race, one state has for centuries formed a self-evident and closed continuum'* (fairy-tale countries, in other words). But they emphasise that the region known as 'The Low Countries' has always been a culturally distinct area on the map of Europe, an area with an impressive civilisation and strong economic activity, a lively political life and an admirable adaptability. The book's conclusions even make a virtue of necessity by linking the cultural and economic dynamism of the Low Countries with their very diversity, their polyglot nature and multi-ethnicity, their amalgam of sometimes contradictory elements. In an ever-changing world, it is suggested, this diversity is not a problem: it is a trump card.

The ten authors invited to contribute – all noted historians from Belgium, the Netherlands and Luxembourg – thus embark on their task with few qualms. In as many chapters they tell the story of the Low Countries, from Julius Caesar and the Merovingian dynasty to the recent constitutional reforms in Belgium and the turbulent 1960s in the Netherlands. Up to the Revolt of the sixteenth century, which heralded the end of the unity established by Charles V, the Low Countries are discussed as a whole. Thereafter – save for the revolutionary era of 1780-1830 – they are treated as distinct entities, with separate chapters on the North (first the Republic, later the Kingdom of the Netherlands) and the South (first the Southern Netherlands, later Belgium). The entire history is most carefully reconstructed in a balanced style, though the critical reader will undoubtedly get annoyed about the anachronisms that have crept into the book, deplore the prominently political input in certain chapters, and be surprised to find no account of the eighteenth-century Republic.

Such criticisms, however, are out of tune with the lofty sentiments that dominate the book – sentiments of wonder and admiration at the power and beauty of the civilisation here portrayed. It is an idealised portrait: not only Holland's Golden Age in the seventeenth century, but the whole history of the Low Countries is lit with a golden glow. But at the same time the book is permeated with nostalgia. It is written out of an awareness that there is an unbridgeable gulf between late-twentieth-century workaday reality and the civilisation of the past. *The Drama of the Low Countries* is indeed a Sunday book; here history is stilled to a precious memory.

Even more than in the main body of the book, this is apparent in the fifty or so short articles which are scattered throughout and supplement the main chapters. Each devoted to one specific aspect of the past – one event, one figure, one oeuvre, one place – together they form an inventory of the patrimony of the Low Countries. They condense history into a series of symbolic highpoints upon which memories of that increasingly alien civilisation have fastened, an index of what is worth remembering from that history. In short, they offer a guided tour of those spots where the people of the Low Countries like to linger in memory.

Within that canon, it seems, cultural history is far and away the most important. Almost half the short articles are on architecture and the visual arts, literature and the sciences. And within that category painting and architecture have the lion's share, with pieces on, for example, gothic architecture, the Flemish Primitives, miniatures, Bosch and Bruegel, Art Nouveau and Functionalism, Van Gogh, Ensor, Magritte and Mondrian. The memory in question is thus above all a visual memory; literature, here represented only by articles on the languages and works of the early Middle Ages, medieval Dutch mysticism, the Plantijn publishing house and – leaping the centuries – the twentieth-century comic strip hero Tintin, has left little mark on it. But cultural history has no monopoly on the historical memories of the Low Countries. They also attach themselves, as other contributions show, to themes from political, social-economic, religious and colonial history such as the monarchy, the nineteenth-century industrial revolution, the crusades and the Congo. Finally, there are many articles devoted to the structure of the landscape of the Netherlands, to urban life and the confrontation with Nature and the elements.

The choice of articles, though, does more than demonstrate the thematic range of collective memory in the Low Countries; it also shows how certain periods of the past have won themselves a privileged place in that memory. Chief among these are the High and the Late Middle Ages, the Burgundian Age, Holland's Golden Age, and in Belgium the nineteenth, in the Netherlands the twentieth century. Even more striking, though, are the differences between North and South. A case in point is the way the region's development is perceived. The South's memory is urban (they recall the rebellious Ghent of medieval times, the baroque metropolis of Antwerp, the prince-bishopric of Liège, Ghent again, this time as a cotton town during the Industrial Revolution, and the rebellious, artistic Brussels of the nineteenth century and the *fin de siècle).* The memory of the – equally urbanised – North is concerned primarily with the countryside, the polders and the dikes (one of the articles is entitled 'The Netherlands as a structure of hydraulic engineering'). This is only one of the surprises one comes upon when strolling through the Low Countries' Hall of Memories.

In this way *The Drama of the Low Countries* offers not only an overview of the history of the Low Countries but also a sample of what elements from that history the people who live there have absorbed into their memory. It is this rare duality that makes the book, which is splendidly produced and lavishly illus-

Peter Paul Rubens, *The Garden of Love.* 1630. Canvas, 198 x 283 cm. Prado, Madrid.

trated, so interesting and so attractive.

JO TOLLEBEEK
Translated by Tanis Guest

The Drama of the Low Countries, Twenty Centuries of Civilization between Seine and Rhine. Antwerp: Fonds Mercator – Paribas, 1996; 404 pp. ISBN 90-6153-3740.

The Drama of the Low Countries, Twenty Centuries of Civilization between Seine and Rhine. Antwerp: Fonds Mercator – Paribas, 1996; 404 pp. ISBN 90-6153-3740.

Language

Europe, Dutch and the Dutch Language Union Taking the Bull by the Horns

Europe. Still the name evokes the image of the virgin on the back of the bull; the Greek god Zeus carrying off the beautiful Europa. Today, however, most Europeans will think rather of the euro, the single currency which is planned for 1999, of the bureaucracy in Brussels, of the increasingly far-reaching powers which the member states share with or transfer to the Council of Europe. Forty years on, the 'free traffic of people, goods and services' which the six European nations pledged to work towards in 1958 has grown into supranational regulation and legislation which, in an increasing number of areas, applies to fifteen member states. But while European unity influences the daily lives of Europe's citizens to an ever greater extent, one thing has remained unchanged: linguistic diversity. This is in fact one of the European Union's main problems as a political and economic community; one which for several years it has been trying to turn, at the instigation of the French, into a trump card. The Dutch language can benefit from this – indeed, it *must* turn this situation to its advantage because it is under threat.

In practical terms there is much to be said for using

a single language for internal communication within the European Community. From the point of view of language politics, however, it is simply not feasible. If a single language were to be chosen it would, logically speaking, have to be English: a world language and the most widely-learned language in Europe, particularly among the younger generation. Under no circumstances, however, would France renounce French, traditionally the largest cultural language in Europe and, until Britain joined the Community, the main working language. And if the French and British adhere to the principle of equal status for their languages, German cannot be excluded either. German is the language with the most native speakers in Europe, and Germany is the largest contributor to the EU. A three-language regime, then? Spain and Italy are protesting strongly against that. They feel that they belong to the 'Big Five'. France likes to support them in this, to ensure that the EU's focal point does not move too far northward.

Dutch is therefore left in a very vulnerable position. It is Europe's sixth largest language in terms of the number of native speakers, and the official language of two economically important member states (Belgium and the Netherlands). It is also one of the two official languages of the European capital, Brussels. But it has considerably fewer native speakers than Italian and Spanish. Moreover, unlike the Italians and Spanish, many native speakers of Dutch are able to communicate in at least two of the three main European languages (English, French and German). As regards mutual comprehension, therefore, the frequent lack of interpreting and translating into and out of Dutch does not create too many problems for day-to-day European cooperation. However, this situation needs to be monitored for language-political reasons. Unlike the Dutch, who for centuries have been used to being governed, judged and taught in their own language, the Flemish are very aware of the dangers which can threaten the position of a language. Therefore, the status of Dutch in Europe is high on the agenda of the Dutch Language Union, within which the Dutch and Flemish governments pursue a common policy with regard to the Dutch language.

In order to pursue an effective policy, it is important to establish exactly where the greatest risks and opportunities lie. It is often said that, in the highly-developed and wealthy society of Western Europe, knowledge and information are the most important capital for the future. Well then, knowledge and information are both stored largely in language. In the multilingual society which Europe is and chooses to remain, all languages – including Dutch – must therefore be able to participate fully in both sectors. That is why the Dutch Language Union has focused its attention on these two fields in recent years.

In communications and information technology, radical developments are taking place at the technical level and therefore also at user level. More and more people are using the new technologies to supply or obtain information. That is why the quality of the information and its accessibility are of vital importance. The fact that information is language-specific is an important factor in supply via and access to the new channels of communication. It is not simply a question of the language in which the texts are available, but also of search functions and structure, standards, and terminology. World-wide there is a great deal of interest in systems which transcend the language barrier by means of artificial (i.e. not linked to a natural language) 'intermediate languages' or 'metalanguages', through uniform standards or automatic conversion from one language into another. That is why Europe is striving, under the impetus of the European Commission and in cooperation with industry and education, to develop high-quality multilingual technology. Dutch now has the opportunity to participate in this – and it must seize this opportunity. The Dutch Language Union is working to bring together the relevant partners and encourage the Dutch and Flemish governments to provide joint funding. A prerequisite for participation in these developments is that all basic language facilities for Dutch should be available in an appropriate electronic form. By basic language facilities we mean: dictionaries, terminology, grammatical and semantic databases, corpora, thesauruses. The European Commission is assuming that each language area will provide these itself. Whether this is a realistic assumption is another matter. But, in any case, the Dutch and Flemish governments must respond.

Dutch as a language of administration in Europe could benefit from the desired progress in the field of multilingual communication and information technology. For it is precisely in the 'grey area' where sometimes all languages, but often only some, are designated as 'working languages' that standardised multilingual technology creates opportunities for working more quickly and more cheaply.

Knowledge, the second of the fields mentioned above, has many aspects, but for the sake of brevity I shall confine myself to education and science. University exchange schemes within the various university programmes initially appeared to lead to an increased use of English in higher education. However, it is increasingly becoming compulsory for exchange students to follow an intensive course in the language of their host country. This has gradually led to an increasing demand for high-quality course material for highly-educated 'beginners' in Dutch. In this context the Dutch Language Union supports the umbrella organisation University Language Centres for Dutch (Nederlandstalige Universitaire Talencentra), which has been working for several years to produce a good supply of such courses, and also to draw the attention of the European Commission to the importance of such courses. In addition the Dutch Language Union is encouraging university departments abroad to offer exchange students a language course before they leave for Flanders or the Netherlands. In 1996, for example, for the first time, the University of Porto in Portugal held an intensive summer course in Dutch for students from all the universities in the region. These developments have also increased interest abroad in Dutch studies; the number of students studying it as an optional or subsidiary subject is increasing considerably in certain places. This is partly due to the fact that, through the existence of the European Union, there is more translation and interpreting into and out of Dutch than ever before. Learning a middle-scale language such as Dutch therefore enhances the career prospects of many students abroad.

A further important development in the field of education is the recent endorsement by most member states of the objective that students in higher education 'should learn at least two foreign languages'. In some countries, Dutch has consequently become an attractive subject in schools, particularly in the regions bordering the Netherlands and Flanders. In the past, there has been little interest in the teaching of Dutch as a foreign language. From a historical perspective this is understandable. But now prompt action needs to be taken to remedy this situation, and the Dutch Language Union is therefore working to bring together the fragmented expertise which exists in this field to form 'a centre of expertise for Dutch as a foreign language'. Within this context, it will then be possible to establish what additional forms of expertise need to be developed, how teachers can be trained, and what learning materials are needed.

The Dutch Language Union (see *The Low Countries* 1993-94: 267) considers the identification and monitoring of developments in the language politics of Europe to be an important part of its job. In that way it can focus its attention on those sectors where the influence of language choices is, or is becoming, significant. The Union's activities will, then, be further geared towards bringing together the relevant organisations, institutions, disciplines or people to initiate particular projects or developments. The most important instruments in this 'fly-wheel' role are efficient coordination and incentive subsidies. The Dutch Language Union must show that it is flexible enough to respond quickly to new developments, and dogged enough to pursue its chosen course until it is successful. The more strategic support it can find in Europe, the more successful it will be.

GREETJE VAN DEN BERGH
Translated by Yvette Mead.

A Decade of Dutch Studies in Leiden

After other foreign students in Leiden had tried in vain, about 1980 Mjong Soek Djie from South Korea succeeded in obtaining her Master's in Dutch. She was to go on to make a name for herself with her translation into her mother-tongue of Multatuli's *Max Havelaar*. The poor success rate of foreign students in the Dutch Department gave the Faculty of Arts food for thought. This brought them, in the eighties, to the idea of developing a completely separate four-year programme for foreigners, which led to the establishment of the inde-

pendent Department of Dutch Studies, which began work in September 1986.

The new course, which the university was prepared to finance for a few years until it could stand on its own feet, was open only to foreign students. From existing contacts with Chinese and Indonesian universities, it was expected that this new line of study could be a viable proposition. In 1986 ten or so students registered, mainly Indonesians and Chinese, the latter at that time still in pre-capitalist Mao-style dress.

The aim was to give students an education which would equip them to function in their country of origin as university lecturers in Dutch language and culture. To this end the curriculum was developed roughly as follows.

In the first year of preliminary study considerable attention is paid to all aspects of language skills. In addition, there are lectures in the art history of the Low Countries (the only lectures that are given in English), and in Dutch culture and society, supplemented by a programme of excursions. This first year is also followed on occasion by students who are studying in Leiden for one year only, often in conjunction with a Dutch course in their own foreign university.

In the second year of study, attention is still paid to language acquisition, but there are also introductory courses in modern and historical Dutch linguistics, in Dutch literature, and the history of the Netherlands. Students are familiarised with the bibliographical apparatus of the various subjects, and they are required to do a lot of reading. Students also take a course in linguistics outside their own department.

In the third and fourth years students diversify. In two years they must specialise in one of the subject areas of linguistics, literature, history of the Low Countries and art history. During this time, in most cases, courses are followed outside the Dutch Studies

Department, but within the Leiden University Faculty of Arts. Within the Dutch Studies Department there are classes in composition, reading earlier Dutch, especially seventeenth-century Dutch, and the didactics of what may be broadly termed Dutch Studies. A final piece of work in the area of specialisation completes the study, and this must be written in Dutch.

In addition, the Department also provides language courses for students who have come to Leiden with a specific aim, for example, students from the European Union on exchange programmes within the Erasmus or Socrates frameworks. There are also close contacts with foreign universities; after all, this is where most of the students must be recruited. The Department helps as well in developing Dutch programmes in foreign universities, such as the universities of Jakarta (Indonesia), Wroclaw (Poland) and Debrecen (Hungary). Finally, doctoral studies of university lecturers abroad are supervised – often at long range.

The growth of the group has been explosive: in 1996 more than seventy students were registered. Their motives for choosing Dutch Studies vary. Apart from those students sent by their home universities as part of a course in Dutch, some are the children of emigrants in search of their roots, others have friends in the Netherlands, or are drawn by curiosity about social or cultural phenomena; and finally there is the occasional individual who has the same scholarly interest in Dutch language and culture as impels the Dutch to study Greek or Chinese. In the last decade forty or so students have obtained their MA. In the course of those ten years students have come from an increasing number of countries, from Australia to the United States, from Russia to Ireland. If the emphasis originally lay on teaching, research has come to play an ever greater role, and three former students of the Department have gone on to gain their Doctorates from the University of Leiden: a Chinese on the historical relations between Taiwan and the Republic in the time of the United East India Company, another Chinese on a generative linguistics topic, and an Indonesian on a comparative lexicological study of Indonesian and Dutch. Graduates have mostly found posts in a foreign university, or a position in business or in the service of their own government, for instance in the diplomatic service.

The Department was also given a permanent establishment, appropriate to its growth, of one professor, three university lecturers with research responsibilities, and a number of language lecturers. What began as an emergency programme for foreign students who had tried unsuccessfully before 1986 to get a degree in Dutch Studies has resulted in a fully-fledged, flourishing department.

JAN W. DE VRIES
Translated by Sheila M. Dale.

ADDRESS
Dutch Studies Department
Leiden University / P.O. Box 9515 / 2300 RA Leiden / The Netherlands
tel. +31 71 5272233 / fax +31 71 5272615

Nescio, a Great Author of a Small Oeuvre

'His work constitutes the greatest small oeuvre in Dutch literature,' Reinder P. Meijer said in his *Literature of the Low Countries* – and rightly so. In fact, in this respect Nescio *('I don't know'* – pen name of J.H.F. Grönloh, 1882-1961) can be compared to Emily Brontë in Britain and Alain-Fournier in France. For most of his life he was completely neglected by the reading public, though admired and loved by a few discerning colleagues as the author of a single book of 128 pages, containing three stories: 'Little Poet' ('Dichtertje'), 'The Sponger' ('De Uitvreter') and 'Young Titans' ('Titaantjes'), published in 1918 in an edition of 500 copies and not sold out till fifteen years afterwards. And hardly anybody knew who was the man behind these novellas. Only in 1929, four years before a second edition appeared, which did not sell either, was he obliged to reveal his name because his book had been wrongly attributed to another man in a dictionary of pseudonyms. In spite of this disclosure Grönloh was and remained a maverick: he never mixed in literary circles. Nor in any other circles for that matter.

In the course of the late forties, however, after a second publication, *Mene Tekel,* an even tinier book than its predecessor, he became somewhat better-known. And in 1961, just before he died, a third book, *Above the Valley* (Boven het dal) appeared, thanks to the efforts of some relatives and friends. Since that time Nescio's reputation as well as his popularity have increased steadily: by now more than thirty editions of his first three stories have been published and more than twenty of *Above the Valley:* the Netherlands had at long last discovered one of its outstanding authors. Some of his sentences, such as *'Boys we were, but nice boys',* have even become proverbial.

One might wonder why it has taken such a long time for one of our most distinguished and original authors to get through to the general reader. It can certainly not have been on account of his style. On the contrary: his style is deceptively realistic and simple, often near-colloquial, free from any attempt at literary finesse, but nevertheless subtle and remarkably effective. Although more than eighty-five years have elapsed since his first story was published ('The Sponger' in 1911) his way of writing has suffered very little from the passage of time and the changing language. And one might say that, although the world around us has altered almost beyond recognition, the world evoked in Nescio's stories has remained intact. In 'Young Titans' he writes about a band of five young friends, nineteen or twenty years old: two painters, two aspiring writers and one man with no special artistic ambitions, who dream of changing the world utterly, although they have no idea in which way and into what. Of course they are cheated and defeated by the harsh realities of life: *'Wise men we have become, pitiably wise. Except for Bavink [one of the painters], who has gone crazy'.*

The exceptional merit of Nescio's stories is not to be found in their plots, but in their empathy and in their style, in the fusion of (self)irony, mockery and sarcasm with vague longings and melancholy. Most probably it was this blend which proved too heady for most of his contemporaries, who were accustomed to downright realism or romantic aestheticism.

Moreover, his stories were thought irreverent if not sacrilegious. A highly respectable literary journal refused to publish 'Young Titans' because of its unconventional representation of God's way with the world and with new generations of young Titans who *'will always keep trying to thrust Him from His elevated position'* and who, of course, will be defeated and put in their place in the same way as their predecessors. And what were the high-priests of literature to think of the opening passage of 'Little Poet', where *'the God of the Netherlands' – 'your God, the God of your boss and of your father-in-law and of your boss' bookkeeper and of the restaurant manager of The New Cherry Tree. The God of your aunt'* – is strolling about in Amsterdam. But of course 'religious projection' was only discovered some decades after Nescio wrote his tale. One might say that nowadays *'the God of your aunt'* has become as popular as His creator.

Few people seem to have noticed at the time that Nescio was a mystic at heart. His sensitive awareness of nature in all its manifestations is virtually unique. He looked at everything around him with an unequalled intensity. Some of his characters may say that *'God is eternally repeating Himself'*, but the reader is made intensely aware of the life-long fascination that God's world with its endless variety of ever-changing shapes must have had for Nescio. No author I know has evoked the changes of His light on sea, rivers and trees, on cities, villages and meadows, so convincingly.

Now, at last, Nescio's *Collected Work* has appeared in an exemplary edition and all these qualities are exhibited one more. The editor, Dr Lieneke Frerichs, who had already written a thesis on the genesis of 'The Sponger', was allowed access to the whole of Nescio's literary heritage and compiled two volumes of 700 and 400 pages, together with 300 pages of commentary. The first volume contains the stories we already knew, some 200 pages altogether, plus 500 pages of sketches – for the most part unfinished stories. Nescio had a curious way of working: unlike most authors he didn't start from a more or less general scheme which he gradually developed and rewrote. He started writing a story with both feet forward as it were, and when he got stuck he left it as it was, using parts of it later, sometimes in a wholly different context. And as the plot is only of secondary interest in his work, these unfinished sketches are often as fascinating as the stories he succeeded in rounding off. The second volume contains his 'Nature diary'. From 1945 till 1955 Nescio made notes of his regular walking or cycling tours, mostly in the vicinity of Amsterdam. At first these notes are purely matter of fact, but gradually they become more and more 'subjective': he writes down his sensations and his so to say mystical experience of the countryside in

a way that will not fail to leave a deep impression on the sensitive reader. It is a telling fact that the first edition (6,000 copies) of Nescio's *Collected Work,* sold out, despite its price, within three months.

A.L. SÖTEMANN

FURTHER READING
Nescio, *Verzameld werk* (2 vols.) Amsterdam, 1996.

Johan Snapper and *Vantage Points*
A Festschrift for *'eine bunte Eminenz'*

On 20 October 1971 the Princess Beatrix Chair of Dutch Language, Literature and Culture – later renamed the Queen Beatrix Chair – was formally inaugurated at the University of California at Berkeley. This Dutch Studies Program was, and still is, the fruit of a joint funding initiative by the university itself and the Dutch government.

As soon as the chair had been established the search for a professor began. After lengthy consideration the choice fell on Johan Snapper (1935-), an assistant professor of Dutch extraction from Berkeley's own ranks. Snapper, then a Germanist engaged in the study of eighteenth-century German literature with a particular interest in the *Sturm und Drang* movement, threw himself into his new task with real energy and enthusiasm. The brand-new Princess Beatrix Professor blossomed into a *'self-made Netherlandist',* but he did more than acquire the necessary knowledge of his subject; under his inspiring leadership the Dutch Studies Program grew and expanded, until today it is possible to gain a Master of Arts degree in Dutch-Flemish Studies at Berkeley. It was Snapper who attracted the well-known Dutch writers Cees Nooteboom and Harry Mulisch to the UCB campus as Regents' Lecturers, as well as organising numerous other events. From 1985 biennial international conferences have been held, alternately on the literature and the language of the Low Countries. And since 1982 the Belgian government has funded a Peter Paul Rubens Chair for the History and Culture of the Lowlands, held each year by a Visiting Professor from one of the Flemish universities.

In 1996 the Dutch Studies Program celebrated 25 years of its existence. The Festschrift published to mark the occasion was compiled – according to its editors, almost as a matter of course – *'mainly to honor that person who has made the Program possible and who has directed its progress to flourishing success'.* Snapper has in the past been decorated by the American, Belgian and Dutch governments. Now, with *Vantage Points,* he is being honoured by friends and colleagues from the Netherlands, Flanders, Germany, Great Britain and the United States.

It is not surprising, then, that the volume puts several of Johan Snapper's hobby-horses on parade. Francis Bulhof in his contribution discusses Otto Christian Friedrich Hoffham, an eighteenth-century 'Dutch' writer who was by birth a Prussian subject. Bulhof explains his choice as follows: *'As Johan Snapper combines a scholarly interest in German Enlightenment and Sturm und Drang with his specialty in Dutch literature, it seems fitting to introduce this eighteenth-century German "Gastarbeiter" in a Festschrift in his honor.'* Hoffham, whose name is indeed *'not exactly a household word'* in Dutch literary history, wrote among other things *Toward a Theory of Dutch Poetry* (Proeve eener theorie der Nederduytsche poëzy, 1788), an entertaining poetics of Dutch classicist literature. In this masterpiece, written when he had returned to his homeland after years spent working as a businessman in Amsterdam, Hoffman quotes and discusses some sixty poets. He does this with great expertise, and has no hesitation in cutting some established reputations down to size. For instance, he argues for a rational prose because the tyranny of rhyme damages the author's integrity. He also likes to turn his biting sarcasm on the weaknesses in Joost van den Vondel's verse, such as his use of high-flown language. Bulhof rightly

Johan P. Snapper (1935-).

calls attention to the value of Hoffmann's work: the Prussian Dutchman, *'a critical mind who kept his sanity amidst the adulation',* views his subject with the unbiased eye of an outsider, and is thus in some sense *'the godfather of Neerlandica extra muros'.*

In 'Gerard Reve and Romantic Irony' Ton Anbeek investigates exactly what we mean by irony in the work of this author, of whom Snapper has made a detailed study. Among the passages Anbeek quotes is one from *Mother and Son* (Moeder en zoon, 1984), in which Reve praises the excellences of the past as follows: *'The times were not nearly as disastrous as they are now. Young people were still willing to work, still had respect for authority, and didn't yet treat their parents as old trash. Nor had they succumbed to alcohol abuse, senseless destruction, drugs, or the shameless fornication in the woods, parks, and on the beaches.'* The standard definition of romantic irony as a *'conscious ironic manner of writing from which it appears that the author distances himself from his statements'* does not work here. In Anbeek's view this definition is too static. The hallmark of romantic irony is above all uncertainty on the part of the reader, who is often not quite sure whether the author is or is not distancing himself from his own values (always assuming, of course, that those values exist). In other words: *'we speak of romantic irony when we are not sure whether it is really a matter of irony at all.'* In this respect the combination of the exalted and the down-to-earth in Reve's work can also be characterised as typically romantic; the mixture of styles expresses *'a deep sense of underlying chaos'.*

Joris Duytschaever begins his 'Canon refiguration in the Low Countries' by drawing our attention to another of Snapper's passions, Flemish literature: *'Although proud to be of Dutch extraction, Snapper was always eager to advance the idea of Dutch Studies in the widest sense by taking Flemish writers and colleagues as seriously as those from Holland.'* Among other things Duytschaever discusses the manipulation of the Flemish literary canon for political ends by the adherents of *'the dark side of Flemish nationalism'*: *'To them it's an "added value" for an artist or writer to have been on the wrong side at least once (…), such as Wies Moens and Felix Timmermans. Admittedly both were important writers at a certain stage of their career, but that they went downhill as they got into the poisoning orbit of Nazism is still anathema to many Flemish whose powers of denial are amazing. Hero worship seems to remain an intractable problem of the Flemish movement (…). Therefore the Flemish movement can only be qualified as "a relatively noble cause" (…).'* Duytschaever's indignation is certainly justified, but 'a partially noble cause' might be a more appropriate way of putting it. After all, a sizable element of the Flemish movement, both past and present, has no truck with the reactionary political and cultural ideas of *'the dark side'.*

'Lambert van Bos should definitely be numbered among the most unfortunate of Dutch writers ever' is the intriguing opening sentence of the late André

Lefevere's 'History, Institution, Imagination: The Epic in the Dutch Republic and What It Teaches Us'. In the middle years of the seventeenth century Van Bos wrote three epics which aroused no interest whatsoever among his contemporaries. His work was never reprinted, and even in later times he has never been a 'hot topic' among the historians of literature. The same goes, for that matter, for most seventeenth-century and later Dutch epic, which receives decidedly niggardly treatment from contemporary literary history. In this context Lefevere strongly criticises modern literary scholarship for assaulting the texts with 'theories' and 'supertheories': literature is subjected to deconstructionist, psychoanalytical, marxist etc. screening so as to prove a preconceived theory. In the process people have lost sight of the fact that literature can also be regarded as a balanced system. Every work is a product of its time, of an interplay between authors, readers, and *a generally accepted set of conventions which are primarily literary in kind*. For this reason Lefevere argues strongly for the revaluation of works such as those of Lambert van Bos, curiosities though they may seem. He closes with this plea: *'If we believe that literature can teach us how to live, we shall have little time for the Dutch epic, or for any literature that is not "great". If we believe that literature can teach us how other people lived, and how they used this sophisticated system of communication, we shall be able to deal with literature that is not necessarily "great", but is, and was "meaningful". I believe that we have priests and ministers for the first option, therapists and psychiatrists, and of late, even theorists. For the second option, we have scholars.'*

In *Vantage Points* those scholars have acquitted themselves of their task in a manner that is often surprising and refreshing. They write on a range of topics: from the Golden Age to the present day, on symbolism and modernism, poetry and epic, on colonial literature, postmodernism and feminism in Dutch-language literature. The result is a varied collection of articles on Flemish and Dutch literature, a fitting tribute to Johan Snapper, the *'bunte Eminenz'* of Dutch Studies at Berkeley.

FILIP MATTHIJS
Translated by Tanis Guest.

Vantage Points. Festschrift for Johan P. Snapper (ed. Blake Lee Spahr, Thomas F. Shannon and Wiljan van den Akker). Publications of the American Association for Netherlandic Studies vol. 10. Lanham (MD): University Press of America, 1996; 266 pp. ISBN 0-7618-0421-8.

Harry Mulisch's The Discovery of Heaven
An International Success

The publication of Harry Mulisch's novel *The Discovery of Heaven* (De ontdekking van de hemel) in 1992 (the author's 65th year) brought a virtually unanimous reaction from Dutch literary critics: here was a master-piece. The novel was awarded the Multatuli Prize by the Municipality of Amsterdam in 1993, and the Mekka Prize by Dutch and Flemish literary critics. The rear flap describes the book as a 'total novel': *'This monumental book, in which all the themes and obsessions from the work of Harry Mulisch are brought together in 65 chapters, is at one and the same time a psychological novel, a philosophical novel, a temporal novel, a Bildungsroman, an adventure novel and an all-embracing mystery play.'*

All this may seem a lot to say about one book, and yet the novel most certainly does contain all these facets. The novel's great national and international success is undoubtedly rooted in the mix of narrative genres. An American reviewer in *Kirkus Reviews* even wrote: *'Mulisch's bid for a masterpiece works commandingly, on every level. Could be one of the best novels of the last 20 years'*. And the *Washington Post* added the following plaudit: *'The standard danger lurking in monster-long novels is loss of control. This is not a problem for Mulisch'*. The reviewer at the *Wall Street Journal* even places the novel in the tradition of 'very great' literature by writing that Mulisch, like Homer, Dante and Milton, uses the cosmos as his stage and history and the meaning of everything as his theme.

The twelfth print run of the novel was published in the spring of 1997 by Mulisch's Amsterdam publishing house De Bezige Bij, taking the total circulation at that time to 140,000 copies. Following its appearance in the German language area (in 1993, aided by the media publicity generated by the Frankfurt Book Fair), the book's circulation there also rose rapidly to more than 100,000 copies.

Many German literary critics also emphasised the masterly character of this weighty novel. Harry Mulisch was 'discovered' as a writer and placed in the literary traditions of the great European storytellers. Or, perhaps more appropriately: it was precisely in Germany that the high philosophical content of the novel was appreciated – and not only because of the allusions to Goethe and Thomas Mann's *Doktor Faustus*. Mulisch raises explicit questions about the relationship between God and man; he examines the relationship between good and evil. But in this book he does it all in literary fashion. Mulisch does not present a philosophical tract here, but a book in which all manner of literary 'tricks' are used, so that it becomes above all a *gripping* book to read. Literary critics in Germany appreciate that. *Die Zeit* praises Mulisch's virtuosity: *'Mulisch's powers of combination, exercised in a way which is entertaining, surprising, comical, sombre, crazy, as idiosyncratic as it is light-footed, can no longer be ignored after this novel.'* The *Frankfürter Allgemeine Zeitung* is equally lyrical about Mulisch's narrative qualities: *'Mulisch is a brilliant storyteller, an author who knows his craft through and through. His work has an untiring, often refreshing meticulousness of detail, even – indeed especially – in the highest spheres.'* The *Süddeutsche Zeitung* – rightly – places Mulisch in a somewhat broader Dutch-language perspective and regards itself as fortunate that Germany has two neighbours, namely Harry Mulisch and Cees Nooteboom, '*who, each in their own way, can tell us something about God and the world and about Europe and Germany and about the labyrinth in our breast*'.

The Discovery of Heaven is an exceptional book in modern Dutch-language literature, not only because of its size (over 800 pages), but above all because of the breadth of its themes. No other modern Dutch author has devised such a coherent philosophical system with a claim to universal applicability as Harry Mulisch in his essays, and in particular, in *The Composition of the World* (De compositie van de wereld, 1980). *The Discovery of Heaven* can be regarded as the fictional counterpart to this philosophical-scientific *magnum opus*. The discovery of technology has in fact caused mankind to 'lose touch with God', and placed him on an inevitable path to his own end. What Mulisch proved scientifically (or at least claimed to prove) in *The Composition of the World*, he now 'proves' in a Heaven and Earth created by himself, with a God created by himself (although, interestingly, that God

Harry Mulisch (1927-)(Photo by Klaas Koppe).

Siegfried Woldhek, *Harry Mulisch and J.H. Donner*. 1977. Ink on paper, 15.5 x 24 cm. Letterkundig Museum, The Hague.

remains invisible: the angels carry out the policy of 'the Boss').

The novel can be read as an expression of a pessimistic vision: mankind is doomed to extinction. The writing is literally on the wall; after all, the divine assignment is being carried out and the agreement once forged between God and mankind – symbolised in the testimony of Moses' Stone Tablets containing the Word of God, the Ten Commandments – is cancelled and sent back to where it came from: Heaven.

But the novel also has a rational / optimistic vision: mankind has taken over a world in which there is no longer a place for a God, a fundamental metaphysical pattern underlying all things – mankind can now after all do everything of which God has ever been considered capable. The angel / narrator is not satisfied with this prospect, however; he refuses to be pensioned off and demands a new assignment in order to save mankind from his technological side-track and lead him back to the original source of everything: the Word. In the words of the Gospel according to St John: '*In the beginning was the Word, and the Word was with God, and the Word was God. The same was in the beginning with God. All things were made by Him; and without Him was not anything made that was made.*' This is a rather tautological formulation, something with which Bible texts have no problem. The return of the testimony to Heaven is not the last word on the matter, however: the testimony returns in the world of the story, the world of words, the world of the spirit... As so often in his work, Mulisch refers here to the mythical / magical, the Godly force, which he sees as inherent in 'writing'.

The philosophical layer of meaning is one which can intrigue readers, particularly because of the lightness with which serious themes are treated. With equal irony, however, Mulisch looks back in his novel at his own writing career and presents a chronology, both reviews covering the period 1967-1985. With the emphasis on the man's world in which the adventures take place in the first instance, the novel becomes a monument to and of friendship: the friendship between the astronomer Max Delius and the linguist Onno Quist. Their meeting, arranged as a 'chance' event by the angels, stands at the beginning of a series of events which are designed to lead to the creation of the *Wunderkind* Quinten and thus to the carrying out of the divine assignment. The description of Quinten's development into adulthood contains all the hallmarks of a *Bildungsroman*: growing up in the almost fairy-tale ambience of a castle (*'a gift from Heaven'*), it is – literally – child's play for him to learn those things which he will need later, both psychologically and physically, in order to carry out his allotted task.

For the writer / philosopher Mulisch, these scenes allow him every opportunity to display his knowledge in a wide range of fields, but always in a playful tone, since they are seen through the eyes of a growing boy. Mulisch plays an exceptionally refined game with fiction and reality on these narrative levels. In his essays, autobiographical writings and interviews, Mulisch has never made a secret of his life. In his narrative worlds, he places recognisable events from his own life in ever-changing perspectives. This applies to this novel, too, in which Mulisch creates his alter ego Max Delius by means of a mirror-biography, placing him opposite Onno Quist, a faithful representation of Mulisch's friend, the Dutch chess grand master Jan Hein Donner (1927-1988).

Mulisch's political involvement with the Cuba of Fidel Castro, a figure so greatly admired by him in the 1960s, is also given a literary 'treatment': it is precisely on this island, on a moonlit night in January 1968, during one of those eternal Communist international friendship conferences, that the god-child Quinten is conceived by the two friends Max and Onno. That is Max' betrayal of friendship, or at least that is the way he sees it for the rest of his life, because on that fateful night he has sex with his former girlfriend, who at that moment is Onno's girlfriend. She also sleeps with Onno on that same night.

Another, *literary* event takes place on Cuba, which is highly typical of Mulisch's way of writing. During the Cuban conference Mulisch places his alter ego, the character Max Delius, eye to eye with a Dutch writer who displays clear traits of the writer Harry Mulisch. Max is drunk and sees the writer double; he asks the question: '*How is it possible in God's name for someone to dream up a novel?*' '*I never dream anything up,*' reply the two mouths coolly. '*I remember. I remember things which have never happened. Just like you when you read my novel.*' And for the reader, too, Mulisch is present here in a double image – as a figure in his own novel being addressed by a character – but he gives a uniform answer to the puzzle of how great 'literature' operates. That operation has to do with universality; then, the unique biographical anecdote of the writer proves to be no more than a leader to a story which is recognisable, or at least imaginable, to many readers.

In his first major (autobiographical) essay collection, *Fodder for Psychologists* (Voer voor psychologen, 1961), Mulisch makes the statement: '*Literature is not a supply in response to demand; rather, it is supply which creates demand.*' That, at least, is how Mulisch's literature works, as is evidenced once again by the reactions to the novel in America (in the English translation by Paul Vincent): critics respond enthusiastically, praise the gripping narrative character (and this is an area where modern American literature has itself recorded not a few achievements), and even (see the *Wall Street Journal*) refer to the literary tradition of Homer, Dante and Milton. This last comment perhaps goes a little too far in describing a writer who presents himself – though of course ironically – with the statement: '*I am world famous in Amsterdam*'. Because that, in turn, was saying much too little about a writer whose book was placed in the following company by John Updike writing in the *New Yorker*: '*Like Joyce's "Finnegans Wake" it is oneirically entangled with the entirety of European history; like Umberto Eco's "Foucault's Pendulum" it proposes a dark trickle of arcana running beneath the surface of that history, and*

gives us a thriller dénouement. Perhaps the great book it most resembles – in its genial ironical tone, in its hospitality to extended arguments, and in the metaphysical height of its sympathy with humanity's spiritual and erotic adventures – is Thomas Mann's "Magic Mountain".' In early 1997 *The Discovery of Heaven* was hailed by the New York Public Library as one of the 25 'Books to Remember 1996'.

In 1995 Harry Mulisch received the highest literary distinction which the Netherlands and Flanders can bestow: the Netherlands Literature Prize. The jury was unanimous: '*The apotheosis of Mulisch's writing career so far is formed by the spectacular "The Discovery of Heaven". This book unites mastery in storytelling with a multi-layered structure. It allows diverse readings which do not contradict each other.*' And that is precisely the paradox about which Mulisch so likes to talk, or rather: about which he writes in this novel. Everything appears to be a contradiction, but everything is in fact interrelated. The establishing of those contrastive bonds, on so many different levels of meaning, must be an activity for the reader. In his *Manifests* from 1958, Mulisch puts it like this: '*It is not the writer, but the reader who must display fantasy. The reader is not a spectator in the theatre, but rather the actor who plays all the roles. What he is reading is very much his own creation. The writer supplies text – but it only becomes a work of art with the talent of the reader.*'

Such a statement is both a great compliment and a challenge to the creative capacity of the reader. The international esteem in which *The Discovery of Heaven* is held emanates at the very least from the scope which this majestic novel, thanks to the talent of the writer, offers to the creativity of the reader.

FRANS DE ROVER
Translated by Julian Ross.

Harry Mulisch, *The Discovery of Heaven* (Tr. Paul Vincent). New York: Viking, 1996; 736 pp. ISBN 0-670-85668-1.

Anne Frank and After

A brief history of Dutch Jews which focuses specifically on the Holocaust, *Anne Frank and After* fills an important niche in English-language works on Dutch history and literature. It provides a succinct introduction for students of Dutch history, culture and literature, balancing brevity with interesting detail taken from both historical and literary sources.

The book begins the story of Jews in the Netherlands with the Dutch Golden Age, briefly mentioning in the first short chapter the reasons why Jews settled in that country. From there it takes the reader through the occupation of the Netherlands by Nazi German forces in May 1940 and the gradual introduction of progressive levels of persecution of the Jews in the occupied Netherlands. It details the difficult choices between allowing oneself and one's family to be deported on the one hand and going into hiding on the other. It

Departure from Westerbork to Auschwitz (Photo Rijksinstituut voor Oorlogsdocumentatie, Amsterdam).

then follows the victims as they are taken away to transit camps such as Westerbork and Vught, describing the conditions there, and on again as they are then deported to different concentration and extermination camps; Theresienstadt, Bergen-Belsen, Auschwitz-Birkenau, Sobibor are the camps listed separately as the most common destinations for deportees from the Netherlands. The story of the Holocaust is rounded out with a brief treatment of survivor's guilt and the problems faced by second-generation survivors which includes references to literature as recent as from the 1980s. The authors append an 'Epilogue' in which they consider the relationship between literature and history, in my view the least successful part of the book.

An interesting structural technique employed in this book is its use of Anne Frank's story as a personalising element, a strategy parallel to that used at the United States Holocaust Memorial Museum, where the viewer is handed a 'passport' at the start of the exhibit and directed from time to time to read a page, on which the stage of the Holocaust shown on a massive scale in the display (persecution in the homeland, deportation, camp, death) is personalised in the experiences of the reader's 'special person'. In *Anne Frank and After*, chapters on the overall history of the Holocaust as experienced by Dutch Jews more or less alternate with 'instalments' in the life of Anne Frank which are easily identified by a different page layout. The intended effect – which I surmise succeeds for most readers – is to make the general history described both more comprehensible (less unmanageable, unfathomable) and more personal, and thus more difficult to read in a distanced mode.

In addition, the authors supply a chronology of the occupation and brief biographies for the authors whose literary texts they cite as illustrations; both are useful reference tools, particularly for those not very familiar with the topic.

Even a casual reader will note that the English is, unfortunately, not flawless. My concern ranges from run-of-the-mill examples of usage which are not so much wrong as just strongly influenced by Dutch idiom, such as '*they put their experiences into words*' (p.11) to awkward constructions ('*The switching from a microlevel...should not confuse the reader...*', p.11) to the unintentionally funny '*This book will confine itself to Holland*' (p.10; I am puzzled at the use of 'Holland' in this work to refer to the country, where I would expect 'the Netherlands').

Such instances are somewhat pedestrian and will annoy native speakers, but should not – assuming a little good will – impede comprehension. Nevertheless, even the possibility of 'unintentionally funny' locutions is unfortunate in a book dealing with a topic as sensitive as the Holocaust, one in which precision counts. I worry, though, that opportunities for misunderstanding occur as well. Thus, when chapter VI bears the title: 'The Paradox of Silence: Survivors and Losers', it is clear that the word 'losers' here refers to those forced to make a difficult decision under duress, and based on incomplete information, and who lost the historic gamble, i.e. lost their lives. But it will be difficult for some readers to suppress the contemporary meaning of the word 'losers.'

The brief description of Andreas Burnier's past raises serious questions about the clarity of the English. This account edges toward an unwarranted suggestion of pathology. The authors write: '*(...) it is estimated that most hidden Jews had to change their address at least three or four times for security reasons. The young Dutch writer Andreas Burnier even had to go into hiding at 16 different addresses. Apart from having to disguise her Jewishness, she also had trouble with her sexual identity: she felt like a boy in the body of a girl, as we can read in her novel, "Het Jongensuur" (Boys' Hour).*' (p. 66-68). The reader must doubt that a character in a novel is really meant to be identified with the author of the work, and whether the implication that '*trouble with her sexual identity*' was somehow caused by the occupation and the character's need to hide and thus to move often, rather than a response to a sexist society. I am certain that such quandaries must be viewed charitably as linguistic problems, but it is unfortunate that these language barriers still exist.

Given the virtues of this book, and its usefulness to a wide range of audiences as an introduction to the occupation of the Netherlands during the Second World War, I would urge readers of English to take the aforementioned barriers in their stride, for this book has much to offer.

JOLANDA VANDERWAL TAYLOR

Dick van Galen Last and Rolf Wolfswinkel, *Anne Frank and After: Dutch Holocaust Literature in Historical Perspective*. Amsterdam: Amsterdam University Press, 1996; 184 pp; ISBN 90-5356-177-3.

FURTHER READING

SCHRAM, D.H., 'An Unfinished Chapter: The Second World War and the Holocaust in Dutch Literature'. In: *The Low Countries. Arts and Society in Flanders and the Netherlands 1994-95* (ed. Jozef Deleu *et al.*), Rekkem, 1994, pp. 195-203.

VANDERWAL TAYLOR, JOLANDA, *A Family Occupation. Children of the War and the Memory of World War II in Dutch Literature of the 1980s.* Amsterdam, 1997.

The TLS Vondel Translation Prize

1996 saw the launch of a new translation prize in England: the Vondel Prize for translations of work originally written in the Dutch language. The prize is worth £2,000. Translations published between 1990 and 1995 were eligible, and up to 20 works were submitted. In future the prize will be awarded every two years for translations published during those two years. The 1996 jury consisted of Anne Chisholm, English author; Francis Jones, linguist at the University of Newcastle and himself a brilliant translator of poetry, and Theo Hermans of University College London – also a translator.

After serious consideration four books were nominated: *The Sorrow of Belgium* by Hugo Claus, translated by Arnold Pomerans (Penguin); *Villa des Roses* by Willem Elsschot, translated by Paul Vincent (Penguin); *The Great Longing* by Marcel Möring, translated by Stacey Knecht (Flamingo) and *Lucifer* by Joost van den Vondel, translated by Noel Clark (Absolute Press).

The judges focused on two aspects: the accuracy of the translation and the quality of the English book. They reached a unanimous decision on the winner of this first Vondel Translation Prize: Stacey Knecht for *The Great Longing. The Times Literary Supplement* which, in addition to prizes for translations from French, German and Italian, can now add the Vondel Translation Prize to this list, described the book as follows: '*A short novel describing the Wanderjahre of a young orphan, Sam, with and without his twin sister Lisa and their elder brother Raph. His odyssey through a post-punk landscape of strip clubs, deserted oilfields, and windblown potato fields cuts rapidly between lyrical recollections of childhood and desolate descriptions of the present. Stacey Knecht's translation manages these jump cuts with the fluency of "water running over the stones", to quote one of the judges.*' Other comments by the judges on the winning translation: '*The translation reads like natural English, the colloquial style well-translated*' and '*This book never reads like a translation, and never sags*'.

Who exactly is Stacey Knecht, the person behind this achievement?

Stacey Knecht (1957-) was born and raised in New York City. She came to the Netherlands in 1980 for a week's vacation – and is still living there. Her first translation, *The Glass Bridge* by Marga Minco, appeared in 1988 (Peter Owen Publishers). This was followed by Lieve Joris' *Back to the Congo* (Macmillan London / New York, 1992), for which she received the James S Holmes Translation Award.

The Great Longing, her translation of Marcel Möring's *Het Grote Verlangen*, was published in 1995 by Harper Collins (London and New York). Her English translation of Hugo Claus' *Het Verlangen*, entitled *Desire*, is due to be published in 1997 by Penguin USA. She will also translate Marcel Möring's latest novel *In Babylon*, since she feels a great affinity with his work and style. Why? His books, according to Knecht, ask many questions which she herself is occupied with; about relationships, memories, attachment and non-attachment. But she also identifies with the longing for that indefinable something, the feeling that something is missing. These questions form the theme of Möring's work.

Stacey Knecht also likes to translate other writers. She is the only translator of a short story by the late W.F. Hermans with whom the great writer did *not* argue. Knecht is a passionately enthusiastic, professional translator. In her own words, spoken at the Vondel presentation in London in 1996: '*I myself am slow, fussy, chaotic, sceptical, and very, very stubborn. In short, a publisher's worst nightmare. But I won't, I can't submit the work until I think it's done. Because I know that if I persevere, there comes a moment when the words on the page stop glaring at me, when they lie there and glow, as if they couldn't have been any other way. A moment when I hear them once again, just as I heard them in the language they were born in, only louder and clearer, because they've been reborn in the language closest to my heart*'.

That is the voice of a true translator. A translator who fully deserves the Vondel Translation Prize with her wonderful translation *The Great Longing*.

RUDI WESTER
Translated by Yvette Mead.

Music

The Royal Carillon School in Mechelen
Chimes from Flanders

In 1921 the Belgian King Albert I made a donation for the establishment of a carillon school , with the words that carillon music was '*un art essentiellement belge, né dans ces beffrois qui symbolisent notre vieux passé communal*' ('an essentially Belgian art, born in those belfries which symbolise our communal past').

The following year the 'Jef Denyn' Royal Carillon School was established in Mechelen by the famous carilloneur Jef Denyn, with financial support from the Americans Herbert Hoover, John D. Rockefeller and William Gorham Rice. The school was the first of its kind in the world, and was under the leadership of, successively, Jef Denyn, Staf Nees and Piet van den Broek. Since 1981 the school has been headed by Jo Haazen (1944-), who also holds the post of town carilloneur. In 1993 this highly talented musician was made an honorary member of the Guild of Carilloneurs

Mechelen - Malines
Het Mekanisme van de belaard met
Meester Jef Denyn.
Le Mécanisme du carrillon avec
Maître Jef Denyn.

Jef Denijn, who established the Royal Carillon School, in front of the carillon of St Rombouts, Mechelen (c.1920).

ate's diploma, the candidates are expected to present a paper on a campanological theme. To be accepted as a student, the candidates must present a certificate of competency covering music theory, music reading and instrumental playing (preferably piano, organ or harpsichord), or pass an entrance examination.

The teaching staff consists of six lecturers who are themselves performing artists: Koen Cosaert, Geert D'Hollander, Jo Haazen (Director), Jan Hadermann, Eddy Mariën and Carlo van Ulft.

In 1984 the School opened a branch at the Catholic University of Leuven. In the same year Queen Fabiola lent her distinguished patronage to the school and carillon culture was taken from Mechelen to Japan for the first time. In 1990 a second branch of the school was opened, in Osaka. In 1991 yet another department was opened in Halle near Brussels, and in 1992 in Roeselare, West Flanders. In the academic year September 1996-June 1997 the school had 58 students, spread across all departments.

The reputation of the Royal Carillon School was further enhanced by the institution of the Queen Fabiola International Carillon Competition. This competition is considered one of the most prestigious of its kind, and carilloneurs from all over the world compete in it. The school also organises a composition contest and publishes carillon scores and literature about bells and carillons.

Partly thanks to the influence of the school and the enthusiasm of its Director, Japan now has a total of four carillons which have come from Flanders, and money is being collected for a carillon for the Cathedral of St Peter and St Paul in St Petersburg. It was no accident that the school was also given the official title of 'Cultural Ambassador' by the Flemish government. Every Summer, on a Monday evening, from a seat in the garden of 'Busleyden', one can hear Jo Haazen and other renowned carilloneurs on one of the two carillons belonging to the imposing cathedral of St Rombouts. And if you are in Brussels, Mechelen is only thirty kilometres away.

LUC DEVOLDERE
Translated by Sheila M. Dale.

ADDRESS
Royal Carillon School
F. de Merodestraat 63 / 2800 Mechelen / Belgium
tel. +32 15 20 47 92

FURTHER READING
André Lehr *et al.*, *The Art of the Carillon in the Low Countries.* Tielt, 1991.

of North America. From its inception the school developed its own style and gained international recognition. Carilloneurs from all over the world (but particularly from Flanders, the Netherlands, French-Flanders and the United States) were trained there, and by virtue of this fact alone the school has continued to set its stamp on international carillon events. In 1927 Frank Percival Price graduated from the school. He became carilloneur at the Michigan University in Ann Arbor where he was also lecturer in campanology. He has made an invaluable contribution to the American art of carillon playing.

The Royal Carillon School is housed in the historic building of 'Het Schipke', 63 Frederik de Merodestraat. There one can find practice keyboards, a unique music library, and an historical archive. The historic 'Hof van Busleyden', next door to the school, where the Collegium Trilingue was established, is home to the school carillon and the school museum with its valuable collection of bells, carillon keyboards, manuscripts and objects of art.

The study programme, spread over six academic years, comprises: carillon playing, music theory, harmony, counterpoint, history of the carillon and campanology, composition and arrangement for the carillon, part-singing, and kinetics. To obtain a laure-

The Beau Hunks *'The best thing from Holland since tulips'*

The statement that Americans don't know about their own culture ('look at how jazz gets marginalised in the USA') is a cliché that mainly testifies to European chauvinism. But that clichés can indeed contain a grain of truth has been amply proved over the past few years by Gert-Jan Blom, bass player, band leader and Dutchman. Blom is a treasure hunter, a scourer of thrift shops and flea markets for old 78 rpm collections. His quarry is the long-lost oddities of the forgotten by-ways of American music, and his trophies are the recreations he compiles from these, and lovingly performs with his orchestra The Beau Hunks. In the United States Blom and his men (he himself disclaims any pretensions to being either *beau* or hunky, by the way) already have quite a fan following.

It all took off with Blom's rediscovery of Leroy Shield, the man who throughout the thirties wrote so many of the catchy and delightful – and frequently uncredited – scores that put the finishing touch to the Laurel & Hardy films. The whole thing began as a one-off, a lark, when Blom devised a Shield sequence for live performance at a Laurel & Hardy festival in Amsterdam. However, reactions were so enthusiastic that the idea soon developed into a longer-term, more serious project. Thus The Beau Hunks (so-named after a Laurel & Hardy film), metamorphosed overnight from a party turn into a permanent ensemble.

A CD followed in 1993. Since the original Shield scores do not survive, the only way to access the music was by transcribing the original sound tracks, a herculean job on which Blom collaborated with other members of the band, with outside help from Laurel & Hardy aficionados. The outcome was this launchpad CD, *The Beau Hunks Play The Original Laurel & Hardy Music* (1993). Two factors contribute to its attraction. Firstly, it reveals that Shield's incidental film music has solid quality and a lasting appeal of its own. Secondly, it stimulates the Ah-ha!-reflex. The Shield legacy, it turned out, already had a place in the collective subconscious of generations of filmgoers with childhood memories of Laurel & Hardy children's matinees. Cartoonist Robert Crumb, for one, declared: '*This is the music I've been looking for all my life!*'

The American music press reacted with similar enthusiasm, and also eagerly welcomed Blom's second Shield release in 1994, which consisted of sophisticated arrangements of soundtracks of the pre-World War II children's series *The Little Rascals*. *Newsweek* said: '*The best thing from Holland since tulips*', while The New Yorker spoke of '*a crackerjack orchestra*', and ex-Beach Boy Brian Wilson confessed that '*The Beau Hunks triggered off a very beautiful sentimental chord in my soul*'. Meanwhile, the *Little Rascals* CD has sold over 35,000 copies in the US alone.

Back in Amsterdam, it did not take Gert-Jan Blom long to decide what the next Beau Hunks venture should be. Not film music, this time, but the innovative small-band compositions of Raymond Scott who, like Shield, was once upon a time an exceptionally prolific and popular composer, and who is likewise virtually forgotten in the US.

Raymond Scott was given to writing complex music disguised to appear easy and playful. His 'novelty jazz' was characterised by a humorous, feather-light touch, underneath which lurked a wealth of rhythmic and melodic intricacy. His titles show a lively and childlike imagination: *War Dance for Wooden Indians*, *The Toy Trumpet*, *New Year's Eve in a Haunted House*. While the technical perfectionism of Scott's instrumentation brings to mind Ellington and Benny Goodman, its coloration evokes a fairy world of magic – like Tchaikovsky's *Nutcracker*, say.

Blom became acquainted with this music through a handful of half-worn-out 78s. When he decided on the Scott project, he was faced with the same problem as with Leroy Shield: sheet music non-existent. Again, he and the Hunks set themselves to the laborious job of transcription. Finding the raw material was another matter, but here he found a particularly rich vein in the sound archives of the University of Missouri in Kansas City, where he was able to tape many original recordings by Scott and his group.

When, after months and months of arranging and re-arranging, and endless rehearsal of try-out upon try-out, The Beau Hunks Sextette's CDs *Celebration on Planet Mars* and *Manhattan Minuet* were released in 1994 and 1996 respectively, history once more repeated itself. Again the American press marvelled that it took the Dutch to jog America into awareness of this forgotten, but still very much alive 'chamber jazz'. And, as before, critics noted that the music sounded amazingly familiar. No wonder: all during the forties Warner Bros utilised countless Scott fragments for *Bugs Bunny* and their other popular animations. It was a perfect marriage: the compulsive rhythmic *push*, and the plasticity of the unexpected twists and turns of a piece such as 'Powerhouse', for instance, perfectly match the restless, agitated imagery of the typical classic cartoon.

After Brian Wilson, Elvis Costello too was greatly taken with The Beau Hunks' work. His tribute runs: '*This is surely the beauty of the group: to faithfully bring music from hidden corners and make it part of our lives. No dusty scholarship! Hear how they swing!*'

Swing they certainly do, for which much of the credit must go to drummer Louis Debij for his unerring feel for the thirties. But there's more to it than that. Gert-Jan Blom is meticulous in making sure that the effect captures the original sound as faithfully as possible. In some respects, he says, his way of working is not unlike the techniques involved in playing Baroque music on original instruments. The imprint of this high level of awareness is discernible in every detail of performance and production. For a start, the CDs are '*Newly Recorded in Authentic Lo-Fi*', as the covers proudly proclaim; they use contemporary 30s and 40s instruments wherever they can; they rehearse ruthlessly to get the tempi and the dynamics exactly right, and they avoid all but essential use of advanced studio technology. The end result is a completely balanced, unforced sound which restores this timeless music of a bygone age to the place it deserves in our own time and place.

Blom has cause for satisfaction. In his wake, American musicians are now also showing an interest in what he calls 'the classical entertainment music of this century'. At the end of 1996, for example, the New York clarinettist Don Byron released a CD which includes renderings of 'Powerhouse' and 'Siberian Sleighride'. With this unambivalent accolade, Raymond Scott, who after a brief flash of fame was for so long deprived of recognition, is once again where he deserves to be: at the top of the modern repertoire. One hopes for more such rehabilitations.

ERIK VAN DEN BERG
Translated by Sonja Prescod.

DISCOGRAPHY
The Original Laurel & Hardy Music vol. 1 & 2 (MSA 99003/99025, 1992 / 1993)
The Original Little Rascals Music (Koch Screen 3-8702-2, 1994)
Celebration on Planet Mars (Basta 30-90562, 1994)
On to the Show (Koch Screen 3-8705-2, 1995)
Manhattan Minuet (Basta 30-90362, 1996)

Philosophy

Max Wildiers, Theologian and Cultural Philosopher

17 August 1996 saw the passing of the internationally renowned theologian and cultural philosopher Max Wildiers, for decades one of the most influential champions of culture in the Low Countries. He was born in Antwerp in 1904. After secondary school he joined the Capuchins and studied theology at the Gregoriana in Rome, where he obtained his doctorate with a dissertation on the eschatology of Albert Schweitzer. From 1932 to 1940 he taught theology to his fellow Flemish Capuchins. Afterwards he was employed as an instructor at various colleges, while he himself sat in on lectures in biology. In 1964 he moved to the United States,

Max Wildiers (1904-1996)
(Photo by Paul van den Abeele).

where for many years he was a professor at the University of San Francisco in California. From 1969 to 1974 he taught in the English-language section of the Leuven theological faculty.

The name of this Flemish Capuchin priest will always be associated with the French Jesuit Pierre Teilhard de Chardin. Indeed, it was Wildiers who edited Teilhard's unpublished writings after his death on Easter Day 1955; this, despite the Vatican prohibition. It required a great deal of courage at that time to defy such a veto. Wildiers was able to summon the necessary courage, driven as he was by both his interest in biology, especially the theory of evolution, and his theological concern that the Christian message be interpreted in contemporary terms. This concern was already apparent in a work he published in 1952 on evolution and world view.

Wildiers never met Teilhard personally. He had learned about his ideas from the Flemish Jesuit Claeys-Bouuaert. He was able to contact Teilhard, who was in New York at the time, through his secretary in Paris. Teilhard's prompt reaction was: '*At last a theologian who is interested in my writings*'. Wildiers was given immediate access to the archives of the famous paleontologist and philosopher, and when *The Phenomenon of Man* (Le phénomène humain) was published in November 1955, it was with a preface by Wildiers. He would write an introduction to each of the separately published parts of the book.

In 1960 Wildiers' book on Teilhard's philosophy was published in Paris, a book that went through many reprints and appeared in many translations. *An Introduction to Teilhard de Chardin* (Inleiding tot Teilhard de Chardin) followed in 1963. In his countless lectures at the universities of San Francisco, Berkeley, Chicago, Alberta (Canada), and Leuven, in his public lectures in Europe and the United States, and in his many publications, Wildiers explained and clarified Teilhard's vision, not as a detached observer and neutral reporter, but as a confirmed though not uncritical defender.

Like Teilhard, Wildiers also set out, using the results of the positive sciences, to discover the unified structure of the universe and to gain insight into the metaphysical problem of the relationship with 'spiritual matter'. It was a daring method and plan, that led to the declaration of '*the law of growing complexity and growing consciousness*' and to the notion of the historical dimension of the universe. This approach was not new, but its content was far from classical. Scholastic philosophy had also been based on contemporary cosmology, but since Copernicus, Galileo, Lamarck and Darwin it had been completely and irrevocably superseded. This explains the unavoidable collision not only with fundamentalist biblical exegesis and neo-scholasticism, but also with the doctrinal authority of the Church.

Wildiers himself had undergone an enormous spiritual evolution over the years. With his theological training at the Gregoriana in Rome, he knew where his roots were. Throughout his life until he was well advanced in years he would continue to read and study,

not only because his sympathies lay with the reconciliation of science and faith, but also because the eternal
search for truth so appealed to him. In this he was faithful to his motto and his ex libris, '*spiritus quiescit
numquam*' – the spirit never rests.

During his many years in the United States his quest
brought him in contact with the notion of process as advanced by the British philosopher A.N. Whitehead and
the American theologian Ch. Hartshorne. Wildiers
gladly subscribed to the concept of the universe as a
continuous process of self-creation set in motion by
God. He became one of the most influential promoters
of process theology in the Low Countries. While in the
United States he wrote his masterpiece, published in
1974, *The Theologian and his Universe: Theology and
Cosmology from the Middle Ages to the Present*
(Wereldbeeld en theologie). In this large tome he
demonstrated how the cosmological concepts that had
been formed throughout the ages had influenced religious thinking and theology. The favourable reception
of this unique work was tremendous.

As he advanced in years, Wildiers, who was a strong
opponent of neo-scholasticism and its related church
dogma, began to regard himself more and more as a
cultural philosopher. This is clearly apparent in his
later publications such as *Farewell to Los Alamos* (Af-
scheid van Los Alamos) about the nuclear age, and *The
Hidden Life of Culture* (Het verborgen leven van de
cultuur). In these essays, as well as in many magazine
articles, Wildiers emerged as a shrewd cultural critic
and an adept natural philosopher. Few were as open to
the signs of the times as he. As the esteemed Teilhard
de Chardin before him, Wildiers was also something of
a visionary. Probing the tradition from whence he
came, his inner dynamic drove him steadily towards
the future: restless yet serene, progressive but always
nuanced, and with a hefty dose of humour. He always
enjoyed a large readership. In acknowledgement of his
scholarly labours he was awarded two honorary doctorates (Antwerp, 1985 and Leuven, 1992).

Wildiers's journalistic work is also worth mentioning. He regularly contributed articles to the Flemish
newspaper *De Standaard*, short features which were
signed 'Scrutator' (there were a few thousand of these
over the years). He also established a prestigious literary section in this newspaper in 1952, *De Standaard
der Letteren*.

The fact that Wildiers' efforts to interpret the faith
in contemporary terms were not gratefully accepted by
the institutional church is more than regrettable, to put
it mildly. Even his 1966 publication *The Church in our
Future World* (De kerk in de wereld van morgen)
stirred up ill-feeling among many church leaders. In
this challenging but soundly-based essay he treated
three themes: the attitude of the Church towards the
natural sciences, towards democracy, and towards plu-
ralism and freedom of conscience. In a critically sound
and direct manner, Wildiers supported a Church with
close ties to the world, a Church that is democratic and
tolerant.

Countless believers were and still are thankful to

him for this open-hearted plea, despite the opinions of
many bishops and other conservatives. The total absence of the official Church at his funeral, in contrast
to the great number of prominent representatives from
political and cultural circles, was simply annoying. But
it was not only his theological vision and his resistance
to abuse of power by the clerical authorities that made
the hierarchy suspicious. It was also his indefatigable
efforts on behalf of the cultural, social and political
emancipation of the Flemish people. His intellectual
labours were related not only to his innate honesty and
drive for freedom; they were socially motivated as
well. This world citizen with his global vision remained
faithful to his radical Flemish convictions until his
death.

Wildiers gave his university and public lectures in
Dutch, French and English, and always with the same
aisance and rich vocabulary, whether he was address-
ing academicians or those with less schooling. With
him we have lost a talented and widely-read writer, an
exceptionally eloquent speaker and, above all, a great
mind.

HERMAN-EMIEL MERTENS
Translated by Nancy Forest-Flier.

TRANSLATIONS
An Introduction to Teilhard de Chardin (Tr. Hubert Hoskins).
New York, 1968.
*The Theologian and his Universe: Theology and Cosmology from the
Middle Ages to the Present*. New York, 1982.

Society

The Memoirs of Aletta Jacobs A Modest Testimony

Aletta Jacobs (1854-1929) was one of the pioneers of
Dutch feminism; not only was she a political activist,
she was also the first Dutch woman to attend an ordinary secondary school and the first woman to study at
a Dutch university. Her arduous struggle to gain ad-
mission to university and her triumph in qualifying as
a doctor are of such significance that for these alone
she merits a place in history. For her to be admitted to
university required a political decision in the public debate as to whether women were constitutionally suited
to higher education. Her case sparked off a heated discussion about the desirability of such a level of learning for women. In her medical studies she came up
against the taboo which held that a respectable woman
could and should have no knowledge of such matters
as sexuality, contraception, venereal disease or prostitution. Since she was always the first in the field, she
invariably became the focus of controversy; not only
about herself but about women in general. Her application to enter university provoked a public debate in
the national press, with political parties taking posi-

Aletta Jacobs (1854-1929)
(Photo IIAV, Amsterdam).

tions for and against, which led in the end to a ministerial ruling by the liberal politician Thorbecke. It took courage for Aletta Jacobs to hold firm and complete her studies under so much pressure, with all eyes upon her.

In her memoirs she defended herself against the suggestion that she was aware of any analogy between her efforts to go to university and the furious debates raging in other countries about access to higher education for women: '*I had virtually no idea of the consequences of what I was doing. How could I? I had been brought up in a village and knew little about the world at large.*'

This village girl was to become more than just the first female student, the first woman doctor, fighting for her own rights; for years she was active in the peace movement, she was among the first to advocate a more woman-friendly approach to medical practice, and it was also she who initiated the large-scale use of the diaphragm (also: Dutch cap!) as a modern means of contraception.

In 1996 the American publishing house The Feminist Press at The City University of New York published a translation of Jacobs' memoirs, which she wrote in 1924, under the title *Memories. My Life as an International Leader in Health, Suffrage and Peace.* This is an account written in her later years by an activist whose personal struggle had led to her becoming part of a world-wide network of feminists and others who strove to improve the position of women.

I still remember with what breathless excitement I read those memoirs years ago, and how I found in Aletta Jacobs' work a source of inspiration for my own feminism. They spell out very clearly how lonely the struggle can be and the enormous importance of solidarity. Now, rereading them, I am struck by how much of the book is devoted to her international contacts in the world of the women's suffrage movement around the turn of the century, and how little she says of her own political and cultural background. This is under-

standable, given that most memoirs belong to a particular literary genre in which the dominant element is whatever is foremost in the author's mind at the time of writing. In Aletta Jacobs' case this means a book which gives the palest outline of her private life and devotes little space to herself as its protagonist. When she wrote it, in 1924, only five years had elapsed since the victory of the suffrage movement in the Netherlands, while in many other countries the battle was still going on. Almost nothing could have meant more to her than that battle at whose heart she had been for two long decades. People writing memoirs of this kind do not concern themselves with the historical setting from which they came; that is meat for future historians.

So how was it possible for the village girl to become such a key figure? Aletta Jacobs is representative of two historical developments. Firstly, she came from the Netherlands' provincial Jewish middle class at a time when it was restyling itself outside Amsterdam, the great centre of Jewish cultural life. Secondly, her progress ties up with the rise of radical liberal thinking in the late nineteenth century. She was born in the far north of the country, in the village of Sappermeer where her father was in practice as a doctor. She was not the only member of the family to break new ground: her sister Charlotte became the first woman pharmacist. When Aletta announced at an early age that she wanted to be a doctor the idea was not dismissed as nonsense. But her upbringing was at first still directed towards a traditional career as a wife and mother. It was unthinkable for her to become a doctor; that it was possible for Jewish men to do so was already a great step forward. Jews in the Netherlands had acquired full citizenship in 1796. The modernists among them believed passionately in equality and embraced the liberal views typical of the time. They strove to free themselves from their disadvantaged position and become integrated in Dutch society; and a precondition for this was access to higher education. The views of Aletta's father were likewise permeated by the idea of all people being equal. But a typical feature of the Jewish circles from which he came was that they saw this idea as closely linked with the importance they attached to upbringing and education. More than just a village doctor, he was involved in the political and cultural developments of his time. His friends and acquaintances were part of a network of prominent Jewish provincials of liberal views, and this network was called into play when Aletta set out to do the seemingly unthinkable. That he supported her in her struggle to be admitted to secondary school and then to university is in line with a striving for equality that was acceptable in his circle. He himself had achieved something which, for a Jew, would have been inconceivable a century earlier. He was a respected citizen, a university-trained doctor; so why should not education allow his daughter also to achieve the unthinkable? In later life Aletta Jacobs' thoughts and opinions were for the most part those of the more radical wing of this liberalism which regarded universal suffrage as the basis for equality and believed that the achievement of this equality for the common people required social commitment and, in political terms, a great deal of social legislation. By then she had moved to Amsterdam, where she married a husband of similarly radical views. Aletta Jacobs was convinced that the right to vote would bring women equality, and she was the first to demand this.

At first glance her actions seem to be these of an individual bent on her own advancement. But there was more to it. Where her demands were in accordance with those of the suffragists she consistently received massive support. But when she turns her attention to social matters and fights for effective contraception for women of the working classes, then she shines out as the lonely pioneer, blithely sticking her neck out and, in many people's view, going much too far. Talking about contraception was all very well, but opening a clinic in a working-class neighbourhood and giving practical help to working-class women was something many people found too much to take. She was also the first to speak up for shop-girls who were forbidden to sit down during opening hours. As a doctor, Aletta Jacobs had to deal with the gynaecological problems they suffered as a result of long days spent on their feet, and she fought hard for the 'Right to Sit'.

In 1903 Aletta Jacobs decided to give up her medical practice and devote herself henceforth to the fight for women's suffrage. During this time she became the most prominent feminist in the Netherlands. In 1908 the Dutch movement played host to the International Woman Suffrage Movement in Amsterdam, and from this in the First World War grew the international women's peace movement. In 1911-1912 she travelled the world with Carrie Chapman Catt, secretary of the American movement, to spread the word on women's suffrage. On these journeys she was at all times also Aletta Jacobs the doctor, concerned with issues of prostitution and women's health. Thus her interests were always wider than the single issue of votes for women.

Aletta Jacobs has gone down in history as a fighter for women's suffrage. Incontrovertibly, it is in that field that she became most famous. But if we ask about the importance of what she did, it is not enough to answer simply: 'Votes for women'. We know now that the vote has not brought equality, that it was only one step along a road leading to many other measures. But in the story of Aletta Jacobs a number of developments converge; these not only affected her as an individual, but were decisive for many women who came after her. This is not simply the result of the striving of one brave individual, or of a father's support for his daughter, or later the support of a radically democratic and free-thinking husband for the wife he so admired. Her memoirs afford us a glimpse of the way in which this unique personality came to be part of a world-wide movement. It is a most modest testimony. Looking at a photo of her parent's house on the day of her seventieth birthday, she wrote: '*Father, it's all right. You often worried that I'd end up landing myself in real trouble. But the little I still have to do is really no cause for concern.*

'*Dr Evaletta Jacobs offers the apple to the learned Adam Cort Esq., and he bites.*' (Political cartoon on the proposed constitutional reform which was to include women's suffrage, 1915).

My work has been successfully completed, thanks to your help and advice. Women can now look forward to a brighter future.'

SELMA LEYDESDORFF
Translated by Tanis Guest.

Aletta Jacobs, *Memories. My Life as an International Leader in Health, Suffrage, and Peace* (ed. Harriet Feinberg & tr. Annie Wright). New York: The Feminist Press at The City University of New York, 1996. ISBN 1-55861-137-1.

Dutch American Voices

For Americans of any ethnic background, it is particularly fascinating to watch something unfolding before our eyes that we all learned in school: the making of our diverse society. *Dutch American Voices* offers a colourful, candid tapestry of not only the first-hand reactions of Dutch immigrants to the culture they found around them, but their enculturation process and – last but by far the most intriguing to those of us who are not of Dutch descent – their contributions to the ongoing process of building this culture.

The selection of letters published here is from the Calvin College Library Archives. Letters from 23 different families over a ten-state area (mostly around the Great Lakes) were chosen to provide a representative panorama. Some twenty pages of introduction give the reader a detailed overview of Dutch immigration patterns to the US in the period of most intense migration. In addition, each of the five chapters offers more specific historical notes, and each immigrant family's letters are preceded by a few identifying paragraphs.

The letters are a faithful reflection of the story familiar from our history books: the rugged rural life in a fertile but demanding country, the clearing of the dense forests in Michigan, the gradual change from an agricultural to a manufacturing economy. Occasionally the immigrants are such conscientious observers and recorders of the life around them that they almost seem to be aware of writing for history. We participate in successes and an affluence beyond the dreams of most immigrants, but also failures and the trials of unfamiliar weather extremes. But the intense religious piety of most of the earlier immigrants gave them a solid basis on which to accept both good and bad.

The Dutch like most other immigrants tended to live in tight communities by religious persuasion, surrounded by 'alien beliefs' and the world referred to by most as 'the English'. It is an interesting footnote that the 'wild people' mentioned in 1867 undoubtedly refers to Indians, but that this same people is referred to in a letter as early as 1905 by our modern term 'Native Americans'.

Most of the immigrants are clearly overwhelmed by the prosperity and the size of the land they find themselves in, and cannot tell their families back home often enough what opportunities await anyone who is willing to work hard. '*Life is free here – You have no one looking over your shoulder*', exults one. But we also hear some early doubts about the callousness and commercialism of American life.

What gives this collection its special interest is the many large and small ways in which the Dutch immigrants faithfully transplanted the cultural attitudes and customs they brought with them. We see the familiar '*verzuiling*' ('pillarisation') pattern of '*Hervormd, Gereformeerd and Rooms Katholiek*'. In their urge to be '*more Dutch than the Dutch*' (a phrase used in the Introduction), the immigrants – particularly the high proportion of Seceders, followers of the 'Afscheiding' – kept these sub-societies even more determinedly sealed off from each other than in the old country. It is only in the most recent times that the lines are finally beginning to fade away.

The book's major division of the rural immigrants into those of 'Sand-soil' and 'Clay-soil' origins will provoke either bafflement or a knowing smile, depending on the reader's familiarity with the importance of these to the agriculture, and therefore the distinct cultures, that had evolved in each in the Netherlands. At first glance many of these earlier immigrants sound conspicuously obsessed with possessions and earnings. Over and over again, the letters parade their success in securing an economically comfortable life in the new country. Then it may dawn on the reader that they are using the only means at their disposal to convey a crucial idea to the families they left: this relative affluence, in the new country within the reach of all, implies a social status that simple people like themselves could never have aspired to back home. This in turn justifies the painful decision to emigrate.

The chapters are further subdivided into 'Rural to rural' , 'Rural to urban', and 'Urban to urban' to show the patterns of environments the immigrants left and entered. In following the patterns of most immigrants, they are adding their skills, their customs, and their attitudes to the evolving 'American way of life'.

The conscientious translation makes this collection accessible to the wide audience it deserves. The reader will, to be sure, be amused at an occasional reminder of the Dutch original: 'by you' instead of 'where you are', 'farmeress', 'eight to fourteen days', 'half a foot', the inappropriate overuse of the word 'beautiful' and a reluctance to use the progressive where it would seem called for.

WILLIAM Z. SHETTER

Herbert J. Brinks (ed.), *Dutch American Voices: Letters from the United States, 1850-1930*. Documents in American Social History. Ithaca / London: Cornell University Press, 1995; 480 pp. ISBN 0-8014-3063-1.

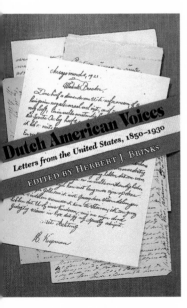

Small, Incomplete but Charming The Museum of Decorative Art in Ghent

In the middle of the last century, the growing textile industry in the Flemish city of Ghent made it the Manchester of the European continent. At that time the new Ghent entrepreneurs particularly welcomed artistic signs of prosperity. In 1903, a group of textile barons and a few art lovers founded a museum of applied art in the city. It is no coincidence that the considerable textile collection features prominently in the summary catalogue of 1909. The enterprising association Union des Arts Industriels et Décoratifs also praised its library, which was housed with the collection in an upper room of the Academy of Fine Arts.

If today, just a few years short of its centenary, the collection of the Museum of Decorative Art gives the impression of being rather fragmentary and incomplete, this is in large measure due to a lack of continuity in policy. It is therefore enlightening to take a brief look at the museum's history.

At first sight, 1903 seems quite early to found a museum of applied art, yet an applied arts movement had already developed in England and France many years before this date. The British Arts & Crafts Movement, permeated with socialist ideology, did not fail to have an impact on the avant-garde art group Les Vingt, established in Brussels in 1883. But this influence was particularly felt among artists, the most important of whom were Henry van de Velde (see *The Low Countries* 1994-95: 244-251), George Lemmen and Theo van Rysselberghe, especially in the narrow field of poster and cover design. Of these three, only Henry van de Velde emerged as an all-rounder, designing buildings, clothes and furniture as well as everyday objects. The Brussels Art Nouveau architects, such as Paul Hankar and Victor Horta (see *The Low Countries* 1996-97: 39-45), also had an eye for the design of the living environment. Unfortunately, however, the collecting policy of the new Ghent museum of applied art was not oriented towards contemporary creations. Between 1913 and 1931, a less conservative wind blew through the museum and there was interest in the work of contemporary designers. 1913 was also the year in which the Museum received a bequest from the collector and artist Fernand Scribe (who also contributed to the collection of the Museum of Fine Arts in Ghent). With this enlargement of its collection and the acquisitions it made at the Ghent World Exhibition of 1913, the Museum was in urgent need of larger premises; but it was not until 1922 that the city of Ghent offered the Hotel de Coninck in Jan Breydelstraat as its new home.

The Museum is still housed in this eighteenth-century merchant's house with its imposing facade in Balegem sandstone. It was in this spacious house with its large courtyard that the De Coninck family ran a flourishing wholesale business in linen. The part of the building along the street was left virtually as it was, except for the installation of a magnificent Louis XVI-style staircase, and houses the dining room of F.J. De Coninck. The former coach house on the other side of the courtyard proved suitable for the temporary exhibitions that the Museum frequently organised in the 1920s.

Unfortunately, the interesting and fairly large Art Nouveau and Art Deco collection did not find favour with the curator who took up office in the 1930s. The items were not exhibited and some of them were probably sold. Moreover, the city council, which in the meantime had taken over administration of the museum, decided to close it temporarily in 1958 in order to carry out restoration work. The Museum did not reopen until 1973 after undergoing only some refurbishment. When it later emerged that the coach house could not be restored, a new museum wing sprang up in its place and was brought into use in 1992. This airy new wing offers flexibility and space and contrasts sharply with the cramped eighteenth-century part, which is still used for exhibiting Ancien Régime furniture. Two floors in the new building are reserved for exhibitions on contemporary applied arts. The tradition of holding temporary exhibitions was re-

The Jan Frans Allaert dining room (1761) in the Ghent Museum of Decorative Art.

The new wing of the Ghent Museum of Decorative Art.

sumed in the 1970s and some interesting individuals were featured, including the Belgian architect-designers Gaston Eysselinck and Huib Hoste. Hoste was an important figure in Belgian modernism and in 1928 he signed the La Sarraz manifesto of the Nieuwe Bouwen (New Building), along with his fellow architect Victor Bourgeois. Eysselinck was a more retiring character who worked in Ostend and, particularly, Ghent. As was often the case with architects, he too, like Hoste, designed some inspired pieces of furniture. Eysselinck's tubular chairs and Hoste's simple, colourful furniture rightly gained a place in the permanent exhibition alongside the famous designs of Le Corbusier, Marcel Breuer and Mies van der Rohe, which rank as milestones in modernism.

The new part also houses the small, but nevertheless valuable Art Nouveau collection. The arrangement of the collection emphasises the constructive tendency and the importance of functional logic in the Belgian furniture designs of, in particular, Paul Hankar, Gustave Serrurier-Bovy and Henry van de Velde. This contrasts with the more decorative trend of Art Nouveau in neighbouring countries, illustrated in the Museum by smaller decorative objects.

The blind spot in the furniture collection is undoubtedly the absence of any examples of the influential Scandinavian furniture design, with Alvar Aalto as its main exponent. American design, such as the work of Charles & Ray Eames, also deserves a place, and all the more so since the shell forms used were a source of inspiration in the 1960s, which are also not represented in the display.

There are many examples of Italian design, which caused such a sensation in the early 1980s with the frivolous designs of the Memphis Group, the Studio Alchimia and Alessi. The work of more recent great names such as Borek Sipek can also be seen. Also on view is the work of the Flemish furniture designers Peter de Bruyne, Emiel Veranneman (see *The Low Countries* 1995-96: 303-305) and André Verroken, representing some of the few bright spots in the post-war period. And running through the exhibition like a leitmotif is the display of Flemish carpets.

Although the Ghent Museum of Decorative Art could have come a lot further if it had not been for its fitful history, some of its pieces will nevertheless be the envy of museums with more resources at their disposal. Its present location in the historic centre of Ghent is an added bonus.

ERIC BRACKE
Translated by Gregory Ball.

ADDRESS
Museum of Decorative Art
Jan Breydelstraat 5 / 9000 Ghent / Belgium
tel. +32 9 225 66 76
Opening hours: 9 a.m.-5.15 p.m. (closed on Mondays)

The Jan van Goyen Quartercentenary and Britain

On 15 January 1596, the great landscapist Jan van Goyen was born in Leiden, the son and grandson of simple shoemakers. In the spring of 1996, the London gallery of Richard Green, reviving a nearly extinct tradition of scholarly dealer-shows, celebrated the 400th anniversary of this remarkable Dutch Golden Age painter with a special exhibition of no less than 40 works, many rarely seen. And from October 1996 to 13 January 1997 the Lakenhal Museum in the artist's birth-place offered a sumptuous commemorative oeuvre-show.

As a talented youth, Van Goyen was apprenticed to a number of established painters, both at Leiden and elsewhere. In his development he progressed from charming but traditional anecdotal town- and country-scenes to being influenced by such pioneer artists as Esaias van de Velde, Salomon Ruysdael and Jan Porcellis. Thus he became expert in the atmospheric understatement that from the early 1630s so strikingly characterised his later sky-dominated compositions. With their ever lower horizons and delicate colour schemes they made him into an undisputed champion of the new Dutch landscape painting.

Van Goyen was the most peripatetic Dutch artist of his day, filling dozens of sketchbooks with pictorial records in black chalk. He was also incredibly prolific, turning out innumerable canvasses. But with his more than 1,000 pictures he never made any money, depending financially on his dealings in art, real estate, and even tulips (until the ruinous Tulipomania crash of 1636). He was a great family-man, though, and one of his daughters married his ex-pupil Jan Steen (see *The Low Countries* 1996-97: 304-305). In 1632, none too happy in his Roman Catholic parents' largely Protestant Leiden, he moved to the more liberal The Hague where he died in 1656 – deeply in debt.

The reason why this painter should not go unnoticed in the pages of our Yearbook is not only that, from the eighteenth century onwards, Van Goyen gradually became more and more popular among British connoisseurs, but also that in 1833 the then supremo of English landscape and marine painting, J.M.W. Turner RA, exhibited a picture with the intriguing title of *Antwerp. Van Goyen looking out for a Subject*.[1]

From his early youth, Turner had been a great fan of the Dutch School.[2] More than once he added the name of one of its Masters to a sketch, e.g. *'Quite a C[u]yp'* on an impression of the Amsterdam skyline[3], or included it in the title of a picture to which he had been inspired by the memory of their style, e.g. *Port Ruysdael*.[4]

Van Goyen's superb *View of Antwerp*, dated 1648 and owned at one time by George Wilbraham of Northwich, Cheshire, was auctioned in 1830. Turner regularly visited collections and sales to view recent acquisitions. In the 1830s Antwerp was in the news in connection with the military consequences of the Belgian Revolt against Dutch rule and the fact that the British

Jan van Goyen, *View of Antwerp.* 1648. Canvas, 74.5 x 118.5 cm. Private collection.

Government was leaving the King of the Whitehall-created United Netherlands in the lurch. Van Goyen's *Antwerp* was an outstanding example of the Master's silver-grey palette. Coming across the picture by pure chance, perhaps at an auction, must have fascinated Turner at once. And as one of his principles was *'I never lose an accident'*[5], it is more than likely that the combination of outraged pro-Dutch feelings and the 'accident' of his confrontation with so surprisingly beautiful a Dutch depiction of the Flemish city at this politically testing moment prompted him to another of his occasional symbolic compositions.

This time the message clearly was *'Let art reconcile what regional fanaticism seems ready to destroy'*. The plume-hatted figure of Van Goyen, standing on the deck of a Dutch yacht with 'VAN G' on her stern sailing towards a Belgian waterfront, is facing not the shore but the viewer and clearly embodies this unspoken message – while a man-of-war (with guns run out!) is anchoring on the left, presumably just in case ....[6]

Antwerp was no *terra incognita* for either Van Goyen or Turner. Both were great travellers who made hundreds of sketches for future reference, among which there are several of Antwerp. With certain types of landscape in mind, Turner will have greeted wholeheartedly the Dutch Master's style and technique in his picture, but the sight of Antwerp as his subject probably acted as a trigger; Turner was, after all, a great newspaper-reader.

Following on Richard Green's show, the Leiden exhibition enabled the public to form an excellent impression of the Master in his career from overcrowded, conventional beginnings to unique near-monochrome panoramas of dunes and countryside, especially since it included 46 carefully selected sketches and drawings. These greatly enhance the value of the catalogue, as do the reproductions of related works by contemporary Dutch artists.

Ideally it would be most revealing if exhibitions could show examples of the art of the Dutch Masters

Gerard Terborch, *Portrait of Jan van Goyen.* c.1652-1655.   Collection Prince of Lichtenstein, Vaduz Castle.

who inspired British landscapes and marines next to these works themselves. But this may well have to remain wishful thinking. As it is, we can only be grateful for small mercies – realising that, in Van Goyen's quatercentenary, 'small' was remarkably 'great'.

FRED G.H. BACHRACH

NOTES
1. Frick Collection, New York.
2. See *The Low Countries 1995-96*, pp. 198-207.

3. *Holland Sketchbook,* 1825, f. 117 (Tate Gallery, London).

4. Royal Academy 1827 *(Yale Center for British Art,* New Haven, Connecticut).

5. Ruskin, J., *Modern Painters.* 1860 (ed. Barrie 1989, V, p. 504).

6. Bachrach, Fred G.H., 'Turner's Tale of Two Cities'. In: *Turner Society News,* August 1996, pp. 11-15.

FURTHER READING

Christiaan Vogelaar (ed.), *Jan Van Goyen* (Catalogue with English summary). Zwolle, 1996.

Rubens' Landscapes The Private Works of a Public Artist

From 16 October 1996 to 19 January 1997 the National Gallery, London, held the exhibition *Rubens' Landscapes,* in which Chief Curator Christopher Brown presented a rare overview of this lesser-known segment of the oeuvre of a painter who is chiefly associated with monumental altar pieces, and religious and allegorical scenes on an equally heroic scale. In his own time, too, it was for these that Peter Paul Rubens (1577-1640) was primarily celebrated. Indeed, demand was so great that in order to keep up with his many commissions he maintained a full staff of assistants and students in his large studio workshop in Antwerp.

Today, particularly in England, Rubens is not generally appreciated: his work is too hermetically allegorical and explicitly counter-reformatory in character to appeal to current tastes. However, with this exhibition, reinforced by an impressive catalogue, Brown has certainly made a strong case for the disdained Antwerp *maestro's* prompt reinstatement in the public's favour. In fact, modern viewers enjoy considerably more access to Rubens' landscapes (which include paintings as well as drawings and oil sketches) than did the bulk of his contemporaries. For these were, as Brown repeatedly stressed in his opening talk to the press view, *'the private works of a public artist'.* The prince of Flemish art created them chiefly to please himself. They were not commercial works, but painted to adorn his own home, or as personal gifts for his friends, acquaintances and patrons.

The exhibition presented the landscapes in the dual context of the Flemish landscape tradition, and of Rubens' output as a whole. Thus, the first section of the exhibition included works by other painters of the first half of the sixteenth century, among them Joachim Patinir and Pieter Bruegel, who were likewise from Antwerp. This was the generation which developed landscape painting into an art form in its own right, in contrast to their immediate predecessors such as Hugo van der Goes, for instance, for whom landscape had been no more than a backdrop for religious and allegorical subjects. Patinir mainly painted panoramic, or high viewpoint, scenes in which human figures appear as tiny and insignificant specks in the face of an overwhelming nature. Landscapes, that is, conceived in imitation of God's view of the earth. Bruegel, too, initially worked with this bird's eye perspective, but he progressively adopted a more naturalistic vantage point as – particularly in his woodland scenes – he began to paint nature for its own sake.

Rubens was familiar with the work of Patinir and Bruegel, which he had studied in the studios of the older school of painters like Joos de Momper and Jan Bruegel the Elder, in the course of his apprenticeship with Tobias Verhaecht. Nonetheless, he was to paint no landscapes himself until after his stay in Italy between 1600 and 1608. In the interim, the political situation in his home country had changed completely. The truce negotiated between Spain and the breakaway Dutch Republic became effective on 9 April

Peter Paul Rubens, *Pond with Cows and Milkmaids.* c.1614. Panel, 76 x 107 cm. Collection Prince of Lichtenstein, Vaduz Castle.

Peter Paul Rubens, *An Autumn Landscape with a View of Het Steen in the Early Morning.* c.1636. Panel, 131.2 x 229.2 cm. National Gallery, London.

1609, ushering in a twelve-year remission in the war which had raged since 1565. Under the governorship of 'the Archdukes', Albert and Isabella, the Southern (Spanish) Netherlands experienced a renewed hope in the future.

As economic recovery set in, the flame of Catholicism was rekindled anew by the Jesuits and Dominicans. For the nation to be wooed back to the One True Faith, the Church would have to dazzle and overwhelm the popular imagination with all the pomp and splendour at its command. To this end, the best of local artistic talent was put to work. For Rubens, orders flowed in for one altarpiece after another. At the same time, he rediscovered the natural beauties of his own land. This is manifest from those works which were not commissioned. *Pond with Cows and Milkmaids*, and *The Farm at Laeken*, for instance, two composite landscapes in which he integrates original sketches with elements from older masters, are veritable paeans to the rich fertility of the Flemish countryside. Wholesome country lasses and glossy cattle animate the scene, while wheel-barrows and panniers bulging with fruits and vegetables bear witness to the prosperity of the Southern Netherlands under the benevolent surveillance of the Holy Mother and the archducal couple. The strength of these works, in common with the great landscapes of his later years, lies in their exquisite finish and sensitive detail. To achieve this, Rubens almost habitually painted his landscapes on oak panel as canvas, by then the standard support medium, could not match the smooth texture of wood as the ideal surface for delicate brushwork.

Rubens' joyous conception of nature is similarly manifest in the series of woodland scenes painted between 1618 and 1625. From 1626, however, there were to be no more landscapes for a number of years. The death of his first wife, and the increasing demands of his diplomatic commitments, left Rubens with neither the inclination nor the time for landscape painting.

In 1630 he remarried, and took up permanent residence at Het Steen, his Brabant country estate at Elewijt, between Mechelen and Brussels, with his new bride, the sixteen-year-old Hélène Fourment. Here he spent the remaining fifteen years of his life quietly among his family. He began again to produce 'private works', among them some of his greatest landscapes, including *Autumn Landscape with a View of Het Steen in the Early Morning*, which Brown describes as '*a wealthy town dweller's view of the countryside and its inhabitants*'. Painted in the world-view tradition of Patinir, these pictures powerfully convey his delight in the Brabant scenery.

A new departure for Rubens in this period was the pastoral landscape. Yet Rubens' personal Arcadia does not always confine itself to the precepts of a completely artificially constructed, mythical scenario. Thus in *Sunset Landscape with a Shepherd and his Flock*, we see a synthesis of pastoral features with actual, identifiable landscape elements.

As the landscapes had such limited circulation, their commercial potential emerged only when his personal collection was sold following his death. Soon the art market was awash with prints and etchings after the master's landscapes. In England towards the end of the eighteenth century, Rubens landscapes came to be keenly sought-after collectors' items. Thomas Gainsborough, for one, was a great admirer, and painted his own *The Watering Place* in homage to Rubens', while John Constable, in a lecture of 1833, declared: '*In no other branch of art is Rubens greater than in landscape.*'

Granted this degree of enthusiasm in informed English circles, it can hardly come as a surprise that a good many of the works featured in this wholly admirable exhibition should have come from the National Gallery's permanent stock. For that matter, Trafalgar Square houses a formidable Flemish collection which ranges from the Primitives to Rubens and Van Dyck. When the North Gallery refurbishments now in progress have been completed, these will appear to even greater advantage in the new Flemish Room, which is being supported by the Flemish government and a number of leading Flemish corporations. Another eagerly awaited date on the international Flemish art agenda is the exhibition which Christopher Brown is preparing to mark the 400th anniversary of the birth of Van Dyck. This will be opening at the Antwerp Museum voor Schone Kunsten in 1999, after which it travels to the Royal Academy in London.

FILIP MATTHIJS
Translated by Sonja Prescod.

FURTHER READING
Christopher Brown, *Rubens's Landscapes*. London, 1996.

Simply Marblelous On Sir Lawrence Alma-Tadema

In 1912 the society artist Lawrence Alma-Tadema RA died in London. Distinguished in death, as in life he was fêted and knighted, he was laid to rest in St Paul's Cathedral.

Quite an achievement, it must be said, for a lad named Laurens Alma from the depths of Friesland, who moved to England, was naturalised, garnered wealth and renown, and knew how to husband his good fortune with a true instinct for business. All the same, soon after his demise his reputation plummeted. In 1934, briefly, his star flickered once more in Hollywood, when Cecil B. De Mille, in his classic *Cleopatra*, re-enacted the spectacular procession in the painting *Spring* on celluloid. But thenceforth, the march of Modernism, for at least the time being, extinguished any further interest in the kind of fancy *tableaux* set in antiquity, and executed with a precision of an archaeological reconstruction, that were the Alma-Tadema hallmark. Unless you count their occasional re-emergence on a biscuit tin, that is. His works were relegated to the attic or, worse still, put out with the lumber. In the seventies, however, he was rediscovered, and his ratings took an upturn. Now, as the current *fin de siècle* is upon us, saleroom prices are rocketing, while high street figures show a healthy demand for poster versions of his work. Furthermore, a comprehensive retrospective exhibition displayed his talents in Amsterdam (29 November 1996-2 March 1997) and Liverpool (21 March-8 June 1997).

Alma-Tadema's career began in 1852 at the age of sixteen when, having first been rejected by the academies in Amsterdam and The Hague, he entered the Kunstacademie in Antwerp. There he found ideal mentors in Louis de Taeye, an erudite expert on antiquity, and Henri Leys. The latter, who had a reputation as a stickler for detail as an artist, and as a demanding taskmaster for his students, presently engaged him as an assistant. The first of Tadema's works to attract notice, was his large-scale *The Education of the Children of Clovis*. In Autumn 1863 he married and set off for Italy on a prolonged working honeymoon. That Italian winter was to be his rubicon.

The Italy which fascinated Alma-Tadema was not Piranesi's land of haunted ruins and spectral decay, but

Lawrence Alma-Tadema, *Coign of Vantage*. 1895. Canvas, 64 x 44.5 cm. Private collection.

the land of archaeological revelation. Pompeii especially, where antiquity is so palpably present, was to remain fresh in his mind for as long as he lived. In the domestic architecture and frescoed walls of Pompeii (which he documented comprehensively on camera) Alma-Tadema had found a personal artistic habitat which, endlessly magnified, endlessly recycled and elaborated, he recreated time and time again.

On his return, he was discovered and launched by Ernest Gambart, the leading Belgian international art dealer of the day. Even when negotiating this first, highly lucrative, contract, Tadema already had the confidence to stipulate that rather than conform with the fashion for medieval scenarios, his pictures would depict the world of antiquity. In 1865 he moved to Brussels, which at that time rivalled Paris as a centre of art and sophistication. All set now for the big time, he produced almost sixty canvasses in the next five years. A fresh move, this time to London, followed in 1870. The motive for this was mixed. His wife had died in the interim, and his career was not going quite as he wished. In his native Netherlands his work was not sought after, because it lacked the fashionable attributes of 'atmosphere' and 'mood'. In France he was well enough established, but not collected. Presumably the Franco-Prussian War must also have influenced his decision. London, in the event, was to bring him both fame and a second wife.

Antiquity was by now Tadema's acknowledged professional terrain: Egypt, ancient Greece and, above all, Rome. However, the Rome which Tadema made his own is a far cry from Winckelmann's classical age of 'noble simplicity and silent grandeur'. Tadema's epoch is the late Empire, in which display, luxury and refinement might reign supreme, but decline and fall are always imminent. Thus one of his best-known and most opulent canvasses, *The Roses of Heliogabalus*, depicts a lavish banquet scene just at the point when the blizzard of rose petals under which this most spectacularly degenerate of late Roman emperors proposes to asphyxiate his guests begins to descend. On the whole, though, a few exceptions aside, Alma-Tadema's preferred domain is not the arena of history's more epic moments, but the private realm of intimate interiors from which languorous damosels, their eyes filled with patrician *ennui*, look out into the middle distance. Furthermore, although details of his settings are authentic in themselves (the artist kept his photographic archive catalogued according to subject), he has no compunction about juxtaposing styles and objects from different periods if this will enhance the interest value of a given composition. The elements, in other words, have historical verisimilitude, even if they are often blown up and distorted, but the assembly as a composite is a montage, a created construct. Tadema's treatment of the 'historical' is perhaps best defined by Marguerite Yourcenar in *Memoirs of Hadrian*: '*No matter how, one always reconstructs the monument in one's own fashion. To use nothing but authentic stones means a lot already.*' The function of archaeology, in Tadema's vocabulary, is to make the past tangible.

The past as conjured up by Tadema held up a flattering mirror to the clientele to which his art addressed itself: moneyed Victorians with time, leisure, pretensions to culture, and a zest for travel. What he gave them was that sense of a remote antiquity of which they had gained some impression on their travels, the matt marble and the infinite blue of the sea, and finer and more comprehensible than it had ever been in reality. In plain fact, the trio of lustrous Roman beauties looking out from their belvedere high over the sea in *Coign of Vantage* (in real life Axel Munthe's Villa San Michele in Capri; the bronze beast is a free interpretation of the Egyptian sphinx which Munthe kept on the balcony), are a dressed-up threesome of Victorian *belles*. Tadema's productions pandered to an escapist mentality among the beneficiaries of the industrial age: a desire to flee the very machines and commerce to which they owed their wealth and their identity as a class. In addition, the Tadema *genre* was suffused with a brand of socially acceptable erotic titillation, wrapped in the pseudo-mythical and morally-approved trappings of another time and place. A Tadema picture can be seen as a high-class version of what the butler saw. Ultimately, however, the appeal of Tadema goes deeper. In transposing his own culture into a distant and highly admired civilisation which, like his own, took an inordinate pride in the ownership and conspicuous display of material possessions, Tadema effec-tively placed Victoria's England first in the line of succession to Rome.

As a painter, Lawrence Alma-Tadema was blessed with a matchless technique and craftsmanship, learned the hard, painstaking way in Europe, where apprentices were still schooled by masters in the time-honoured tradition. This he combined with a vivid sense of realism, and a sensual imagery which was set off by a mannered style of composition, and enlivened by daring *découpage* and unexpected perspectives. And last but not least, he was successful because he happened to be in the right place at the right time, and attracted the right people.

Tadema's personal lifestyle was no less opulent than that of his clients. He cultivated the role of a jovial, generous society host, and was proverbial for the lavish entertainments he staged at his palatial Regent's Park residence. However, he also had a quirky reputation for not allowing a soul to lay a hand on any object whatsoever in either his home or his studio.

One wonders whether in the end Tadema may not have felt himself trapped in his own craft and phenomenal success. To a friend he confided: '*I paint a piece of marble, and they want nothing but marble; a blue sky, and they want nothing but blue skies; an Agrippa, and they want nothing but Agrippas; an oleander bush, and they want nothing except oleanders. Arrgh! A man isn't a machine!*'

LUC DEVOLDERE
Translated by Sonja Prescod.

FURTHER READING

BECKER, EDWIN (ed.), *Sir Lawrence Alma-Tadema* (Exhibition Catalogue, Van Gogh Museum, Amsterdam / Walker Art Gallery, Liverpool). Zwolle, 1996.

LIPINCOTT, LOUISE, *Lawrence Alma Tadema: Spring.* Malibu, 1990.

SWANSON, VERN G., *The Biography and Catalogue Raisonné of the Paintings of Sir Lawrence Alma-Tadema.* London, 1990.

Two World Press Photo Prizes for Stephan Vanfleteren

The Flemish press photographer Stephan Vanfleteren (1969-), a regular freelance for the newspaper *De Morgen*, won awards in two categories of the World Press Photo international photography competition. Vanfleteren's work was chosen by the nine members of the jury from almost 36,000 entries. The series concerned are 'Hobos in the USA' (first prize in the 'Daily Life Stories' category) and 'AIDS and Prostitution' (second prize in the 'People Stories' category).

For the first series Vanfleteren went to the United States with the journalist Jan Hertoghs to report on railroad drifters for the *Humo* weekly magazine. As Vanfleteren put it: '*We spent a fortnight with them on the trains, a fortnight of shared joy and sorrow.*'

The second series was shot for *De Morgen* in Kenya, where international aid campaigns succeeded in stemming the tide of the AIDS epidemic. '*The main aim of that report was to demonstrate that the aid campaigns were achieving results, not just to show the misery of that country for the umpteenth time*', said Vanfleteren. Photos from these series were published in the World Press Photo yearbook, presented to the public in Amsterdam on 28 April 1997.

The World Press Photo Foundation, a non-profit-making organisation based in Amsterdam, was founded in 1955 and is intended to provide an independent platform for international press photography. This platform consists of an annual photographic competition, from which emerge a yearbook and an exhibition. This exhibition normally tours the whole world, on condition that all the winning entries are shown, without any form of censorship. The World Press Photo jury is traditionally made up of internationally renowned photographers, the chairman in 1996 being Neil Burgess from Great Britain. The international nature of the competition is guaranteed by the International Advisory Board, which includes experts and photographers from all over the world. The image cho-

sen as 'Photo of the Year' was a portrait by the Italian Francesco Zizola. The jury considered his picture of children in a trauma centre for war victims in the Angolan town of Quito to be the best of 1996. Quito was bombarded for nine months during the Angolan civil war; 25,000 people were killed.

The first prize in each category includes a sum of money, but the World Press Photo prizes are regarded primarily as prestigious honours at an international level. The competition has 18 categories in all, and this year was its fortieth anniversary. No less than 3663 photographers from 119 countries took part.

It is not the first time that a photographer has won prizes in several categories, but according to the Dutch organisers of the WPP it is exceptional. Last year Vanfleteren had already won a third prize in the Sport category, with a report on young Cuban boxers. In the same year he won the annual Gemeentekrediet press prize, and was honoured in Charleroi for a series on the genocide in Rwanda. To find another Belgian World Press Prize winner we have to go back in time to 1976, when Françoise de Mulder won the top prize with a harrowing war report shot in Beirut.

Sensation is by no means the chief element in Vanfleteren's work. The celebrated photographer, who has been working professionally for four years since graduating from the St Lucas College, tells us that in each shot he is looking for the perfect balance between composition and content. Even when the subject tempts one to go the other way, as during the report on the AIDS epidemic in Kenya. Vanfleteren said: '*I am rather intrigued by the way people live. Or survive. I want to know who, where and why, how someone has ended up in a particular situation. So I suppose I do have a certain social commitment. But that does not necessarily mean one has to seek out the sensational. For example, in their own way the hobos in America are perfectly happy, despite the severe conditions they have to cope with every day as nomads on the railway network. The same applies to the Kenya report: there is more than just the horror. One cannot deny that harrowing scenes sometimes take place there, but it seems to me the easy way out to depict only the negative aspects of any situation. Then you might just as well take pictures of the people dying in their beds in the hospitals, but in that case you can count me out. Unless there's a very good reason. To me, a successful photo must combine an event with an approach relevant to the content. The one without the other, or the purely aesthetic approach, does not interest me. And of course you also have to have a bit of luck.*'

STEVEN HEENE
Translated by Gregory Ball.

Hobos in the USA (Photo by Stephan Vanfleteren).

AIDS and Prostitution (Photo by Stephan Vanfleteren).

Panorama Mesdag A Dutch Mega-Painting

The name Mesdag requires no explanation in the Netherlands. Not because of the story of the banker who gave up his career to become a maritime painter, and who almost immediately landed a gold medal in the famous Paris Salon. Nowadays, that information is known only to art lovers. Nor, even, because of the charming Museum Mesdag which he had built in The Hague, and which houses the largest collection of early French modern landscape art anywhere outside France. What everyone in the Netherlands is familiar with is the Panorama Mesdag, that cylindrical mega-painting which shows how the fishing village of Scheveningen looked in 1881. As one of the few panoramas left in the world, it is among the top attractions in The Hague.

Every year thousands of people climb the narrow little stairway to the wooden platform at the centre of the tiny, circular exhibition building, in order to take a plunge into the past. It's as if they had just climbed up Seinpostduin (Signal Station Dune) to look out over the sea and beach, as Hendrik Willem Mesdag (1831-1915) did just over a century ago. How beautiful and untouched Scheveningen was then! How enchanting those picturesque little fishermen's cottages, tucked away amid the dunes. Those typical Scheveningen-type, round-bellied vessels, which used to be hauled ashore by horses, with the fishermen and their wives all about. A group of hussars is exercising on the wet sand, and in the distance the contours of The Hague delineate themselves, as yet unscathed by bombings, new buildings, and high-rise architecture.

A fine, nostalgic illusion, that mega-painting, 120 m in length, and 14 m high. The commission for the panorama was made to measure for Mesdag. Not only was the sea 'his' theme but, shortly before he commenced work on it, he had documented the Seinpostduin area in innumerable sketches upon hearing that the municipality proposed razing the Dune to develop the site for building. Thus this authentic view was in danger of being lost. Mesdag saved it for the general public in his panorama. As a true Hague School painter, he was more inclined towards rural and nostalgic subject matter, than the depiction of the dynamics of the great, modern city.

His peaceful representation of Scheveningen beach is now unique. Panorama Mesdag is the only panorama extant that does not feature a battle. The panorama was the first mass medium. These 'views of the world' with lifelike images of famous cities, distant landscapes, and historical events, were in their time just as novel and sensational an experience as the IMAX giant-screen film, or virtual reality, are today. The visitors found themselves, just for a while, in a different, just-like-real reality, which completely embraced them.

What is remarkable is that the painting was preserved. Of the hundreds of panoramas painted in the last century, virtually all perished because they were intensively used: they travelled from city to city and from festival to festival. But Panorama Mesdag was only shown outside its home twice. Apart from that, it hung quietly in its circular residence with the great light dome on Zeestraat in The Hague, now a monument to industrial iron and glass architecture. It is thanks to that tranquil existence that the gigantic artwork is still completely intact.

That is not what Mesdag himself expected. He estimated its life span at some twenty-five years. But thanks to the recent restoration, during which heavy layers of dust were removed and a specially-developed type of resilient nylon textile was applied to the half-decayed canvas, his painting is once again in top condition.

Mesdag received 60,000 guilders for the painting. The commissioning party, the Belgian Société Anonyme du Panorama Maritime de la Haye, anticipated a box office success. For the painter, it was money well-earned: in only four months (!) he had it finished. He himself executed the beach and the sea, his speciality. His wife, Sientje Mesdag-van Houten, put her brush to work for Scheveningen village. For the cavalry, they enlisted their painter friend Georg Hendrik Breitner, who specialised in hussars, while Theophile de Bock, a lesser-known member of the Hague School of painters, painted in one hundred and twenty metres of dunes, and the one hundred and twenty metres of sky. To perfect the illusion, a lookout post was constructed at the centre of the rotunda, with around it an artificial dune. Thus the transition between reality and representation was almost imperceptible.

At the end of the last century, Mesdag was an important person. The landscapes of the Hague School created a furore around the world, and he was regarded as its most famous exponent. Today, his lively seascapes are not considered quite as brilliant and original as they were then, even if the Panorama re-

Part of Hendrik Willem Mesdag's Panorama of Scheveningen beach (1881).

mains a fantastic document. Now it is in his capacity as a collector that he is most valued.

Thanks to his money and his love of modern art, he bought many works by his colleagues as well as by famous contemporaries. As a result, the Netherlands now possesses a unique collection of works by Hague School painters, and by their great exemplars, the French landscape painters of the Barbizon School. Aside from France, nowhere else in the world is such an extensive collection of works by Millet, Daubigny, Dupré, Rousseau and Corot to be found.

In his own time this collection was even more remarkable, as modern art was scarcely to be seen in the Netherlands. Mesdag's collection was semi-public as, on Sundays, he received visitors by appointment. He took visitors around in person. First he would show them his studio which, apart from his own canvasses, contained Oriental artworks, exotic textiles, and arts and crafts in all manner of styles. Then, via a connecting door, they would enter the museum which he had built specially for his collection in 1887.

As the collection expanded, the Mesdags conceived a plan to donate it to the Dutch state. The matter was finalised in 1903. Mesdag himself was the first director. Since then, the building on Laan van Meerdervoort has been a little pearl among Dutch museums, even if it did become dusted-over and forgotten in the course of time. The Van Gogh Museum, however, which in 1990 took over its administration, removed the dust and grime, installed a dehumidification system, and emptied out the depot in the garden. The collection was completely re-inventorised, and described in an English-language catalogue. By a stroke of luck, it proved possible to purchase the adjoining building as well, Mesdag's one-time private home, so that the original link between the artist's home and the museum could be restored.

In Autumn 1996 Museum Mesdag reopened, to great interest from the international press. A few weeks later the Panorama's restoration was completed. So 1996 was quite a Mesdag year.

INEKE SCHWARTZ
Translated by Sonja Prescod.

ADDRESSES

Panorama Mesdag
Zeestraat 65 / 2518 AA The Hague / The Netherlands
tel. +31 70 3642563
Opening hours: 10 a.m.-5 p.m. (Monday to Saturday)
12 a.m.-5 p.m. (Sundays)

Museum Mesdag
Laan van Meerdervoort 7f / 2517 AB The Hague / The Netherlands
Opening Hours: 12 a.m.-5 p.m. (Tuesday to Sunday)

The Ghent Altarpiece A Great Miniature

On the frame of *The Adoration of the Lamb*, the great polyptich in the Cathedral of St Bavo in Ghent, there is a quatrain in somewhat clumsy Latin: it tells us that this work was begun by Hubertus van Eyck and completed by Jan van Eyck. The final line incorporates a chronogram stating that the altarpiece was presented to the church authorities on 6 May 1432. Straightforward as all this may seem, the authorship of *The Adoration of the Lamb*'s 20 constituent panels is still quite a bone of contention in the art historical community.

What no one disputes is Jan van Eyck's hand in the work. Van Eyck (c.1390-1441) is the most celebrated and also the most innovative of the fifteenth century Flemish painters. He was also the first Flemish Primitive to sign his works. Well-known, for instance, is the jaunty little inscription '*Johannes de Eyck fuit hic*', in *Jan Arnolfini and His Wife*, in the National Gallery, London. In all, the number of works ascribed to him with certainty is nine.

Hubertus van Eyck, on the other hand, is another kettle of fish altogether. He is something of an enigma. Absolutely nothing is known of his life or anything else he may have painted. Who was he, anyway? Was he an older brother? Did he execute the greater part of *The Adoration*, or was it Jan who was responsible for the majority of the panels? Was Hubertus, indeed, even a painter? Or could he, perhaps, have been a sculptor who constructed a frame for the polyptich? Did he, in fact, exist at all?

One author who resolutely refuses to venture into any such '*controversial Eyckian questions*', and who declines to add to the already numerous and conflicting interpretations of this complex work – which the French poet Paul Claudel once described as '*a great miniature*' – is Alfons Lieven Dierick. Rather, he takes as the motto for his magnificent book *The Ghent Altarpiece* the words of Hieronymus Muenzer, the distinguished humanist physician from Nuremberg who, having seen the work in 1495, wrote: '*Not only a painting is there to be seen, but the whole art of painting.*'

Dierick views *The Adoration of the Lamb* as a double artistic zenith: a highpoint in the art of Jan van Eyck, and a highpoint in the history of art. His book sets out to show how the artist used line and colour to recreate the totality of the Divine Creation and at the same time give expression to his personal, emotional conception of life. The reader must therefore not expect any involved and elaborate theories, but accept the author's stated aim of giving his readers the opportunity to *see* the painting '*by means of sharp life-size photographs in authentic colour*'.

Dierick shot the photographs by natural daylight over a period from 1975 to July 1986, and also processed all the negatives and transparencies himself. The book makes use, for the first time, of a new lithographic procedure which dramatically improves the quality of detail in the reproduction. Even with a magnifying glass, the plates show no trace of pixellation. Dierick's reputation as a photographer of painting is, of course, already well-established, notably through his earlier series of five 'imaginary museums', featuring life-sized reproductions of the complete works of Jan van Eyck, Rogier van der Weyden, Hugo van der

Goes, Hieronymus Bosch and Pieter Bruegel the Elder.

The Ghent Altarpiece comprises 36 true-to-size (30 x 23 cm) plates of individual fragments. Each in its own right represents '*an open window into the painting*', while collectively they aim '*to convey both the vision and the skill of the painter*'. As Dierick wanted to show the polyptich as it originally was, he first had to identify 36 fragments in a suitable state of preservation. This was by no means easy, given the retable's tumultuous history. To begin with, the cleaning and restoration which the work has at various times undergone was not always as competent as it might have been. The eponymous lamb in the central panel, for example, shows some crude overpainting. Furthermore, the work has on several occasions been broken up. In 1794, the four central panels were removed to Paris on Napoleon's instructions. They were returned after his defeat at Waterloo, but the following year (1816) saw the sale of the side panels while the then Bishop of Ghent was out of town. The panels eventually ended up in a Berlin museum where they were sawn through lengthwise to enable the simultaneous display of the front and back. Two other panels depicting Adam and Eve – so admired by Dürer on his visit to Ghent in 1550 that for two centuries thereafter the polyptich as a whole was known as the Adam and Eve Altarpiece – were sold to the Belgian state in 1861. In their place were inserted two new panels which showed the first man and his wife decorously garbed in animal skins. Not until 1920 could Ghent display the complete polyptich in all its glory. Then, in 1934, the 'Just Judges' panel disappeared altogether as a result of a still unexplained robbery. An accurate copy was put in its place, and remains there for the original has never been found. During the Second World War all the panels were appropriated by the occupying German forces and sent off to an unknown destination which proved to be a disused Austrian salt mine, where they were discovered, together with thousands of other looted art treasures, in May 1945. A succession of cleaning projects now followed, in the course of one of which, in 1978, the until then best-preserved panel (that of John the Baptist) was damaged when somebody dropped it. Today *The Adoration of the Lamb,* securely encased in bullet-proof glass, is housed under high-security conditions in one of the St Bavo side chapels.

Dierick had the good fortune to be able to take his photographs prior to 1986, when the retable was still unglassed, and still in its original location in the Vijd Chapel, so named after Joos Vijd, sheriff of Ghent and warden of St Bavo, who commissioned the work from Van Eyck. This is of special significance because the direction of the light in the panels appears to correspond with how the light falls in that chapel. The eyes and jewellery of the figures which originally faced the windows quite unmistakably reflect the light, whereas the figures turned away from the light source cast a backward shadow.

In the past it was often asserted that the medium of painting in oil was discovered by Van Eyck. Although this is now disproved, there can be no doubt that he

Jan and (?) Hubertus van Eyck, *The Adoration of the Lamb* (detail from the central panel).

1432. Cathedral of St Bavo, Ghent.

perfected the technique. Dierick's pictures show the extent to which the painter achieves a life-like effect through an accumulation of tiny, meticulous details – the glow of jewellery and precious metal, for instance, the precisely identifiable flower and plant species, a censer dangling from an angel's hand, the torn-out tongue of St Livinus, the beard stubble and the wart on the face of Joos Vijd. He focuses attention on the still life seen in the panel next to 'Mary in the Annunciation Room', which serves not only as an example of Van Eyck's technical mastery, but also prefigures what was to become a major autonomous genre in the art of the Low Countries some two hundred years later, in the seventeenth century. Van Eyck also experiments with perspective in *The Adoration.* In the central panel with the Lamb, we see numerous churches and cathedrals in the background, depicted in what Dierick reveals to be the new discovery of aerial perspective, with '*the sky fading into the hazy blue of the distance in contrast with the sharply defined foreground*'. Remarkable, too, is the differentiation between the realistically portrayed and sharply defined flowers in the foreground and the almost impressionistic dots and dabs of the background.

Even though Dierick patently knows his subject inside out, he deliberately confines his commentary to precise and detailed descriptions and explanations of the photographs. And there is no cause for complaint in this; for, as we said earlier, *The Ghent Altarpiece* is not intended to be a piece of hermeneutic analysis. The author is simply in love with the work, and wants to share his perception of its beauty with the reader. Or, as Dierick puts it himself: *'May Van Eyck's sound sense of beauty be a comfort to you and a joy for ever.'*

FILIP MATTHIJS
Translated by Sonja Prescod.

A.L. Dierick, *The Ghent Altarpiece* (tr. Herman Brondeel). 1996. Published privately by the author, Hofstraat 363, Ghent, Belgium.

A New Encyclopedia of Dutch Art

Sheila D. Muller, editor of *Dutch Art: an Encyclopedia* (1997) writes in her Preface that *'this encyclopedia mirrors the state of our knowledge about Dutch art in the mid-1990s'*. She points out, correctly, that in the present decade Dutch art has an established place in many American college and university courses, and that it is also well represented in a number of public and private collections in the USA. The study of Dutch art has become an international and interdisciplinary concern, *'a rapidly growing field'* within which the contributors to this encyclopedia *'have written entries that include knowledge that is changing and developing'*.

Since the mid-sixties there have been a number of important general studies of Dutch art in English. In Muller's view, these *'represent the state of research on Dutch art at specific times in the last half of the twentieth century, and together they show the evolution of the field as a result of a diversity of approaches, changing perspectives, and the posing of new questions'*. To illustrate this she refers to three of this encyclopedia's eminent predecessors. In 1966 Jakob Rosenberg, Seymour Slive and E.H. ter Kuile published *Dutch Art and Architecture 1600-1800* (last reprinted in 1993), which according to Muller is primarily *'a book about reputations'*: the three great names – Hals, Rembrandt and Vermeer – are each allotted a chapter to themselves; the minor masters are discussed in chapters which focus on particular towns or subjects. The response was a flood of monographs between 1966 and 1980 about painters of these local schools. 1978 saw the publication of Rudi Fuchs' *Dutch Painting* (last reprinted in 1989), a study of Dutch painting from its origins in late-fifteenth-century Haarlem to the seventh decade of our own century. For art dating from before 1800 Fuchs works mainly by subject categories such as genre painting, history painting, still life etc. Central to his work is the idea of Dutch Realism as a kind of *'mock realism that functions to disguise meaning as metaphor'*, with a consequent emphasis on formal analysis. Lastly, Bob Haak in his *The Golden Age: Dutch Painters of the Seventeenth Century* (1984) elaborates on the monographs that appeared in the wake of *Dutch Art and Architecture 1600-1800*. He locates the 'Three Greats' within the Dutch tradition and thus shifts the accent to the local schools, within which he discusses the major and minor masters.

In the 1990s the general survey has become something of a *rara avis*. New information is fragmented and scattered across articles in periodicals, monographs, dissertations, exhibition catalogues and the like. Hence this new publication, since *'(…) to interpret the diversity of viewpoints and topical treatments for general use requires an encyclopedia'*. This encyclopedia builds on the three works mentioned above. Its approach to the subject-matter is one of schools and subject categories, but the history of reputations also has its place. The monographic entries on e.g. Rembrandt and Karel Appel do, however, invariably discuss the artists in their national and international context. An important feature here is the *'see also'* heading which in most entries precedes the brief bibliography. Anyone reading the article on 'Contemporary Art (1980-1990)' is not only pointed towards the entries on Carel Visscher and Marlene Dumas, but can also consult those on 'Feminist Issues' or 'State Patronage'. The entry on Rembrandt directs the reader, among other things, to a long piece on 'Art History', where he will learn that *'the Rembrandt Research Project gave an important stimulus to strengthening the ties between art history and the restoration sciences'*.

Dutch Art: An Encyclopedia is an easy book to use. There are illustrations, concise bibliographies, an extensive index of names and concepts, and also a 'Reader's Guide' in which the entries are grouped by major category (e.g. 'Biography', 'Internationalism' and 'Writing about Art'. In addition there is an Introduction which demarcates the book's subject area by defining such concepts as 'Dutch' and 'Low Countries'. In geographical terms the book confines itself to art produced in the area now known as the Netherlands. It thereby excludes Flanders, the Dutch-speaking part of Belgium, though there is a separate entry on 'Belgium'. Nobody will deny the existence of genuine differences between 'Dutch art' and 'Flemish art'. But there are so many references in the entries to 'Flemish' artists such as Jan van Eyck and Pieter Bruegel that one does wonder, to say the least, whether this strict demarcation is entirely justifiable.

FILIP MATTHIJS
Translated by Tanis Guest.

Sheila D. Muller (ed.), *Dutch Art: An Encyclopedia.* New York / London: Garland Publishing, Inc., 1997; 489 pp. ISBN 0-8153-0065-4.

Bibliography

of Dutch-Language Publications translated in English (traced in 1996)

Armando (pseud. of: Herman Dirk van Dodeweerd)
From Berlin / Armando; [transl. from the Dutch by Susan Massotty]. London: Reaktion, 1996. 144 p. (Topographics)
Contains an anthology of texts of: Uit Berlijn. 1982, Krijgsgewoel. 1986, Machthebbers: verslagen uit Berlijn en Toscane. 1983, and: Wij waren zo heerlijk jong.

Bartimaeus.
Bartimaeus / ill. by Kees de Kort; [transl. from the Dutch]. Bennekom: Foundation Art Bible Child, 1996.
[27] p. (What the Bible tells us)
Transl. of: Bartimeüs. 1967.

Bergeijk, Herman van
Town hall Hilversum, W. M. Dudok / Herman van Bergeijk, Paul Meurs; [photogr.: Herman van Doorn; ed.: Arjen Oosterman; transl. from the Dutch]. Naarden: V+K Publishing; [Wormer]: Inmerc, cop. 1995. 48 p.
Transl. of: Raadhuis Hilversum, W. M. Dudok. 1995.

Berlage, Hendrik Petrus
Hendrik Petrus Berlage: thoughts on style, 1886-1909 / introd. by Iain Boyd Whyte; transl. [from the Dutch] by Iain Boyd Whyte and Wim de Wit. [Santa Monica, CA]: The Getty Center for the History of Art and the Humanities, cop. 1996. 331 p. (Texts & documents)

Bernlef, J. (pseud. of Hendrik Jan Marsman)
Eclipse / J. Bernlef; transl. [from the Dutch] by Paul Vincent. London [etc.]: Faber and Faber, 1996.

149 p.; (FF original)
Transl. of: Eclips. 1993.

Bloem, Marion
The cockatoo's lie / Marion Bloem; transl. from the Dutch by Wanda Boeke. 1st ed. Seattle, WA: Women in Translation, 1996. VIII, 239 p.
Transl. of: De leugen van de kaketoe. 1993.

Blok, L.
Tulipa / L. Blok & Jasper Wiedeman; autochromes and spectracolors by L. Blok; photogr. Jasper Wiedeman; text Maria Heiden; transl. [from the Dutch] Stacey Knecht, Marcea R. Hennecke; concept and composition Frido Troost, Willem van Zoetendaal; ed. and introd. Blok Frido Troost. Amsterdam: Van Zoetendaal, 1994.
[48] p. (Lindeseries; 1)
Transl. of: Tulipa. 1994.

Blotkamp, Carel
Mondrian: the art of destruction / Carel Blotkamp; [transl. from the Dutch by Barbara Potter Fasting]. London: Reaktion Books, 1994. 261 p.
Transl. of: Mondriaan: destructie als kunst. 1994.

Bonnefantenmuseum
Bonnefantenmuseum / [ed. by Rik van Wegen and Ton Quik; transl. from the Dutch by Beth O'Brien ... et al.]. Maastricht: Bonnefantenmuseum, 1995. 383 p.
Transl. of: Bonnefantenmuseum. 1995.

Bont, Ad de
Mirad: a boy from Bosnia / Ad de Bont; transl. [from the Dutch by] Marian Buijs; ed. Roy Blatchford. London: Longman, 1995. XIV, 147 p. (Longman literature)

Transl. of: Mirad: een jongen uit Bosnië.

Borchert, Bruno
Mysticism: its history and challenge / Bruno Borchert; [transl. from the Dutch by Transcript, Ltd.]. York Beach, Maine: Weiser, 1994. 456 p.
Transl. of: Mystiek: geschiedenis en uitdaging. 1989.

Braay, C.P.
Windmills of Holland / [text: C.P. Braay; photos: Herman Scholten ... et al.; ill.: G. Pouw ... et al.; comp.: Jaap Kooijman; transl. from the Dutch: CopyTrust]. Koog a/d Zaan: Kooijman International Trade, [1994]. 31 p.
Transl. of: Molens in Nederland. [1994].

Bredero, Adriaan H.
Bernard of Clairvaux: between cult and history / Adriaan H. Bredero; [transl. from the Dutch]. 1st ed. Grand Rapids, Mich: W.B. Eerdmans, 1996.
Transl. of: Bernardus van Clairvaux (1091-1153): tussen cultus en historie: de ontoegankelijkheid van een hagiografisch levensverhaal. 1993.

Broos, Ben
Johannes Vermeer / [authors: Ben Broos and Arthur K. Wheelock, Jr.; with a contribution from Albert Blankert ... et al.; ed.: Arthur K. Wheelock, Jr.; transl. from the Dutch by Jack Horn]. Zwolle: Waanders, cop. 1995. 229 p.
Publ. on occasion of the exposition: "Johannes Vermeer" in The National Gallery of Art, Washington, November, 12th 1995 - February, 11th 1996, and in the Mauritshuis, The Hague, March, 1st - June, 2nd 1996.

Broos, Ben
The Mauritshuis: Royal Cabinet of Paintings, Mauritshuis and Gallery

Prince William V / Ben Broos; [transl. from the Dutch by Phil Goddard; ed. by Quentin Buvelot and Jane Havell]. London: Scala, 1994. 128 p.
Transl. of: Mauritshuis 's-Gravenhage. 1988.

Brouwers, Will
Europe in the past: a general survey from Ancient time till the Middle Ages / Will Brouwers; Marty Monteiro (ed.); [transl. from the Dutch: Maja Keizers ... et al.]. 1st ed. Amsterdam: International Institute of Interdisciplinary Integration, cop. 1995. XIV, 148 p. (Projects / International Institute of Interdisciplinary Integration. Vol. 1, History; pt. 1A)
Transl. of: Europa in het verleden: een algemeen overzicht vanaf de Sumeriërs t.e.m. de Romeinen. 1992.

Chabot, H.Th.
Kinship, status and gender in South Celebes / H.Th. Chabot; [transl. from the Dutch]; with an introd. by Martin Rössler and Birgitt Röttger-Rössler. Leiden: KITLV Press, 1996. 281 p., [11] p. pl. (Translation series / Koninklijk Instituut voor Taal-, Land- en Volkenkunde; 25)
1st English ed.: New Haven, Ct.: HRAF, 1961 / transl. from the Dutch by Richard Nause.
Transl. of.: Verwantschap, stand en sexe in Zuid-Celebes. 1950. Thesis Djakarta.

Chapman, H. Perry
Jan Steen: painter and storyteller / H. Perry Chapman, Wouter Th. Kloek, Arthur K. Wheelock, Jr.; with contributions by Martin Bijl ... [et al.]; ed. by Guido M.C. Jansen; [partly transl. from the Dutch by Michael Hoyle]. Washington: National Gallery of Art; Amsterdam: Rijksmuseum; Zwolle: Waanders, cop. 1996. 272 p.

Publ. on occasion of the exposition "Jan Steen" in the National Gallery of Art, Washington, April 28th, 1996 - August, 18th 1996, and the Rijksmuseum, Amsterdam, September, 21th 1996 - January, 12th 1997.

Choosing
Choosing the better part: Anna Maria van Schurman (1607-1678) / ed. by Mirjam de Baar ... [*et al.*]; [transl. from the Dutch by Lynne Richards]. Dordrecht [etc.]: Kluwer Academic Publishers, cop. 1996. XI, 181 p. (Archives internationales d'histoire des idées = International archives of the history of ideas; 146) Transl. of: Anna Maria van Schurman (1607-1678): een uitzonderlijk geleerd vrouw. 1992.

Claus, Hugo
The swordfish / Hugo Claus; transl. from the Flemish and with an introduction by Ruth Levitt. London: Peter Owen, 1996. 104 p.; 23 cm. Transl. of: De zwaardvis. 1989.

Degenaar, Marjolein
Molyneux's problem: three centuries of discussion on the perception of forms / Marjolein Degenaar; transl. from the Dutch by Michael J. Collins. Dordrecht [etc.]: Kluwer Academic Publishers, cop. 1996. 156 p. (Archives internationales d'histoire des idées = International archives of the history of ideas; 147) Based on: Het probleem van Molyneux. 1992. Thesis Erasmus University Rotterdam.

Dehue, Trudy
Changing the rules: psychology in the Netherlands, 1900-1985 / Trudy Dehue; [transl. and adapt. from the Dutch]. Cambridge: Cambridge University Press, 1995. IX, 204 p. (Cambridge studies in the history of psychology) Transl. and adapt. of: De regels van het vak. 1990.

Dekkers, Midas
Birth day: a celebration of baby animals / Midas Dekkers; [text adapt. by Justine Korman; transl. from the Dutch]. New York: Freeman, cop. 1995. 88 p. (Books for young readers)
Transl. and adapt. of: Het grote moment: hoe dieren geboren worden. 1989.

Dis, Adriaan van
My father's war: a novel / Adriaan van Dis; transl. from the Dutch by Claire Nicolas White. New York: New Press, 1996. 261 p. (The New Press international fiction series) Transl. of: Indische duinen: roman. 1994.

Dresden, Sem
Persecution, extermination, literature / Sem Dresden; transl. [from the Dutch] by Henry G. Schogt. Toronto [etc.]: University of Toronto Press, 1995. VIII, 237 p.
Transl. of: Vervolging, vernietiging, literatuur. 1991.

Duijker, Hubrecht
Bordeaux / Hubrecht Duijker; [transl. from the Dutch: Raymond Kaye]. Utrecht: Het Spectrum, 1994. 143 p. (A wine lover's touring guide)
Transl. of: Bordeaux: een wijn-, reis- en fijnproeversgids. 1994.

Duijker, Hubrecht
Loire / Hubrecht Duijker; [transl. from the Dutch: Paul Goodman]. Utrecht: Het Spectrum, 1994. 143 p. (A wine lover's touring guide) Transl. of: Loire: een wijn-, reis- en fijnproeversgids. 1994.

Dynamics
Dynamics of development: thirty years of SNV / [final ed.: Ton Nijzink ... *et al.*; transl. from the Dutch; photogr.: Angèle Etoundi Essamba]. The Hague: SNV Netherlands development organisation, 1996. 143 p. Transl. of: Dynamiek van

ontwikkeling: dertig jaar SNV. 1995.

E.J.Brill
E. J. Brill: three centuries of scholarly publishing, since 1683 / [comp. by J.M. van Ophuijsen; transl. from the Dutch and rev.]. Leiden [etc.]: Brill, cop. 1994. 38 p.
Publ. on occasion of the exposition in the Municipal Archives at Leiden, September, 1st 1983 - October, 1st 1983 Transl. and adapt. of: Luchtmans & Brill: driehonderd jaar uitgevers en drukkers in Leiden, 1683-1983. 1983.

Esbattement
Een esbattement van smenschen sin en verganckelijcke schoonheit = Man's desire and fleeting beauty / ed., ann. and rev. by Elsa Strietman; transl. from the Dutch by Robert Potter and Elsa Strietman; ed. assistance Sabien van Harten. Leeds: International Medieval Publications, International Medieval Institute, University of Leeds, cop. 1994. XXV, 118 p. (Medieval texts and translations series. Middle Dutch sub-series; 1) (Leeds Medieval studies / Graduate centre for Medieval studies, University of Leeds, England) Bilingual ed. in: Middle-Dutch and English.

Frank, Anne
The diary of a young girl: the definitive edition / Anne Frank; ed. by Otto H. Frank and Mirjam Pressler; transl. [from the Dutch] by Susan Massotty. Thorndike ME: Hall, 1995. 413 p. [Large print ed.]. Transl. of: Het Achterhuis: dagboekbrieven 14 juni 1942 - 1 augustus 1944. 1991

Frank, Anne.
The Diary of Anne Frank: transl. [from the Dutch] by B.M. Mooyaart-Doubleday: forew. by Hugo Gryn. London: Macmillan Children's Books, cop. 1995. 235 p.

1st English ed. publ. as: The diary of a young girl. London: Constellation Books (Vallentine Mitchell & Co.) 1952. Transl. of: Het Achterhuis: dagboekbrieven 14 juni 1942 - 1 augustus 1944. 1947.

Friedman, Carl
The shovel and the loom / Carl Friedman; transl. from the Dutch by Jeannette K. Ringold. New York: Persea Books, 1996. 168 p. Transl. of: Twee koffers vol. 1993.

Gilliams, Maurice
Elias, or the struggle with the nightingales / Maurice Gilliams; transl. from the Dutch by André Lefevere. Los Angeles: Sun & Moon Press, 1995. 115 p. (Words with wings: children's classics) Transl. of: Elias, of Het gevecht met de nachtegalen. 1936.

Gogh, Vincent van
Dear Theo: the autobiography of Vincent Van Gogh / ed. by Irving Stone and Jean Stone; [transl. from the Dutch and French]. New York: Plume, 1995. Abridged transl. of: Brieven aan zijn broeder. 1914.

Gomes da Silva, Aida
The Mozambican press: a historical overview and a political analysis / Aida Gomes da Silva; [transl. from the Dutch]. Nijmegen: Third World Centre/ Development studies, Catholic University of Nijmegen, 1996. VI, 93 p. (Occasional paper / Third World Centre; 54) Transl. of: De Mozambiquaanse pers: een historisch overzicht en een politieke analyse. 1995. Undergraduate thesis Catholic University of Nijmegen.

Good
The good Samaritan / ill. by Kees de Kort; [transl. from the Dutch]. Bennekom: Foundation Art Bible Child, 1996. [28] p. (What the Bible tells us)

Transl. of: De barmhartige Samaritaan. 1968.

Hillesum, Etty
Interrupted life: the diaries 1941-1943, and: Letters from Westerbork / Etty Hillesum; transl. from the Dutch by Arnold J. Pomerans; pref. by Eva Hoffman; introd. and notes by Jan G. Gaarlandt. New York: Henry Holt, 1996. 1st English ed.: Interrupted life: 1984, and: Letters from Westerbork: 1986. Transl. of: Het verstoorde leven: dagboek van Etty Hillesum 1941-1943. 1981, and of: Het denkende hart van de barak: brieven van Etty Hillesum. 1982.

Hoornweg, Ans
Aliens among us / Ans Hoornweg; ed. by Mary Ann & Wolfgang Sell; [transl. from the Dutch: Ananja Wieringa]. Borger: Akasha/3-D Book Productions, [1996], cop. 1997. 95 p. + 56 driedimensionale dia's op acht 3D schijfjes
Transl. of: Wij komen al door de eeuwen heen.... 1995.

Hora Siccama, Fernande
Baskets: indoors, outdoors, practical, decorative / text by Pien Lemstra; arrangements by Fernande Hora Siccama; photogr. by Hans van Ommeren; [transl. from the Dutch by Mieke Wilson-van Leeuwe]. London [etc.]: Simon & Schuster, 1995. 142 p. Transl. of: Manden. 1992.

Huizinga, Johan
The autumn of the Middle Ages / Johan Huizinga; transl. [from the Dutch] by Rodney J. Payton and Ulrich Mammitzsch. Chicago, Ill: University of Chicago Press, 1996. XVIII p., 467 p.
1st English ed. publ. as: The waning of the Middle Ages. London: Arnold, 1924
Transl. of: Herfsttij der middeleeuwen: studie over levens- en gedachten-

vormen der veertiende en vijftiende eeuw in Frankrijk en de Nederlanden. 1919.

Hurenkamp, S.A.P.F.
Hoensbroek Castle / [author: S.A.P.F. Hurenkamp; ed.: C. Bakker-van Berge; draw. and advice: J. Creusen; photogr.: M. van Hoorn; Map: Architectengroep Mertens; transl. from the Dutch by J.P.A. van Rijen]. Hoensbroek: Kasteel Hoensbroek, cop. 1995. 26 p. Transl. of: Kasteel Hoensbroek. 1995.

Huygens, Constantijn
A selection of the poems of Sir Constantijn Huygens (1596-1687) / a parallel text transl., with an introd. and appendices by Peter Davidson and Adriaan van der Weel. Amsterdam: Amsterdam University Press, cop. 1996. XI, 228 p., [1] vouwbl. Bilingual ed. in: Dutch and English, and: Latin and English

Jacobs, Els M.
In pursuit of pepper and tea: the story of the Dutch East India Company / Els M. Jacobs; [transl. from the Dutch: Kist Kilian Communications; photogr.: Frans Hemelrijk ... et al.]. 2nd ed. Amsterdam: Netherlands Maritime Museum; Zutphen: Walburg Pers, [1996]. 96 p. 1st English ed.: 1991. Transl. of: Varen om peper en thee: korte geschiedenis van de Verenigde Oost-indische Compagnie. 1991.

Jagersma, H.
History of Israel to Bar Kochba / H. Jagersma; transl. from the Dutch: J. Bowden. New ed. [S.l.]: SCMP, 1994. [560] p.
1st English ed. publ. as: A history of Israel in the Old Testament period, and: A history of Israel from Alexander the Great to Bar Kochba. 1st Dutch ed. publ. as: Geschiedenis van Israël in het oudtestamentische tijdvak, 1979, and: Geschiedenis van Israël. 2:

van Alexander de Grote tot Bar Kochba. 1985.

Jesus
Jesus and his disciples / ill. by Kees de Kort; [transl. from the Dutch]. Bennekom: Foundation Art Bible Child, 1996. [28] p. (What the Bible tells us) Transl. of: Jezus en zijn leerlingen. 1979.

Jesus
Jesus and the storm / ill. by Kees de Kort; [transl. from the Dutch]. Bennekom: Foundation Art Bible Child, 1996. [28] p. (What the Bible tells us) Transl. of: Jezus en de storm. 1967.

Joris, Lieve
The gates of Damascus / Lieve Joris; transl. [from the Dutch] by Sam Garrett]. Melbourne [etc.]: Lonely Planet, 1996. 306 p. (Lonely Planet journeys) Transl. of: De poorten van Damascus. 1993.

Keizer, Bert
Dancing with Mister D: notes on life and death / Bert Keizer; transl. from the original Dutch by the author.
London [etc.]: Doubleday, 1996. 323 p.
Transl. of: Het refrein is Hein: dagen uit een verpleeghuis. 1994.

Korthals Altes, A.
The forgotten battle: Overloon and the Maas salient, 1944-45 / A. Korthals Altes and N.K.C.A. in't Veld; transl. [from the Dutch] by G.G. van Dam. New York: Sarpedon, 1995. xiii, 226 p. Transl. of: Slag in de schaduw. 1981.

Kossmann-Putto, J.A.
The Low Countries: history of the Northern and Southern Netherlands / J.A. Kossmann-Putto & E.H. Kossmann; [ed. Jozef Deleu ... et al.; transl. from the Dutch by J. Fenoulhet ... et al.]. 6th ed. Rekkem: Flemish-Netherlands Foundation Stichting Ons

Erfdeel, cop. 1996. 64 p. 1st English ed.: 1987. Transl. of: De Lage Landen: geschiedenis van de Noordelijke en Zuidelijke Nederlanden. 1987.

Kouwenhoven, Arlette
Madagascar: the red island / text Arlette Kouwenhoven; photogr. Toussaint Raharison; photo ed. Peter Homan; transl. [from the Dutch] Jacky ter Horst-Meijer; text ed. Amy Newland; overall final ed. Christine T. Waslander. 1st ed. Leiden: WINCO, cop. 1995. 159 p.
Transl. of: Madagascar: het rode eiland. 1995.

Kraan, Hanna
Tales of the wicked witch / Hanna Kraan; ill. by Annemarie van Haeringen; transl. [from the Dutch] by Elisabeth Koolschijn. 1st ed. Arden, North Carolina: Front Street, 1995. 106 p. Transl. of: Verhalen van de boze heks. 1990.

Linden, A.A.M. van der
A revolt against liberalism: American radical historians, 1959-1976 / A.A.M. van der Linden; [transl. from the Dutch by the author]. Amsterdam [etc.]: Rodopi, 1996. 297 p. (Amsterdam monographs in American studies; 6) Transl. of: Opstand onder historici: de Amerikaanse radicale historiografie, 1959-1976. Thesis Utrecht 1994.

Maarseveen, Michel P. van
Vermeer of Delft: his life and times / Michel P. van Maarseveen; transl. [from the Dutch by] M.E. Bennett. Amersfoort: Bekking; Delft: Stedelijk Museum Het Prinsenhof, cop. 1996. 96 p. (Prinsenhof series; dl. 1) Transl. of: Vermeer in Delft: een schilder en zijn stad. 1996.

Magic
The magic of Olympic fame: flashbacks to the history of the Games / ed. by Heleen Sancisi-

Weerdenburg and Thomas van Maaren; [transl. from the Dutch by Peter Mason]. Utrecht: Utrecht University, Bureau Studium Generale, 1996. 112 p. Publ. in cooperation with NOC*NSF Transl. of: De lokroep van Olympia. 1996.

Mahieu, Vincent (pseud. of Jan Boon)
The hunt for the heart: selected tales from the Dutch East Indies / Vincent Mahieu; transl. from the Dutch and introd. by Margaret M. Alibasah. Kuala Lumpur [etc.]: Oxford University Press, 1995. XIV, 206 p. (Oxford in Asia paperbacks) Contains an anthology of texts of: Tjies. 1950, and: Tjoek. 1960.

Marácz, László
Hungarian revival: political reflections on Central Europe / László Marácz; transl. from the Dutch: D.E. Butterman-Dorey. Nieuwegein: Aspekt, 1996. 362 p. (Aspekt non-fiction; no. 2) Transl. of: Hongaarse kentering: een politieke beschouwing over Midden-Europa. 1995.

Mendes, Bob
Vengeance: prelude to Saddam's war / by Bob Mendes; American transl. [from the Dutch] by H.G. Smittenaar. 1st ed. Fairfax Station, Virginia: Intercontinental Publishing, 1995. 303 p. Transl. of: Vergelding: voorspel tot Saddams oorlog: faction-thriller. 1991.

Mol, Pauline
The last child / Pauline Mol; transl. [from the Dutch] Jace van der Veen. Amsterdam: International Theatre & Film Books, 1996. 112 p. 18 cm. (Theatre in translation) Transl. of: Het laatste kind.

Mondriaan, Piet
Natural reality and abstract reality: an essay in trialogue form (1919-1920) / Piet Mondrian; transl. [from the

Dutch] and introd. by Martin S. James [... et al.]. New York: Braziller, 1995. 143 p.; 21 cm.
1st English ed. publ. as: The new art, the new life: the collected writings of Piet Mondrian. Boston: Hall, cop. 1986. (The documents of twentieth century art). Transl. of: Natuurlijke en abstracte realiteit. Between June 1919 and August 1920 publ. in: "De Stijl"

Moor, Margriet de
The virtuoso / Margriet de Moor; transl. from the Dutch by Ina Rilke. London: Picador, 1996. 201 p. Transl. of: De virtuoos: roman. 1993. Other ed.: London: Pan, 1996

Mulder, Filips A.
Quality management and result oriented management/RM / Filips A. Mulder and Henk J. Tepper; [transl. from the Dutch by Bothof Translation Service]. Nijmegen: Mulder & Tepper, Business Consultants, cop. 1995. 131 p. Transl. of: Kwaliteitsmanagement en resultaatgerichte bedrijfsvoering/RGB. 1993.

Mulisch, Harry
The discovery of heaven: a novel / Harry Mulisch; transl. [from the Dutch] by Paul Vincent. New York: Viking, 1996. 730 p. Transl. of: De ontdekking van de hemel: roman. 1992.

Nagtegaal, Luc
Riding the Dutch tiger: the Dutch East Indies Company and the northeast coast of Java 1680-1743 / Luc Nagtegaal; transl. [and adapt. from the Dutch] by Beverley Jackson. Leiden: KITLV Press, 1996. 250 p. (Verhandelingen van het Koninklijk Instituut voor Taal-, Land- en Volkenkunde; 171) Transl. and adapt. of: Rijden op een Hollandse tijger: de noordkust van Java en de V.O.C. 1680-1743. 1988. Thesis Utrecht.

Nooteboom, Cees
The following story / Cees Nooteboom; transl. from the Dutch by Ina Rilke. 1st Harvest ed. San Diego: Harcourt Brace, 1996. 115 p. (Harvest in translation) (Harvest book) 1st English ed.: London: Harvill, 1993. Transl. of: Het volgende verhaal. 1991.

Nouwen, Henri J.M.
With open hands / Henri J.M. Nouwen; transl. from the Dutch]. 1st large pr. ed. New York: Walker and Co, 1995.
1st English ed.: Notre Dame, Ind.: Ave Maria Press, 1972. Transl. of: Met open handen: notities over het gebed. 1972.

Osch, Thera van
Eliminating child labour: an action plan for combating child labour as part of the FNV project "A job for the world": towards a fair world labour market" / [text: Thera van Osch and Willy Wagenmans; [transl. from the Dutch by Robyn de Jong-Dalziel; photogr.: Chris Pennarts ... et al.]. Amsterdam: Stichting FNV Pers, 1995. 24 p. Publ. in cooperation with FNV. Transl. of: Afrekenen met kinderarbeid: een actieplan ter bestrijding van kinderarbeid als onderdeel van het FNV-project "Een baan om de aarde, naar een rechtvaardiger wereldarbeidsmarkt". 1995.

Poorterman, H.W.
Thank you Canada: 1945-1995 / H.W. Poorterman; [transl. from the Dutch: K. Hagoort ... et al.]. [S.l.: s.n.], [1994] (Ommen: Larcom). 104 p.
A publication commissioned by the committee "Thank you Canada", Nijverdal. Transl. of: Thank you Canada: 1945-1995. 1994.

Present
A present from Holland: Amsterdam in the forties / [comp.: Roland van Tulder; transl. from the Dutch: Rachel Starkey].

Amsterdam: Amsterdam Publishers, cop. 1995. 81 p. Transl. of: Knippen & scheren voor vier aardappelen: Amsterdam in de jaren veertig. 1995.

Provoost, Anne
My aunt is a pilot whale / Anne Provoost; transl. [from the Dutch] by Ria Bleumer. Toronto: Women's Press, cop. 1994. 163 p. Transl. of: Mijn tante is een grindewal. 1990.

Public
Public space: design, layout and management of public open space in Rotterdam / ed. by Johan Goossens, Anja Guinée and Wiebe Oosterhoff; [comp.: Johan Goossens ... et al.; ed.: Jos van Rosmalen; transl. from Dutch: D'laine Camp ... et al.; interviews Eric Luiten; drawings: Tekenbureau Goossens ... et al.]. Rotterdam: 010 Publishers, 1995. 184 p.
Transl. of: Buitenruimte: ontwerp, aanleg en beheer van de openbare ruimte in Rotterdam. 1995.

Reijen, Hugo J. van
Why not fly cheaper?: everything you need to know about tariffs, mileage premiums, rerouting, refunds, upgradings, reservations, frequent flyer programmes, baggage, complaint procedures, etc. / Hugo J. van Reijen; [final ed. and drawings T.E. Williams; transl. from the Dutch]. Amsterdam: Mets, cop. 1996. 191 p. Transl. of: Vliegt u ook te duur?: alles over tarieven, rerouting, refunds, upgrading, reservering, bagage, klachtenprocedures etcetera. 6th, rev. ed. 1996. 1st Dutch ed.: 1994.

Riel, Cees B.M. van
Principles of corporate communication / Cees B.M. van Riel; [ed. and adapted by Chris Blackburn]. London [etc.]: Prentice Hall, 1995. XIII, 239 p. Transl. of: Identiteit en imago: een inleiding in de

corporate communication. 1992.

Rijckenborgh, J. van (pseud. of Jan Leene)
The Chinese gnosis: a commentary on part I of Lao Tzu's Tao Te Ching / by Jan van Rijckenborgh and Catharose de Petri; [transl. from the Dutch]. Haarlem: Rozekruis Pers, 1996. 459 p. Transl. of: De Chinese gnosis. 1987.

Ritter, Kees
Dutch diary / Kees Ritter; transl. [from the Dutch] by Agnès Ritter. Lewes, Sussex: The Book Guild, 1995. 240 p. Transl. from the Dutch manuscript.

Rooyackers, Paul
101 dance games for children: fun and learning with creative movement / Paul Rooyackers. Alameda, CA: Hunter House, 1995. Transl. of: Honderd dansspelen. 1992.

Rotterdam
Rotterdam / [compilation: Herman Scholten; text: D. van Koten; photogr.: Herman Scholten ... et al.; transl. from the Dutch by: CopyTrust]. Duiven: Van Mastrigt en Verhoeven, [1996]. 32 p. Transl. of: Rotterdam. 1996.

Ruusbroec, Jan van
The spiritual epousals / Jan van Ruusbroec; transl. [from the Dutch] by H. Rolfson; introd. by P. Mommaers; dir. by G. de Baere. Collegeville, Minn.: Liturgical Press, cop. 1995. viii, 119 p. (A Michael Glazier book) Originally publ. as: Die chierheit der gheesteliker brulocht.

Sanden, Wijnand van der
Through nature to eternity: the bog bodies of northwest Europe / Wijnand van der Sanden; [transl. from the Dutch by Susan J. Mellor]. Amsterdam: Batavian Lion International, 1996. 200 p. Transl. of: Vereeuwigd in het veen: de verhalen van de Noordwest-Europese veenlijken. 1996.

Santen, Bettina van
The Utrecht Dom Tower / [Bettina van Santen; transl. from the Dutch by Babel]. Utrecht: Stichting Publicaties Oud-Utrecht; Utrecht: Dienst Stadsbeheer gemeente Utrecht, 1995. 32 p. (Utrechtse monumenten; 3) Transl. of: De Utrechtse Domtoren. 1995.

Schaaf, Ype
On their way rejoicing: history and role of the Bible in Africa / Ype Schaaf; transl. [from the Dutch] by Paul Ellingworth; with an epilogue by Kwame Bediako. Carlisle: Paternoster Press, 1995. xii, 254 p. Publ. in association with the All Africa Conference of Churches. Transl. of: Hij ging zijn weg met blijdschap: over de geschiedenis en de rol van de bijbel in Afrika. 1990.

Scholarly
The scholarly world of Vermeer / [authors: Klaas van Berkel ... et al.; ed.: Ton Brandenbarg ... et al.; transl. from the Dutch: Lysbeth Croiset van Uchelen Brouwer ... et al.]. Zwolle: Waanders; The Hague: Museum van het Boek/Museum Meermanno-Westreenianum, cop. 1996. 79 p.
Publ. on occasion of the exposition "The scholarly world of Vermeer", in the Museum van het Boek/ Museum Meermanno-Westreenianum, The Hague, March, 1st 1996 - June, 2nd 1996
Transl. of: De wereld der geleerdheid rond Vermeer. 1996.

Schuiringa, Klaarke
Nederlands Openlucht-museum: guide / [text: Klaarke Schuiringa, Gem Couwenberg; transl. from the Dutch: Marleen Deurvorst; final ed.: Bert Ockers; photogr.: Martin Wijdenans ... et al.]. Arnhem: Nederlands Openluchtmuseum, cop. 1996. 64 p.
Transl. of: Nederlands

Openluchtmuseum: gids. 1996.

Schulte Nordholt, Jan Willem
The myth of the West: America as the last empire / Jan Willem Schulte Nordholt; transl. [from the Dutch] by Herbert H. Rowen. Grand Rapids, Michigan: Eerdmans, 1995. 227 p.
Transl. of: De mythe van het Westen: Amerika als het laatste wereldrijk. 1992.

Schuyt, C.J.M.
Vulnerable youth and their future: a policy recommendation based on literature research / C.J.M. Schuyt; [transl. from the Dutch: Aileen Stronge]. [Rijswijk: Ministerie van Volks-gezondheid, Welzijn en Sport], 1995. 60 p.
Transl. of: Kwetsbare jongeren en hun toekomst: een beleidsadvies gebaseerd op een literatuurverkenning. 1995.

Smith, Jacqueline
Visions and discussions on genital mutilation of girls: an international survey / Jacqueline Smith; [transl. from the Dutch by Peter Longbottom]. Amsterdam [etc.]: Defence for Children International, Section The Netherlands [etc.], cop. 1995. 216 p.
Transl. of: Visies en discussies rond genitale verminking van meisjes: een inventarisatie in internationaal perspectief. 1992.

Snoek, G.J.C.
Medieval piety from relics to the Eucharist: a process of mutual interaction / by G.J.C. Snoek. Leiden [etc.]: Brill, 1995. XII, 465 p. (Studies in the history of Christian thought; vol. 63)
Transl. of: Eucharistie- en reliekverering in de Middeleeuwen. 1989. Thesis Free University Amsterdam

Soldier
Soldier abroad: stories of the past: bevrijdingsfestivi-

teiten Dreumel / [ed.: Jos van Koolwijk ... et al.; transl. from the Dutch Mari v.d. Berg ... et al.]. Nijmegen: Brakkenstein, [1995]. 48 p. Transl. of: Soldaat in den vreemde: verhalen van toen: bevrijdingsfestiviteiten Dreumel. 1995.

Spijker, Willem van 't
The ecclesiastical offices in the thought of Martin Bucer / by Willem van 't Spijker; transl. [from the Dutch] by John Vriend [text] and Lyle D. Bierma [notes]. Leiden [etc.]: Brill, 1996. XII, 508 p. (Studies in medieval and reformation thought; vol. 57)
Transl. of: De ambten bij Martin Bucer. 2nd ed. 1987. 1st Dutch ed.: 1970. Thesis Free University Amsterdam.

Spruit, Ruud
Artists on Bali: W.O.J. Nieuwenkamp, Rudolf Bonnet, Walter Spies, Willem Hofker, A.J. Le Mayeur, Arie Smit / Ruud Spruit; [transl. from the Dutch by Robert Lankamp]. 1st publ. Amsterdam [etc.]: The Pepin Press, 1995. 128 p.
Transl. of: Kunstenaars op Bali. 1995.

Spruit, Ruud
The land of the sultans: an illustrated history of Malaysia / Ruud Spruit; [transl. from the Dutch: Robert Lankamp]. Amsterdam [etc.]: The Pepin Press, cop. 1995. 144 p.
Transl. of: Het land van de sultans: Maleisië en het kolonialisme. 1989.

Stadhuis/bibliotheek
Stadhuis/bibliotheek: the cityhall and library-complex of Richard Meier in The Hague / Fred Feddes ... [et al.]; photogr.: Michel Boesveld, Thijs Wolzak; [ed.: Simon Franke ... et al.; transl. from the Dutch by Michael O'Loughlin]. Rotterdam: NAi Uitgevers, cop. 1995. 80 p. Publ. in

cooperation with the City of The Hague
Transl. of: Het stadhuis/ bibliotheek-complex van Richard Meier in Den Haag. 1995.

Tennekes, Henk
The simple science of flight: from insects to jumbo jets / Henk Tennekes; [transl. from the Dutch]. 1st ed. Cambridge, Mass. [etc.]: MIT Press, 1996. 137 p.
Transl. of: De wetten van de vliegkunst: over stijgen, dalen, vliegen en zweven. 1992.

Thiel, Pieter J.J. van
Framing in the Golden Age: picture and frame in 17th-century Holland / Pieter J.J. van Thiel and C.J. de Bruyn Kops; transl. [from the Dutch] by Andrew P. McCormick. Amsterdam: Rijksmuseum; Zwolle: Waanders, 1995. 375 p.
Transl. of: Prijst de lijst: de Hollandse schilderijlijst in de zeventiende eeuw. 1984.

Thoes, Peter
Triple / Peter Thoes; [transl. from the Dutch: Margaret Kofod]. 1st ed. Amsterdam: Griekse Eiland, cop. 1994. [32] p.
Transl. of: Driedubbel. 1994.

Top, Bart
Balance or blunder: recommendations for reporting on migrants / Bart Top & Monique Doppert; [transl. from the Dutch: C.E.B. Verheus]. Amsterdam: Working Group Migrants and the Media of the NVJ, cop. 1994. 16 p.
Transl. of: Tussen missie & misser. 1993.

Torfs, Rik
A healthy rivalry: human rights in the church / by Rik Torfs; [transl. from the Dutch]. Louvain: Peeters; [Grand Rapids, MI]: Eerdmans, [1995]. VI, 125 p.; 21 cm.
(Louvain theological & pastoral monographs; 20)
Transl. of: Mensen en rechten in de kerk. 1993.

Uffelen, Aad van
Creative flower arranging with Anthurium / Aad van Uffelen; with flower arrangements by: Aad van Uffelen ... [et al.; transl. from the Dutch by Andes/Van der Velden; photogr. Aad van Uffelen ... et al.; drawings Aad van Uffelen]. Utrecht [etc.]: Kosmos-Z&K, cop. 1996. 96 p. (De groenboekerij)
Transl. of: Creatief bloemschikken met Anthurium. 2e dr. 1993.
1st Dutch ed. 1991.

Vandeputte, O.
Dutch: the language of twenty million Dutch and Flemish people / O. Vandeputte; [transl. from the Dutch and adapted by] P. Vincent, T. Hermans; [ed.: Jozef Deleu ... et al.]. 6th rev. ed. Rekkem: Stichting Ons Erfdeel, cop. 1996. 64 p.
1st English ed.: 1981.
1st Dutch ed.: Nederlands: het verhaal van een taal. 1983.

Velthuijs, Max
Frog is a hero / Max Velthuijs. London: Andersen, cop. 1995. [33] p.
Transl. of: Kikker is een held. 1995.

Ven, Johannes A. van der
Ecclesiology in context / Johannes A. van der Ven; [transl. from the Dutch]. Grand Rapids, Michigan [etc.]: Eerdmans, cop. 1996. XV, 568 p.
Transl. of: Ecclesiologie in context. 1993.

Visker, Rudi
Michel Foucault: genealogy as critique / Rudi Visker; transl. [from the Dutch] by Chris Turner. London [etc.]: Verso, 1995. X, 179 p.; 22 cm.
Transl. of: Genealogie als kritiek: Michel Foucault. 1990.

Vliet, Eddy van
Farewell and fall / Eddy van Vliet; [transl. from the Dutch by Matthew Blake ...

et al.]. Dublin: Dedalus, 1994. 77 p.; 22 cm.
Bilingual ed. in Dutch and English.

Vondel, Joost van den
Mary Stuart, or tortured majesty / Joost van den Vondel; transl. [from the Dutch], with an introd. and notes, by Kristiaan P.G. Aercke. Ottawa: Dovehouse, 1996.
Transl. of: Maria Stuart of gemartelde Majesteit. 1646.

Vos, Dirk de
Hans Memling: the complete works / by Dirk De Vos; [transl. from the Dutch by Ted Alkins]. London: Thames and Hudson, 1994. 431 p.
Transl. of: Hans Memling: het volledige oeuvre. 1994.

Vos, Ida
Dancing on the bridge of Avignon / Ida Vos; transl. [from the Dutch] by Terese Edelstein and Inez Smidt. Boston: Houghton Mifflin, 1995.
Transl. of: Dansen op de brug van Avignon. 1989.

Vries, Anke de
Bruises / Anke de Vries; transl. [from the Dutch] by Stacey Knecht. 1st ed. Arden, NC: Front Street, 1995. 168 p.
Transl. of: Blauwe plekken. 1992.

Vries, Anke de
My elephant can do almost anything / Anke de Vries; [transl. from the Dutch]; paintings by Ilja Walraven. 1st ed. Arden, N.C.: Front Street / Lemniscaat, cop. 1996.
Transl. of: Mijn olifant kan bijna alles. 1995.

Wagenaar, R.R.B.M.
Maastricht: Basiliek Onze Lieve Vrouw "Sterre der Zee" / [R.R.B.M. Wagenaar; English transl. from the Dutch by Katherine Vanovitch]. 2nd rev. ed. Regensburg: Schnell & Steiner, 1995. 15 p. (Art guide; No. 2054)
1st English ed.: München

[etc.]: Verlag Schnell & Steiner, 1993. (Schnell art guide; nr. 2054).
Transl. of: Maastricht: Basiliek Onze Lieve Vrouw "Sterre der Zee". 1993.

Weert, Ad van
Legend of the lighter / Ad van Weert; text by Joop Bromet, Ad & Alice van Weert; [transl. from the Dutch]. New York [etc.]: Abbeville Press [etc.], 1995. 192 p.
Transl. of: Van tondeldoos tot turbo: historie en magie van de aansteker. 1995.

Wessels, Anton
Europe: was it every really Christian?: the interaction between gospel and culture / Anton Wessels; [transl from the Dutch]. London: SCM Press, 1994. IX, 242 p.
Transl. of: Kerstening en ontkerstening van Europa: wisselwerking tussen evangelie en cultuur. 1994.

Wetering, JanWillem van de
The blond baboon / JanWillem van de Wetering.; [transl. from the Dutch]. New York: Soho Press, 1996.
1st American ed.: Boston, Mass.: Houghton Mifflin, 1978.
1st Dutch ed. publ. as: De blonde baviaan. 1978.

Winter, Leon de
Hoffman's hunger / Leon de Winter; transl. [from the Dutch] by Arnold and Erica Pomerans. London: Deutsch, 1995. 246 p.
Transl. of: Hoffman's honger: roman. 1990.

Woudstra, Karst
A black Pole / Karst Woudstra; transl. [from the Dutch] by Paul Clark; photogr.: Herman Selleslags]. Amsterdam: International Theatre & Film Books, 1996. 176 p. (Theatre in translation)
Transl. of: Een zwarte Pool. 1992.

Zee, William R. van der
Curse or blessing?: is something wrong between

God and me? / by William
R. van der Zee; [transl. by
Gerard M. Verschuuren
from the Dutch]. North
Andover, Mass: Genesis
Pub. Co, 1996.
Transl. of: Wie heeft daar
woorden voor?: een pasto-
rale over lijdende mensen
en een leidende god. 1981.

Editor:
Dutch Books in Translation
Koninklijke Bibliotheek
The Hague
The Netherlands

Contributors

Ludo Abicht (1936-)
Lecturer in Philosophy
(PHITC, Antwerp) / Guest
lecturer in Philosophy
(University Institute
Antwerp)
Mechelse Steenweg 212,
2018 Antwerp, Belgium

Dirk van Assche (1955-)
Editorial Secretary *Ons
Erfdeel*
Murissonstraat 260,
8931 Rekkem, Belgium

*Fred G.H. Bachrach
(1914-)*
Emeritus Professor of
English Literature
(University of Leiden)
55 Cole Park Road,
Twickenham TW1 1HT,
United Kingdom

Geert Bekaert (1928-)
Chief Editor (*Archis*)
Koepoortbrug 4,
2000 Antwerp, Belgium

Erik van den Berg (1956-)
Editor *de Volkskrant*
Prinseneiland 99",
1013 LN Amsterdam,
The Netherlands

*Greetje van den Bergh
(1946-)*
Secretary-General of the
Dutch Language
Union
Lange Voorhout 19,
2514 EB The Hague,
The Netherlands

Hana Bobkova (1941-)
Lecturer in Dramaturgy
(University of Amsterdam)
Reyer Anslostraat 11,
1054 KT Amsterdam,
The Netherlands

Pieter Bots (1969-)
Theatre critic

Frederiksstraat 17',
1054 LA Amsterdam,
The Netherlands

Jos Bouveroux (1947-)
Chief editor News (BRTN
Radio)
A. Reyerslaan 52,
1043 Brussels, Belgium

Eric Bracke (1960-)
Journalist *De Morgen*
Wegvoeringstraat 115,
9230 Wetteren, Belgium

Hugo Brems (1944-)
Professor of Modern Dutch
Literature (Catholic
University of Leuven)
Huttelaan 263,
3001 Heverlee, Belgium

Max Bruinsma (1956-)
Art critic / Editor *Eye*
Nieuwe Jonkerstraat 35,
1011 CM Amsterdam,
The Netherlands

*Willy van den Bussche
(1942-)*
Chief curator Provincial
Modern Art Museum
(Ostend)
Romestraat 11,
8400 Ostend, Belgium

Paul Depondt (1953-)
Journalist *de Volkskrant*
Lange Violettestraat 263 B,
9000 Ghent, Belgium

Luc Devoldere (1956-)
Deputy Editor
'Stichting Ons Erfdeel'
Murissonstraat 260,
8931 Rekkem, Belgium

Eduard van Ermen (1956-)
Lecturer in History
(Catholic University of
Leuven)
Tiensevest 68,
3000 Leuven, Belgium

Steven Heene
Journalist *De Morgen*
Savaanstraat 112,
9000 Ghent, Belgium

Peter Hoefnagels (1927-)
Emeritus Professor of
Criminology
and Family Law (Erasmus
University, Rotterdam)
/ former MP
Lindeseweg 25,
7251 NJ Vorden,
The Netherlands

Hans Ibelings (1963-)
Staff member of the
Netherlands Architecture
Institute (Rotterdam)
Curierekade 50,
1013 CH Amsterdam,
The Netherlands

Anton Korteweg (1944-)
Director of the Netherlands
Literature Museum and
Documentation Centre
(The Hague) / Poet
Wasstraat 23,
2313 JG Leiden,
The Netherlands

E.H. Kossmann (1922-)
Emeritus Professor of
History
(University of Groningen)
Thorbeckelaan 180,
9722 NJ Groningen,
The Netherlands

Pascal Lefèvre (1963-)
Staff member Belgian
Centre for Comic Strip
Art (Brussels)
Eikkapellaan 19
3400 Landen, Belgium

Selma Leydesdorff (1949-)
Professor / Director of the
Belle van Zuylen
Institute (University of
Amsterdam)
Hogeweg 58,
1098 CE Amsterdam,
The Netherlands

Gerdin Linthorst (1946-)
Film critic
Admiraal De Ruyter-
weg 274,
1055 MR Amsterdam,
The Netherlands

*Marie Juliette Marinus
(1965-)*
Staff member of the
Antwerp Municipal Archive

Gerard van Laethem-
laan 15,
2650 Edegem, Belgium

Marita Mathijsen
Lecturer in Modern Dutch
Literature
(University of Amsterdam)
Nicolaes Maesstraat 7,
1071 PM Amsterdam,
The Netherlands

Filip Matthijs (1966-)
Editorial Secretary *The Low
Countries*
Murissonstraat 260,
8931 Rekkem, Belgium

*Herman-Emiel Mertens
(1928-)*
Professor of Theology
(University of Leuven)
W. Geetsstraat 12,
2800 Mechelen, Belgium

Louise S. Milne
Lecturer in Humanities
Edinburgh College of Art
(Heriot-Watt University),
Lauriston Place, Edinburgh
EH3 9DE, United Kingdom

*Anne Marie Musschoot
(1944-)*
Professor of Dutch
Literature (University of
Ghent)
Nieuwkolegemlaan 44,
9030 Ghent, Belgium

Frits Niessen (1936-)
Deputy Editor *The Low
Countries*
Rijvoortshoef 265,
4941 VJ Raamsdonksveer,
The Netherlands

Frans Oudejans (1926-)
Journalist
Barnsteenstraat 24,
4817 HS Breda,
The Netherlands

Micky Piller (1950-)
Art critic / Journalist
J.A. Alberdingk
Thijmlaan 62,
2106 EM Heemstede,
The Netherlands

Wim de Poorter (1939-)
Teacher / Film critic
Rijselstraat 280 B,
8200 Bruges, Belgium

Walter Prevenier (1934-)
Professor of History

(University of Ghent)
Vlieguit 14, 9830 Sint-
Martens-Latem, Belgium

Anneke Reitsma (1949-)
Lecturer in Dutch
Dorpsweg 25,
8755 JH Idsegahuizum,
The Netherlands

Marc Reynebeau (1956-)
Editor *Knack*
Kempstraat 35,
9000 Ghent, Belgium

Frans de Rover (1946-)
Professor of Dutch
(Free University of Berlin)
Nassauische Strasse 16 A,
1 Berlin 31, Germany

Marc Ruyters (1952-)
Journalist / Scriptwriter
Drie Eikenstraat 282 / 4,
2650 Edegem, Belgium

Reinier Salverda (1948-)
Professor of Dutch
Language and Literature
(University of London)
University College London,
Gower Street,
London WC1E 6BT,
United Kingdom

Ella B. Schaap
Curatorial associate
(Philadelphia
Museum of Art)
Pennswood Village -
Apt. B 113,
1382 Langhorne Road ,
Newtown, PA 189402401,
USA

*M.A.Schenkeveld-van der
Dussen (1937-)*
Professor of Dutch
Renaissance Literature
(University of Utrecht)
Herman Heijermanslaan 23,
2106 ER Heemstede,
The Netherlands

Ineke Schwartz (1961-)
Journalist
Oudezijds Achterburgwal
171 A,
1012 DJ Amsterdam,
The Netherlands

William Z. Shetter
Emeritus Professor of
Dutch
(Indiana University)
Balantine Hall 644,
Bloomington,
IN 47405-6601, USA

A.L. Sötemann (1920-)
Emeritus Professor of
Modern Dutch Literature
(University of Utrecht)
P. Saenredamstraat 5,
3583 TA Utrecht,
The Netherlands

Bianca Stigter (1964-)
Journalist *NRC
Handelsblad*
Oude Schans 19 / 2,
1011 KR Amsterdam,
The Netherlands

Jo Tollebeek (1960-)
Lecturer in History
(Catholic University of
Leuven)
Blijde Inkomststraat 21-05,
3000 Leuven, Belgium

Hans Vanacker (1960-)
Editorial secretary
Septentrion
Murissonstraat 260,
8931 Rekkem, Belgium

Jolanda Vanderwal Taylor
Assistant Professor of
German and Dutch
(University of Wisconsin)
818 Van Hise Hall,
1220 Linden Drive,
Madison, WI 53706, USA

Jan W. de Vries (1937-)
Professor of Modern
Linguistics / President of
the Dutch Studies
Programme
(University of Leiden)
3e Poellaan 40,
2161 DN Lisse,
The Netherlands

Ingeborg Walinga (1965-)
Art critic
Snikkevaardersgang 4,
9711 RW Groningen,
The Netherlands

Jan Wauters (1939-)
Chief editor Sports (BRTN
Radio)
C. Vankerckhoven-
straat 120,
2880 Bornem, Belgium

Anneke Wertheim (1965-)
Art historian
13 Boulevard Henri IV,
75004 Paris, France

Rudi Wester (1943-)
Director of the Foundation
for the Production and

Translation of Dutch
Literature
Singel 464,
1017 AW Amsterdam,
The Netherlands

Veerle Windels (1965-)
Journalist
Westhoekstraat 16,
8700 Aarsele-Tielt,
Belgium

Christopher Wright (1945-)
Art historian
48 Northumberland Place,
London W2 5AS,
United Kingdom

Aart van Zoest (1930-)
Writer
Broekerwaard 154,
1824 EW Alkmaar,
The Netherlands

Translators

Gregory Ball (B)

A.J. Barnouw (+)

James Brockway (NL)

Sheila M. Dale (UK)

Peter Davidson (UK)

Eric Dickens (NL)

Jane Fenoulhet (UK)

Peter Flynn (B)

Nancy Forest-Flier (NL)

Deborah ffoulkes (D)

Lesley Gilbert (UK)

Tanis Guest (UK)

James S Holmes (+)

Yvette Mead (NL)

Elizabeth Mollison (NL)

Alison Mouthaan-Gwillim
(B)

Arnold Pomerans (UK)

Erica Pomerans (UK)

Sonja Prescod (UK)

Julian Ross (NL)

John Rudge (NL)

Michael Shaw (UK)

Paul Vincent (UK)

Adriaan van der Weel (NL)

Claire Nicholas White
(USA)

Rachel van der Wilden (NL)

Diane L. Webb (USA)

ADVISOR ON ENGLISH
USAGE

Tanis Guest (UK)

As well as the yearbook *The Low Countries*, the Flemish-Netherlands foundation 'Stichting Ons Erfdeel' publishes the following books covering various aspects of the culture of Flanders and the Netherlands:

O. Vandeputte / P. Vincent /
T. Hermans
*Dutch. The Language of
Twenty Million Dutch and
Flemish People.*
Illustrated; 64 pp.

J.A. Kossmann-Putto &
E.H. Kossmann
*The Low Countries.
History of the Northern and
Southern Netherlands.*
Illustrated; 64 pp.

Jaap Goedegebuure &
Anne Marie Musschoot
*Contemporary Fiction of
the Low Countries.*
Illustrated and with
translated extracts from
15 novels; 128 pp.

Hugo Brems &
Ad Zuiderent
*Contemporary Poetry of the
Low Countries.*
With 52 translated poems;
112 pp.

Ludo Bekkers &
Elly Stegeman
*Contemporary Painting of
the Low Countries*
Illustrated in four colour
printing; 128 pp.

320